THE PRONUNCIATION

OF

10,000 PROPER NAMES

THE PRONUNCIATION

OF

10,000 PROPER NAMES

GIVING

FAMOUS GEOGRAPHICAL AND BIOGRAPHICAL
NAMES, NAMES OF BOOKS, WORKS OF ART,
CHARACTERS IN FICTION,
FOREIGN TITLES, ETC.

*NEW EDITION, WITH CORRECTIONS,
AND THE ADDITION OF IMPORTANT WORDS MAKING A
TOTAL OF 12,000 PROPER NAMES*

BY

MARY STUART MACKEY

AND

MARYETTE GOODWIN MACKEY, B.A.

NEW YORK
DODD, MEAD AND COMPANY
1934

PRINTED IN THE U. S. A.

To the Memory

OF

JOHN ROSEBERY MACKEY,

THIS LITTLE BOOK IS DEDICATED

PREFACE TO SECOND EDITION

THIS little book was first compiled in the hope of supplying some useful assistance to the reading public. The modest place which it has kept for more than twenty years seems to show that it has not been without its value.

It was not intended for scholars nor for linguists, who do not need it. It was planned to help the large number of readers who often wander far afield in the world of books, and who know but little of any language than their own. For them the signs and directions have been made as simple as possible, and it is hoped that they will be found clear.

The original edition contained considerably more than the 10,000 words claimed for it, and for this new edition about 1500 words have been added, and the whole work has been carefully revised. The new words are for the most part names of persons, places, characters in literature, etc., which have come into prominence since the publication of the first edition. It may safely be claimed that no other single work contains them all

THE AUTHORS

TABLE OF SIGNS, MARKS, AND ABBREVIATIONS

ā as in fāte, āte.
ă " făt, ăt.
ä " fäther, mämmä.
â " fâre, câre.
à " sodà, àsk.
ē " mēte, wē.
ĕ " mĕt, bĕd.
ẽ " hẽr, fathẽr.
ī " fīle, sīte.
ĭ " fĭll, sĭt.

ō as in nōte, ōpen.
ŏ " nŏt, bŏx.
ô " ôr, fôr.
ǒ " whǒlly.
ōō " fōōl, sōōth.
ŏŏ as in lŏŏk, bŏŏk.
ū " ūse, attenūated.
ŭ " ŭs, flŭsh.
ü " Fr. sur, Ger. über.

adj. for adjective.
Am. " American.
Arab. " Arabic.
Bib. " Bible, Biblical.
Boh. " Bohemian.
class. " classical.
D. " Dutch.
Dan. " Danish.
Eng. " English, England.
Fl. " Flemish.
Fr. " French.
Ger. " German.
Gr. " Greek.
Heb. " Hebrew.
Hind. " Hindu.
Hung. " Hungarian.
I. " Island.
Ice. " Icelandic.

Lat. for Latin.
loc. " local.
L. " Lake.
mod. " modern.
n. " noun.
Nor. " Norwegian.
Pers. " Persian.
pop. " popularly.
Port. " Portuguese.
R. " River.
Russ. " Russian.
Sc. " Scotch.
Shak. " Shakespeare.
Sp. " Spanish.
Sw. " Swedish.
St. " Saint.
Turk. " Turkish.

SOUNDS AND MARKS USED IN GIVING PRONUNCIATION.

ch is pronounced as in choose.

ċh   "   "   *Sc.* loch, *Ger.* aċh.

g is always hard in the pronunciation, as in get.

h   "   an aspirated sound.

‹h is strongly aspirated, as in ‹hither, ‹horrid.

ng is pronounced as in ring.

ṅ   "   "   "   *Fr.* boṅ-boṅ.

oi   "   "   "   oil.

ow   "   "   "   now.

sh   "   "   "   show.

th   "   "   "   thin.

ŧh   "   "   "   ŧhiŧher.

y   "   "   "   a consonant, as in you.

zh   "   "   "   s in treasure.

= indicates a rapid pronunciation or running together of two syllables: as Mercier, mârs-ē-ā′, almost mârs=yā.

′ indicates the principal accent.

″   "   "   secondary, or weaker accent.

NOTES ON SOUNDS IN FOREIGN LANGUAGES.

In all cases foreign sounds should be learned from a native, if possible. In many cases they can be indicated only approximately by English sounds. Some have *no* equivalent in English.

French.

1. **e** and **eu** are both sounded peculiarly in French. They have been indicated in most cases by ẽ as in hẽr. It should be remembered that this is *not the exact* sound.

2. **e** at the end of a French word, and sometimes between two syllables, is pronounced very lightly. At the end of a word this has been indicated by the syllable **yu,** with the tie **-**. Example, **Allemagne, äl-män′-yŭ**. This slight sound is lost in rapid speech, but should be indicated, rather than pronounced, when the word is spoken deliberately.

3. **u** is pronounced like the German **ü**. These sounds are not heard in English, but are between **ū** in flūte, and **wee** in sweet. They are indicated by **ü**.

4. **n** in French has no equivalent in English. It is like a smothered **ng,** and is sometimes so indicated in dictionaries. But it is a worse fault to give it the full **ng** sound than to keep it a simple English **n**. It is indicated by **ṅ**.

5. **r** is rolled in the throat in a way difficult for an English-speaking person to acquire.

German.

1. **ch** is a strongly aspirated sound, and has no equivalent in English. If it is impossible to acquire this sound, it is perhaps best to use hard **c** or **k** instead. It is indicated by **ċh**. Ex. **Berchem, bĕr′-ċhĕm, — bĕr′-kĕm.**

2. **g** at the end of a word has nearly the same sound as **ch,** and has been indicated in the same way. In this case, however, one who cannot pronounce **ċh,** should use hard **g**. Ex. **Altenburg, äl′-tĕn-bōōrċh, — äl′-tĕn-bōōrg.**

3. **ö** is different from any English sound, and resembles **eu** in French. It has been indicated by **ē** as in **hēr,** but this is *not the exact* sound.

4. **ü** has no equivalent in English, but is like **u** in

French and in Dutch. It is a sound between ū in flute, and **wee** in sweet, and is indicated by ü.

Spanish.

1. Spanish vowels are all pronounced, though sometimes syllables are run together rapidly. Ex. **Caimanera, kä-ē-mä-nä-rä.** But the first two syllables are so rapidly spoken that they have the effect of **kī,** and the pronunciation is so given in some dictionaries. But here it has seemed best to keep the value of the vowels in most cases, according to Spanish rules. Sometimes this practice has appeared misleading; accordingly, **Aranjuez, ä-räng-ċhōō-ĕth′,** has been given **ä-räng-hwĕth′,** as less likely to be confusing.

2. **b** and **v** are often interchangeable, and have a sound between **b** and **v,** but as this is difficult for a foreigner, it has been given as a simple **b,** and may be pronounced **b** or **v** according to the letter employed in the Spanish word. It is **b** pronounced without closing the lips.

3. **d** is often softened or almost lost in Spanish, and in most dictionaries has been given as **ŧh.** But it has seemed better to indicate it here as a simple **d.**

4. **j** and **x** are interchangeable in Spanish, and have an aspirated sound much like the German **ċh.** If this is not to be acquired, it is better to use an aspirated **ʻh** as in **ʻhither,** and the sound is indicated by both **ċh** and **ʻh.**

5. **r** is rolled with the tip of the tongue.

Italian.

1. Double consonants in Italian are both pronounced, as the **d's** in **sand dune.** Ex. **libretto, lē-brät′-tō.**

2. Before **t** the letter **n** is distinctly pronounced, the effect being of a pause between **n** and **t.**

10,000 PROPER NAMES

A

Aachen	ä′-ċhĕn.
Aar	är.
Aare	är′-ŭ.
Aaron	är′-ŭn, âr′-ŭn, ā′-rŭn.
Ab	äb.
Abaco	ä′-bä-kō.
Abaddon	ā-băd′-ŭn, ă-băd′-ŏn.
Abana	ăb′-à-nà.
Abassides, see Abbassides	ă-băs′-īdz, ăb′-à-sīdz.
Abate, see Abbate	ä-bä′-tĕ.
Abbas	äb′-bäs.
Abbassides, see Abassides	ă-băs′-īdz, ăb′-à-sīdz.
Abbate, see Abate	ä-bä′-tĕ.
Abbaye	ä-bā′.
Abbeokuta, see Abeokuta	ŭb-ē″-ō-kōō′-tà.
Abbeville	ăb-vēl′.
Abbotsford	ăb′-ŏts-fŭrd.
Abdallah, see Abdullah	äbd-äl′-äh.
Abd-el-aziz, see Abdul-Aziz	äbd″-ĕl-ä-zēz′.
Abd-el-Kader, or Kadir	äbd-ĕl-kä′-dēr.
Abd-el-Wahab	äbd″-ĕl-wä-häb′.
Abd-er-Rahman	äbd-ēr-rä′-män.
Abdiel	ăb′-dĭ-ĕl.
Abdul-Aziz, see Abd-el-aziz	äbd″-ōōl-ä-zēz′.
Abdul-Kerim	äb-dōōl-kĕ-rēm′.
Abdullah, see Abdallah	äbd-ōōl′-ä.
Abdul-Medjid, or Mejid	äbd″-ōōl-mĕ-jēd′.

1

À Becket . . . . . . à-běk'-ět.
Abednego . . . . . . ă-běd'-nē-gō.
Abel . . . . ā'-bel. *Nor.* ä'-běl.
Abelard. Fr. Abélard . ăb'-ē-lärd. *Fr.* ä-bā-lär'.
Abelian . . . . . . ā-běl'-ĭ-ăn.
                    ăb-ĕn'-sĕ-rāj-ĕz.
Abencerrages . . . . *Sp.* ä''-běn-thā-rä'-ċhěs.
Abeokuta, see Abbeokuta   ăb-ē''-ō-kōō'-tà.
Abercrombie . . . . ăb'-ēr-krŭm-bĭ.
Aberdeen . . . . . . ăb-ēr-dēn'.
Abergavenny . . . . ăb-ēr-gā'-nĭ, ăb''-ēr-gă-věn'ĭ.
Abernethy . . . . . ăb'-ēr-něth-ĭ, ăb'-ēr-nē-thĭ.
Abia, or Abiah . . . . à-bĭ'-à.
Abiathar . . . . . . à-bĭ'-à-thär.
Abib . . . . ā'-bĭb.
Abiezar, or Abiezer . . ā- bĭ-ē'-zēr.
Abigail . . . . . . ăb'-ĭ-gāl.
Abihu . . . . à-bĭ'-hū.
Abijah . . . . à-bĭ'-jä.
Abila, see Abyla . . . ăb'-ĭ-lä.
Abimelech . . . . . à-bĭm'-ĕ-lěk.
Abo . . . . ä'-bō. *Sw.* ô'-bō.
Abomey . . . . . . ăb-ō'-mĭ, ä-bō-mā'.
Abonita . . . . . . ä-bō-nē'-tä.
Abookeer, see Aboukir,
   Abukir . . . . . . ä-bōō-kēr'.
Abou-ben-Adhem . . . ä'-bōō-běn-ä'-děm.
Aboukir, see Abookeer,
   Abukir . . . . . . ä-bōō-kēr'.
About, Edmond . . . ěd-môṅd' ä-bōō'.
Abra . . . . ăb'-rà.
Abrantès, (Duc) d' . . dä-brän'-těz.
Abruzzi . . . . . . ä-brŏŏtz'-sē.
Abruzzo . . . . . . ä-brŏŏt'-sō.
Absalom . . . . ، . ̦ ăb'-sà-lŭm.
Abt . . . . äpt.
Abu-Bekr . . . . . . ä''-bōō-běk'-r.

Abukir, see Abookeer,
  Aboukir . . . . . ä-bōō-kēr'.
Abu-l-Hassan . . . . ä'-bōōl-häs'-än, häs-än'.
Abul-Kasim-Mansur . . ä'-bōōl-kä-sēm' (or
                 kä'-sēm) män-sōōr'.
Abydos . . . . . . ă-bĭ'-dŏs, ā-bĭ'dŏs.
Abyla, see Abila . . . ăb'-ĭ-lä.
Abyssinia . . . . . . ăb-ĭ-sĭn'-ĭ-à.
Académie Française, l' . lä-kă-dā-mē' frän-sĕz'.
Accademia delle Belle Arti äk-kä-dā'-mē-à dĕl'-lĕ
                 bĕl'-lĕ är'-tē.
Academus . . . . . äk-ā-dē'-mŭs.
Acadia . . . . . . à-kā'-dĭ-à.
Acadie . . . . . . ä-kä-dē'.
Acapulco . . . . . ä-kä-pōōl'-kō.
Acbar, see Akbar . . . äk'-bēr. Hind. ŭk'-bĕr.
Accademia della Crusca . äk-kä-dā'-mē-à dĕl'-lä
                 krōōs'-kä.
Acciajoli, or . . . . . ä-chä-yō'-lē.
Acciajuoli . . . . . . ä-chä-yōō-ō'-lē.
Accoramboni . . . . . äk-kō"-räm-bō'-nē.
Aceldama . . . . . . à-sĕl'dä-mà.
Acemetae, Acemeti, see
  Acoemitae . . . . . ă-sĕm'-ē-tē, ă-sĕm'-ē-tī.
Acemetic . . . . . . ăs-ē-mĕt'-ĭk.
Achaea, see Achaia . . ā-kē'-yà, ă-kē'-yà.
Achaean, see Achean . ā-kē'-àn, ă-kē'-àn.
Achaia, see Achaea . . ā-kā'-yä, ă-kā'-yà.
Achaian, see Achean . . ā-kā'-yàn, ă-kā'-yàn.
Achan . . . . ā'-kăn.
Achates . . . . . . ă-kā'-tēz.
Achean, see Achaean . . ā-kē'-àn, ă-kē-àn.
Acheloös, or Achelous . ăk-ē-lō'-ŏs, ăk-ē-lō'-ŭs.
Acheron . . . . . . ăk'-ē-rŏn.
Achillean . . . . . . ăk-ĭl-ē'-àn.
Achilles . . . . . . ă-kĭl'-ēz.
Achitophel, see Ahithophel ā-kĭt'-ō-fĕl.

Achmet, see Ahmed . . . ăċh'-mĕt.
Achray (Locḥ) . . . . ăk'-rā.
Acis . . . . ā'-sĭs.
Ackbar, see Akbar . . . äk'-bĕr. *Hind.* ŭk'-bĕr.
Acoemitae, see Acemetae ăs-ē-mĭ'-tē, *or* ă-sĕm'-ĭ-tē.
Adabazar . . . . . ä-dä-bä-zär'.
Adelina . . . . . . ăd-ĕ-lī'-nȧ.
Adeline . . . . . . ăd'-ĕ-līn. *Fr.* ăd-lēn'.
Adis Abeba . . . . . ä'-dĭs ä-bā'-bä.
Adlai . . . . ăd'-lī.
Aegades (Is.) . . . . ē-gā'-dēz.
Aguada . . . . . . ä-gwäd'-thȧ.
Aguilar . . . . . . ä-gē-lär'.
Aguinaldo . . . . . ä-gē-näld'-thō.
Agulhas (Cape) . . . . ä-gōōl'-yäs.
Acre . . . . ā'-kĕr, ä'-kĕr.
Acropolis . . . . . ă-krŏp'-ō-lĭs.
Actaeon . . . . . . ăk-tē'-ŏn.
Actian . . . . ăk'-shĭ-ȧn.
Actium . . . . . . ăk'-shĭ-ŭm, ăk'-tĭ-ŭm.
Acuña . . . . ä-kōōn'-yȧ.
Adalbert . . . . . . ăd'-ăl-bĕrt.
Adam (Mme.) . . . . ä-däṅ'.
Adamawa . . . . . ä-dä-mô'-wä.
Adamic . . . . . . ă-dăm'-ĭk.
Adamowski . . . . . ä-dä-mŏf'-skĭ.
Adar . . . . ā'-där.
Ade (Geo.) . . . . . ād.
Adela . . . . ăd'-ē-lȧ.
Adelaide . . . . . . ăd'-ĕ-lād.
Adélaïde (Princess) . . *Fr.* ä-dä-lä-ēd'.
Adelaïde (Beethoven) . . *Ger.* ä-dä-lä-ē'-dŭ.
Adelheid . . . . . . ä'-dĕl-hīt.
Adelphi, or Adelphoe . . ă-dĕl'-fī, ă-dĕl'-fē.
Aden . . . . ä'-dĕn, ā'-dĕn.
Adeona . . . . . . ăd-ē-ō'-nȧ.
Adige . . . . ăd'-ĭj-ē. *It.* ä'-dē-jĕ.

Adjanta, Adjunta, see
 Ajuntah . . . . .   ă-jŭn'-tå.
Adjuntas . . . . . .   äd-hōōn'-täs.
Adlai . . . .   ăd'-lī, ăd'-lē-ī.
Adler . . . .   äd'-lĕr.
Admetos, or Admetus .   ăd-mē'-tŏs, ăd-mē'-tŭs.
Adonai . . . .   ăd-ō-nā'-ī, ä-dō-nī'.
Adonais . . . . . .   ăd-ō-nā'-ĭs.
Adonic . . . .   å-dŏn'-ĭk,
Adonijah . . . . . .   ăd-ō-nī'-jå.
Adoniram . . . . . .   ăd-ō-nī'-răm.
Adonis . . . .   ă-dō'nĭs, ā-dō'-nĭs.
Adoni-zedec . . . .   å-dō'-nī-zē'-dĕk.
Adraste . . . . . .   ä-dräst'.
Adrian . . . .   ā'-drĭ-ån.
Adriana . . . . . .   ā-drĭ-ā'-nå.
Adrianople . . . .   ā-drĭ-ăn-ō'pl.
Adriatic . . . . . .   ā-drĭ-ăt'-ĭk, ăd-rĭ-ăt'-ĭk.
Adrienne Lecouvreur .   ä-drē-ĕn' lē-kōōv-rēr'.
Adullam . . . . . .   å-dŭl'-åm.
Aeacides . . . . . .   ē-ăs'-ĭ-dēz.
Aeacus . . . .   ē'-å-kŭs.
Aegadian (Is.) . . .   ē-gā'-dĭ-ån.
Aegates . . . . . .   ē-gā'-tēz.
Aegean, see Egean .   ē-jē'-ån.
Aegeria, see Egeria .   ē-jē'-rĭ-å.
Aegina, see Aigina . .   ē-jī'-nå.
Aeginetan . . . . .   ē-jĭ-nē'-tån.
Aeginetic . . . . . .   ē-jĭ-nĕt'-ĭk.
Aegis . . . .   ē'-jĭs.
Aeneas, see Eneas . .   ē-nē'ås.
Aeneid . . . .   ē-nē'-ĭd.
Aeolian, see Aiolian .   ē-ō'-lĭ-ån.
Aeolic, see Eolic . .   ē-ŏl'-ĭk.
Aeolis, see Eolis . .   ē'-ō-lĭs.
Aeolus . . . .   ē'-ō-lŭs.
Aerschot . . . . . .   är'-skŏt.

Aeschines . . . . . . ĕs'-kĭ-nēz.
Aeschylean . . . . . ĕs-kĭ-lē'-ȧn.
Aeschylus . . . . . . ĕs'-kĭ-lŭs.
Aesculapius, see Asklepios ĕs-kū-lā'-pĭ-ŭs.
Aesir . . . . ā'-sēr, mod. ē'-sēr. Ice. ī-sēr.
Aesop, see Esop . . . ē'-sŏp.
Aethelberht, see Ethelbert ăth'-ĕl-bĕrht.
Aethelwulf, see Ethelwulf ăth'-ĕl-woolf.
Aether . . . . ē'-thēr.
Aëtion . . . . ā-ē'-shĭ-ŏn.
Aetna, see Etna . . . ĕt'-nȧ.
Aetolian . . . . . . ē-tō'-lĭ-ȧn.
Afer . . . . ā'-fēr.
Afghan . . . . ăf'-găn.
Afghanistan . . . . . af-găn-ĭs-tän', af-găn-ĭs-tän'.
Afium-Kara-Hissar . . ä-fē-oom'-kä-rä'-hĭs-sär'.
Africaine, L' . . . . . lăf-rē-kĕn'.
Africander, see Afrikander ăf'-rĭ-kăn-dēr.
Africanus . . . . . . ăf-rĭ-kā'-nŭs.
Afridis . . . . ä-frē'-dĭz.
Afrikander, see Africander ăf'-rĭ-kăn-dēr.
Agades, Agadez, see Agdas ä'-gä-dĕz.
Agag . . . . ā'-găg.
Agamemnon . . . . . ăg-ā-mĕm'-nŏn.
Agaña . . . . ä-gän'-yä.
Agassiz . . . . . . ăg'-ăs-sĭ, ăg'-ăs-ē. Fr.
　　　　　　　　　　ä-gä-sē'.
Agdas, see Agades . . . ăg'-dȧs.
Agen . . . . ä-zhŏn'.
Agenor . . . . ă-jē'-nôr.
Agésilas . . . . . . Fr. ä-zhä-sē-läs'.
Agesilaos, or . . . . . ă-jĕ-sĭ-lā'-ŏs.
Agesilaus . . . . . . ă-jĕ-sĭ-lā'-ŭs.
Aghrim, see Aughrim . . ôg'-rĭm.
Agincourt, see Azincourt . ăj'-ĭn-kōrt. Fr.
　　　　　　　　　　äzh-ăn-koor'.
Aglaia . . . . ăg-lā'-yä.

Agnolo	än'-yō-lō.
Agnus Dei	ăg'-nŭs dē'-ī.
Agoncillo, Felipe . . .	fā-lē'-pā ä-gōn-thēl'-yō.
Agonistes	ăg-ŏn-ĭs'-tēz.
Agora	ăg'-ō-rà.
Agoult (Comtesse d') . .	dä-gōō'.
Agra	ä'-grà.
Agram	ä'-gräm.
Agricola	ă-grĭk'-ō-lä.
Agrigentum	ag-rĭ'-jĕn'-tŭm.
Agrippina	ăg-rĭ-pĭ'-nà.
Aguadilla	ä-gwä-dēl'-yä.
Aguado	ä-gwä'-dō.
Aguadores	ä-gwä-dō'-rās.
Aguas Buenas	ä'-gwäs bōō-ä'-näs.
Aguas Calientes . . .	ä'-gwäs kä-lē-ĕn'-tĕs.
Ahab	ā'-hăb.
Ahasuerus	ă-hăz-ū-ē'-rŭs.
Ahaz	ā'-hăz.
Ahimelech	ă-hĭm'-ĕ-lĕk.
Ahithophel, see Achitophel	ă-hĭth'-ō-fĕl, ā-hĭth'-ō-fĕl.
Ahmed, see Achmet . .	äh'-mĕd.
Ahmedabad	ä-mĕd-ä-bäd'.
Ahmednuggur	ä-mĕd-nŭg'-ēr.
Ahriman	ä'-rĭ-män.
Aï, see Ay	ä'-ē, ī. *Bib.* ā'-ī
Aibonito, see Aybonito .	ä-ē-bō-nē'-tō.
Aïda	ä-ē'-dä.
Aïdé	ä-ē-dä'.
Aidenn	ā'-dĕn.
Aidin	ī-dēn'.
Aigina, see Aegina . . .	ī'-gĭ-nä.
Aiglon, L'	lä-glôṅ'.
Aiguille du Midi . . .	ā gē'=yŭ dü mē dē'.
Aiguillon (Duc) d' . . .	dä-gē-yôṅ'
Aijalon, see Ajalon . .	ăj'-à-lŏn.
Aintab	īn-täb'.

Aiolian, see Aeolian . . ā-ō'-lǐ-àn.
Aire . . . . âr.
Aisha . . . . ä'-ē-shä.
Aisne . . . . ĕn.
Aix . . . . island, ā. city, ĕks, ās.
Aix-la-Chapelle . . . . ĕks-lä-shä-pĕl'.
Aix-les-Bains . . . . ĕks-lā-băṅ'.
Ajaccio . . . . . . ä-yä'-chō.
Ajalon, see Aijalon . . ăj'-à-lŏn.
Ajax . . . . ā'-jăks.
Ajmere, or Ajmir . . . äj-mēr'.
Ajuntah, see Adjanta . . ă-jŭn'-tà.
Akbar, or . . . . . .
Akber, see Ekber . . . äk'-bĕr. *Hind.* ŭk'-bĕr.
Akiba (Rabbi) . . . . ä-kē'-bä.
Akimenko . . . . . ä-kē-mĕn'-kō.
Akra . . . . äk-rä'.
Aksakoff, or Aksakov . . äk-sä'-kŏf.
Akyab . . . . äk-yäb'.
Al Aaraaf, see Al Araf . äl-är'-äf.
Alabama . . . . . . ăl-à-bä'-mà.
Alabamian . . . . . ăl-à-bä'-mǐ-àn.
Alacoque . . . . . . ä-lä-kŏk'.
Aladdin, or Ala-ed-Din . à-lăd'-ĭn, ä-lä'-ĕd-dēn'.
Alamanni, see Alemanni . ăl-à măn'-ī.
Alamannic, see Alemannic ăl-à-măn-ĭk.
Alameda . . . . . . ä lä-mā'-dä.
Alamo . . . . ä'-lä-mō.
Al Araf, see Al Aaraaf . äl är'-äf.
Alarcon y Mendoza . . ä-lär-kōn'ē mĕn-dō'-thä.
Alaric . . . . ăl'-är-ĭk.
Alastor . . . . ă-lăs'-tôr.
Alba (Duke of), see Alva . ăl'-bà. *Sp.* äl'-bä.
Alba Longa . . . . . ăl'-bà lŏng'-gà.
Alban, St. . . . . . . ăl'-băn, ôl' bàn.
Albani (Mme.) . . . . äl-bä'-nē.
Albania . . . . . . äl-bā'-nǐ-à.

Albano	äl-bä'-nō.
Albai, or Albay	äl-bä'=ē.
Alberic	ăl'-bĕr-ĭk.
Albert (of Belgium) . .	ăl-bâr'.
Albert, D'	däl-bâr'.
Albertinelli	äl-bâr-tē-nāl'-lē.
Albertini	äl-bâr-tē'-nē.
Albert Nyanza	ăl'-bĕrt nyăn'-zȧ.
Albi, see Alby	äl-bē'.
Albigenses	ăl-bĭ-jĕn'-sēz.
Albion	ăl'-bĭ-ŏn.
Alboin	ăl'-boin.
Alboni (Mme.)	äl-bō'-nē.
Albrecht	äl'-brĕcht.
Albret, Jeanne d' . . .	zhän däl-brā'.
Albuera	äl-bōō-ā'-rä.
Albuquerque	ăl'-bū-kĕrk
	Sp. äl-bōō-kâr'-kā.
Alby, see Albi	äl-bē'.
Alcaeus	ăl-sē'-ŭs.
Alcalá de Henares . . .	äl-kä-lä' dä ā-nä'-räs.
Alcamenes	ăl-kăm'-ĕ-nēz.
Alcantara	äl-kän'-tä-rä.
Alcázar	äl-kä'-thär.
Alceste	ăl-sĕst'.
Alcibiades	ăl-sĭ-bī'-ȧ-dēz.
Alcinous	ăl-sĭn'-ō-ŭs.
Alcmaeon	ălk-mē'-ŏn.
Alcmaeonidae	ălk-mē-ŏn'-ĭ-dē.
Alcmene	ălk-mē'-nē.
Alcoran, see Alkoran . .	ăl'-kō-răn, ăl-kō-răn'.
Alcott, (Bronson) . . .	ôl'-kŭt.
Alcuin	ăl'-kwĭn.
Alcyone, see Halcyone .	ăl-sī'-ō-nē.
Aldebaran	äl-dĕb'-ȧ-răn, äl-dĕ-bä-rän'.
Alderney	ôl'-dĕr-nĭ.
Aldershot	ôl-dĕr-shŏt.

Aldine . . . .   ăl'-dĭn, ôl'-dīn.
Aldobrandini . . . . .   äl-dō-brän-dē'-nē.
Aldus Manutius   . . .   ăl'-dŭs mă-nū'-shĭ-ŭs.
Alecto . . . .   ă-lĕk'-tō.
Aleksyeev, see Alexeieff .   ä-lĕk-sā'-yĕf.
Alemanni, see Alamanni .   ăl-ē-măn'-ī.
Alemannic, see Alamannic   ăl-ē-măn'-ĭk.
Alembert, D'   . . . .   dä-lŏn-bâr'.
Alençon . . . . . .   ä-lĕn'-sŭn. Fr. ä-lŏn-sôn'.
Alethea . . . . . .   ăl-ē-thē'-à.
Aleutian . . . . . .   ā-lū'-shĭ-ăn, ăl-ē-ū'-shĭ-ăn.
Aleuts . . . .   ăl'-ē-ūts.
Alexeieff, see Aleksyeev .   ä-lĕk-sā'-yĕf.
Alfadir . . . .   äl-fà'-dĭr.
Alfieri, Vittorio . . . .   vēt-tō'-rē-ō äl-fē-ā'-rē.
Alfio . . . .   äl-fē'-ō.
Alfonso, see Alphonso   ăl-fŏn'-sō, ăl-fŏn'zō. Sp.
                                äl-fōn'-sō.
Alford . . . .   ôl'-fŭrd.
Alger . . . .   ăl'-jĕr, ôl'-gĕr.
Algerian . . . . . .   ăl-jē'-rĭ-àn.
Algerine . . . . . .   ăl'-jĕ-rēn.
Algiers . . . .   ăl-jērz'.
Algoa (Bay) . . . .   ăl-gō'-à.
Algonkin, or Algonquin .   ăl-gŏn'-kĭn, ăl-gŏn'-kwĭn.
Alhambra . . . . . .   ăl-hăm'-brà.
Ali Baba . . . . . .   ä'-lē bä'-bä.
Alicante . . . . . .   äl-ē-kän'-tā.
Alighieri . . . . . .   ä-lē-gē-ā'-rē.
Aliwal . . . .   äl-ē-wäl'.
Alkmaar . . . . . .   älk-mär'.
Alkoran, see Alcoran . .   ăl'-kō-ràn, ăl-kō-rán'.
Allah . . . .   ăl'-ä.
Allahabad . . . . . .   äl-ä-hä-bäd'.
Alleghany, or Allegheny .   ăl'-ē-gā-nĭ, ăl'-ē-gĕn-ĭ.
Allegri . . . .   äl-lā'-grē.
Allemagne   . . . . .   ăl-măn'=yŭ.

Allenstein . . . . . . äl'-ĕn-shtīn.
Alleyne . . . . . . ăl'-ĕn.
Aller . . . . äl'-ĕr.
Allobroges . . . . . ăl-ŏb'-rō-jēz.
Almacks . . . . . . ôl'-măks.
Almagest . . . . . . ăl'-mȧ-jĕst.
Almahide . . . . . . äl-mä-ēd'.
Almansa, see Almanza . äl-män'-sä.
Al Mansour, Al Mansur . äl män-sōōr'.
Almanza, see Almansa . äl-män'-thä.
Alma-Tadema . . . . äl'-mä tä'-dŏ-mä.
Almeida . . . . . . äl-mā'-ē-dä.
Almeyda (Bay) . . . äl-mā'-dä.
Almirante Oquendo . . äl-mē-rän'-tä ō-kĕn'-dō.
Almohades . . . . . ăl'-mō-hädz.
Almoravides . . . . . ăl-mō'-rȧ-vīdz.
Alnwick . . . . . . ăn'-ĭk.
Aloiadae, or Aloidae . . ă-lō-ī'-ȧ-dē, ă-lō-ī'-dē
Aloysius . . . . . . ăl-ō-ĭsh'-ĭ-ŭs.
Alpes-Maritimes . . . älp-mär-ē-tēm'.
Alph . . . . ălf.
Alpheius, or Alpheus . . ăl-fī'-ŭs, ăl-fē'-ŭs.
Alphonse . . . . . . ăl-fôns'.
Alphonso, see Alfonso . ăl-fŏn'-sō, ăl-fŏn'-zō.
. . . . Sp. äl-fōn'-sō.
Alpini . . . . äl-pē'-nē.
Alpujarras, or Alpuxaras . äl-pōō-ċhär'-räs.
Alsace-Lorraine . . . . äl-zăs' lōr-rŏn'.
Al Sirat . . . . . . äl sē-rät'.
Altai . . . . äl-tī'.
Altaic . . . . ăl-tā'-ĭk.
Alter Fritz . . . . . äl'-tĕr frĭts.
Althaea . . . . . . ăl-thē'ȧ.
Althing . . . . . . äl'-tĭng.
Alton Locke . . . . . ôl'-tŭn lŏk.
Altstrelitz . . . . . . ält-shtrā'-lĭtz.
Alva, Duke of, see Alba . ăl'-vȧ. Sp. äl'-bä.

Alvarado . . . . . . äl-bä-rä′-dō.
Alvares . . . . . . äl′-bä-rĕs.
Alvarez . . . . . . *Port.* äl′-vä-rĕz.
                   Sp. äl′-bä-rĕth.
Alvary . . . . äl-vä′-rĭ.
Alvinczy, or Alvinzi . . ôl′-vĭn-tsē.
Alwar, see Ulwar . . . äl′-wär.
Amadeo . . . . . . ä-mä-dä′-ō.
Amadeus . . . . . . ăm-ȧ-dē′-ŭs.
Amadis of Gaul . . . . äm′-ȧ-dĭs ŭv gôl.
Amalfi . . . . ä-mäl′-fē.
Amalia, Anna . . . . än′-ä ä-mä′-lē=ä.
Aman-Jean . . . . . ä-mäṅ′-zhäṅ′.
Amants Magnifiques, Les lä zä-mäṅ′ män-yē-fēk′.
Amaryllis . . . . . . ăm-ȧ-rĭl′-ĭs.
Amasa . . . . ăm′-ȧ-sȧ.
Amati . . . . ä-mä′-tē.
Amaury . . . . . . ă-mô′-rĭ. *Fr.* ä-mō-rē′.
Amazulu . . . . . . ä-mä-zōō′-lōō.
Ambois . . . . . . äṅ-bwä′.
Amboise . . . . . . äṅ-bwäz′.
Ambrogio, San . . . sän äm-brō′-jō.
Ambrosius, (St.) . . . ăm-brō′-zhĭ-ŭs.
Ambur . . . . ȧm-bōōr′.
Amenhotep . . . . . ä-mĕn-hō′-tĕp.
Amerigo Vespucci . . . ä-mĕr-ē′-gō vĕs-pōō′-chē.
Amerongen . . . . . ȧm′-ĕr-ông-ĕn.
Amicis, De . . . . . dā ä-mē′-chēs.
Amiel . . . . ā′-mĭ-ĕl.
Amiel, Henri Frédéric . ŏṅ-rē′ frä-dā-rēk′ ă-mē-ĕl′.
Amiens . . . . ă-mē-äṅ′.
Amistad . . . . . . *Sp.* ä-mēs-täd′.
Amlwch . . . . . . ăm′-lōōk.
Amneris . . . . . . äm-nä′-rēs.
Amoor, see Amur . . . ä-mōōr′.
Amor . . . . ā′-môr.
Amoret . . . . . . ăm′-ō-rĕt.

Amorites	ăm′-ō-rīts.
Amory (Blanche) . . .	ā′-mō-rĭ.
Amoskeag	ăm-ŏs-kĕg′.
Amoy	ä-moi′.
Ampère	äṅ-pâr′.
Amphictyonic	ăm-fĭk-tĭ-ŏn′-ĭk.
Amphictyony	ăm-fĭk′-tĭ-ŏn-ĭ.
Amphion	ăm-fī′-ŏn.
Amphipolis	ăm-fĭp′-ō-lĭs.
Amphitrite	ăm-fī-trī′-tē.
Amphitryon	ăm-fĭt′-rĭ-ŏn.
Amritsar, see Umritsir .	ȧm-rĭt′-sär.
Amundsen	ä′-mŏŏnt-sĕn.
Amur, see Amoor . . .	ä-moōr′.
Amurath	ä-moō-rät′.
Amyot	ä-mē-ō′.
Anabasis	ȧ-năb′-ȧ-sĭs.
Anacreon, see Anakreon .	ă-năk′-rē-ŏn.
Anadyomene	ăn-ȧ-dĭ-ŏm′-ĕ-nē.
Anagni	än-än′-yē.
Anahuac	ä-nä′-wäk.
Anak	ā′-năk.
Anakim	ăn′-ă-kĭm.
Anakreon, see Anacreon .	ă-năk′-rē-ŏn.
Anam, see Annam . . .	ăn-ăm′, än-äm′.
Ananias	ăn-ȧ-nī′-ȧs.
Añasco	än-yäs′-kō.
Anastasius	ăn-ȧs-tā′-shĭ-ŭs.
Anathoth	ăn′-ȧ-thŏth.
Anatolian	ăn-ȧ-tō′-lĭ-ȧn.
Anaxagoras	ăn-ăks-ăg′-ō-rȧs.
Anaximander	ăn-ăks-ĭ-măn′-dĕr.
Anaximenes	ăn-ăks-ĭm′-ĕ-nēz.
Anchises	ăn-kī′-sēz.
Ancillon	äṅ-sē-yôṅ′.
Anckarström	äng′-kär-strĕm.
Ancona	än-kō′-nä.

Ancre (Marquis) d' . . däṅ'-kr.
Ancus Marcius . . . . ăng'-kŭs mär'-shĭ=ŭs.
Andalucia . . . . . . *Sp.* än-dä-lōō-thē'-ä
Andalusia . . . . . ăn-dȧ-lū'-shĭ-ȧ,
        ăn-dȧ-lōō'-zĭ-ȧ.
Andaman . . . . . . ăn'-dȧ-mȧn.
Andelys, Les . . . . lä zäṅ=dŭ-lē's
Andermatt . . . . . än'-dĕr-mät.
Andernach . . . . . än'-dĕr-näċh.
Andersen, Hans . . . häns än'-dĕr-sĕn.
Andes . . . . ăn'-dēz.
Andorra . . . . . . än-dŏr'-rä.
Andrássy . . . . . . ŏn'-drä-shē.
André . . . . än'-drä, ăn'-drĭ. *Fr.*
        äṅ-drä'.
Andrea del Sarto . . . än-drä'-ä dĕl sär'-tō.
Andrea Ferrara . . . . ăn'-drē-ȧ fĕr-rä'-rä.
Andrée . . . . äṅ'-drä.
Andreieff (-eyev) . . . ȧn-drä'-yĕf.
Androclus . . . . . . ăn'-drō-klŭs.
Andromache . . . . . ăn-drŏm'-ȧ-kē.
Andromaque . . . . . *Fr.* äṅ-drō-măk'.
Andromeda . . . . . ăn-drŏm'-ĕ-dȧ.
Andromède . . . . . äṅ-drō-mĕd'.
Andronicus . . . . . ăn-drō-nī'-kŭs.
        Shak. ăn-drŏn'-ĭ-кŭs.
Anelida . . . . ă-nĕl'-ĭ-dȧ.
Angara (R.) . . . . . än-gä-rä'.
Angelico, Fra . . . frä än-jĕl'-ē-kō.
Angélique . . . . . . äṅ-zhä-lēk'.
Angelo . . . . ăn'-jĕ-lō. *It.* än'-jä-lō.
Angelus . . . . . . ăn'-jĕ-lŭs.
Angers . . . . ăn'-jĕrs. *Fr.* äṅ-zhä'.
Angevin, or Angevine . . ăn'-jē-vĭn, ăn'-jē-vīn.
Anghiari . . . . . . än-gē-ä'-rē.
Anglesea (-sey) . . . . ăng'-gl-sē.
Angra Pequeña . . . . äng'-grä pä-kän'-yȧ.

Annas	ăn'-ás.
Annecy	än-sē'.
Anse	äṅs.
Antares	ăn-tā'-rēz.
Antigone	ăn-tĭg'-ō-nē.
Antigonus	ăn-tĭg'-ō-nŭs.
Antigua	än-tē'-gwä.
Antilles	än-tĭl'-lēz. *Fr.* äṅ-tēl'.
Antilochus	ăn-tĭl'-ō-kŭs.
Anti-Macchiavel . . .	ăn-tĭ-măk͵-ĭ-à-vĕl.
Antin (Duc) d'	däṅ-täṅ'.
Antinous	ăn-tĭn'-ō-ŭs.
Antioch	ăn'-tĭ-ŏk.
Antiochus	ăn-tĭ'-ō-kŭs.
Antiope	ăn-tĭ'-ō-pē.
Antipas, Herod	hĕr'-ŏd ăn'-tĭ-păs.
Antipater	ăn-tĭp'-à-tēr
Antiphanes	ăn-tĭf'-ă-nēz.
Antiphon	ăn'-tĭ-fŏn.
Antipodes	ăn-tĭp'-ō-dēz, ăn'-tĭ-pōds.
Antipolo	än-tē-pō'-lō.
Antistates	ăn-tĭs'-tă-tēz.
Antium	ăn'-shĭ-ŭm.
Antivari	än-tē'-vä-rē.
Antofagasta	än"-tō-fä-gäs'-tä.
Antoine de Bourbon . .	äṅ-twăn' dē boōr-bôṅ'.
Antokolsky	än-tō-kŏl'-skē.
Anton Ulrich	ăn'-tōn oōl'-rĭch.
Antonelli Giaccomo (Cardinal)	jä'-kō-mō än-tō-nĕl'-lē.
Antonello da Messina .	än-tō-nĕl'-lō dä mĕs-sē'-nä.
Antonina	ăn-tō-nī-nä.
Antoninus Pius	ăn-tō-nī'-nŭs pī'-ŭs.]
Antonio	än-tō'-nē-ō.
Antraigues, see Entraigues	äṅ-trāg'.
Antwerp	ănt'-wĕrp.
Anubis, see Anoobis . .	ă-nū'-bĭs.
Anvers	äṅ-vârs'.

Anzac . . . . ăn'-zăk.
Aosta . . . . ä-ŏs'-tä.
Apache, or . . . . . ä-pä'-chä.
Apaches . . . . . . *pop.* ä-păch'-ēz.
Apari, or Aparri . . . . ä-pär-rē'.
Apelles . . . . . . ă-pĕl'-ēz.
Apemantus . . . . . ăp-ĕ-măn'-tŭs.
Apennines . . . . . ăp'-ĕ-nīnz.
Aphrodite . . . . . . ăf-rō-dī'-tē.
Apia . . . . ä'-pē-ä.
Apicius . . . . . . ă-pĭsh'-ĭ=ŭs.
Apocalypse . . . . . ȧ-pŏk'-ȧ-lĭps.
Apocrypha . . . . . ȧ-pŏk'-rĭ-fȧ.
Apollinare in Classe . . ä-pōl-lē-nä'-rĕ ĭn kläs'-sĕ.
Apollino . . . . . . ă-pŏl-lē'-nō.
Apollo Belvedere . . . ȧ-pŏl'-ō bĕl-vē-dēr'.
   It. ä-pōl'-lō bāl-vā-dä'-rĕ.
Apollo Chresterios . . . ȧ-pŏl'-ō krĕs-tē'-rĭ-ŏs.
Apollo Citharoedus . . ȧ-pŏl'-ō sĭth-ȧ-rē'-dŭs.
Apollo Sauroktonos . . ȧ-pŏl'-ō sôr-ŏk'-tō-nŏs.
Apollodorus . . . . . ȧ-pŏl''-ō-dō'-rŭs.
Apollonius . . . . . ăp-ŏl-ō'-nĭ-ŭs.
Apollyon . . . . . . ă-pŏl'-yŏn, ā-pŏl'-ĭ-ŏn.
Apoxyomenos . . . . ăp''-ŏks-ĭ-ŏm'-ĕ-nŏs.
Appalachian . . . . . ăp-ȧ-lăch'-ĭ-ăn,
   ăp-ā-lā-chĭ-ăn.
Appii Forum . . . . . ăp'-ĭ-ī fō'-rŭm.
Appomattox . . . . . ăp-ō-măt'-ŏks.
Apponyi . . . . . . ŏp'-pōn-yē.
Appuleius, see Apuleius . ăp-ū-lē'-ŭs.
Apraxin . . . . . . ä-präk'-sĭn.
Apries . . . . ā'-prē-ēz.
Apuleius, see Appuleius . ăp-ū-lē'-ŭs.
Apulia. It. Puglia . . . ȧ-pū'-lĭ-ȧ.
Aquae Sextiae . . . . ā'-kwē sĕk'-stĭ-ē.
Aquambo . . . . . . ä-kwäm-bō'.
Aquapim . . . . . . ä-kwä-pēm'.

Aquarius . . . . . . à-kwā'-rĭ-ŭs.
Aquednek, or . . . . ă-kwĕd'-nĕk.
Aquidneck . . . . . à-kwĭd'-nĕk.
Aquila . . . . ä'-kwē-lä.
Aquinas . . . . . . à-kwī'-nàs.
Aquitaine . . . . . ăk-wĭ-tän'. *Fr.* ä-kē-tän'.
Arab . . . . ăr'-àb.
Arabia Petraea . . . à-rā'-bĭ-ä pē-trē'-ä.
Arabic . . . . ăr'-à-bĭk.
Arabi Pasha . . . . ä-rä'-bē păsh-ô', pà-shä',
    or päsh'-à.
Araby . . . . ăr'-à-bĭ.
Ara Celi, or Coeli . . . ā'-rä sē'-lī.
Arachne . . . . . . à-răk'-nē.
Araf, Al, see Al Aaraaf . äl ä'-ràf.
Arafat . . . . ä-rä-fät'.
Arago . . . . ăr'-à-gō. *Fr.* ä-rä-gō'.
Aragon . . . . ăr'-à-gŏn. *Sp.* ä-rä-gōn'.
Araktcheyeff . . . . . ä-räk-chā'-yĕf.
Aral (Sea) . . . . . ăr'-àl.
Aram (Eugene) . . . . ā'-ràm.
Aramaic . . . . . . ăr-à-mā'-ĭk.
Aramis . . . . ä-rä-mēs'.
Aranjuez . . . . . . ä-räng-'hwĕth'.
Arany János . . . . . ŏr-ŏn-yē' yä'-nōsh.
Arapaho, or Arapahoe . à-răp'-à-hō.
Arar . . . . ā'-rär.
Ararat . . . . ăr'-ă-răt.
Arayat . . . . ä-rä'=ē-ät.
Arbaces . . . . . . ăr'-bă-sēz, är-bā'-sēz.
Arbate . . . . är-bät'.
Arbela . . . . är-bē'-lä.
Arblay (Mme.) d' . . . där-blä'.
Arbois . . . . är-bwä'.
Arbuthnot . . . . . . är'-bŭth-nŏt. *Sc.*
    är-bŭth'-nŏt.
Arcades . . . . . . är''-kà-dēz.

Arcady . . . . är'-ka-dĭ.
Arc de Triomphe de L'Étoile ärk dŭ trē-ônf' dŭ lā-twäl'.
Arc de Triomphe du Car-   ärk dŭ trē-ônf' dü
rousel . . . . . kä-rōō-zĕl'.
Archangel . . . . . . ärk-ān'-jĕl.
Archangelsk . . . . . är-ċhäng'-gĕlsk.
Archelaus . . . . . . är-kē-lā'-ŭs.
Archias . . . . är'-kĭ-ȧs.
Archidamus . . . . . är-kĭ-dā'-mŭs.
Archilochus . . . . . är-kĭl'-ō-kŭs.
Archimage . . . . . är'-kĭ-māj.
Archimago . . . . . . är-kĭ-mā'-gō.
Archimedean . . . . . är-kĭ-mē-dē'-ȧn.
Archimedes . . . . . är-kĭ-mē'-dēz.
Arcis-sur-Aube . . . . är-sē'-sür-ōb'.
Arcite . . . . är'-sīt.
Arco dei Leoni . . . är'kō dā'-ē lā-ō'-nē.
Arco della Pace . . . är'-kō dĕl'-lä pä'-chĕ.
Arcola, or Arcole . . . är'kō-lä, är'-kō-lĕ.
Arcot . . . . är-kŏt'.
Arcturus . . . . . . ärk-tū'-rŭs.
Arcueil . . . . är-kē'=yŭ.
Ardahan . . . . . . är-dä-hän'.
Ardennais . . . . . är-dĕn-nā'.
Ardennes . . . . . . är-dĕn'.
Arditi, Luigi . . . . lōō-ē'-jē är-dē'-tē.
Ardres . . . . ärdr.
Ardrossan . . . . . . är-drŏs'-ȧn.
Arduin . . . . ärd'-wĭn.
Are, see Ari . . . . . ä'-rĕ.
Arecibo . . . . ä-rä-sē'-bō.
Arenas Gordas, Las . . läs ä-rä'-nȧs gōr'-dȧs.
Arensky . . . . . . ä-rĕn'-shkē.
Areopagite . . . . . ăr-ē-ŏp'-ȧ-jīt.
Areopagitica . . . . ăr″-ē-ō-pă-jĭt'-ĭ-kä.
Areopagus . . . . . ā-rē-ŏp'-ă-gŭs.
Arequipa . . . . . . ä-rä-kē'-pȧ.

Ares	ā′rēz.
Arethusa	ăr-ē-thū′-sä.
Aretine	ăr′-ĕ-tĭn.
Aretino, Guido . . .	gwē′-dō ä-rā-tē′-nō.
Arezzo	ä-rĕt′-sō.
Argam, see Argaum . .	är-gäm′.
Argan	är-gäṅ′.
Argante (Spenser) . .	är-găn′tĕ.
Argante (Molière) . .	är-gäṅt′.
Argantes	är-gän′-tĕs.
Argaum, see Argam . .	är-gôm′.
Argenis	är′-jĕ-nĭs.
Argenson, d'	där-zhŏṅ-sôṅ′.
Argenteau	är-zhôṅ-tō′.
Argenteuil	är-zhŏṅ-tē′=yŭ.
Argentina	är-jĕn-tē′-nä. *Sp.*
	är-ċhĕn-tē′-nä.
Argentine	är′-jĕn-tīn, är′-jĕn-tēn.
Argives	är′-jīvz.
Argolis	är′-gō-lĭs.
Argonauts	är′-gō-nôtz.
Argonnes	är-gŏn′.
Argüelles	är-gwĕl′-yĕs.
Argyle, or Argyll . .	är-gīl′.
Ari, see Are	ä′-rē.
Ariadne	ăr-ĭ-ăd′-nē. ā-rĭ-ăd′-nē.
Arian	ā′-rĭ-ȧn.
Ariane	ä-rē-ȧn′.
Arians	ā′-rĭ-ȧnz, ȧ′-rĭ-ȧnz.
Ariège	ä-rē-ĕzh′.
Ariel	ā′-rĭ-ĕl.
Aries	ā′-rĭ-ēz.
Ariete	ä-rē-ĕ′-tä.
Ariguanabo	ä-rē-gwä-nä′-bō.
Arimathaea, or Arimathea	ăr-ĭ-mä-thē′-ä.
Arion	ă-rī′-ŏn.
Ariosto	ăr-ĭ-ŏs′-tō. *It.* ä-rē-ŏs′-tō.

Arista (Gen.) . . . . . ä-rēs'-tä.
Aristagoras . . . . . ăr-ĭs-tăg'-ō-ràs.
Aristarchus . . . . . ăr-ĭs-tär'-kŭs.
Ariste . . . . ä-rēst'.
Aristeides, or Aristides . ăr-ĭs-tī'-dēz.
Aristippus . . . . . . ăr-ĭs-tĭp'-ŭs.
Aristobulus . . . . . ăr"-ĭs-tō-bū'-lŭs.
Aristodemus . . . . . ăr"-ĭs-tō-dē'-mŭs.
Aristogeiton, or Aristogiton ăr"-ĭs-tō-jī'-tŏn.
Aristophanes . . . . . ăr-ĭs-tŏf'-à-nēz.
Aristotle . . . . . . ăr'-ĭs-tŏtl.
Arius . . . . ăr'-ĭ-ŭs, ā'-rĭ-ŭs.
Arjish . . . . är-yĭsh'.
Arkansas . . . . . . är'-kăn-sô, är-kăn'-zàs.
Arles . . . . ärlz. *Fr.* ärl.
Arlésienne, L' . . . . lär-lä-zē=ĕn'.
Arline . . . . är'-lēn.
Armada . . . . . . är-mä'-dä.
Armado, Don . . . . dŏn är-mä'-dō.
Armageddon . . . . . är-mà-gĕd'-ŏn.
Armagh . . . . . . är-mä'.
Armagnac . . . . . . àr-màn-yàk'.
Armande Béjart . . . . är-mänd' bä-zhär'.
Armentières . . . . . är-mŏn-tē=är'.
Armida . . . . . . är-mē'-dä.
Armide et Renaud . . . är-mēd' ä rē-nō'.
Arminius . . . . . . är-mĭn'-ĭ-ŭs.
Armorel of Lyonesse . . är'-mō-rĕl ŭv lī'-ŏn-ĕs.
Armorica . . . . . . är-mŏr'-ĭ-kä.
Armorican . . . . . . är-mŏr'ĭ-kàn.
Arnauld . . . . . . är-nō'.
Arnaut . . . . är'-nôt.
Arnim, Bettina von . . bĕt-tē'-nä fŏn är'-nĭm.
Arno . . . . är'-nō.
Arnolfo di Cambio . . . är-nōl'-fō dē käm'-bē-ō.
Arnolfo di Lapo . . . . är-nōl'-fō dē lä'-pō.
Arnolphe . . . . . . är-nōlf'.

Arondight	ā'-rŏn-dīt.
Aroostook	ȧ-rōōs'-tŏŏk.
Arouet	ȧ-rōō-ā'.
Arpachshad, see Arphaxad	är-păk-shăd'.
Árpád	är'-päd.
Arphaxad, see Arpachshad	är-făk'-săd.
Arquà	är-kwä'
Arques	ärk.
Arras	är-räs'.
Arrhidaeus	ăr-ĭ-dē'-ŭs.
Arrivabene	är-rē-vä-bā'-nĕ.
Arroyo Molinos	är-rō'yō mō-lē'nōs.
Arsaces	är'-să-sēz, är-sā'-sēz.
Arsacidae	är-săs'-ĭ-dē.
Arsames	är'-sā-mēz.
Arsenieff	är-sĕn'-yĕf.
Arsiero	är-sē-ā'-rō.
Arsinoë	är-sĭn'-ō-ē.
Ars Poetica	ärz pō-ĕt'-ĭ-kȧ.
Artachshast	är-tăk-shăst'.
Artagnan, D'	där-tän-yäṅ'.
Artamène	är-tä-mĕn'.
Artaphernes	är-tȧ-fēr'-nēz.
Artaxerxcs	är-tăks-ērks'-ēz.
Artegal	är'-tē-gȧl.
Artemas	är'tē-mȧs.
Artemidorus	är-tē-mĭ-dō'-rŭs.
Artemis	är'-tē-mĭs.
Artemisia	är-tē-mĭsh'-ĭ=ä.
Artemisium	är-tē-mĭsh'-ĭ=ŭm.
Artevelde, Van	văn är'-tĕ-vĕl-dĕ.
Artiago	är-tē-ä'-gō.
Artichofsky	är-tē-shōv'-skē.
Artois	är-twä'.
Aruba	ä-rōō'-bä.
Arundel	ăr'ŭn-dĕl.
Aruwimi	är-ōō-wē'-mē.

Arviragus . . . . . . är-vĭr'-à-gŭs.
Aryan . . . . är'yàn, är'-ĭ=än.
Asaph . . . . ā'-sàf.
Asben . . . . äs-bĕn'.
Asboth . . . . ăs'-bŏth. *Hung.* ŏsh'-bōt.
Ascagne . . . . . . äs-kän'=yŭ.
Ascalon, see Askelon . . ăs'-kă-lŏn.
Ascanio . . . . . . äs-kä'-nē=ō.
Aschaffenburg . . . . ä-shäf'-ĕn-bōōrċh.
Ascham . . . . . . ăs'-kăm.
Asdrubal, see Hasdrubal ăs'-drŭ-bàl.
Asenath . . . . . . ăs'ē-năth, ā-sē'-năth.
Aserraderos . . . . . ä-sâr-rä-dä'-rōs.
Asgard . . . . ăs'-gärd.
Ashango . . . . . . ä-shän'-gō.
Ashantee or Ashanti . . ä-shän'-tē, ă-shăn'-tē.
Ashby-de-la-Zouch . . ăsh'bĭ-dĕl-à-zōōch'.
Ashestiel . . . . . . ăsh'-ĕs-tēl.
Ashtaroth, Ashteroth . . ăsh'-tà-rŏth.
Ashtoreth, see Ashtaroth ăsh'tō-rĕth.
Asia . . . . ā'shĭ=ä, ā'-zhĭ=ä.
Asiago . . . . ä-sē-ä'-gō.
Asiatic . . . . ā-shĭ-ăt'-ĭk, ā-zhĭ-ăt'-ĭk.
Asisi, see Assisi . . . ä-zē'-zē.
Askabad . . . . . . äs-kä-bäd'.
Askelon, see Ascalon . . ăs'-kĕ-lŏn.
Askew (Anne) . . . . ăs'-kū.
Asklepios, see Aesculapius ăs-klē'pĭ-ŏs.
Asmodeus . . . . . ăs-mō-dē'-ŭs, ăs-mō'-dē-ŭs.
Asnières . . . . . . ä-nē=âr'.
Asola . . . . ä-zō'lä.
Asolando . . . . . . ăs-ō-lăn'-dō.
Asolo . . . . ä'-zō-lō.
Asolone . . . . . . ä-sō-lō'-nä.
Aspasia . . . . . . ăs-pā'-shĭ=à.
Aspromonte . . . . . äs-prō-mōn'-tĕ.
Asquith . . . . . . ăs'-kwĭth.

Assam	ăs-săm'.
Assaye, see Assye . . .	äs-sī'.
Assen	äs'-ĕn.
Assini	äs-sē'-nē.
Assiniboia	ăs''-ĭn-ĭ-boi'-ä.
Assisi, see Asisi . . .	ä-sē'-zē.
Assommoir, L'	lä-sŏm-wär'.
Assouan, Assuan, or Asswan	äs-swän'.
Assuay, see Azuay . . .	äs-sōō-ī'.
Assye, see Assaye . . .	äs-sī'.
Astarte	ăs-tär'tē.
Asterabad, see Astrabad .	äs-tĕr-ä-bäd'.
Asti	äs'tē.
Astolat	ăs'-tō-lăt.
Astolfo, or Astolpho . .	ăs-tŏl'fō.
Astorga	äs-tōr'-gä.
Astrabad, see Asterabad .	äs-trä-bäd'.
Astraea, or Astrea Redux	ăs-trē'ä rē'dŭks.
Astrakhan	äs-trä-ċhän'.
Astrée	äs-trä'.
Astrolabe	ăs'-trō-lāb.
Astrophel	ăs'-trō-fĕl.
Asturias	äs-tōō'-rē-äs.
Astyages	ăs-tī'á-jēz.
Astyanax	ăs-tī'-á-năks.
Asuncion	ä-sōōn-thē-ōn'.
Asurbanipal . , . . .	ä-sōōr-bä'-nĭ-päl.
Atacama	ä-tä-kä'-mă.
Atahualpa	ä-tä-wäl'pä.
Atak, see Attock . . .	ăt-ăk'.
Atala	ä-tä-lä'.
Atalanta in Calydon . .	ăt-á-lăn'-tä ĭn kăl'-ĭ-dŏn.
Ataliba	ăt-ă-lē'-bä.
Atalide	ät-ä-lēd'.
Atbara	ät-bä'-rä.
Ate	ā'-tē.
Aterno	ä-tĕr'-nō.

Athalaric, see Athalric . ăth-ăl'-à-rĭk.
Athaliah . . . . . . ăth-à-lī'-ä.
Athalie . . . . ä-tä-lē'.
Athalric, see Athalaric . ăth-ăl'-rĭk.
Athanasian . . . . . ăth-à-nā'-zhĭ-zăn.
Athanasius . . . . . ăth-à-nā'-shĭ=ŭs.
Atharvaveda . . . . . ăt-här-vä-vā'-dä.
Athena . . . . ă-thē'-nä.
Athenaeum, see Atheneum ăth-ĕ-nē'-ŭm.
Athene . . . . ă-thē'-nē.
Athene Parthenos . . . ă-thē'-nē pär'-thĕ-nŏs.
Athene Polias . . . . ă-thē'-nē pŏl'-ĭ-ăs.
Atheneum, see Athenaeum ăth-ĕ-nē'-ŭm.
Athol . . . . ăth'-ŏl.
Athos (Mt.) . . . . . ăth'ŏs.
Athos (Dumas) . . . . ä-tōs'.
Atlantean . . . . . . ăt-lăn-tē'-àn.
Atlantides . . . . . ăt-lăn'-tĭ-dēz.
Atreus . . . . ā'-trūs, ā'-trē-ŭs.
Atri . . . . ä'-trē.
Atria . . . . ä'-trē-ä.
Atridae . . . . . . ă-trī'dē.
Atropos . . . . . . ăt'-rō-pŏs.
Attalia . . . . ăt-à-lī'-ä.
Attalus . . . . ăt'-à-lŭs.
Attar . . . . ăt-tär'.
Atticus . . . . ăt'-ĭ-kŭs.
Attila . . . . ăt'-ĭ-lä.
Attis, see Atys . . . . ăt'-ĭs.
Attock, see Atak . . . ăt-tŏk'.
Atys, see Attis . . . . ăt'-ĭs.
Aubanel . . . . . . ō-bä-nĕl'.
Aubé, Jean Paul . . . zhŏṅ pōl ō-bā'.
Auber (D. F. E.) . . . ō-bâr'.
Auberge Rouge . . . . ō-bârzh' rōōzh'.
Aubert . . . . ō-bâr'.
Aubigné, D' . . . . . dō-bēn-yā'.

Aubusson . . . . . . ō-büs-ôǹ'.
Aucassin et Nicolette . . ō-kǎ-sǎǹ'nä nē-kō-lĕt'.
Auch . . . . ōsh.
Aude . . . . ōd.
Audefroy le Bastard . . ōd-frwä' lē bȧs-tär'.
Audenarde, see Oudenarde ōd-närd'.
Audh, see Oudh, Oude . owd.
Audouin . . . . . ō-dōō-ǎǹ'.
Audran . . . . . . ō-dräǹ'.
Audrey . . . . . . ôd'-rǐ.
Aue, Hartmann von . . härt'män fŏn ow'-ŭ.
Audubon . . . . . ô'-dū-bŏn.
Auerbach . . . . . ow'-ĕr-bäċh.
Auersperg . . . . . ow'-ĕrs-pĕrċh.
Auerstädt or Auerstedt . ow'ĕr-stĕt.
Auf der Höhe . . . owf dĕr hē'-yŭ.
Augarten . . . . . ow'-gär-tĕn.
Augean . . . . . ô-jē'-ȧn.
Augeas . . . . . ô'-jē-ǎs, ô-jē'-ǎs.
Auger . . . . . . *Fr.* ō-zhä'.
Augereau . . . . . ōzh-rō'.
Aughrim, see Aghrim . . ôg'-rǐm.
Augier, Émile . . . ä-mēl' ō-zhē=ä'.
Augsburg . . . . . ôgz'-bĕrg. *Ger.*
owgs'-bōōrċh.
Augusta Victoria . . . ô-gŭs'tä vǐk-tō'-rǐ-ȧ.
Ger. ow-gōōs'-tä,
fēk tō'-rē-ä.
Augustenburg . . . ow-gōōs'tĕn-bōōrċh.
Augustine . . . . . ô-gŭs'-tǐn, ô'-gŭs-tǐn.
Augusti y Davila . . . ä=ōō-gōōs'-tē ē dä'-bē-lä.
Augustovo . . . . ow-gōōs-tō'-vō.
Augustulus . . . . ô-gŭst'-yū-lŭs.
August Wilhelm . . . *Ger.* ow'-gōōst vǐl'-hĕlm.
Aulis . . . . . . ô'-lǐs.
Aulnoy, or Aunoy . . ō-nwä'.
Aumale, Duc d' . . . . dük dō-mǎl'.

Aurangabad, see Auren-
gabad . . . . . . ow-rŭng-gȧ-bäd'.
Aurelle de Paladines . . ō-rĕl'dŭ pä-lä-dēn'.
Aurengabad, or Aurungabad ow-rŭng-gȧ-bäd'.
Aureng-zebe, or Aurung-zeb ô'-rŭng-zĕb'.
Aurigny . . . . . . ō-rēn-yē'.
Aus der Ohe . . . . . ows dĕr-ō'-ŭ.
Aussa . . . . ow'-sä.
Austerlitz . . . . . . ows'-tĕr-lĭts.
Austrasia . . . . . . ôs-trā'-shĭ=ȧ, ôs-trā'-zhĭ=ȧ
Austria-Hungary . . . ôs'-trĭ-ä-hŭng'-gä-rĭ.
Auteuil . . . . . . ō-tĕ'=yŭ.
Autolycus . . . . . . ô-tŏl'-ĭ-kŭs.
Automedon . . . . . ô-tŏm'-ĕ-dŏn.
Autriche . . . . . . ō-trēsh'.
Auvergnat . . . . . ō-vârn-yä'.
Auvergne . . . . . . ō-vârn'=yŭ.
Aux Cayes, see Cayes . ō kä.
Auxerre . . . . . . ōks-âr'.
Auxerrois . . . . . . ōks-âr-wä'.
Avalon or Avallon . . . ăv'-ä-lŏn.
Avalos, D' . . . . . dä-vä'-lŏs.
Avare, L' . . . . . . lă-văr'.
Ave Maria . . . . . ā'-vē mȧ-rī'-ȧ. It. ä'-vä
mä-rē'-ä.
Avenel . . . . āv'-nĕl.
Aventine . . . . . . ăv'-ĕn-tĭn.
Avenue de l'Opéra . . . ăv-nü' dŭ lō-pā-rä'.
Ave Roma Immortalis . ā'-vē rō'-mȧ ĭm-ôr-tä'-lĭs.
Averrhoës or Averroës . ă-vĕr'-ō-ĕz.
Avesnes . . . . . . ä-vän'.
Avicenna . . . . . . ăv-ĭ-sĕn'-ä.
Avignon . . . . . . ä-vēn-yôṅ'.
Avila . . . . ä'-vē-lä.
Avilion, see Avalon . . ă-vĭl'yŏn.
Aviz . . . . Port. ä-vēz'; Sp. ä'-vĭth.
Avlona . . . . äv-lō'-nä.

Avogadro	ä-vō-gä′-drō.
Avon	ā′-vŏn, *local Am.* ăv′-ŏn.
Avre	ävr.
Ayala, Pero López . . .	pä′-rō lō′-pĕth ä-yä′-lä.
Axayacatl, or	ă-tchä-yä-kä′-tl.
Axayacatzlin	ä-tchä-yä-kătz-lēn′.
Axim	äks′-ĭm, ä-shēng′.
Axminster	äks′-mĭn-stēr.
Ay, see Aï	ä′=ē.
Ayacucho	ä=ē-ä-kōō′-chō.
Ayala	ä-yä′-lä.
Aybonito, see Aibonito .	ä=ē-bō-nē′-tō.
Ayesha	ä-yĕ′-shä.
Aymon	ā′-mōn.
Ayoub Khan, see Ayub Khan	ä-yōōb′ khän.
Ayr	âr.
Ayscue	ās′-kū.
Aytoun	ā′-tōōn.
Ayub Khan, see Ayoub Khan	ä-yōōb′ khän.
Azarael, or Azareel . .	ăz′-à-rä-ĕl, äz′-à-rĕ-ĕl.
Azarias	ăz-à-rī′-às.
Azazel	ă-zä′-zĕl.
Azaziel	ă-zä′-zĭ-ĕl.
Azeglio, D'	däd-zäl′-yō.
Azerbaijan	äz-ĕr-bī-jän′.
Azimgarh	ă-zĭm-gŭr′.
Azincourt, see Agincourt .	ăz′-ĭn-kōrt. *Fr.* äzh-ăṅ-kōōr′.
Azof, or Azoff, see Azov .	ä′-zŏf.
Azor	*Sp.* ä-thōr′.
Azores	ă-zōrz′.
Azorin	ä-sō-rēn′.
Azov, see Azof . . .	ä′-zŏf.
Azrael, or Azrail . . .	ăz′-rä-ĕl, äz′-rä-ĭl.
Aztecas	ăz′-tĕk-àz.
Azuay, see Assuay . . .	ä-thōō-ī′.
Azucena	äd-zōō-chä′-nä.

B

Baal	bā′-ȧl.
Baalbac, or Baalbak . .	bäl′-băk, bäl-băk′.
Baalbec, or Baalbek . .	bäl′-běk, bäl-běk′.
Baalim	bā′-ȧ-lĭm.
Bab	bäb.
Baba, Ali	ä′-lē bä′-bä.
Bab-el-Mandeb	bäb-ĕl-män′-děb.
Baber, see Babur . . .	bä′-bĕr.
Babieca, see Bavieca . .	bä-bē=ā′-kä.
Babington	băb′-ĭng-tŏn.
Babist	bäb′-ĭst.
Babur, see Baber . . .	bä′-bĕr.
Babúyan (Is.)	bä-bōō′-yän.
Babylonic	băb-ĭ-lŏn′-ĭk.
Bacchae	băk′-ē.
Bacchante	băk-kăn′-tē.
Bacchus	băk′-ŭs.
Bacchylides	bă-kĭl′-ĭ-dēz.
Bacciochi	bä-chŏk′-kē.
Baccio della Porta . . .	bä′-chō děl′-lä pōr′-tä.
Bach, J. S.	bäċh.
Bache	bāch.
Backergunge, see Baker-	
ganj	bäk-ĕr-gŭnj.
Backhuysen	bäk′-hoi-zĕn.
Bacolod	bä-kō-lōd′.
Bacolor	bä-kō-lōr′.
Bacoor, see Bakoor . .	bă-kōōr′.
Bacsânyi	bä′-chän-yē.
Bactriana	băk-trĭ-ā′-nä.
Badagry	bä-dä-grē′.
Badajos, or Badajoz . .	bäd-ä-hōs′. *Sp.*
	bä-dä-hōth.
Badebec	bäd-běk′.
Baden	bä′-děn.

Baden-Powell	bā-dĕn-powl'.
Badinguet-Radot . . .	bä-dăṅ-gā' rä-dō'.
Badon (Mt.)	bā'-dŏn.
Badoura	bă-dōō'-rä.
Baedeker	bā'-dĕk-ĕr. *Ger.* bâ'-dĕk-ĕr.
Baena	*Sp.* bă-ā'-nä; *Port.* bä-yā'-nä.
Baer, Von	fōn bâr.
Baez	bä'-āth.
Bafing, Ba-Fing . . .	bä-fēng'.
Bagalor	bä-gä-lŏr'.
Bagamoyo	bä-gä-mō'-yō.
Bagdad or Baghdad . .	bäg-däd', *commonly* băg'-dăd.
Bagehot	băj'-ŏt.
Baghdad or Bagdad . .	bäg-däd', *commonly* băg'-dăd.
Bagheria	bä-gā-rē'-ä.
Baguio	bä'-gē-ō.
Bagnacavallo . . .	bän"-yä-kä-väl'-lō.
Bagni di Lucca . . .	bän'-yē dē lōōk'-kä.
Bagration	bä-grä-tsē-ōn', bä-grä'-shŭn.
Bahamas	bā-hā'-máz.
Bahar, see Behar, Bihar .	bă-här'.
Bahari	bä-hä-rē'.
Bahawalput	bä-hä-wäl-pōōr'.
Bahia	bä=ē'-ä.
Bahia Honda . . .	bä=ē'-ä ōn' dä.
Baiae	bā'-yē.
Baikal	bī'-käl, bī-käl'.
Bailleul	bä=ē-yēl'.
Baillie	bā'-lē.
Baillot	bä=ē-yō'.
Bailly	bā'-lē. *Fr.* bä-yē'.
Baiquiri	bä=ē-kē'-rē.
Bairam, see Beiram . .	bī-räm'.
Baireuth, see Bayreuth .	bī'rūth. *Ger.* bī-roit'.

Bairut, see Beirut, or Bey-
rout . . . . bā-rōōt'.
Baja . . . . bä'-yä.
Bajazet, see Bayazid . . băj'-ā-zĕt, băj-ā-zĕt'。
Bajza . . . . bŏy'-zä.
Bakerganj, see Backergunge bäk'-ēr-gánj.
Bakhuyzen . . . . . bäk'-hoi-zĕn.
Bakoor,or Bakor, see Bacoor bă-kōōr'.
Baku . . . . bä-kōō'.
Balaam . . . . . . bā'-lăm.
Balábac . . . . . . bä-lä'-bäk.
Balaclava, or Balaklava . bä-lä-klä'-vä.
Balafré, Le . . . . . lŭ bä-lä-frā'.
Balaguer . . . . . . bä-lä-gâr'.
Balakireff . . . . . . bä-lä-kēr'-ĕf.
Balaklava, or Balaclava . bä-lä-klä'-vä.
Balasore, Balasur . . . băl-à-sōōr'.
Balaustion . . . . . bă-lôs'-chŏn.
Balbek, see Baalbec . . bäl'-bĕk, bäl-bĕk'.
Balbo . . . . bäl'-bō.
Balboa, De . . . . . dā bäl-bō'-ä.
Balchen (Admiral) . . . bôl'-chĕn.
Baldassare . . . . . bäl-däs-sä'-rā.
Balder, Baldur . . . . bôl'-dēr.
Bâle, see Basle . . . . bäl.
Baleares . . . . . . bā-lē-ā'-rēz.
Balearic . . . . . . băl-ē-ăr'-ĭk.
Baléchou . . . . . . bä-lä-shōō'.
Baler . . . . bä-lâr'.
Balestier . . . . . . băl-ĕs-tēr'.
Balfe . . . . bălf.
Balfour . . . . . . băl'-fōōr, băl'-fēr.
Balimghem . . . . . bä-lăṅ-găṅ'.
Balin and Balan . . . bā'-lĭn, ănd bā'-lăn.
Baliol, see Balliol . . . bā'-lĭ-ŏl. *Fr.* bäl-yōl'.
Baliuag . . . . . . bäl-ē'-wäg.
Balize . . . . bä-lēz'.

Balkan . . . . bôl'-kăn, bäl-kän'.
Ballarat . . . . . . băl-å-răt'.
Ballari . . . . bäl-lä'-rē.
Ballesteros . . . . . bäl-yĕs-tä'-rōs.
Balliol, see Baliol . . . bā'-lĭ-ŏl. *Fr.* bäl-yōl'.
Balliol (College) . . . băl'-yĕl.
Ballo in Maschera . . . bäl'-lō ēn mäs'-kā-rä.
Balmaceda . . . . . bäl-mä-thä'-dä.
Balmoral . . . . . . băl-mŏr'-ăl, băl-mō'-răl.
Balmung . . . . . . bäl'-mŏŏng.
Balsamo . . . . . . băl-sä'-mō. *Fr.* bäl-sä-mō'.
Balthasar, or Balthazar . băl-thä'-zär, bäl'-tä-zär.
Baluchistan, see Beluchis-
    tan, or Beloochistan . băl-ōō-chĭs-tän'.
Balwhidder . . . . . băl-whĭth'-ẽr.
Balzac . . . . băl-zăk', *commonly* băl'zăk.
Bamberg . . . . . . bäm'-bĕrċh.
Banana . . . . bä-nä'-nä.
Banaras, see Benares . . bă-nä'-räs.
Banat . . . . bä'-nät.
Bancroft . . . . . . băn'-krŏft.
Banér, see Banner . . . bä-nâr'.
Bangkok . . . . . . băng-kŏk'.
Bangor (Me.) . . . . băn'-gŏr.
Bangor (Wales) . . . . băng'-gẽr.
Bangweolo . . . . . băng-wē-ō'-lō.
Banner, see Banér . . . bä-nâr'.
Banquo . . . . . . băn' kwō, băng'-kwō.
Bantam . . . . . . bän-täm'.
Bantu . . . . bän'-tōō.
Banville (Théodore de) . bäṅ-vēl'.
Banyoro . . . . . . bä-nyō'-rō.
Bapaume . . . . . . bă-pōm'.
Bara Banki . . . . . bä'-rä bän'-kē.
Barabas, or Barabbas . . bā-răb'-ås.
Barabra, see Berabra . . bä-rä'-brä.
Baracoa . . . . . . bä-rä-kō'-ä.

Baraguay d'Hilliers . . bä-rä-gä′ dē-yä′.
Barataria . . . . . . bär-á-tä′-rĭ-ä. *Sp.*
                    bä-rä-tä-rē′-ä.
Barbadoes, or Barbados . bär-bä′-dōz.
Barbarelli . . . . . bär-bä-rĕl′-lē.
Barbarossa . . . . . bär-bá-rŏs′-ä.
Barbaroux . . . . . bär-bä-rōō′.
Barbary . . . . . bär′-bá-rĭ.
Barbauld . . . . . bär′-bôld. *Fr.* bär-bō′.
Barbazon, see Barbison . bär-bä-zôṅ′.
Barberini . . . . . bär-bä-rē′-nē.
Barbey d'Aurevilly . . . bär-bä′ dō=rĕ-vē-yē′.
Barbier de Séville, Le . lŭ bär-bē=ä′ dŭ sä-vēl′.
Barbiere de Seviglia, Il . ēl bär-bē-ä′-rĕ dä sä-vēl′-yä.
Barbison, see Barbazon . bär-bē-zôṅ′.
Barbusse, Henri . . . ôṅ-rē′ bär-büs′.
Barcellona . . . . . bär-chĕl-lō′-nä.
Barcelona . . . . . bär-sĕ-lō′-nä. *Sp.*
                    bär-thä-lō′-nä.
Barclay de Tolly . . . bär-klä′ dŭ tō-lē′.
Bardera . . . . . . bär-dä′-rä.
Bardi, Bardo de′ . . . bär′-dō dä bär′-dē.
Bardolph . . . . . bär′-dŏlf.
Bardwan, see Burdwan . bárd-wän′.
Bareja . . . . . . bä-rä′-ċhä.
Barère de Vieuzac . . . bä-râr′ dŭ vē=ē-zä′.
Baretti . . . . . . bä-rät′-tē.
Barfleur . . . . . bär-flĕr′.
Bargello . . . . . bär-jĕl′-lō.
Bargiel . . . . . . bär′-gēl.
Bariatinski . . . . . bär-yä-tēn′-skē.
Baring . . . . . . bä′-rĭng, bâr′-ĭng.
Baring-Gould . . . . bâr′-ĭng-gōōld′.
Barlaymont . . . . . bär-lä-môṅ′.
Bar-le-Duc . . . . . bär-lē-dük′.
Barmecides . . . . . bär′-mē-sīdz.
Barnabas . . . . . . bär′-ná-bás.

Barnato	bär-nä'-tō.
Barnay	*Ger.* bär'-nī.
Barnett	bär'-nĕt.
Barneveld	bär'-nĕ-vĕlt.
Baroccio, see Barozzio	bä-rŏch'-ō.
Baroda	bä-rō'-dä.
Baroja	bä-rō'-chȧ.
Baron	*Fr.* bä-rôṅ'. *Ger.* bä-rōn'.
Baronin	bä-rō'-nēn.
Baronne	bä-rŏn'.
Baroque	bä-rŏk'.
Barotse Land . . .	bà-rŏt'-sĕ-lȧnd.
Barozzi	bä-rŏt'-sē.
Barozzio, see Baroccio	bä-rŏt'-sē-ō.
Barrackpur	bär-äk-pōōr'.
Barradas	bär-rä'-däs.
Barragan	bär-rä-gän'.
Barranquilla	bär-rän-kēl'-yä.
Barranquitas	bär-rän-kē'-täs.
Barras	bä-räs'. *Fr.* bä-rä'.
Barré	bä-rä'.
Barrès, Maurice . . .	mō-rēs' bär-rĕz'.
Barrie	bär'-ĭ.
Barrili	bär-rē'-lē.
Barrot	bä-rō'.
Barrundia	bä-rōōn'-dē-ä.
Barry, Mme. du . . .	mä-dăm' dü bär-rē'.
Bar-sur-Aube . . .	bär-sür-ōb'.
Bartas	bär-tä'.
Barth	bärt.
Barthélemy-Saint-Hilaire	bär-tāl-mē'-săṅ-tē-lâr'.
Bartholdi	bär-tōl-dē'.
Bartholo	bär-tō-lō'.
Bartholomé	bär-tō-lō-mä'.
Bartimeus	bär-tĭm-ē'-ŭs.
Bartol	bär-tŏl'.
Bartoli	bär'-tō-lē.

Bartolommeo . . . . . bär-tō-lŏm-mā'-ō.
Bartolozzi . . . . . . bär-tō-lōt'-sē.
Baruch . . . . bā'-rŭk.
Bärwalde . . . . . . bâr'-väl-dŭ.
Barye . . . . bä-rē'.
Barzillai . . . . . . bär-zĭl'-ā-ī, bär'-zĭl-ā.
Baseelan, see Basilan . bä-sē'-län.
Basel . . . . bä'-zĕl.
Bashan . . . . . . bā'-shȧn.
Bashee, or Bashi (I.) . . bä-shē'.
Bashi-Bazouk . . . . băsh'-ĭ-bă-zōōk'.
Bashkirtseff, Marie . . mă-rē' bäsh-kērt'-sĕf.
Basil . . . . bā-'zĭl, băz'-ĭl.
Basilan, see Baseelan . bä-sē'-län.
Basilicon Doron . . . bă-sĭl'-ĭ-kŏn dō'-rŏn.
Baskunchak . . . . . bäs-kōōn-chäk'.
Basque . . . . bȧsk.
Basra, see Bussora . . bäs'-rä.
Bassanio . . . . . . bä-sä'-nĭ-ō.
Bassano (Duke of) . . bäs-sä'-nō.
Basses-Alpes . . . . bäs-zälp'.
Basses-Pyrénées . . . bäs-pē-rä-nā'.
Basse-Terre . . . . . bäs-târ'.
Bassi . . . . bäs'-sē.
Bassompierre . . . . bä-sôṅ-pē=âr'.
Bastian . . . . . . bäs'-tē=än.
Bastiat . . . . bäs-tē=ä'.
Bastien-Lepage . . . . bäs-tē=ĕṅ' lē-păzh'.
Bastile, or Bastille . . . băs'-tēl. *Fr.* bäs-tē'=yŭ.
Basundi . . . . . . bä-sōōn'-dē.
Basutoland . . . . . bä-sōō'-tō-lănd.
Bataan . . . . bä-tä-än'.
Batabano . . . . . . bä-tä-bä'-nō.
Batalha . . . . . . bä-täl'-yä.
Batan (I.) . . . . . . bä-tän'.
Batanes . . . . . . bä-tä'-nĕs.
Batangas . . . . . . bä-tän'-gäs.

Batavia	bȧ-tä′-vĭ-ȧ. *Jav.* bä-tä′-vĭ-ȧ.
Báthori, see Batory . .	bä′-tō-rē.
Bathsheba	băth-shē′-bä, băth′-shĕ-bȧ.
Batignolles	bȧ-tēn-yŏl′.
Baton Rouge	băt′-ŭn rōōzh. *Fr.* bä-tôn′
	rōōzh.
Batory, see Báthori . .	bä′-tō-rē.
Battenberg	băt′-tĕn-bĕrg. *Ger.*
	bät′-tĕn-bĕrch.
Battersea	băt′-ĕr-sē.
Batthyányi	bŏt′-yän-yē.
Batum, or Batoum . .	bä-tōōm′.
Baucis	bô′-sĭs.
Baudelaire	bōd-lâr′.
Baudissin	bow′-dĭs-sēn.
Baudricourt	bō-drē-kōōr′.
Baudry	bō-drē′.
Bautista	bä=ōō-tēs′-tä.
Bautzen	bowt′-sĕn.
Bavieca, see Babieca .	bä-bē=ä′-kä.
Bayambang	bī-äm-bäng′.
Bayamo	bä-yä′-mō.
Bayamon	bä-yä-mōn′.
Bayard (Chevalier) . .	bä′-ärd. *Fr.* bä-yär′.
Bayard (James A.) . .	bī′-ärd.
Bayazid, see Bajazet . .	bä-yä-zēd′.
Bayeux , ...	bä-yē′.
Bayle	bäl.
Bayombong	bä=ēŏm-bōng′.
Bayonne	bā-yŏn′, bī′-yŭn. *Fr.*
	bä-yŏn′.
Bayreuth, see Baireuth .	bī′-rŭth. *Ger.* bī-roit′.
Baza	bä′-thä.
Bazaine	bă-zĕn′.
Bazalgette, Léon . .	lä-ōn′ bă-zăl-zhĕt′.
Bazan, Don Cesar de .	dôn sä-zär′ dŭ bä-zän′.
Bazán, Emilia . . .	ä-mēl′-ē-ä bä-thän′.

Bazarof . . . . . . bä-zär'-ŏf.
Bazin . . . . bă-zăn'.
Beaconsfield . . . . bē'-kŏnz-fēld, bĕk'-ŏnz-fēld
Béarn . . . . bā-är'.
Béarnais, Le . . . . lē bā-är-nā'.
Beata Beatrix . . . bē-ā'-tä bē'-ä-trĭks.
Beaton . . . . . . bē'-tŏn. *Sc.* bā'-tŏn.
Beatrice . . . . . . bē'-à-trĭs. *Fr.* bā-ä-trēs'.
                                 It. bā-ä-trē'-chĕ.
Beatrice Cenci . . . . bā-ä-trē'-chĕ chĕn'-chē.
Beatrice Portinari . . . bā-ä-trē'-chĕ pōr-tē-nä'-rē.
Beatrix . . . . . . bē'-à-trĭks.
Béatrix . . . . . . bē'-à-trĭks. *Fr.* bā-ä-trēks'.
Beattie . . . . . . bē'-tĭ. *Sc.* bā'-tĭ.
Beau Brummel . . . . bō brŭm'-ĕl.
Beaucaire . . . . . . bō-kâr'.
Beauchamp (Alphonse de) *Fr.* bō-shän'.
Beauchamp (Philip) . . *Eng.* bē'-chăm.
Beauclerc, or Beauclerk . bō-klärk', bō'-klärk.
Beaufort . . . . . *Eng.* bō'-fŭrt. *Fr.* bō-fōr'.
Beaufort-en-Vallée . . bō-fōr'-tôn-väl-lā'.
Beaufort (Sir Francis) . bŭ'-fŭrt.
Beaugency . . . . . bō-zhŏn-sē'.
Beauharnais, Eugène de . ē-zhĕn' dŭ bō-är-nā'.
Beauharnais, Joséphine de zhō-zā-fēn' dŭ bō-är-nā'.
Beauharnais, Hortense de ōr-tŏns' dŭ bō-är-nā'.
Beaujeu, Anne de . . . ăn dē bō-zhē'.
Beaulieu . . . . . . bō-lē=ē'.
Beaumanoir . . . . . bō-mä-nwär'.
Beaumarchais . . . . bō-mär-shā'.
Beaumont . . . . . *Eng.* bō'-mŏnt, *or*
                                 bū'-mŏnt. *Fr.* bō-môn'.
Beaumont-sur-Oise . . bō-môn'-sür-wäz'.
Beaune . . . . . . bōn.
Beaune-la-Rolande . . bōn-lä-rō-länd'.
Beauregard . . . . . bō'-rĕ-gärd. *Fr.* bō=rĕ-gär'.
Beaurepaire . . . . . bō=rĕ-pâr'.

Beauvais . . . . . . bō-vā′.
Beaux . . . . bō.
Bebel . . . . bā′-běl.
Beccafumi . . . . . běk-kä-foo′-mē.
Beccari . . . . . . běk′-kä-rē.
Beccaria . . . . . . běk-kä-rē′-ä.
Becher . . . . běćh′-ĕr.
Bechuanaland . . . . bět-choo-ä′-nä-lănd.
Bechuanas . . . . . bět-choo-ä′-näs.
Becket (Thomas) à . . à běk′-ĕt.
Bécquer . . . . . . bā′-kĕr.
Becquerel . . . . . . běk-rĕl′.
Bedaween, see Bedouin . běd′-à-wēn.
Bede . . . . bēd.
Bedel (Timothy) . . . bē′-děl.
Bedivere . . . . . . běd′-ĭ-vēr.
Bedouin, see Bedaween . běd′-oo-ĭn.
Bedreddin Hassan . . . běd-rěd-dēn′ häs′-sän.
Beelzebub, see Belzebub . bē-ĕl′-zē-bŭb.
Beerbohm . . . . . bēr′-bōm.
Beersheba . . . . . bē-ēr-shē′-bà, bē-ēr′-shě-bà.
Beethoven, Van . . . . fän bā′-tō-věn.
Befana . . . . bā-fä′-nä.
Béguinage . . . . . . bā-gē-näzh′.
Beguins, or Béguines . . běg′-ĭnz or bā′gĭnz.
Behaim . . . . . . bā′-hīm.
Behar, see Bahar, Bihar . bě-här′.
Behechio . . . . . . bā-ä′-chē=ō, bā-ě-chē′-ō.
Behn (Mrs. Aphra) . . bān.
Behring, see Bering . . bē′-rĭng. Dan. bā′-rĭng.
Beira . . . . bā′-rä.
Beiram, see Bairam . . bī-räm′.
Beirut, see Bairut and Bey-
  rout . . . . bā-root′.
Béjart, Armande . . . är-mänd′ bā-zhär′.
Bejol . . . . bā-ćhōl′.
Bejucal . . . . . . bā-ćhoo-käl′.

Belarius . . . . . . bĕ-lā′-rĭ-ŭs.
Belaspoor, see Bilaspoor . bē-läs-pōōr′.
Belchite . . . . . . bĕl-chē′-tä.
Beleek . . . . bĕl-ēk′.
Belfagor, see Belphegor . bĕl′-fà-gôr.
Belfast (Ireland). . . bĕl-fäst′, bĕl-făst′.
Belfast (Maine) . . . . bĕl′-făst, bĕl-făst′.
Belfort . . . . *Fr.* bĕl-fōr′.
Belgian . . . . . . bĕl′-jĭ-ăn.
Belgiojoso . . . . bĕl-jō-yō′-zō.
Belgique . . . . . . bĕl-zhēk′.
Belgium . . . . . . bĕl′-jŭm.
Belgrad . . . . . . bĕl-gräd′.
Belgrade . . . . . . bĕl-grād′.
Belial . . . . bē′-lĭ= ăl.
Belianis (of Greece) . . bā-lē-ä′-nēs.
Belisario . . . . . . bā-lē-zä′-rē-ō.
Belisarius . . . . . . bĕl-ĭ-sā′-rĭ-ŭs.
Bélise . . . . bā-lēz′.
Beliza . . . . bĕ-lē′-zä.
Bellagio . . . . . . bĕl-lä′-jō.
Bellario . . . . . . bĕl-lä′-rĭ-ō.
Bellarmine . . . . . bĕl-lär-mēn′.
Bellatrix . . . . . . bĕl′-à-trĭks, bĕl-lā′-trĭks.
Bellay . . . . bĕ-lā′.
Belle Alliance, La . . . lä bĕl äl-lē-äṅs′.
Belleau . . . . . . bĕl-lō′.
Belle Île, or Belle Isle-en-
 Mer . . . . . . bĕl ēl′ ôṅ mâr′.
Belle-Isle (Newfoundland) bĕl-īl′.
Belle Jardinière, La . . lä bĕl zhär-dēn-ē=âr′.
Belle Laitière, La . . . lä bĕl lâ-tē=âr′.
Bellerophon . . . . bĕ-lĕr′-ō-fŏn.
Belliard . . . . . . bĕl-yär′.
Bellingham . . . . bĕl-ĭng-àm.
Bellini . . . . bĕl-lē′-nē.
Bello, Andres . . . bĕl′-yō. *Sp.*än-drĕs′bāl′-yō.

Belloc, Hilaire . . . . ē-lâr′ bĕl-ŏk′.
Bellona . . . . . . bĕl-ō′-nȧ.
Beloeil . . . . . . bĕl-ē′=yŭ.
Belon . . . . bĕ-lôṅ′, blôṅ.
Beloochistan, see Beluchis-
  tan, Baluchistan . . . bĕl-ōō-chĭs-tän′.
Belphegor, see Belfagor . bĕl′-fĕ-gôr.
Belphoebe . . . . . bĕl-fē′-bē.
Belshazzar . . . . . bĕl-shăz′-är.
Beluchistan, see Baluchis-
  tan, Beloochistan . . bĕl-ōō-chĭs-tän′.
Belvedere . . . . . bĕl-vĕ-dēr′. It.
             bāl-vā-dā′-rĕ.
Belvoir . . . . Eng. bē′-vẽr.
Belzebub, see Beelzebub . bĕl′-zē-bŭb.
Belzoni . . . . . . bĕl-tsō′-nē.
Bemba (L.) . . . . . bĕm′-bä.
Bembesi . . . . . . bĕm-bā′-zē.
Benaiah . . . . . . bĕ-nā′-yä.
Benalcazar, see Velalcazar bā-näl-kä′-thär.
Benares, see Banaras . . bĕ-nä′-rĕz.
Benbow (Admiral) . . . bĕn′-bō.
Bendavid . . . . . bĕn-dä′-fĭd.
Bender-Abbas, or . . . bĕn′-dĕr-äb′-bäs.
  Bender Abbasi . . . bĕn′-dĕr-äb-bä-sē′.
Benedetto da Majano . . bā-nā-dāt′-tō dä mä-yä′-nō.
Benedicite . . . . . bĕn-ĕ-dĭs′-ĭ-tē.
Beneke . . . . . . bĕ′-nĕ-kŭ.
Benevento . . . . . bĕn-ĕ-vĕn′-tō. It.
             bā-nā-vān′-tō.
Bengal . . . . bĕn-gôl.
Bengali . . . . . . bĕn-gô-lē′.
Benguela . . . . . . bĕng-gä′-lä.
Ben-hadad . . . . . bĕn-hä′-dăd.
Benicia . . . . . . bē-nĭsh′-ĭ-ȧ.
Beni-Mansur . . . . bā-nē-män-sōōr′.
Benin . . . . bĕ-nēn′.

Ben Ledi . . . . . . běn lĕd'-ĭ.
Ben Nevis . . . . . běn nĕv'-ĭs.
Bennigsen . . . . . běn'-nĭg-sĕn.
Benoît . . . . bĕ-nwä'.
Ben-oni . . . . . . běn-ō'-nĭ.
Bentham . . . . . . běn'-thȧm, běn'-tȧm.
Bentinck . . . . . . běn'-tĭngk.
Bentivoglio . . . . . běn-tē-vōl'-yō.
Bentzon, Théodore . . tä-ō-dōr' bôṅt-zôṅ'.
Benue, see Binue . . . běn-wē'.
Benvenuto Cellini . . . bän-vä-nōō'-tō chĕl-lē'-nē.
Ben Vorlich . . . . . běn vôr'-lĭċh.
Beowulf . . . . . . bä'-ō-wŏŏlf, bē'-ō-wŏŏlf.
Berabra, see Barabra . . bĕ-rä'-brä.
Béranger, de . . . . . dŭ bā-räṅ-zhä'.
Berar . . . . bā-rär'.
Berat . . . . bā-rät'.
Berber . . . . bēr'-bēr.
Berbera . . . . . . bēr-bā'-rä.
Berceo, Gonzalo de . . gŏn-thä'-lō dä bâr-thä'-ō.
Berchem, see Berghem . bĕrċh'-hĕm.
Berea . . . . bĕ-rē'-ȧ.
Berengaria . . . . . bĕr-ĕn-gâr'-ĭ-ȧ,
　　　　　　　　　bā-rĕn-gä'-rē-ä.
Berengarius . . . . . bĕr-ĕn-gâr'-ĭ-ŭs.
Bérenger . . . . . . bā-rŏṅ-zhä'.
Berenice . . . . . . bĕr-ĕ-nī'-sē.
Bérénice . . . . . . bā-rā-nēs'.
Beresford . . . . . . bĕr'-ĕs-fŭrd.
Beresina, or Berezina . . bĕr-ĕ-zē'-nä.
Bergami, Bartolomeo . . bär"-tō-lō-mä'-ō bâr'-gä-mē.
Bergamo . . . . . . bâr'-gä-mō.
Bergen-op-Zoom . . . bĕr'-ċhĕn-ŏp-zōm'.
Bergerac, Cyrano de . . sĭr-ä-nō' dŭ bĕrzh-răk'.
Berghem, see Berchem . bĕrċh'-hĕm.
Bergsö . . . . bĕrg'-sē.
Bergson, Henri . . . . ôṅ-rē' bârg-sôṅ'.

Berhampur	bĕr′-ăm-pōōr.
Bering, see Behring . .	bā′-rĭng, *or* bē′-rĭng. *Dan.* bā′-rĭng.
Bériot	bā-rē-ō′.
Berkeley	bĕrk′-lĭ, bärk′-lĭ.
Berlichingen, Götz von .	gĕts fŏn bĕr′-lĭćh-ĭng-ĕn.
Berlin	bĕr-lĭn′. *Ger.* bĕr-lēn′.
Berliner Tageblatt . . .	bâr-lē′-nĕr tä′-gä-blät.
Berlioz	bĕr-lē-yŏz′.
Bermoothes	bĕr-mōō′-thĕs.
Bermudas	bĕr-mū′-dȧz.
Bern, see Berne . . .	bĕrn. *Ger.* bĕrn.
Bernadotte	bĕr′-nȧ-dŏt. *Fr.* bĕr-nä-dŏt′.
Bernard	bĕr′närd, bĕr-närd′. *Fr.* bâr-när′.
Bernardin de St. Pierre .	bĕr-när-dăṅ′ dŭ săṅ pē=âr′.
Bernardine	bĕr′-när-dĭn.
Bernardo del Carpio . .	bĕr-när′-dō dĕl kär′-pē=ō
Berne, see Bern . . .	bĕrn. *Fr.* bĕrn.
Bernese	bĕr-nēs′, bĕr-nēz′.
Bernhardi	bârn-här′-dē.
Bernhardt, Sarah . . .	sā′-rä bĕrn′-härt. *Fr.* sä-rä′ bâr-när′.
Bernice	bĕr-nī′-sē.
Bernini	bĕr-nć′-nē.
Bernoulli, *or* Bernouilli .	bĕr-nōō′-yē.
Bernson, Bernhardt . .	bârn′-härt bârn′-sŏn.
Bernstorff	bârns′-tôrf.
Berri, *or* Berry	bĕr′-ĭ. *Fr.* bĕr-rē′.
Berruguete	bĕr-ōō-gä′-tĕ.
Bertha	*Ger.* bâr′-tä.
Berthelot	bĕr=tĕ-lō′.
Berthier	bĕr-tē=ä′.
Berthollet	bĕr-tō-lä′.
Bertin	bĕr-tăṅ′.
Bertrand	bĕr-träṅ′.
Bertuccio	bâr-tōōch′-ō.

Berwick . . . . . . bĕr'-ĭk.
Berzelius . . . . . . bĕr-zē'-lĭ-ŭs. *Sw.*
     bĕr-zĭl'-ĭ-ōŏs.
Besançon . . . . . bĕ-zän-sôn'.
Besant (Walter) . . . bĕs'-ȧnt.
Besant (Annie) . . . . bĕz'-ȧnt.
Besnard . . . . . . bĕs-när'.
Bessaraba . . . . . bĕs-ä'-rä-bä.
Bessarabia . . . . . bĕs-ȧ-rä'-bĭ-ȧ.
Bessières . . . . . . bĕs-ē=âr'.
Betelgeux, or . . . . bĕt-ĕl-gē'.
Betelgeuze . . . . . bĕt-ĕl-gēz'.
Betelguese . . . . . bĕt-ĕl-gēz', bĕt'-ĕl-gēz,
     or -gēs.
Bethabara . . . . . bĕth-ăb'-ȧ-rȧ.
Bethesda . . . . . . bĕ-thĕz'-dȧ, bĕ-thĕs'-dȧ.
Bethincourt . . . . . bĕ-tăn-kōōr'.
Bethlehem . . . . . bĕth'-lē-ĕm, bĕth'-lē-hĕm.
Bethmann-Hollweg . . bāt'-män hŏl'-vȧċh.
Bethpeor . . . . . . bĕth-pē'-ôr.
Bethphage . . . . . bĕth'-fä-jē, bĕth'-fäj.
Bethsaida . . . . . . bĕth-sā'-ĭ-dȧ, bĕth-sā'-dȧ.
Bethuel . . . . . . bē-thū'-ĕl.
Bethune . . . . . . bĕ-thūn'.
Béthune . . . . . . bā-tün'.
Bettina von Arnim . . . bĕt-tē'-nä fŏn är'-nĭm.
Bettws-y-Coed . . . . bĕt"-üs-ē-kō'-ĕd.
Beulah . . . . bū'-lä, bē-ū'-lä.
Beust, von . . . . . fŏn boist.
Bevis . . . . bē'-vĭs.
Bewick . . . . . . bū'-ĭk.
Bey . . . . bā.
Beyle . . . . bāl.
Beyle, Henri . . . . . ôn-rē' bĕl.
Beyme, von . . . . . fŏn bī'-mŭ.
Beyrout, see Bairut, Beirut bā'-rōōt. *Turk.* bī'-rōōt.
Beza . . . . bē'-zȧ.

Bezaleel	bĕ-zăl'-ē-ĕl.
Bèze, or Besze	bĕz.
Béziers	bā-zē=ā'.
Bhagalpur, see Boglipoor .	bhä-gäl-pōōr', bôg-ŭl-pōōr'.
Bhagavadgita . . .	bhă"-gă-văd-gē'-tä.
Bhagavatapurana . . .	bhä"-gà-vă-tà-pōō-rä'-nä.
Bhartpur, see Bhurtpore .	bhŭrt-pōōr'.
Bhawalpur	bhä'-wäl-pōōr.
Bheel, or Bhil	bēl.
Bhopal	bhō-pôl'.
Bhurtpore, see Bhartpur .	bhĕrt-pōr'.
Biafra	bē-ä'-frä.
Biagrassa	bē-ä-gräs'-sä.
Bianca Capello . . .	bē-än'-kä kä-pāl'-lō.
Bianchi	bē-än'-kē.
Biarritz	bē-är-rēts'.
Bias	bī'-às.
Bibbiena	bēb-bē-ā'-nä.
Biblical	bĭb'-lĭ-kl.
Bibliothèque Nationale .	bēb-lē-ō-tĕk' năs-ĭ=ō-näl'.
Bicester	bĭs'-tēr.
Bichat	bē-shä'.
Bicor	bē-kŏr'.
Bidassoa	bē-däs-sō'-ä.
Biddeford (Me.) . . .	bĭd'-ĕ-fōrd.
Bideford (Eng.)	bĭd'-ĕ-fŭrd.
Biela	bē'-lä.
Bierstadt	bēr'-stät.
Bigelow	bĭg'-lō.
Bigod	bĭg'-ŏd.
Bihac	bē'-häċh.
Bihar, see Bahar, Behar .	bĭ-här'.
Bilaspoor, see Belaspoor .	bē-läs-pōōr'.
Billardière	bē-yär-dē=âr'.
Billot (Gen.)	bē-yō'.
Bimani, or	bē-mä-nē'.
Bimini	bē-mē-nē'.

Bingen . . . . bĭng'-ĕn.
Biondi . . . . bē-ōn'-dē.
Binondo . . . . . . bē-nŏn'-dō.
Binue, see Benue . . . bĭn'-wē.
Biot . . . . bē-ō'.
Birejik . . . . bēr-ĕ-jĭk'.
Birmingham . . . . . bēr'-mĭng-àm.
Birnam . . . . . . bēr'-nàm.
Biron . . . . bĭr'-ŏn. *Fr.* bē-rôṅ'.
Bisayas . . . . . . bē-sä'-yäs.
Bismarck, or Bismarck-
  Schönhausen . . . . bĭz'-märk shĕn'-how-zĕn.
Bithynia . . . . . . bĭ-thĭn'-ĭ=à.
Bitolj . . . . bē-tŏl'=yŭ.
Biton . . . . bī'-tŏn.
Bivar, Rodrigo de . . . rōd-rē'-gō dä bē-bär'.
Bizet . . . . bē-zā'.
Björnson, Björnstjerne . be=ērn'-shâr-nŭ bē-ērn'-sŏn
Blackstone . . . . . blăk'-stŭn.
Blaise . . . . blĕz.
Blanc . . . . bläṅ.
Blanchard . . . . . bläṅ-shär'.
Blanche . . . . . . blănch. *Fr.* bläṅsh.
Blanco . . . . blän'-kō.
Blandamour . . . . . blän'-dä-mo͞or.
Blanqui . . . . . . bläṅ-kē'.
Blasius . . . . blä'-zĭ-ŭs.
Blavatsky . . . . . . blä-vät'-skĭ.
Blaze de Bury . . . . blăz dŭ bü-rē'.
Bléneau . . . . . . blä-nō'.
Blenheim, see Blindheim blĕn'-ĭm.
Blida, Blidah . . . . blē'-dä.
Blifil . . . . blĭ'-fĭl.
Blind . . . . *Ger.* blĭnt.
Blindheim, see Blenheim *Ger.* blĭnt'-hīm.
Bloemaert . . . . . blo͞o'-märt.
Bloemen . . . . . . blo͞o'-mĕn.

Bloemfontein	blōōm′-fŏn-tĭn.
Blois	blwä.
Bloomfield-Zeisler . . .	blōōm′-fēld-tsīs′-lĕr.
Blouet	blōō-ā′.
Blowitz	blō′-vĭts.
Blücher	blōō′-kēr. *Ger.* blü′-ċhĕr.
Blum	blōōm.
Blumenbach	blōō′-mĕn-bäċh.
Blumenthal	blōō′-mĕn-täl.
Blythe	*Eng.* blī.
B'nai B'rith	b′-nā brĭth.
Boabdelin	bō-äb′-dĕ-lĭn.
Boabdil	bō-äb-dēl′.
Boadicea	bō-à-dĭ-sē′-à.
Boanerges	bō-à-nēr′-jēz.
Boas	bō′-äs.
Boaz	bō′-ăz.
Bobadil	bŏb′-à-dĭl.
Bobadilla	bō-bä-dēl′-yä.
Boboli	bō′-bō-lē.
Boca Chica	bō′-kà chē′-kà.
Boca del Drago . . .	bō′-kä dĕl drä′-gō.
Boca del Sierpe . . .	bō′-kä dĕl sē-ĕr′-pā.
Boccaccio	bŏk-käch′-ō.
Boccardo	bŏk-kär′-dō.
Boccherini	bŏk-kā-rē′-nē.
Boche	bŏsh
Böckh	bēk.
Böcking	bēk′-ĭng.
Böcklin	bēk′-lēn.
Bode	bō′-dŭ.
Bodin	bō-dăṅ′.
Bodleian	bŏd-lē′-àn, bōd′-lē-àn.
Boece	bō-ēs′, bois.
Boehm	bēm.
Boellmann	bēl′-män.
Boeotia	bē-ō′-shà.

Boeotian . . . . . . bē-ō'-shȧn.
Boer . . . . bōōr.
Boerhaave . . . . bōr'-häv. D. bōōr'-hä-vě.
Boethius . . . . . . bō-ē'-thĭ-ŭs.
Bogdanovitch . . . . bŏg-dä-nō'-vĭch.
Boglipoor, see Bhagalpur . bôg-lĭ-pōōr'.
Bogotá . . . . bō-gō-tä'.
Bogra . . . . bŏg-rä'.
Bohemond, Bohemund . bō'-hē-mŭnd.
Bohio . . . . bō-yō'.
Böhme . . . . bē'-mŭ.
Bohol, see Sp. Bojol . . bō-hŏl'.
Bohun . . . . bō'-ŭn.
Boiardo, Bojardo . . . bō-yär'-dō.
Boiëldieu . . . . . . bwä=ĕl-dē=ŭ'.
Boii . . . . bō'-ĭ-ī.
Boileau-Despréaux . . bwä-lō'-dä-prä-ō'.
Bois de Boulogne . . . bwä dŭ bōō-lōn'=yŭ.
Boisdeffre . . . . . bwä-dĕfr'.
Bois de Vincennes . . . bwä dŭ văṅ-sĕn'.
Boise (Idaho) . . . . boi'-zě.
Bois Guilbert . . . . bwä gēl-bâr'.
Boisrobert . . . . . bwä-rō-bâr'.
Boito . . . . bō-ē'-tō.
Bojador (Cape) . . . bŏj-ȧ-dōr'.
Bojer . . . . bô'-yěr.
Bojol, see Bohol . . . bō-hŏl'.
Bokhara, see Bukhara, Bu-
charia . . . . . . bōk-hä'-rä, bō-ćhä'-rä.
Boldini . . . . bōl-dē'-nē.
Boleyn, or Bellen . . . bōŏl'-ĕn.
Bolingbroke . . . . . bŏl'-ĭng-brŏŏk.
Bolívar . . . . Sp. bō-lē'-vär.
Bologna . . . . . . bō-lōn'-yä.
Bolognese . . . . . bō-lōn-yēs', bō-lōn-yēz'.
Bolsena . . . . . . bŏl-sā'-nä.
Bolshevik . . . . . . bŏl'-shĕ-vēk.

Bolsheviki	bŏl′-shĕ-vē-kē.
Bolshevist	bŏl′-shĕ-vĭst.
Bolshevism	bŏl′-shĕ-vĭzm.
Bolsover (Castle) . . .	bŏl′-sō-vẽr, bow′-zẽr.
Bombastes Furioso . .	bŏm-băs′-tēz fū-rĭ-ō′-sō.
Bom Jesus	*Port.* bŏṅ zhā′-zŏŏsh.
Bonaca, or Bonacca . .	bŏn-ăk′-kä.
Bonacieux	bō-nä-sē=ē′.
Bonalde, Pérez	pā′-rĕs bō-näl′-dä.
Bonaparte, see Buonaparte	bō′-nȧ-pärt. *It.*
	bō-nä-pär′-tĕ.
Bonapartist	bō′-nȧ-pärt″-ĭst.
Bonaventura	bō″-nä-vän-tōō′-rä.
Bonci	bōn′-chē.
Bonheur	bŏn-ẽr′.
Bonhomme Richard . .	bŏn-ŏm′ rē-shär′.
Boniface	bŏn′-ĭ-fās.
Bonifacio	bō-nē-fä′-chō.
Bonn	bŏn. *Ger.* bŏn.
Bonnat	bŏn-nä′.
Bonnivard	bŏ-nē-vär′.
Bonnivet	bŏ-nē-vä′.
Bononcini, see Buononcini	bōn-ōn-chē′-nē.
Bonpland	bôṅ-pläṅ′.
Bon Silène	bôṅ se-lĕn′.
Bontemps	bôṅ-tôṅ′.
Bony	*Fr.* bō-nē′.
Boomplaats	bōm′-pläts.
Boötes	bō-ō′-tēz.
Booth	bōōth.
Borachio	bō-rä′-chē=ō, bō-rä′-chō.
Bordeaux	bōr-dō′.
Bordereau (The) . . .	bōr=dĕ-rō′.
Bordone	bōr-dō′-nĕ.
Boreas	bō′-rē-ȧs.
Borghese	bōr-gā′-zĕ.

Borgia . . . . bŏr′-jä.
Borgo . . . . bŏr′-gō.
Borneo . . . . bôr′-nē-ō.
Borodin . . . . . . bō-rō-dēn′.
Borodino . . . . . . bōr-ō-dē′-nō.
Borrioboola-gha . . . bŏr″-ĭ-ō-bōō′-lä-gä′.
Borromean (Is.) . . . bŏr-ō-mē′-àn.
Borromée . . . . . . bŏr-rō-mā′.
Borromeo . . . . . . bŏr-rō-mā′-ō.
Borromini . . . . . . bŏr-rō-mē′-nē.
Bosanquet . . . . . bō′-zăn-kĕt.
Bosboom . . . . . . bŏs′-bōm.
Boscawen (Admiral) . . bŏs′-kà-wĕn.
Boscobel . . . . . . bŏs′-kō-bĕl.
Boshof . . . . bŏs′-hŏf.
Bosna-Serai . . . . . bŏs″-nä-sĕ-rī′.
Bosnia . . . . bŏz′-nĭ-ä.
Bosphorus, or . . . . bŏs′-fō-rŭs.
Bosporus . . . . . . bŏs′-pō-rŭs.
Bossuet . . . . bŏ-sü=ā′.
Boston . . . . bŏs′-tŭn, bôs′-tŭn.
Boswell . . . . bŏz′-wĕl.
Botetourt . . . . . . bŏt′-ĕ-tōōrt.
Botha (Gen.) . . . . bō′-tă.
Bothwell . . . . . . bŏth′-wĕl, bŏŧh′-wĕl.
Botolph (St.) . . . . . bō-tŏlf′, bō′-tŏlf.
Botticelli . . . . . . bŏt-tē-chĕl′-lē,
                        bŏt-tē-shĕl′-lē
Boturini Benaduci . . . bō-tōō-rē′-nē bä-nä-dōō′-chē.
Botzaris, see Bozzaris . bōt′-sä-rēs, *pop.* bŏ-zăr′-ĭs.
Botzen, Bozen . . . bŏts′-ĕn.
Boucher de Perthes . . bōō-shä′ dŭ pârt′.
Boucicault . . . . . bōō′-sē-kō.
Boudinot . . . . . . bōō′-dĭ-nŏt.
Boufflers . . . . . . bōō-flâr′.
Bougainville . . . . . bōō-găṅ-vēl′.
Bouguereau . . . . . bōōg-rō′, bōō-gēr=ō′

Bouillé	bōō-yā'.
Bouillon	bōō-yôṅ', bōōl-yôṅ'.
Boulainvilliers . . .	bōō-lăṅ-vē-yā'.
Boulak, see Bulak . .	bōō-läk'.
Boulanger	bōō-läṅ-zhā'.
Boulevard des Italiens	bōōl-vär' dā zē-täl-ē=ěṅ'.
Boulogne, or	bōō-lōn'. _Fr._ bōō-lōn'=yŭ.
Boulogne-sur-Mer . .	bōō-lōn'-sür-mâr'.
Bourbon	bōōr'-bŭn. _Fr._ bōōr-bôṅ'.
Bourbon (Kentucky) . .	_pop._ bēr'-bŭn.
Bourbon l'Archambault	bōōr-bôṅ' lär-shäm-bō'.
Bourdaloue	bōōr-dä-lōō'.
Bourdon	bōōr-dôṅ'.
Bourgeois (Sir Francis) .	bŭr-jois'.
Bourgeois (François) . .	bōōr-zhwä'.
Bourgeois Gentilhomme, Le	lē bōōr-zhwä' zhôṅ-tēl-ŏm'.
Bourges	bōōrzh.
Bourget, Paul . . .	pōl bōōr-zhā'.
Bourgogne	bōōr-gōn'=yŭ.
Bourrienne, de	dŭ bōō-rē-ěn'.
Bourse, La	lä bōōrs.
Boutet de Monvel . .	bōō-tā' dŭ môṅ-věl'.
Bouvier	bōō-vēr'. _Fr._ bōō-vē=ā'.
Bouvines, see Bouvines	bōō-vēn'.
Bovary, Madame . .	mä-dăm' bō-vä-rē'.
Bovines, see Bouvines	bō-vēn'.
Bowditch	bow'-dĭch.
Bowdoin	bŏ'-dn.
Bowring	bow'-rĭng.
Boyacá	bō-yä-kä'.
Boyesen	boi'-ě-sěn.
Boylesve, René . . .	rē-nā' bwä-lāv'.
Boz	bŏz.
Bozzaris, see Botzaris .	bŏt'-sä-rēs, _pop._ bŏ-zär'-ĭs.
Brabançonne, La . . .	lä brä-bäṅ-sŏn'.
Brabant	brä-bănt', brä-bànt. _Fr._ brä-bäṅ'.

Brabant (Gen.) . . . . brä'-bănt.
Brabantio . . . . . . bră-băn'-shĭ=ō.
Bracciano . . . . . . bräch-ä'-nō.
Bradlaugh . . . . . brăd'-lô.
Braccio da Montone . . bräch'-ō dä mŏn-tō'-ně.
Bradwardine . . . . . brăd'-wär-dĭn.
Bragança . . . . . . brä-gän'-sä.
Braganza . . . . . . brä-gän'-zä.
Bragelonne . . . . . brăzh=ě-lŏn'.
Braham . . . . . . brä'-àm.
Brahe, Tycho . . . . tī'-kō brā or brä. *Dan.* brä'-ě.
Brahma . . . . . . brä'-mä.
Brahman . . . . . . brä'-màn.
Brahmaputra . . . . brä-mà-pōō'-trà.
Brahmasamaj, see Brah-
mosomaj . . . . . brä''-mä-sä-mäj'.
Brahmin . . . . . . brä'-mĭn.
Brahminism . . . . . brä'-mĭn-ĭzm.
Brahmosomaj, see Brah-
masamaj . . . . . brä''-mō-sō-mäj'.
Brahms . . . . . . brämz.
Braila . . . . brà-ē'-là.
Bramante . . . . . . brä-män'-tä.
Brandegee . . . . . brăn'-dě-gē.
Brandeis . . . . . . brăn'-dīs.
Brandenburg . . . . . brän'-děn-bōōrċh.
Brandes, Georg . . . yä-ôrċh' brän'-děs.
Branicki . . . . . . brän=yĭt'-skē.
Brantôme . . . . . . brän-tōm'.
Brasenose (Coll.) . . . brāz'-nōz.
Brassington . . . . . bràs'-n.
Brauwer, see Brouwer . brow'-ěr.
Bravo . . . . brä'-vō.
Brazil. Sp. Brasil . . . bră-zĭl'. *Port.* brä-zēl'.
Brazos . . . . brä'-zōs.
Brazza . . . . brät'-sä.

Breadalbane . . . . . brĕd-ôl'-bān.
Brébeuf . . . . . . brā-bēf'.
Breda . . . . *D.* brā-dä'.
Brederode . . . . . brā'-dä-rō"-dĕ.
Bregenz . . . . . . brā-gĕnts'.
Breisgau . . . . . . brīs'-gow.
Breitenfeld . . . . . brī'-tĕn-fĕlt.
Breitmann, Hans . . . hänts brīt'-män.
Brema, Marie . . . . mä-rē' brā'-mä.
Bremen . . . . . . brĕm'-ĕn. *Ger.* brā'-mĕn.
Bremer (Frederika) . . brām'-ēr. *Sw.* brĭm'-ēr.
Bremerhafen, or . . . brā'-mēr-hä"-fĕn.
Bremerhaven . . . . brĕm'-ēr-hä"-vĕn.
Brentano . . . . . . brĕn-tä'-nō.
Brera . . . . brā'-rä.
Brescia . . . . . . brĕ'-shä.
Breshkovskaya (-ia) . . brĕsh-kŏf'-skä-yä.
Breslau . . . . . . brĕs'-low, brĕs'-lō.
Brest . . . . brĕst
Brest-Litovsk . . . . brĕst-lē-tofsk'.
Bretagne . . . . . . brĕ-tän'=yŭ.
Breteuil . . . . . . brĕ-tē'=yŭ.
Bretigny . . . . . . brĕ-tēn-yē'.
Breton (Cape) . . . . brĭt'ŭn, brĕt'-ŭn.
Breton, Jules . . . . zhül brĕ-tôn'.
Breughel . . . . . . brē'-chĕl.
Brian Borohma, Boroihme,
 or Boru . . . . . . brī'-ȧn bŏ-rō'-mä, bŭ-rōō'.
Briance . . . . . . brē-än'-chĕ.
Briançon . . . . . . brē-än-sôn'.
Briand . . . . brē-än'.
Brian de Bois Guilbert . brē-än' dĕ bwä gēl-bâr'.
Briareus . . . . . . brī-ā'-rē-ŭs, brī'-ā-rūs.
Bridlington . . . . . bĕr'-lĭng-tŭn.
Brie . . . . brē.
Briel . . . . brēl.
Brieux, Édouard . . . ā-dōō-är' brē-ē'.

Brighthelmstone, Brighton brī'-tŭn.
Brignoli . . . . . . brēn-yō'-lē.
Brihuega . . . . . . brē-wā'-gä.
Bril . . . . brēl.
Brilessus . . . . . brĭ-lĕs'-ŭs.
Brillant . . . . . brē-yäṅ'.
Brillat-Savarin . . . brē-yä' sä-vä-räṅ'.
Brindisi . . . . . brēn'-dē-zē.
Brinvilliers . . . . brăṅ-vēl-yä'.
Briseis . . . . . . brī-sē'-ĭs.
Brissot de Warville . . brē-sō' dŭ vär-vēl'.
Britannia . . . . . brĭ-tăn'-ĭ-à.
Britomart, or Britomartis . brĭt'-ō-märt, brĭt-ō-mär'-tĭs.
Brobdingnag . . . . . brŏb'-dĭng-năg. [-nä'-jĭ-ăn.
Brobdingnagian . . . . brŏb-dĭng-năg'-ĭ-ăn,
Brody . . . . . . brō-dē'.
Broek . . . . . . brōōk.
Broglie, de . . . . . dŭ brōg-lē   Fr. dŭ brôg-lē'.
Broke (Sir Philip) . . . brŏŏk.
Bromley . . . . . brŭm'-lĭ.
Brontë . . . . . . brŏn'tē, brŏn'-tĕ.
Brough . . . . . brŭf.
Brougham . . . . . brōō'-àm, brōōm, brō'-àm.
                    Sc. brōŏċh'-àm.
Broughton (Hugh & Thos.) brô'-tŭn.
Broughton (Rhoda) . . brow'-tŭn.
Brougniart . . . . . brōōn-ē=är'.
Brouwer, see Brauwer . brow'-ēr.
Brown-Séquard . . . . brown-sā-kär'.
Bruch . . . . . . brōŏċh.
Brueys . . . . . . brü-ā'.
Bruges . . . . . . brōō'-jĕz.   Fr. brüzh.
Brugsch Bey . . . . . brōōksh, or brōōsh bā.
Brühl . . . . . . brül.
Bruis, see Bruys . . . brü-ē'.
Brumaire . . . . . brü-mâr'.
Brummell . . . . . brŭm'-ĕl.

Brunehaut . . . . . brün-ŭ=ō'.
Brunehild . . . . . . broō'-nŭ-hĭlt.
Brunehilde, see Brunhild   broō"-nŭ-hĭl'-dŭ.
Brunelleschi . . . . . broō"-nĕl-lĕs'-kē.
Brunetière . . . . . brün-tē=âr'.
Brunetto Latini . . . broō-nāt'-tō lä-tē'-nē.
Brunhild, see Brunehild . broōn'-hĭlt.
Brunhilde . . . . . . broōn-hĭl'-dŭ.
Brünig . . . . brü'-nĭċh.
Brunn . . . . brün.
Druno . . . . broō'-nō.
Brunswick-Wolfenbüttel . brünz'-wĭk-vŏl'-fĕn-büt"-tĕl.
Brussiloff (-ov) . . . . broō-sē'-lŏf.
Brut . . . . broōt.
Bruxelles . . . . . . brüs-sĕl', brüks-ĕl'.
Bruycker, Jules de . . zhül dē broi'-kĕr.
Bruys, see Bruis . . . brü-ē'.
Brydges . . . . . . brĭj'-ĕz.
Bryn Mawr (Pa.) . . . *pop.* brĭn mär'.
Bryn Mawr (Wales) . . brŭn-mowr'.
Buccleugh . . . . . bŭ-klū'.
Bucentaur . . . . . bū-sĕn'-tôr.
Bucephalus . . . . . bū-sĕf'-à-lŭs.
Bucer, see Butzer . . . bū'-sĕr.
Buch, von . . . . . . fŏn boōċh.
Buchanan . . . . . . bŭk-ăn'-ăn, bū-kăn'-ăn.
Bucharest, see Bukharest   boō-kà-rĕst', bū-kà-rĕst'.
Bucharia, see Bokhara . bū-kä'-rĭ-à.
Büchner . . . . . . büċh'-nĕr.
Buckingham . . . . . bŭk'-ĭng-àm.
Bucolics . . . . . . bū-kŏl'-ĭks.
Buczacz . . . . . . boōċh'-äch.
Buda Pesth . . . . . bū'-dà-pĕst. *Hung.*
                    boō'-dä-pĕsht.
Budaun . . . . . . boō-dä-ōōn'.
Buddha . . . . . . boōd'-à, boō'-dä, bŭd'-à.
Buddhist . . . . . . boōd'-ĭst, boōd'-ĭst, bŭd'-ĭst.

Buddism . . . . . . bŏŏd'-ĭzm, bōōd'-ĭzm,
                       bŭd'-ĭzm.
Budweis . . . . . . bŏŏd'-vīs.
Buena Vista . . . . bū'-nȧ vĭs'-tȧ. Sp.
                       bwä'-nä vĭs'-tä.
Buen Ayre . . . . . bwän ī'-rä.
Buencamino . . . . . bwän-kä-mē'-nō.
Buenoș Aires . . . bō' nŭo ā' rĭn. βρ.
                       bwä'-nōs ī'-rĕs.
Buffon . . . . bŭf'-ŭn. Fr. büf-ôǹ'.
Bugeaud de la Piconnerie bü-zhō' dŭ lä pē-kŏn=ĕ-rē'.
Bug Jargal . . . . . büg zhär-gäl'.
Buitenzorg . . . . . boi'-tĕn-zôrk.
Bukhara, see Bokhara, Bu-
  charia . . . . . . bōō-ċhä'-rä.
Bukharest, see Bucharest bōō-kä-rĕst', bū-kä-rĕst'.
Bukowina . . . . . . bōō-kō-vē'-nä.
Bulacan . . . . . . bōō-lä-kän'.
Bulak, see Boulak . . . bōō-läk'.
Bulawayo, see Buluwayo . bōō-lä-wä'-yō.
Bulgaria . . . . . . bŏŏl-gä'-rĭ-ȧ.
Bullen, see Boleyn . . . bŏŏl'-ĕn.
Buller (Gen.) . . . . bŏŏl'-ĕr.   [bü'-lŏv.
Bülow, Hans von . . . hänts fŏn bü'-lō. Ger.
Bultfontein . . . . . bŭlt'-fŏn-tīn.
Buluwayo, see Bulawayo . bōō-lōō-wä'-yō.
Bundelcund, Bundelkhand bŭn-dĕl-kŭnd',
                       bŭn-dĕl-känd'.
Bundesrath . . . . . bŏŏn'-dĕs-rät.
Bunsen . . . . bŭn'-sĕn. Ger. bŏŏn'-zĕn.
Bunwool . . . . . . bŭn'-wŏŏl.
Buola . . . . bōō-ō'-lä.
Buonaparte, see Bonaparte bōō=ōn-ä-pär'-tĕ.
Buonarroti . . . . . bōō=ōn-är-rō'-tē.
Buononcini, see Bononcini bōō=ōn-ōn-chē'-nē.
Buonsignori . . . . . bōō=ōn-sēn-yō'-rē.
Burano . . . . bōō-rä'-nō.

Burbon	bēr'-bun.
Burdett-Coutts	bēr-dĕt'-ko͞ots'.
Burdwan, see Bardwan .	bŭrd-wän'.
Burgdorf	bo͞org'-dôrf.
Bürger	bürg'-ĕr.
Burgh, Hubert de . . .	hū'-bĕrt dĕ bērg or bo͞org.
Burghley, see Burleigh .	bŭr'-lĭ.
Burgkmair	bo͞ork'-mīr.
Burgos	bo͞or'-gōs.
Burgundy	bŭr'-gŭn-dĭ.
Burleigh, see Burghley .	bŭr' lĭ.
Burleson	bēr'-lĕ-sŭn.
Burrhus, or Burrus . .	bŭr'-ŭs.
Burschenschaft	bo͞or'-shĕn-shäft.
Bury, Blaze de	blăz dŭ bü-rē'.
Busento	bo͞o-sĕn'-tō.
Bushiri bin Salim . . .	bo͞o-shē'-rē bĭn sä-lēm'.
Busiris	bū-sī'-rĭs.
Bussorah, see Basra . .	bŭs'-sō-rä.
Busuanga	bo͞o-swäng'-gà.
Bussy-Rabutin	büs-c̄'-rä-bü-tăṅ'.
Bustamante	bo͞os-tä-män'-tĕ.
Bustee	bŭs'-tē.
Butauan	bo͞o-tä═o͞o-än'.
Buteshire	būt'-shĭr.
Butte	būt.
Buttes de Chaumont . .	büt dē shō-mòṅ'.
Buturlin	bo͞o-to͞or-lēn'.
Butzer, see Bucer . . .	bo͞ot'-zĕr.
Buxhöwden	bo͞oks-hĕv'-dĕn.
Byblis	bĭb'-lĭs.
Byelostok	b-yĕ-lŏs-tŏk'.
Bysshe	bĭsh.
Byzantian	bī-zăn'-shĭ-àn.
Byzantine	bĭ-zăn'-tĭn, bĭz'-àn-tĭn, bī-zăn'-tĭn.
Byzantium	bĭ-zăn'-shĭ-ŭm.

C

Caaba, see Kaaba . . .	kä'-bȧ, kā'-ȧ-bȧ.
Cabal	kă-băl'.
Cabala, see Kabbala . .	kăb'-ȧ-lä.
Caballero, Fernan . . .	fâr-nän' kä-bäl-yä'-rō.
Caballos	kä-bäl'-yōs.
Cabanagem	kä-bä-nä'-zhām.
Cabañas	kä-bän'-yäs.
Cabanel	kä-bä-nĕl'.
Cabanilla	kä-bä-nēl'-yä.
Cabanis	kä-bä-nēs'.
Cabanos	kä-bä'-nŏs.
Cabatuan	kä-bä-tōō-än'.
Cabazera	kä-bä-thā'-rä.
Cabeça de Vaca, see Cabeza	kä-bä'-thä dā bä'-kä.
Cabell	kă'-bĕl.
Cabet	kä-bā'.
Cabeza de Vaca, see Cabeça	kä-bä'-thä dā bä'-kä.
Cabezas	kä-bä'-thäs.
Cabiao	kä-bē-ä'=ō.
Cabiria	kȧ-bē'-rĭ-ȧ.
Cabo Rojo	kä'-bō rō'ċhō.
Cabot	kăb'-ŏt.
Cabral	kä-bräl'.
Cabrera	kä-brä'-rä.
Cabul, see Kabul . . .	kä-bōōl'.
Cacama	kä'-kä-mä.
Cáceres	kä'-thä-rĕs.
Cadena	kä-dā'-nä.
Cadenus	kă-dē'-nŭs.
Caderousse	käd-rōōs'.
Cadillac	kăd'-ĭl-ăk. *Fr.* kă-dē-yăk'.
Cadiz	kā'-dĭz. *Sp.* kä'-dēth.
Cadmean	kăd-mē'-ȧn.
Cadorna	kä-dōr'-nä.
Ca' d'Oro	kä dō'-rō.

Cadoudal	kă-dōō-däl'.
Cadwalader	kăd-wäl'-à-dĕr.
Caedmon	kăd'-mŏn, kĕd'-mŏn.
Caelian	sē'-lĭ-àn.
Caen	kän.
Caerleon	kär-lē'-ŏn.
Caernarvon, see Carnarvon	kär-när'-vŏn.
Caesalpinus	sĕs-ăl-pī'-nŭs.
Caesarea	sĕs-ā-rē'-à, sĕz-à-rē'-ä.
Caesarian, see Cesarian .	sē-zā'-rĭ-ăn.
Caesarion	sē-zā'-rĭ-ŏn.
Caffarelli	käf-fä-rĕl'-lē.
Caffre, see Kaffir . . .	kăf'-ēr.
Cagayan	kä-gä-yän'.
Cagliari	käl-yä'-rē.
Cagliostro	käl-yōs'-trō. Fr. kä-yō-trō'.
Cagnes	kän'=yŭ.
Caguas	kä'-gwäs.
Cahors	kä-ōr'.
Cahuenga	kä-wĕng'-gà.
Caiaphas	kā-yà-fàs, kī'-à-fàs.
Caibarien	kä=ē-bä'rē=ĕn.
Caicos, see Caycos . .	kī'-kōs. Sp. kä'=ē-kōs.
Caillou, Le	lē kä=ē-yōō'.
Caillebotte	kä=ē-yē-bŏt'.
Caimanera	kä=ē-mä-nä'-rä.
Caimanes	kä=ē-mä'-nĕs.
Ça ira	sä ē-rä'.
Cairo (Egypt) . . .	kī'-rō.
Cairo (U. S.)	kā'-rō.
Caius Cestius . . .	kā'-yūs sĕst'-ĭ=ŭs.
Caius (College)	kēz, kēs.
Cajetan, or	kăj'-ĕ-tăn.
Cajetano, or	It. kä-yā-tä'-nō.
Cajetanus	kăj-ĕ-tā'-nŭs.
Cajigal	kä-ċhē-gäl'.
Calabar	kăl-à-bär', kä-lä-bär'.

Calabria . . . . . . ă. kă-lā'-brĭ-ȧ.
Calais . . . . kăl'-ĭs. *Fr.* kä-lā'.
Calajan . . . . . . kä-lä- hän'.
Calame . . . . . . kä-läm'.
Calamianes . . . . . kä″-lä-mē-ä'-nĕs.
Calaveras . . . . . . kăl-ȧ-vā'-räs, kȧ-lä-vā'-räs.
Calayan . . . . . . kä-lä-yän'.
Calchas . . . . . . kăl'-kȧs.
Calderari . . . . . . käl-dā-rä'-rē.
Calderon . . . . . . kăl'-dĕr-ŏn. *Sp.*
                      käl-dā-rōn'.
Calderon de la Barca . . kăl'-dĕr-ŏn dŭ lä bär'-kȧ.
                      Sp. käl-dā-rōn' dā lä
                      bär'-kä.
Caldiero . . . . . . käl-dē-ä'-rō.
Calgary . . . . . . kăl'-găr-ĭ.
Caliban . . . . . . kăl'-ĭ-băn.
Calif, see Caliph, Khalif . kā'-lĭf.
Caligula . . . . . . kă-lĭg'-ū-lȧ.
Caliph, see Calif, Khalif . kā'-lĭf.
Callao . . . . käl-lä'-ō, käl-yä'-ō, *pop.*
                      kăl-lā-o'.
Calle Obispo . . . . . kăl'-yĕ ō-bēs'-pō.
Callias . . . . kăl'-ĭ-ăs.
Callicrates . . . . . kăl-lĭk'-rȧ-tēz.
Callimachus . . . . . kăl-lĭm'-ȧ-kŭs.
Calliope . . . . . . kăl-lī'-ō-pē.
Callirrhoë . . . . . . kăl-lĭr'-ō-ē.
Callisthenes . . . . . kăl-lĭs'-thĕ-nēz.
Callisto . . . . . . kăl-lĭs'-tō.
Callistratus . . . . . kăl-lĭs'-trȧ-tŭs.
Callot . . . . kä-lō'.
Calmar, see Kalmar . . käl'-mär.
Calne . . . . kôn.
Calpurnia . . . . . . kăl-pẽr'-nĭ-ȧ.
Caltagirone . . . . . käl-tä-jē-rō'-nä.
Caltanissetta . . . . . käl″-tä-nē-sät'-tä。

Calumet	kăl'-ū-mĕt.
Calvados	käl-vä-dōs'.
Calvart, Calvaert . . .	käl'-värt. *Fr.* käl-vär'.
Calvé	käl-vä'.
Calvo, Baldassare . . .	bäl-dä-sä'-rĕ käl'-vō.
Calydon	kăl'-ĭ-dŏn.
Calypso	kă-lĭp'-sō.
Camacho	kä-mä'-chō.
Camaguey	kä-mä-gä'=ē.
Camanche, see Comanche	kă-măn'-chē.
Cámara (Admiral) . . .	kä'-mä-rä.
Camaralzaman	kăm-à-răl'-zà-măn.
Cambacerès	kän-bä-sä-rĕs'.
Cambay	kăm-bä'.
Cambert	kän-bâr'.
Cambon, Jules	zhül kän-bôn'.
Cambrai (-bray) . . .	kăm-brä. *Fr.* kän-brâ'.
Cambria	kăm'-brĭ-ä.
Cambronne	kän-brōn'.
Cambuscan	kăm-bŭs-kăn',
	kăm-bŭs'-kàn.
Cambyses	kăm-bī'-sēz.
Camelot	kăm'-ĕ-lŏt.
Camerarius	kä-mä-rä'-rē-ōōs.
Cameroon, see Kamerun .	kăm-ēr-ōōn', kä-mĕ-rōōn'.
Camille	kä-mēl'.
Camillo	*It.* kă-mĭl'-lō. *Sp.*
	kä-mĭl-yọ.
Caminha	kä-mēn'-yä.
Camino Real	kä-mē'-nō rä-äl'.
Camisards	kăm'-ĭ-zärdz.
Camoens, or	kăm'-ō-ĕns.
Camões	*Port.* kä-môn'-ēsh.
Camorra	kä-mōr'-rä.
Campagna di Roma . .	käm-pän'-yä dē rō'-mä.
Campan	kän-pän'.
Campanini	käm-pä-nē'-nē.

Campaspe . . . . . kăm-păs'-pē.
Campbell . . . . . kăm'-bĕl. *Sc.* kăm'-ĕl.
Campeador, El . . . . āl käm″-pā-ä-dōr'.
Campeachy, or Campeche kăm-pē'-chĭ, käm-pā'-chä.
Campeggio . . . . käm-pĕj'-ō.
Camperdown . . . kăm-pēr-down'.
Campo Formido . . käm'pō fōr-mē'-dō.
Campo Formio . . . käm'-pō fōr'-mē-ō.
Campo Santo . . . käm'-pō sän'-tō.
Campos, Martínez . . . mär-tē'-nĕth käm'-pōs.
Campus Martius . . . kăm'-pŭs mär'-shĭ-ŭs.
Camtoos . . . . . käm-tōs', käm-tōōs'.
Canaan . . . . . . kā'-nȧn, kā'-nā-ăn.
Canale, or Canaletto . . kä-nä'-lĕ, kä-nä-lāt'-tō.
Canalizo . . . . . kä-nä-lē'-thō.
Canaris, see Kanaris . . kä-nä'-rĭs.
Cancao, see Kang-Kao . kän-kow'.
Cancelleria . . . . kän″-chĕl-lä-rē'-ä.
Candace . . . . . kăn'-dȧ-sē.
Candahar, see Kandahar . kän-dä-här', kăn-dȧ-här'.
  or Candehar . . . kän-dĕ-här', kăn-dĕ-här'.
Candeish, see Khandesh . khän-dāsh'.
Candide, ou l'Optimisme . käṅ-dēd' ōō lŏp-tē-mēs'=mŭ.
Candolle . . . . . käṅ-dŏl'.
Canea, see Khania . . kă-nē'-ä.
Caney, El . . . . . āl kä'-nā.
Can Grande . . . . kän grän'-dā.
Canisius . . . . . kä-nē'-sē=ŭs.
Cannæ . . . . . . kăn'-ē.
Cannes . . . . . . kän.
Canon, Hans . . . . hänts kä'-nōn.
Canopus . . . . . kä-nō'-pŭs.
Canossa . . . . . kä-nŏs'-sä.
Canova . . . . . . kä-nō'-vä.
Cánovas del Castillo . . kä'-nō-väs dāl käs-tēl'-yō.
Canrobert . . . . . käṅ-rō-bâr'.
Cantabrian (Mts.) . . . kăn-tā'-brĭ-ȧn.

Cantacuzene . . . . . kăn″-tà-kū-zēn'. *Gr.*
                      kän-tä-koo̅'-zĕ-nĕ.
Cantacuzenus . . . . kăn″-tà-kū-zē'-nŭs.
Cantal . . . . käǹ-täl'.
Canto . . . . kän'-tō.
Canton (China) . . . kăn-tŏn'.
Canton (Ohio) . . . kăn'-tŭn.
Cantú, Cesare . . . chä'-zä-rĕ kän-too̅'.
Canuck, see Kanuck . . kă-nŭk'.
Canute, see Cnut . . . kà-nūt'.
Capaneus . . . . . . kà-pā'-nūs.
Cape Breton . . . . . b" ĭt'-ŏn, brŏt'-ŏn.
Capel . . . . kăp'-ĕl.
Capella . . . . . kă-pĕl'-là.
Capelle, von . . . . fŏn kä-pĕl'-à.
Capello . . . . . kä-pāl'-lō.
Capernaum . . . . kă-pĕr'-nā-ŭm.
Capet . . . . . . kăp'-ā, *or* kā'-pĕt. *Fr.*
                      kä-pā'.
Capetian . . . . . . kà-pē'-shàn.
Cape Verd, or Verde . . kāp vĕrd.
Cap Haitien . . . . . kăp ä=ē-sē-ĕǹ'.
Capistrano . . . . . kä-pĭ-strä'-nō.
Capitoline . . . . . kăp'-ĭ-tō-līn'.
Capitolinus . . . . . kăp-ĭ-tō-lĭ'-nŭs.
Capiz . . . . . . kä-pēth'.
Capo d'Istria, or . . . kä'-pō dēs'-trē-ä.
Capodistrias . . . . kä-pō-dēs'-trē-às.
Caponsacchi . . . . . kä-pōn-säk'-kē.
Caporetto . . . . . kä-pō-rāt'-tō.
Cappadocia . . . . . kăp-à-dō'-shĭ=à.
Cappello, see Capello . . kä-pāl'-lō.
Capreae . . . . . . kā'-prē-ē.
Caprera . . . . . . kä-prā'-rä.
Capri . . . . . . kä'-prē.
Capricornus . . . . . kăp-rĭ-kôr'-nŭs.
Caprivi, von . . . . . fŏn kä-prē'-vē.

Capua . . . . kăp'-ū-à. *It.* kä'-pōō-ä.
Capuchins . . . . . kăp'-ū-chǐnz.
Capucines . . . . . kă-pü-sēn'.
Capulet . . . . . . kăp'-ū-lĕt.
Capus, Alfred . . . . ăl-frĕd' kă-pü'.
Carabagh, see Kara-Bagh,
  or Karabagh . . . . kä-rä-bäg'.
Caracalla . . . . . . kăr-à-kăl'-à.
Caracallus . . . . . kăr-à-kăl'-ŭs.
Caracas . . . . . . kä-rä'-käs.
Caractacus . . . . . kăr-ăk'-tà-kŭs.
Cara-Mustafa, see Kara
  Mustapha . . . . . kä'-rä *or* kä-rä' mŏŏs'-tä-fä.
Caravaca . . . . . . kä-rä-vä'-kä.
Caravaggio . . . . . kä-rä-väd'-jō.
Carbonari . . . . . . kär-bō-nä'-rē.
Carcassonne . . . . . kär-käs-sŏn'.
Cárdenas . . . . . . kär'-dā-näs.
Cardonnel . . . . . kär-dŏn'-ĕl.
Carducci . . . . . . kär-dŏŏch'-ē.
Carême . . . . . . kă-rĕm'.
Carib . . . . kăr'-ĭb.
Caribbean . . . . . kăr-ĭ-bē'-àn.
Caribbees . . . . . . kăr'-ĭ-bēz.
Carignan . . . . . . kä-rēn-yäṅ'.
Carisbrooke . . . . . kăr'-ĭs-brŏŏk.
Carlén (Madame) . . . kär-län'.
Carlier, Don Diego . . dōn dē-ä'-gō kär-lē̄=âr'.
Carlisle . . . . . . kär-līl'.
Carlovingian, see Karlovin-
  gian . . . . kär-lō-vǐn'-jǐ-àn.
Carlowitz, see Karlowitz . kär'-lō-vǐts.
Carlsbad, see Karlsbad . kärlz'-bät.
Carlsruhe, see Karlsruhe kärlz'-rōō-ŭ.
Carlyle . . . . . . kär-līl'.
Carmagnole, La . . . . lä kär-män-yŏl'.
Carnarvon, see Caernarvon kär-när'-vŏn.

Carnaval de Venise . . kär-nä-väl′ dŭ vĕ-nēz′.
Carnegie . . . . . . kär′-nĕ-gĭ, kär-nä′-gĭ,
    kär-nĕg′-ē.
Carniola . . . . . . kär-nĭ-ō′-lä.
Carnot, Sadi- . . . sä-dē′-kär-nō′.
Carolina . . . . . . kăr-ō-lī′-nȧ.
Carolinian . . . . kăr-ō-lĭn′-ĭ-ȧn.
Carolus Duran . . . kăr-ō-lüs′ dü-räṅ′.
Carpaccio . . . . . . kär-päch′-ō
Carpeaux . . . . . . kär-pō′.
Carpio, Bernardo del . . bĕr-när′dō dĕl kär′-pē=ō.
Carracci, Agostino . . . ä-gōs-tē′-nō kär-räch′-ē.
Carracci, Annibale . . . än-nē-bä′-lĕ kär-räch′-ē.
Carranza . . . . . . kär-rän′-sä.
Carrara . . . . . . kär-rä′-rä.
Carreño, Teresa . . . tä-rä′-sȧ kär-rĕn′-yō.
Carrière . . . . . . kăr-rē=âr′.
Carriès, Jean . . . . zhäṅ kăr-rē=ĕs′.
Carrousel . . . . . . kär-ōō-zĕl′.
Cartagena, see Carthagena kär-tȧ-jē′-nȧ. *Sp.*
    kär-tä-ċhä′-nä.
Cartesian . . . . . . kär-tē′-zhĭ=ȧn.
Carthagena, see Cartagena kär-thȧ-jē′-nȧ. *Sp.*
    kär-tä-ċhä′-nä.
Carthaginian . . . . . kär-thȧ-jĭn′-ĭ-ȧn.
Carthusian . . . . . kär-thū′-zhĭ=ȧn.
Cartier, Jacques . . . zhäk kär-tē=ā′.
Caruso . . . . kă-rōō′-sō.
Caryatides . . . . kă-rĭ-ăt′-ĭ-dēz.
Casabianca . . . . kä″-zä-bē=än′-kä.
Casa Braccio . . . . . kä′-zä bräch′-ō.
Casa d'Oro . . . . kä′-zä dō′-rō.
Casa Guidi . . . . kä′-zä gwē′-dē.
Casas, Las . . . . läs kä′-säs.
Casaubon . . . . . . kă-sô′-bŏn. *Fr.* kä-zō-bôṅ′.
Cascine . . . . . . kä-shē′-nä.
Caserta . . . . . . kä-zâr′-tä.

Cases, Las . . . . . läs käz.
Cashmere, see Kashmere,
   Kashmir . . . . . kăsh-mēr'.
Casiguran (Bay) . . . kä″-sē-gōō-rän'.
Casimir . . . . . . kăs'-ĭ-mēr.
Casimir-Périer . . . . kăz-ē-mēr' pä-rē=ā'.
Cassagnac, Granier de . grä-nē=ā' dŭ kăs-sän-yäk'.
Cassibelaunus, see Cassi-
   vellaunus . . . . . kăs″-ĭ-bĕ-lô'-nŭs.
Cassiepeia . . . . . kăs″-ĭ-ĕ-pē'-yȧ.
Cassio . . . . kăsh'-ō.
Cassiopeia . . . . . kăs-ĭ-ō-pē'-yȧ.
Cassius . . . . . . kăsh'-ŭs.
Cassivellaunus, see Cassi-
   belaunus . . . . . kăs″-ĭ-vĕ-lô'-nŭs.
Castagno . . . . . . käs-tän'-yō.
Castaigne . . . . . . käs-tän'.
Castaños . . . . . . käs-tän'-yōs.
Castelar . . . . . . käs-tā-lär'.
Castelfranco . . . . . käs-tĕl-frän'-kō.
Castellamare . . . . käs'-tĕl-lä-mä'-rä.
Castellane, de . . . . dē kăs-tĕl-ăn'.
Castellon . . . . . . käs-tĕl-yōn'.
Castelnau . . . . . . käs-tĕl-nō'.
Castelnaudary . . . käs-tĕl″-nō-dä-rē'.
Castiglione . . . . . käs-tēl-yō'-nĕ.
Castilla, Sp. for Castile . käs-tēl'-yä.
Castillejo . . . . . . käs-tēl-yä'-ċhō.
Castillo . . . . . . käs-tēl'-yō.
Castlereagh . . . . kăs'-ĕl-rä.
Castro del Rio . . . käs'-trō dĕl-rē'-ō.
Catanduanes . . . . . kä″-tän-dōō-ä'-nĕs.
Catania . . . . . . kä-tä'-nē-ä.
Catarina Cornaro . . kä-tä-rē'-nä kōr-nä'-rō.
Catawba . . . . . . kȧ-tô'-bȧ.
Cateau Cambrésis . . kă-tō' kăṅ-brä-zē'.
Cathay . . . . kă-thā'.

Catiline	kăt'-ĭ-lĭn.
Cattack, see Cuttack, Katak	kŭt-tăk', kŭt-täk'.
Cattaro	kät-tä'-rō.
Cattegat, see Kattegat .	kăt'-ĕ-găt.
Caucasians	kô-kā'-shȧnz, kô-kăsh'-ȧnz.
Caucasus (Mts.) . . .	kô'-kȧ-sŭs.
Cauldon	kôl'-dŭn.
Caulincourt, de	dŭ kō-lăṅ-kōōr'.
Cauterets	kōt-rä'.
Cauto (River)	kä'=ōō-tō.
Cavaignac	kä-vän-yăk'.
Cavalcanti, Guido . . .	gwē'-dō kä-väl-kän'-tē.
Cavalieri, Lina	lē'-nä kä-vä-lē-ä'-rē
Cavalleria Rusticana . .	kä"-väl-lä-rē'-ä
	rōōs-tē-kä'-nä.
Cavan	kăv'-ȧn.
Cavaradossi	kä"-vä-rä-dōs'-sē.
Cavell	kȧ-vĕl'.
Cavendish	kăv'-ĕn-dĭsh, kăn'-dĭsh.
Cavey	kä-bā'=ē.
Caviedes	kä-bē=ĕd'-äs.
Cavité	kä-bē-tä'.
Cavour	kä-vōōr'.
Cawein (Madison) . . .	kā-wīn'.
Cawnpore, or Cawnpur .	kôn-pōr', kôn-pōōr'.
Cay	kä'=ē.
Caycos, see Caicos . .	kī'-kōs. *Sp.* kä'=ē-kōs.
Cayenne	kä-yĕn', kī-ĕn'.
Cayes, see Aux Cayes .	ō kä.
Cayister	kä-ĭs'-tēr.
Caylus	kā-lüs'.
Caymans	kī'mȧnz. *Sp.* kä=ē-mänz'.
Cayo Cocas	kī'-ō kō'-käs.
Cayor, see Kayor . . .	kī-ōr', *or* kī-ôr'.
Cay Smith	kī smĭth.
Cayster	kā-ĭs'-tēr.
Cazembe	kä-zĕm'-bĕ.

Cazin . . . . kä-zăṅ'.
Ceadda, see Chad . . . kĕ=äd'-dä.
Cean-Bermudez . . . thā-än' bĕr-moō'-t̄hĕth.
Ceará . . . . sē-ä-rä'.
Ceballos . . . . . . thā-bäl'-yōs.
Cebú, see Zebú . . . . sĕ-boō'. *Sp.* thā-boō .
Cecil . . . . sĕs'-ĭl, sĭs'-ĭl.
Cécile . . . . *Fr.* sā-sēl'.
Cecilia . . . . sē-sĭl'-ĭ-à. *It.* chā-chēl'-yä.
Cecily . . . . sĕs'-ĭ-lĭ.
Cecrops, see Kekrops . . sē'-krŏps.
Ced (St.), or . . . . . kĕd.
Cedda . . . . . . kĕd'-dà.
Cedric of Rotherwood . kĕd'-rĭk, sĕd'-rĭk ŭv
  rŏth'-ēr-woŏd.
Cedron, see Kedron, Kidron sē'-drŏn.
Cefalú . . . . chā-fä-loō'.
Celadon . . . . . . sĕl'-à-dŏn.
Celebes (Is.) . . . . . sĕl'-ĕ-bĕs, *or* sĕl'-ĕ-bēz.
Celia . . . . sē'-lĭ-ä.
Célimène . . . . . . sā-lē-mĕn'.
Cellini, Benvenuto . . . bān-vā-noŏ'-tō chĕl-lē'-nē.
Celsius . . . . . . sĕl'-sĭ-ŭs, sĕl'-shĭ=ŭs
Celts, see Kelts . . . . sĕlts, kĕlts.
Cenci . . . . chĕn'-chē.
Cendrillon . . . . . sôṅdrē-yŏṅ'.
Cenis, Mont . . . . . môṅ sĕ=nē'.
Cephalonia . . . . . sĕf-à-lō'-nĭ-à.
Cephas . . . . . . sē'-fàs.
Cephisodotus . . . . sĕf-ĭ-sŏd'-ō-tŭs.
Cerberian . . . . . . sēr-bē'-rē-àn.
Cerberus . . . . . . sēr'-bĕ-rŭs, sēr'-bē-rŭs.
Cerdic . . . . kēr'-dĭk.
Ceres . . . . sē'-rēz.
Ceri, di . . . . . . dē chā'-rē.
Cernawoda (-voda) . . chĕr'-nä-vō-dä.
Cerquozzi . . . . . . châr-kwŏt'-zē.

Cerro (The) . . . . . thĕr'-rō.
Cerro Gordo . . . . . sĕr'-rō gôr'-dō. *Sp.*
                 thĕr'-rō gōr'-dō.
Certosa, La . . . . . lä chĕr-tō'-zä.
Cervantes Saavedra . . sĕr-văn'-tēz, sä-ä-vä'-drä.
                 Sp. thâr-bän'-tĕs
                 sä-ä-bā'-drä.
Cervera . . . . . . thâr-bā'-rä.
César Birotteau . . . . sā-zär' bē-rŏt-tō'.
Cesare . . . . chā'-zä-rĕ.
Cesari . . . . chā'-zä-rē.
Cesarian, see Caesarian . sē-zā'-rĭ-àn.
Cesario . . . . . . sĕ-zä'-rĭ-ō.
Cesnola . . . . . . chĕs-nō'-lä.
Céspedes, de . . . . dā thĕs'-pā-dĕs.
Cetewayo, see Cettiwayo,
  Ketshwayo . . . . sĕt ĭ wä'-yō.
Cetigne, or Cettinje, or tsĕt-tĭn'-yĕ, *or* chĕ-tēn'-yā.
  Cettigno . . . . .   *It.* chĕt-tēn'-yō.
Cettiwayo, see Cetewayo,
  Ketshwayo . . . . sĕt-ĭ-wä'-yō.
Ceuta . . . . sū'-tä. *Sp.* thā'=ōō-tä.
Cévennes . . . . . . sā-vĕn'.
Ceylon . . . . . . sē-lŏn', sĕ-lŏn'.
Cézanne . . . . . . sä-zăn'.
Chabaud . . . . . . shă-bō'.
Chabert, Le Colonel . . lē kō-lō-nĕl' shä-bâr'.
Chablis . . . . . . shä-blē'.
Chabot . . . . . . shä-bō'.
Chachapoyas . . . . chä-chä-pō'-yäs.
Chacon y Castellon . . chä-kōn' ē käs-tāl-yōn'.
Chad (Lake), see Tchad,
  Tsad, Tschad . . . . chäd.
Chad (St.), see Ceadde . chăd.
Chaeronea, or . . . . kĕr-ō-nē'-à.
Chaeroneia . . . . . kĕr-ō-nē'-yà.
Chagres . . . . . . chä'-grĕs.

Chaillé-Long . . . . . shä-yā'-lôṅ'.
Chaillu, du . . . . . dü shä-yü'.
Chalcis . . . . . . kăl'-sĭs.
Chaldea . . . . . kăl-dē'-à.
Chaldean . . . . . kăl-dē'-àn.
Chaldee . . . . . kăl'-dē.
Chalgrin . . . . . shäl-grăṅ'.
Challemel-Lacour . . . shăl-mĕl'-lä-kōōr'.
Chalmers . . . . . chăl'-mĕrz, chä'-mĕrz.
             Sc. chô'-mĕrz.
Châlons . . . . . . shä-loṅ'.
Cham . . . . kăm.
Chamba . . . . . chăm'-bà.
Chambertin . . . . shäṅ-bĕr-tăṅ'.
Chambéry . . . . shäṅ-bā-rē'.
Chambezi . . . . . chăm-bē'-zĭ.
Chambord . . . . shäṅ-bōr'.
Chaminade . . . . shă-mē-năd'.
Chamisso . . . . . shä-mēs'-sō.
Chamonix, or . . . shä-mō-nē'.
Chamouni, or Chamouny . shä-mōō-nē'.
Champagne . . . . shăm-pān'. Fr.
             shäṅ-pän'=yŭ.
Champaigne, de . . . dŭ shäṅ-pān'=yŭ.
Champaran, see Chumparun chŭm-pä-rŭn'.
Champ-de-Mars . . . shäṅ-dŭ-märs'.
Champfleury . . . . shäṅ-flĕ-rē'.
Champigny . . . . shäṅ-pēn-yē'.
Champlain . . . . shăm-plān'. Fr. shäṅ-plăṅ'
Champollion . . . . shăm-pōl'-ĭ-ŏn. Fr.
             shäṅ-pŏl-yôṅ'.
Champs-Élysées . . . shäṅ-zā-lē-zā'.
Chanda . . . . . . chän'-dä.
Chang Chau . . . . . chäng'-chow'.
Changsha . . . . . chäng'-shä'.
Chanoine . . . . . shä-nwăn'.
Chanson de Geste . . . shäṅ-sôṅ' dŭ zhĕst'.

Chanson de Roland . . shän-sôn′ dŭ rō-län′.
Chanson de Roncevaux . shän-sôn′ dŭ rôns-vō′.
Chantecler . . . . . shän=tē-klĕr′.
Chantilly . . . . . . shän-tē-yē′.
Chapdelaine . . . . shäp=dē-lĕn′.
Chapelain . . . . . . shăp-lăn′.
Chapu . . . . chä-pōō′, shä-pōō′.
Chapultepec . . . . chä-pōōl″-tĕ-pĕk′.
Chardin . . . . . . shär-dăn′.
Chardonne, Jacques . . zhăk shär-dŏn′.
Charente . . . . . . shä-rŏnt′.
Chargé d'Affaires . . . chär-zhä′ dăf-fâr′.
Charlemagne . . . shär′-lĕ-mān. Fr.
  shärl-män′=yŭ.
Charleroi . . . . . . shär=lē-rwä′.
Charleville . . . . . shärl-vēl′.
Charlevoix . . . . . shär=lē-vwä′.
Charmian . . . . . . kär′-mĭ-án.
Charon . . . . . . kä′-rŏn.
Charpentier . . . . . shär-pôn-tē=ā′.
Chartier, Alain . . . ä-lăn′ shär-tē=ā′.
Chartism . . . . . . chär′-tĭzm.
Chartres . . . . . . shärtr.
Chartreuse . . . . . shär-trēz′.
Charybdis . . . . . kä-rĭb′-dĭs.
Chasles . . . . . . shäl.
Chasseloup-Laubat . . shäs-lōō′-lō-bä′.
Chassepot . . . . . shäs-pō′.
Chastelard, de . . . . dŭ shät-lär′.
Chasteler, du . . . . dü shät-lä′.
Châtaignerie, La . . . lä shä-tān=yŭ-rē′.
Chateaubriand . . . shä-tō-brē-än′.
Château d'If . . . . . shä-tō′ dēf′.
Château Lafitte . . . shä-tō′lä-fēt′.
Château Margaux . . . shä-tō′ mär-gō′.
Châteauroux . . . . . shä-tō-rōō′.
Château-Thierry . . . shä-tō′-tē=âr-rē′.

Châtelet . . . . . . shät-lā'.
Chatham . . . . . . chăt'-àm.
Châtillon . . . . . . shä-tē-yôṅ'.
Châtillon-sur-Seine . . shä-tē-yôṅ'-sür-sĕn'.
Chatrian . . . . . . shä-trē-äṅ'.
Chaucer . . . . . . chô'-sēr.
Chaulnes . . . . . . shōn.
Chaumont . . . . . shō-mŏṅ'.
Chautauqua . . . . . shô-tô'-kwà.
Chauvinism . . . . . shō'-vĭn-ĭzm.
Chavannes, Puvis de . . pü-vēs' dŭ shä-vän'.
Chedorlaomer . . . . kē''-dôr-lä-ō'-mĕr,
             lā'-ō-mĕr.
Che-kiang . . . . . chē-kyäng'.
Chemin des Dames . . shĕ-măṅ' dā dăm'.
Chenab, Chenaub, see
   Chinab . . . . . . chē-nôb'.
Chénier . . . . . . shä-nē=ā'.
Cheops . . . . . . kē'-ŏps.
Chephren . . . . . kĕf'-rĕn.
Cher . . . . shâr.
Cherbourg . . . . . shēr'-bĕrg. *Fr.* shâr-bo͞or'.
Cherbuliez . . . . . shâr-bü-lē=ā'.
Cherniavsky . . . . . tschĕr-nĭ-äf'-skĭ.
Chersonesus . . . . . kĕr-sō-nē'-sŭs.
Chertsey . . . . . . chĕs'-sĭ, chĕrt'-sĭ.
Cherubini . . . . . . kä-ro͞o-bē'-nē.
Chevalier . . . . . . shĕ-vä-lē=ā'.
Chevalier de Maison-Rouge shĕ-vä-lē=ā' dŭ mā-zôṅ'-
             ro͞ozh.
Chevalier de Saint George shĕ-vä-lē=ā' dŭ săṅ zhŏrzh'.
Chevalier d'Harmental . shĕ-vä-lē=ā' där-mŏṅ-täl'.
Chevillard . . . . . shĕ-vē-yär'.
Cheviot . . . . . . chĕv'-ĭ-ŭt, chĭv'-ĭ-ŭt.
Chevreuse . . . . . shĕv-rĕz'.
Chevy Chase . . . . chĕv'-ĭ-chās.
Cheyenne . . . . . . shī-ĕn'.

Cheyne	chān, chīn.
Chhatisgarh	chŭt-tēs-gär'.
Chiaja, La	lä kē-ä'-yä.
Chianti	kē-än'-tē.
Chicago	shĭ-kô'-gō.
Chichester	chĭ'-chĕs-tēr.
Chicot	shē-kō'.
Chienne	shē-ĕn'.
Chieveley	chĭv'-lĭ'.
Chih-li, see Chi-li . . .	chē'-lē'.
Chihuahua	chē-wä-wä.
Chi-li, see Chih-li . . .	chē'-lē'.
Chile or Chili	chĭl'-ĕ, chĭl'-ĭ. *Sp.* chē'-lĭ.
Chilkat	chĭl'-kăt.
Chillon	shĭl'-ŏn. *Fr.* shē-yôn'.
Chilpéric	chĭl'-pĕ-rĭk. *Fr.* shēl-pā-rēk'.
Chimæra	kī-mē'-rä.
Chimay	shē-mä'.
Chimborazo	chĭm-bō-rä'-sō.
Chinab, see Chenab . .	chē-nŏb'.
Chinese	chī-nēz', chī-nēs'.
Chingachgook . . .	chĭn-gäk'-gŏŏk.
Chingleput	chĭng-glĕ-pŭt'.
Chin-kiang	chĭn-kē-äng'.
Chinon	shē-nôn'.
Chinook	chĭ-nŏŏk'.
Chioggia, see Chiozza	kē-ŏd'-jä.
Chios, see Scio . . .	kī'-ŏs.
Chiozza, see Chioggia	kē-ŏt'-sä.
Chippewa, or . . .	chĭp'-pē-wä, chĭp'-pē-wä.
Chippeway	chĭp'-ĕ-wä.
Chiron	kī'-rŏn.
Chisholm	chĭzm.
Chisleu	kĭs'-lū.
Chiswick	chĭz'-ĭk.
Chita	chē'-tä.

Chitral . . . . chĭt-räl', *or* chī'-tràl.
Chittagong . . . . . chĭt-tà-gŏng'.
Chittim, see Kittim . . kĭt'-ĭm.
Chivery . . . . . chĭv'-ĕ-rĭ.
Chloe . . . . . . klō'-ē, *or* klō'-ĭ.
Chlom . . . . ċhŏlm.
Chlopicki . . . . . ċhlō-pĭt'-skē.
Chlotar, see Clotaire . . ċhlō'-tär.
Chmielnicki . . . . ċhmē=ĕl-nĭt'-skē.
Chocano, Santos . . . sän'-tōs chō-kä'-nō.
Cho-Cho-San, (see Cio-Cio) chō-chō-sän.
Choiseul . . . . . shwä-zēl'.
Choiseul-Praslin . . . shwä-zēl'-prä-lăṅ'.
Choisy . . . . . . shwä-zē'.
Cholmondeley . . . chŭm'-lĭ.
Chopin . . . . . . shŏ-păṅ'.
Chorazin . . . . . kō-rä'-zĭn.
Chosroes . . . . . . kŏs'-rō-ēz, kŏs'-rō-ĕz.
Chota, see Chutia . . . chō'-tä.
Chouans . . . . . . shōō'-ànz. *Fr.* shōō-äṅ'.
Chrestien, or Chrétien de
Troyes . . . . . . krä-tē-ĕṅ' dŭ trwä'.
Chriemhild, see Kriemhild krēm'-hĭlt.
Christe eleïson . . . krĭs'-tē ĕ-lä'-ĭ-sŏn.
Christian . . . . . krĭst'-yăn, *or* krĭst'-ĭ=àn.
Christianity . . . . krĭst-yăn'-ĭ-tĭ,
　　　　　　　　　 krĭst-ē=ăn'-ĭ-tĭ.
Christus . . . . . . krĭs'-tŭs.
Chronos . . . . . . krō'-nŏs.
Chryseis . . . . . . krī'-sē-ĭs.
Chrysostom . . . . krĭs'-ŏs-tŏm, krĭs-ŏs'-tŏm
Chumie . . . . . . chōō'-mē.
Chumparun, see Champaran chŭm-pà-rŭn'.
Chur, see Coire . . . . kōōr.
Churubusco . . . . . chōō-rōō-bōōs'-kō.
Chusan . . . . . . chōō-sän'.
Chutia, see Chota . . . chōō'-tē-ä.

Cialdini	chäl-dē'-nē.
Cibo (Cardinal)	thē'-bō.
Cibola, see Sibola . . .	sē'-bō-lä.
Cibrario	chē-brä'-rē-ō.
Cicero	sĭs'-ĕ-rō.
Cid, El	ĕl sĭd. *Sp.* äl thĭd.
Cid, Le	*Fr.* lĕ sēd.
Cienfuegos	thē-än"-fōō=ā'-gōs.
Ciergnon	sē-ârn-yôn'.
Cifuentas	thē-fōō=ĕn'-läs.
Cimabue	che-mä-bōō'-ā.
Cima da Conegliano . .	chē'-mä dä kō-nāl-yä'-nō.
Cimarosa	chē-mä-rō'-zä.
Cimmeria	sĭ-mē'-rĭ-à.
Commerian	sĭm-mē'-rĭ-àn.
Cimon	sī'-mŏn.
Cincinnati	sĭn-sĭn-nä'-tĭ.
Cincinnatus	sĭn-sĭn-nā'-tŭs.
Cingalon	thēn-gä-lōn'.
Cinq-Mars	săn-mär'.
Cinque Ports	sĭngk pōrts.
Cintra	sōn'-trä
Cio-Cio-San, (see Cho-Cho)	chō-chō-sän.
Cipango	sĭ-päng'-gō.
Cipriani	chē-prē-ä'-nē.
Circaean, see Circean . .	sēr-sē'-àn.
Circe	sēr'-sē.
Circean, see Circacan . .	sēr-sē'-àn.
Cisleithania	sĭs-lī-thä'-nĭ-à, sĭs-lī-tä'-nĭ-à.
Cisneros	thēs-nä'-rŏs.
Cispadane	sĭs-pä'-dän.
Cissey	sē-sä'.
Città della Pieve . . .	chēt-tä' dĕl'-lä pē=ā'-vĕ.
Ciudad Bolívar	sē-ōō-däd' bō-lē'-vär.
Ciudad de Cadiz . . .	thē=ōō-däd' dä kä'-dĭth.
Ciudad Real	thē=ōō-däd' rä-äl'.
Ciudad Rodrigo	thē=ōō-däd' rōd-rē'-gō.

Cività Vecchia, Civitavecchia chē-vē-tä′ vĕk′-kē-ä.
Claes . . . . kläz.
Clairault, or Clairaut . . klā-rō′.
Clairvaux . . . . . . klår-vō′.
Claretie . . . . . . klăr-tē′.
Claude, Georges . . . zhōrzh klōd.
Claudel, Paul . . . . pōl klō-dĕl′.
Claude Lorraine . . . klōd lō-rĕn′.
Claverhouse . . . . . klăv′-ēr-ŭs.
Cléante . . . . . . klā-äṅt′.
Cleishbotham . . . . klēsh′-bŏℏ-ȧm.
Cleisthenes, see Clisthenes klĭs′-thĕ-nēz.
Clélie . . . . klā-lē′.
Clémenceau . . . . . klā-mŏṅ-sō′.
Clément . . . . . . klā-môṅ′.
Clemente, San . . . . sän klā-mĕn′-tĕ.
Clementi . . . . . . klā-mĕn′-tē.
Clementine . . . . . klĕm′-ĕn-tĭn, klĕm′-ĕn-tēn,
                        or klĕm-ĕn-tēn′.
Cleobis . . . . . . klē′-ō-bĭs.
Cleopas . . . . . . klē′-ō-păs.
Cleopatra . . . . . . klē-ō-pā′-trȧ.
Cléopâtre . . . . . . klā-ō-pătr′.
Cleves, or . . . . . . klēvz.
Clèves . . . . Fr. klåv.
Clio . . . . klĭ′-ō.
Clisthenes, see Cleisthenes klĭs′-thĕ-nēz.
Clitandre . . . . . . klē-täṅdr′.
Clive . . . . klīv.
Cloaca Maxima . . . . klō-ā′-kȧ măk′-sĭ-mȧ.
Cloisonné . . . . . . klwä-zŏn-nā′.
Clonmel . . . . . . klŏn-mĕl′.
Clos Vougeot . . . . klō vōō-zhō′.
Clotaire, see Chlotar . . klō-tår′.
Clouet . . . . klōō-ā′.
Clough . . . . klŭf.
Cluseret (Gen.) . . . . klü=zĕ-rā′.

Clusium	klū'-sĭ-ŭm, klū'-shĭ-ŭm.
Cnidian	nĭd'-ĭ-àn.
Cnidus	nī'-dŭs.
Cnut, see Canute . . .	knōōt.
Coachella	kō-à-chĕl'-à.
Coahuila	kō-à-wē'-là.
Coamo	kō-ä'-mō.
Coanza, see Kuanza, Quanza	kō-än'-zä.
Cobi, see Gobi . . .	kō'-bē.
Coblenz, or Coblentz . .	kō'-blĕnts.
Cobre, El	ĕl kō'-brā.
Cochin China	kō'-chĭn chī'-nà.
Cockagne, or Cockaigne .	kŏk-ān'.
Cockburn	kō'-bŭrn.
Cocles	kō'-klēz.
Cocytus	kō-sī'-tŭs.
Codrus	kō'-drŭs.
Cœlebs	sē'-lĕbz.
Coelho, or Coello . . .	kō-ĕl'-yō.
Coelian Hill	sē'-lĭ-àn.
Coeur d'Alène	kĕr dă-lĕn'.
Coeur de Lion	kĕr dŭ lī'-ŏn. *Fr.* kĕr dŭ lē-ôn'.
Cognac	kōn-yäk'.
Cohoes	kō-hōz'.
Coimbatore, see Koimbatur	kō-ĭm"-bà-tōr'.
Coire, see Chur	kwär.
Coke	kōk, *originally* kŏŏk.
Colapur, see Kolhapur .	kō-lä-pōōr'.
Colbert	*Fr.* kōl-bâr'.
Colenso	kō-lĕn'-sō.
Coleone, see Colleoni . .	kō-lā-ō'-nā.
Colesberg	kōlz'-bĕrg.
Colet	kŏl'-ĕt.
Coligni, or Coligny . .	kō-lēn'-yē. *Fr.* kō-lēn-yē'.
Colin Clout	kŏl'-ĭn klowt.
Coliseum, see Colosseum .	kŏl-ĭ-sē'-ŭm.

Colleoni, see Coleone . . kōl-lä-ō'-nē.
Colletta . . . . . . kŏl-lĕt'-tä.
Colmar, see Kolmar . . kōl-mär'.
Cologne . . . . . . kä-lōn'. *Fr.* kō-lōn'=yŭ.
Colon . . . . kŏ-lŏn'. *Sp.* kō-lōn'.
Colon Cristóbal . . . . krēs-tō'-bäl kō-lōn'.
Colonel Chabert . . . kō-lō-nĕl' shä-bâr'.
Colonna . . . . . . kō-lŏn'-nä.
Coloocan . . . . . . kŏl-ō'-kăn.
Colorado . . . . . . kŏl-ō-rä'-dō.
Colosse . . . . kō-lŏs-sē.
Colosseum, see Coliseum kŏl-ō-sē'-ŭm.
Colquhoun . . . . . kŏ-hōōn'.
Comacchio . . . . . kō-mäk'-kē=ō.
Comanche, see Camanche kō-măn'-chē.
Combe . . . . kōm, kōōm.
Comédie Française . . . kō-mä-dē' frän-sĕz'.
Comédie Humaine . . . kō-mä-dē' ü-mĕn'.
Comeiro . . . . . . kō-mä'=ē-rō.
Comines, or Commines . kŏ-mēn'.
Commodus . . . . . kŏm'-mō-dŭs.
Commune . . . . . . kŏm'-yūn. *Fr.* kŏm-ün'.
Comneni . . . . . . kŏm-nē'-nī.
Comnenus . . . . . kŏm-nē'-nŭs.
Comorin . . . . . . kŏm'-ō-rĭn.
Compagnie Général— kôṅ-pän-yē' zhä-nä-răl'
    Transatlantique . . . tränz-ät-läṅ-tēk'.
Compiègne . . . . . kôṅ-pē-ān'=yŭ.
Comte . . . . kôṅt.
Comtesse de Rudolstadt . kôṅ-tĕs' dŭ rü-dŏl-stät'.
Comtist . . . . . kŏm'-tĭst. *Fr.* kōṅ-tēst'.
Comus . . . . kō'-mŭs.
Concas . . . . kōng'-käs.
Concepcion . . . . . kŏn-sĕp'-shŏn. *Sp.* kōn-
    thäp″-thē-ōn'.
Conchita . . . . . kōn-chē'-tȧ.
Conciergerie . . . . . kōn-sē=ĕr-zhē-rē'.

Concini . . . . *It.* kŏn-chē'-nē. *Fr.*
kŏn-sē-nē'.
Concone . . . . . . kōn-kō'-nā.
Concordat . . . . . kŏn-kôr'-dăt. *Fr.*
kŏṅ-kōr-dä'.
Condé . . . . kôṅ-dā'.
Condé-sur-Noireau . . kôṅ-dā'-sür-nwä-rō'.
Condillac . . . . . . kôṅ-dē-yäk'.
Condorcet, de . . . . du kôṅ-dōr-sā.
Conegliano, Cima da . . chē'-mä dä kō-nāl-yä'-no.
Confessio Amantis . . . kŏn'-fĕsh'-ō ā-măn'-tĭs.
Conflans . . . . . . kôn-fläṅ'.
Congreve . . . . . . kŏng'-grev.
Coniston . . . . . . kŏn'-ĭs-tŭn.
Connaught . . . . . kŏn'-nôt.
Conradin . . . . . . kōn'-rä-dēn.
Consalvi . . . . . . kōn-säl'-vē.
Constable . . . . . . kŭn'-stà-bl.
Constant de Rebecque . kôṅ-stäṅ' dŭ rē-bĕk'.
Constantine (Emperor) . kŏn'-stàn-tīn.
Constantine (Algeria) . . kôn-stäṅ-tēn'.
Constanza . . . . . . kŏn-stän'-zä.
Consuelo . . . . . . kŏn-sōō-ä'-lo. *Fr.*
kŏṅ-sü=ā-lŏ'.
Conte . . . . kōn-tā.
Contel . . . . kŏn-tĕl'.
Contes d'Hoffmann . . kōnt dŏf-män'.
Contessa . . . . . . kōn-tĕs'-sä.
Conti . . . . kônt-tē'.
Contreras . . . . . . kōn-trä'-räs.
Conybeare . . . . . . kŭn'-i-bĕr.
Coomassie, see Kumassi . kōō-mäs'-sē.
Coombe . . . . . . kōōm.
Copenhagen . . . . . kō-pĕn-hā'-gĕn. *Dan.*
kō-pĕn-hä'-gĕn
Copernicus . . . . . kō-pēr-'nĭ-kŭs.
Cophetua . . . . . . kō-fĕt'-ū-à.

Coppée François . . . . frän-swä' kŏp-pā'.
Coquelin . . . . . . kōk-lăn'.
Corcyra . . . . . . kôr-sī'-rà.
Corday d'Armans . . . kôr-dā där-män'.
Cordeliers . . . . . kōr-dĕ-lē=ā'.
Cordilleras . . . . kôr-dĭl'-ēr-àz. Sp.
          kōr-dĕl-yā'-räs.
Córdoba, or Cordova . . kôr'-dō-vä. Sp.kōr'-dō-bä.
Cordovan . . . . . . kôr'-do-vàn.
Corea, see Korea . . . kō-rē'-à.
Corean, see Korean . . kō-rē'-àn.
Corfu . . . . kŏr-fōō', kŏr-fŭ'.
Cori . . . . kō'-rē
Coriolanus . . . . . kō"-rĭ-ō-lā'-nŭs.
Corioli . . . . . . kō-rī'-ō-lē.
Corleone . . . . . . kōr-lā-ō'-nā.
Cornaro . . . . . . kōr-nä'-rō.
Corneille . . . . . . kŏr-nāl. Fr. kōr-nā'=yŭ.
Cornelis . . . . . . kŏr-nā'-lĭs.
Cornice, or . . . . . It. kōr'-nē-chä.
Corniche . . . . . . Fr. kôr-nēsh'.
Corona Borealis . . . kō-rō'-nä bō-rē-ā'-lĭs.
Corozal . . . . . . kō-rō-säl'.
Corot . . . . kō-rō'.
Correa . . . . kōr-rā'-ä.
Correggio . . . . . . kŏr-rĕd'-jō.
Corregidor . . . . . kŏr"-rāċh-ē-dōr'
Corrèze . . . . . . kŏr-râz'.
Corrientes . . . . . kŏr-rē-ĕn'-tĕs.
Cortes (The) . . . . . kŏr'-tĕs.
Cortés (Fernando) or . . kŏr tās'.
Cortez . . . . kŏr'-tĕz.
Coruña, La . . . . . lä kō-rōōn'-yä.
Corunna . . . . . . kō-rŭn'-à.
Corvisart-Desmarets . . kōr-vē-zär' dā-mä-rā'.
Corydon . . . . . . kŏr'-i-dŏn
Cosette . . . . . . kō-zet'.

Cosimo	kō'-zē-mō.
Cosmati	kōs-mä'-tē.
Cosmo de Medici . . .	kōs'-mō dä mä'-dē-chē.
Cossack	kŏs'-ăk, kŏz-ăk'.
Costa Rica	kŏs'-tä rē'-kä. *Sp.*
	kōs'-tä.
Costis	kŏs'-tĭs.
Côte d'Azur	kŏt dă-zür'.
Côte d'Or	kŏt'- dōr'.
Cotes du Nord	kŏt'-dü-nōr'.
Cottin	kōt-tăṅ'.
Coucy	kōō-sē'.
Coulanges	kōō-läṅzh'.
Coulommiers	kōō-lŏm-ē=ā'.
Couperin	kōō-pē-răṅ'.
Couperus	kōō-pâr'-ōōs.
Courbet	kōōr-bä'.
Courcelles	kōōr-sĕl'.
Courcy	kōōr-sē'.
Courland	kōōr'-lănd.
Courtenay	kẽrt'-nā, kōŏrt'-nā.
Courtois	kōōr-twä'.
Courtrai, or Courtray . .	kōōr-trā'.
Cousin, Victor . . .	vēk-tōr' kōō-zăṅ'
Cousin Pons	kōō-zăṅ' pôṅ.
Cousine Bette . . .	kōō-zēn' bĕt.
Coutances	kōō-täṅs'.
Coutras	kōō-trä'.
Couture	kōō-tür'.
Covent (Garden) . . .	kŭv'-ĕnt.
Coventry	kŭv'-ĕn-trĭ.
Correa	kŏr-rā'-ä.
Correggio	kŏr-rĕd'-jō.
Corregidor	kŏr"-rāch-ē-dōr'.
Corrèze	kŏr-rĕz'.
Coxsackie	kōŏk-sô'-kĭ.
Coysevox	kwäz-vŏks'.

Craigenputtoch, or . . . *Sc.* krä-gĕn-pŭt'-ŏċh.
Craigenputtock . . . . krä-gĕn-pŭt'-ŏk.
Cramer . . . . . . *Ger.* krä'-mĕr.
Cranach (Lucas), see Kranach krăn'-ȧk, krä'-näċh.
Craonne . . . . . . krä-ŏn'.
Crapaud . . . . . . kră-pō'.
Cratylus . . . . . . krăt'-ĭ-lŭs.
Crébillon . . . . . . krä-bē-yôṅ'.
Créçy, see Cressy . . . krĕs'-ĭ. *Fr.* krä-sē'.
Credi . . . . krä'-dē.
Crédit Lyonnais . . . krä-dē' lē-ŏn-ĕ'.
Crédit Mobilier . . . . krĕd'-ĭt mō-bē'-lĕ-ēr. *Fr.*
     .krä-dē' mō-bē-lē=ä'.
Crémieux . . . . . . krä-mē-ē'.
Cremona . . . . . . krē-mō'-nä. *It.* krä-mō'-nä.
Crespy, or Crêpy-en-
 Laonnais . . . . krä-pē' ôṅ lä=ō-nä'.
Cressida . . . . . . krĕs'-ĭ-dȧ.
Cressy, see Créçy . . . krĕs'-ĭ.
Creusa . . . . krē-ū'-sȧ.
Creuse . . . . krēz.
Creusot, or Creuzot . . krē-zō'.
Crèvecœur . . . . . kräv-kēr'.
Crichton . . . . . . krī'tŏn.
Crillon . . . . krē-yôṅ'.
Crimea . . . . . . krĭ-mē'-ȧ, krī-mē'-ȧ.
Crispi . . . . krĭs'-pē.
Cristóbal Colón . . . krēs-tō'-bäl kō-lōn'.
Cristofori . . . . . . krĭs-tō-fō'-rē.
Critias . . . . krĭsh'-ĭ-ȧs.
Crito . . . . krī'-tō.
Crivelli . . . . . . krē-vel'-lē.
Crna Gora, see Czernagora chĕr'-nä gō'-rä.
Croat . . . . krō'-ăt.
Croatia . . . . . . krō-ā'-shē=ȧ.
Cromwell . . . . . . krŏm'-wĕl, krŭm'-wĕl.
     pop. krŭm'-l.

Cronaca	krōn'-ä-kä.
Cronjé	krŏn'-yĕ.
Cronstadt, see Kronstadt .	krŏn'-stăt. *Ger.* krōn'-stät.
Cronus, or Cronos, see	
Kronos	krō'-nŭs.
Cruz	krōōth.
Ctesias	tē'-shĭ=às.
Cuba	kū'-bä. *Sp.* kōō'-bä.
Cuchulain, (or -lin, etc.) .	kōō-'hōō'-lĕn.
Cuddalore	kŭd-dȧ-lōr'.
Cuddapah, see Kadapa .	kŭd'-dȧ-pä.
Cuenca	kōō̄—ĕn'-kä.
Cuernavaca	kwĕr-nä-vä'-kä.
Cui, César	tsä'-zär kwē.
Culebra	kōō-lä'-brȧ.
Culiacan	kōō-lē-ä-kän'.
Culion	kōō-lē-ōn'.
Culloden	kŭl-lō'-dĕn.
Culmbach, see Kulmbach	kŏŏlm'-bäċh.
Cumae	kū'-mē.
Cumaean	kū-mē'-ȧn.
Cumières	kü-mē=âr'.
Cunctator	kŏŏngk-tä'-tôr.
Cuneo	kōō-nä'-ō.
Cupey	kōō-pä'=ē.
Curaçao, or Curazao, or .	kōō-rä-sä'-ō, kū'-rȧ-sō,
Curaçoa	kū'-rȧ-sō''-a, kōō-rä-sō'-ä, kōō-rä-sō'.
Curico	kōō-rē-kō'.
Curie	kü-rē'.
Curtius	*Ger.* kōōr'-tsē-ŏŏs. *Lat.* kĕr'-shĭ-ŭs.
Curzon	kĕr'-zŭn.
Cush	kŭsh.
Custine	küs-tēn'.
Custoza, or	kŏŏs-tōd'-sä.
Custozza	kŏŏs-tōt'-zä.

Cüstrin, see Küstrin . . küs-trēn'.
Cuttack, see Cattack, Kutak kŭt-tăk', kŭ-täk'.
Cuvier . . . . kü-vē=ā'.
Cuxhaven . . . . . kŭks-hā'-věn. *Ger.*
       kōōks'-hä-fěn.
Cuyo . . . . kōō'-yō.
Cuyos . . . . kōō'-yōs.
Cuyp, see Kuyp . . . . koip.
Cuzco . . . . kōōz'-kō.
Cwm . . . . kōōm.
Cyaxares . . . . . sī-ăx'-ā-rēz.
Cybele . . . . . . sĭb-ē'-lē, sĭb'-ĕ-lē.
Cyclades . . . . . sĭk'-lā-dēz.
Cyclop . . . . . . sī'-klŏp.
Cyclopean . . . . sī-klŏ-pē'-ȧn.
Cymbeline . . . . sĭm'-bĕ-lĭn, *or* sĭm'-bĕ-līn.
Cymry, see Kymry . . kĭm'-rĭ.
Cynewulf . . . . . kĭn'-ĕ-wŏŏlf.
Cyprian . . . . . sĭp'-rĭ-ȧn.
Cyrano de Bergerac . . sĭr-ä-nō' dŭ bâr=zhĕ-räk'.
Cyrene . . . . . . sī-rē'-nē.
Cyrenian . . . . . sī-rēn'-ĭ-ȧn.
Cyril . . . . sĭr'-ĭl.
Cythera . . . . . sī-thē'-rȧ.
Cytherean . . . . sĭth-ēr-ē'-ȧn.
Cyzicus . . . . . sĭz'-ĭ-kŭs.
Czajkowski, Czaykowski . chī-kŏv'-skē.
Czar . . . . zär, tsär.
Czardas . . . . . chär'-däsh.
Czarevitch, see Tsarovitch zär'-ĕ-vĭch, tsär'-ĕ-vĭch.
Czarevna, see Tsarevna . zär-ĕv'-nä, tsär-ĕv'-nä.
Czarina, see Tsarina . . zär-ē'-nä, tsär-ē'-nä.
Czaritza . . . . . zär-ĭt'-zä, tsär-ĭt'-zä.
Czarniecki . . . . chärn-yĕt'-skē.
Czarowitch . . . . zär'-ō-vĭch, tsär'-ō-vĭch.
Czarowitz, see Tsarowitz . zär'-ō-vĭtz, tsär'-ō-vĭtz.
Czartoryski . . . . chär-tō-rĭ'-skē.

Czaykowski, Czajkowski .	chī-kŏv'-skē.
Czecho-Slovak	chĕk'-ō slō'-văk.
Czechs, see Tsech . . .	chĕċhs, chĕks.
Czermak	chĕr-mäk'.
Czernagora, or Crna Gora	chĕr"-nä-gō'-rä.
Czernin	tchĕr-nēn'.
Czernowitz	chĕr'-nō-vĭts.
Czerny	chĕr'-nē.
Czibulka	chē-bōōl'-kä.

D

Dablon	dä-blôṅ'.
Dacca, see Dhaka . . .	dăk'-ȧ.
Dacia	dā'-shĭ=ä.
Daedalian	dē-dā'-lĭ-ȧn.
Daedalus	dē'-dȧ-lŭs, dĕd'-ȧ-lŭs.
Daeye, Hippolyte . . .	ēp-ō-lēt' dä'=yŭ.
Daghestan	dä-gĕs-tän'.
Dagnan-Bouveret . . .	dän-yäṅ'-bōōv-rä'.
Dagobert	dăg'-ō-bērt. Fr. dä-gō-bâr'.
Dagon	dā'-gŏn.
Dagonet, or Daguenet .	dăg'-ō-nĕt, or dăg'-ĕ-nĕt.
Daguerre	dä-gâr'.
Dagupan or Dagúpan . .	dä-gōō-pän', dä-gōō'-pän.
Dahlgren	dăl'-grĕn. Sw. däl'-grĕn.
Dahn	dän.
Dahomey	dä-hō'-mĭ, dä-hō'-mä.
Dail Eirann	dĭl ē'-rän.
Daimio	dī'-mē=ō.
Daiquiri	dä=ē-kē'-rē.
D'Albert	däl-bâr'.
D'Alembert	dä-lôṅ-bâr'.
Dalgetty	dăl'-gĕt-ĭ.
Dalgleish	dăl-glēsh'.
Dalhousie	dăl-hōō'-zĭ, dăl-how'-zĭ.
Dalida	dăl'-ĭ-dȧ.

Dalin . . . . dä'-lĭn.
Dalkeith . . . . . . dăl-kēth'.
Dalles . . . . dălz.
Dall' Ongaro . . . . . däl ŏng'-gä-rō.
Dalmatia . . . . . . däl-mä'-shĭ-à.
Dalmores . . . . . . dăl-mō-rĕz'.
Dalou, Jules . . . . . zhül dä-lōō'.
Dalrymple . . . . . dăl-rĭm'-pl.
Daman, see Damaun . . dä-män'.
Damaraland . . . . . dä-mä'-rä-lănd.
Damaris . . . . . . dăm'-à-rĭs.
Damascene . . . . . dăm'-ă-sēn.
Damasus . . . . . . dăm'-à-sŭs.
Damaun, see Daman . . dä-môn'.
Dame aux Camélias, La . lä däm ō kä-mä-lē=ä'.
Damiano . . . . . . dä-mē-ä'-nō.
Damien . . . . . . dä-mē=ĕṅ'.
Damis . . . . dä-mēs'.
Damnation de Faust . . däm-nä-sē=ôṅ' dŭ fowst.
Damoclean . . . . . dăm-ō-klē'-àn.
Damocles . . . . . . dăm'-ō-klēz.
Damon . . . . . . dā'-mŏn.
Dampier . . . . . . dăm'-pēr.
Dampt . . . . dämpt.
Damrosch . . . . . däm'-rŏsh.
Danaë . . . . dăn'-ā-ē.
Danai . . . . dăn'-ā-ī.
Danaïdes . . . . . . dă-nā'-ĭ-dēz, dā-nā'-ĭ-dēz.
Danaoi . . . . dăn'-ā-oi.
Dandin, George . . . zhŏrzh däṅ-dăṅ'.
Dandolo . . . . . . dän'-dō-lō.
Danegeld . . . . . . dān'-gĕld.
Danelagh, Danelaw . . dān'-lô.
Dannecker . . . . . dän'-nĕk-ĕr.
D'Annunzio, Gabriele . . gä-brē-ā'-lä
　　　　　　　　　　dän-nōōn'-dzē-ō.
Danse Macabre . . . . däṅs mä-kăbr'.

Dante Alighieri . . . . dăn'-tĕ ăl"-ĭ-gĭ=â'-rĭ. *It.*
                     dän'-tā ä"-lē-gē=ā'-rē.
Dantean . . . . . . dăn'-tē-àn.
Dantès . . . . dän-tĕs'.
Danton . . . . . . dăn'-tŏn. *Fr.* dän-tôn'.
Dantsic, Dantzic, or Danzig dănt'-sĭk. *Ger.* dänt'-sĭćh.
Daphne . . . . . . dăf'-nē.
Daphnis . . . . . . dăf'-nĭs.
Darbhangah, see Durbunga dä-bän'-gä.
D'Arblay, Madame . . mä-dăm' där-blä'.
Darc, or D'Arc, Joanne . zhän därk.
Dardanelles . . . . där-dà-nĕlz'.
Dardanus . . . . . . där'-dà-nŭs.
Dar-es-Salam . . . där"-ĕs-sä-läm'.
Darfor or Darfur . . . där'-fōr, där'-fōōr.
Dargomijsky . . . . där-gō-mĭzh'-skĭ.
Darien . . . . dä'-rĭ-ĕn. *Sp.* dä-rē-ĕn'.
Darío, Rubén . . . rōō-bĕn' dä-rē'-ō.
Darius . . . . dà-rī'-ŭs.
Darjeeling (-jiling) . . . där-jē'-lĭng.
Darwar, see Dharwar . . där'-wär.
D'Aubigné, Merle . . . mĕrl dō-bēn-yä'.
Daubigny . . . . . dō-bēn-yē'.
Daudet, Alphonse . . . ăl-fŏňs' dō-dā'.
Daudet, Léou . . . . lā-ôň' dō-dä'.
Daun . . . . down.
Dauphin . . . . . . dō'-fĭn. *Fr.* dōfăň'.
Dauphiné . . . . . . dō-fōn-ä'.
Dauphiness . . . . . dô'-fĭ-nĕs.
Dauphiny . . . . . . dô'-fĭ-nĭ.
Daur, or Dauria . . . dä-ōōr', dä-ōōr'-rē-ä.
Davalos . . . . . . *Sp.* dä-bä'-lŏs.
David, Gheerardt . . . gä-rärt' dä'-vēt.
David, Felicien . . . fä-lē-sē-ĕň' dä-vēd.
David, (L. J.) . . . . dä-vēd'.
Davila . . . . dä'-vē-lä.
Da Vinci, Leonardo . . lā-ō-när'-dō dä vēn'-chē.

Davoust . . . . . . dä-vōō'.
De Aar . . . . . . dĕ ar.
Deák . . . . dā-äk'.
De Amicis . . . . . dā ä-mē'-chēs.
De Amicitia . . . . dē ăm-ĭ-sĭsh'-ĭ=ä.
Débeney . . . . . . dāb-nā'.
Débonnaire, Louis le . . lōō-ē' lē dā-bŏn-ār'.
Deborah . . . . . dĕb'-ō-rȧ.
Debreczin . . . . . dā-brĕt'-sĭn, or
　　　　　　　　　　dā-brĕt'-sĭn.
De Bruycker, Jules . . zhül dē broi'-kĕr.
Debussy, Claude . . . klōd dē-büs-ē'.
Decameron . . . . . dē-kăm'-ĕr-ŏn.
Decamerone . . . . dā-kä-mā-rō'-nä.
Decamps . . . . . . dē-kän'.
Decazes . . . . . . dŭ-kăz'.
Deccan, see Dekkan . . dĕk'-ȧn.
Decelean . . . . . . dĕs-ē-lē'-ȧn.
Deffand, Marquise du . mär-kēz'-dü dĕf-fän'.
Defregger . . . . . dā-frĕg'-ĕr.
Degas . . . . dē-gä'.
Delhi, see Delhi . . . dā'-lē.
Dehra Dun . . . . . dĕh'-rä dōōn.
Deianira, see Dejanira. . dē-yȧ-nī'-rȧ.
De Imitatione Christi . . dē ĭm"-ĭ-tā-shĭ-ō'-nĕ
　　　　　　　　　　krĭs'-tĭ.
Deiphobus . . . . . dē-ĭf'-ō-bŭs.
Dejanira, see Deianira . dĕj-ȧ-nī'-rȧ.
Dejean . . . . dŭ-zhôn'.
Dekkan, see Deccan . . dĕk'-ȧn.
De Koven . . . . . dē ko'-vĕn.
Delacroix . . . . . dŭ-lä-krwä'.
Delagoa . . . . . . dĕl-ȧ-gō'-ȧ.
Delambre . . . . . dŭ-länbr'.
Deland (Margaret) . . dē-lănd'.
De la Ramée . . . . dŭ lä rä-mā'.
Delaroche . . . . . dŭ-lä-rŏsh'.

Delaunay . . . . . . dē-lō-nā'.
Delavigne . . . . . . dŭ lä-vēn'=yŭ.
Declassé . . . . . . dĕl-kăs-ā'.
Deledda, Grazia . . . grätz'-ē-à dā-lād'-dä.
Delegorgue . . . . . dē=lē-gōrg'.
Delft . . . . dĕlft.
Delgado . . . . . . dĕl-gä'-dō.
Delhi, see Dehli . . . dĕl'-hī.
Delian . . . . dē'-lī-àn.
Délibes . . . . . . dā-lēb'.
Délila . . . . . . Fr. dā-lē-lä'.
Delilah . . . . . . dē-lī'-lä.
Della Cruscan . . . . dĕl'-là krŭs'-kàn.
Delorme, Marion . . . mä-rē-ôṅ' dŭ lôrm'.
Delos . . . . dē'-lŏs.
Delphi . . . . dĕl'-fī.
Delphic . . . . . . dĕl'-fĭk.
Delphine . . . . . . Fr. dĕl-fēn'.
Del Pino . . . . . . dĕl pē'-nō.
Delsarte . . . . . . dĕl-särt'.
Del Sarto, Andrea . . än-drā'-ä dāl sär'-to.
De Lussan, Zélie . . . zā-lē' dŭ lüs-sän'.
Delyannis . . . . . . dĕl-ĭ-ăn'-ĭs.
Demange, Maître . . . mätr dŭ-mäṅzh'.
Demerara, or Demerary . dĕm-ȩ-rä'-rà, dĕm-ȩr-rä'-rĭ.
Demeter . . . . . . dĕ-mē'-tēr.
Demetrius . . . . . . dĕ-mē'-trĭ-us.
Demidoff, Demidov . . dĕm'-ē-dŏf.
Democritus . . . . . dē-mŏk'-rĭ-tŭs.
Demogorgon . . . . . dē-mō-gôr'-gŏn.
Demos . . . . dē'-mŏs.
Demosthenes . . . . dē-mŏs'-thĕ-nēz.
Denderah . . . . . . dĕn'-dĕr-ä.
Deneb . . . . dē'-nĕb, dĕn'-ĕb.
Den Haag . . . . . . dĕn häch.
Denikin . . . . . . dyĕ-nē'-kĭn.
Denis, St., see Denys . . sānt dĕn'-is. Fr. säṅ dē-nē.

Dent du Midi . . . . . dŏṅ dü mē-dē'.
Denys, St., see Denis . . sānt dĕn'-ĭs. *Fr.* sän dŭ-nē'
D'Épinay . . . . . . dā-pē-nā'.
Dépit Amoureux, Le . . lē dā-pē' tä-mōō-rē'.
De Prés, Josquin, see
    Desprez . . . . . . zhŏs-kăṅ' dŭ prä'.
De Profundis . . . . dē prō-fŭn'-dĭs.
Deptford . . . . . . dĕt'-fŭrd.
De Quincey . . . . . dŭ kwĭn'-zĭ.
Derajat . . . . . . dĕr-à-jăt'.
Derby . . . . dĕr'-bĭ, där'-bĭ.
Dercetas . . . . . . dĕr'-sĕ-tàs.
Der Fliegende Holländer . dĕr flē'-gĕn-dà hŏl'-ĕn-dĕr.
Dernburg . . . . . . dĕrn'-bōōrch.
Dernier Chouan, Le . . lŭ dĕr-nē=ā' shōō-äṅ'.
Déroulède . . . . . . dā-rōō-lĕd'.
De Ruyter . . . . . . dē rī'-tĕr. *D.* dŭ roi'-tĕr.
Dervis, Dervise, or Dervish dĕr'-vĭs, dĕr'-vĭsh.
Desaix de Veygoux . . . dŭ-sā' dŭ vā-gōō'.
Descartes . . . . . . dā-kärt'.
Deschamps . . . . . dā-shäṅ'.
Desdemona . . . . . dĕz-dĕ-mō'-nä.
Desdichado . . . . . dĕs-dĭ-chä'-dō.
Deseada . . . . . . dĕs-ĕ-ä'-dä.
Des Grieux . . . . . dā grē-ē'.
Désirade . . . . . . dā-zē-răd'.
Des Lys, Gaby . . . . gă-bē' dā lēs'.
Des Moines . . . . . dĕ-moin.
Desmoulins . . . . . dā-mōō-lăṅ'.
Despenser . . . . . . dĕ-spĕn'-sĕr.
Desprez, Josquin, see De
    Prés . . . . zhŏs-kăṅ' dā-prä'.
Dessalines . . . . . dĕs-ä-lēn'.
Dessau . . . . dĕs'-sow.
Dessauer, ... dĕs'-sow-ĕr.
De Staël-Holstein . . . dŭ stä'-ĕl-hŏl'-stīn.
                        Fr. dŭ stä-ĕl-ōl-stăn'.

D'Este	dās'-tĕ.
De Stendhal	dŭ stŏṅ-däl'.
Destinn (Emmy). . . .	dĕs'-tĭn.
Destouches	dā-tōōsh'.
Detaille	dŭ-tä'=yŭ.
De Tocqueville	dŭ tŏk'-vĭl. *Fr.*
	dŭ tōk-vēl'.
Deucalion	dū-kā'-lĭ-ŏn.
Deutsch	doich.
Deutsche Tages-Zeitung .	doich'-ŭ tä'-gĕs tsī'-tōŏng.
Deux-Ponts	dē pôn.
Deux-Sèvres	dē sĕvr.
Deventer	dā-vĕn'-tĕr.
Devereux	dĕv'-ēr-ōō, dĕv'-ēr-ŭ.
De Vigny	dŭ vēn-yē'.
Devizes	dē-vī'-zĕz.
D'Ewes	dūz.
De Wet	dā-vĕt'.
Dewetsdorp	dā-vĕts'-dŏrp.
De Wette	dĕ wĕt'-tĕ. *D.* dĕ vĕt'-tĕ.
De Witt	dĕ wĭt. *D.* de vĭt.
Dhaka, see Dacca . . .	dhä'-kä.
Dhar	dhär.
Dharwar, see Darwar . .	där'-wär.
Dhawalaghiri	dhȧ-wäl″-ă-ghēr'-ē.
Dolphur	dhŏl-pōōr'.
Diabelli	dē-ä-bĕl'-lē.
Diable, Robert le . . .	rō-bâr' lĕ dē=äbl'.
Diadochi	dī-ăd'-ō-kī.
Diane de Poitiers . . .	dē-ăn dŭ pwä-tē=ā'.
Diarbekir, or Diarbekr .	dē-är″-bĕ-kēr', dē-är-bĕkr'
Dias	dē'-äs.
Diavolo, Fra	frä dē-ä'-vō-lō.
Diaz	*It.* dē'-ätz. *Mex.* dē'-äs.
	Sp. dē'-äth.
Diderot	dēd-rō'.
Didot	dē-dō'.

Didymus . . . . . . dĭd'-ĭ-mŭs.
Diederichs, von . . . . fŏn dē'-dā-rĭks.
Diego . . . . dē-ā'-gō.
Dieppe . . . . dē-ĕp'.
Dies Irae . . . . . . dī'-ēz ī'-rē.
Dieskau   . . . . . dēs'-kow.
Dietrich von Bern . . . dē'-trĭċh fŏn bĕrn.
Dijon . . . . dē-zhôṅ'.
Dilke . . . . dĭlk.
Dimitri . . . . dē-mē'-trē.
Dinan . . . . dē-näṅ'.
Dinant . . . . dē-nänt'.   Fr. dē-näṅ'.
Dingaan . . . . . . dĭn-gän', or dĭng-gän'.
Diodorus Siculus . . . dī-ō-dō'-rŭs sĭk'-ŭ-lŭs.
Diogenes . . . . . . dī-ŏj'-ĕ-nēz.
Diomedes . . . . . . dī-ō-mē'-dēz.
Dionysia . . . . . . dī-ō-nĭsh'-ĭ-à.
Dionysius . . . . . . dī-ō-nĭsh'-ĭ-ŭs.
Dionysus . . . . . . dī-ō-nī'-sŭs.
Dioscuri . . . . . . dī-ŏs-kū'-rī.
Dippel . . . . dĭp'-pĕl.
Dirce . . . . dĕr'-sē.
Discobolus. . . . . . dĭs-kŏb'-ō-lŭs.
Disraeli . . . . . . dĭs-rā'-li, diz-rē'-li.
Dives . . . . dī'-vēz.
Divina Commedia . . . dē-vē'-nä kōm-mä'-dē-ä.
Dixmude . . . . . . dē-müd'.
Dmitri . . . . d-mē'-trē.
Dnieper, or Dniepr . . . nē'-pĕr. Russ. dynĕp'-ĕr.
Dniester, or Dniestr . . nēs'-tĕr. Russ. dnyĕs'-tĕr.
Dobrudja . . . . . . dō-brōō'-jä.
Dodona . . . . dō-dō'-nä.
Dogali . . . . dō-gä'-lē.
Doiran . . . . doi'-rän.
Dolce . . . . dŏl'-chĕ. It. dŏl'-chā.
Dolci . . . . dŏlchĭ. It. dŏl'-chē.
Dolgorouki, or Dolgoruki . dŏl-gŏ-rōō'-kē.

Döllinger	dĕl'-ĭng-ĕr.
Dolomite	dŏl'-ō-mīt.
Dolores	dō-lō'-rĕs.
Domenichino	dō''-mā-nē-kē'-nō.
Domingue	dŏ-mäng'.
Dominguez	*Mex.* dō-mĭn'-gĕs. *Sp.* dō-mĭn'-gĕth.
Dominica	dŏm-ĭn-ē'-kȧ.
Dominical	dō-mĭn'-ĭ-kȧl.
Dominique, La	lä dōm-ē-nēk'.
Domitian	dō-mĭsh'-ĭ=ȧn.
Domo d'Ossola	dō'-mō dŏs'-sō-lä.
Dom Pedro	dōm pā' drō. *Pg.* dōṅ.
Domremy-la-Pucelle . .	dôṅ-rā-mē'-lä-pü-sĕl'.
Doña	dōn'-yä.
Donalbain	dōn'-ăl-bān.
Donatello	dōn-ä-tĕl'-lō.
Donati	dō-nä'-tē.
Donauwörth	dō'-now-vĕrt.
Don César de Bazan . .	dôn sā-zär' dŭ bä-zäṅ'.
Donegal	dŏn'-ē-gôl.
Don Giovanni	dŏn jō-vän'-nē.
Dongola	dŏng'-gō-lä.
Donizetti	dō-ne-dzĕt'-tē.
Don Juan	dŏnjū'-ȧn.*Sp.*dōn 'hōō-än'.
Donna	dŏn'-nä.
Donnay	dŏn-ā'.
Donne (John)	dŭn.
Don Pasquale	dōn päs-kwä'-lä.
Don Pedro de Alcántara .	dōn pā'-drō dä äl-kän'-tä-rä.
Don Quixote. Sp. Quijote	dŏn kwĭks'-ŏt. *Sp.* dōn kē-ćhō'-tä.
Dorado, El	äl dō-rä'-dō.
Dordogne	dôr-dōn'. *Fr.* dōr-dōn'=yŭ.
Dordrecht	dôr'-drĕćht.
Doré	dō-rä'.

Dorgelès . . . . . . dŏr-zhĕ-lĕz'.

Doria . . . . dō'-rē-ä.

Dorian . . . . dō'-rĭ-àn.

Doric . . . . dôr'-ĭk, dŏr'-ĭk.

D'Orleans . . . . . dŏr-lä-äṅ'.

Dorothea . . . . . . dŏr-ō-thē'-à.
  Ger. dō-rō-tä'-ä.

Dorothée . . . . . . dō-rō-tä'.

D'Orsay, Quai . . . . kä dôr-sä'.

Dort . . . . dôrt.

D'Orthez, see Orthez . . dŏr-tĕss' *or* -täz'.

Dossi, Dosso . . . . . dŏs'-sō dŏs'-sē.

Dossier, The . . . . . dŏs-sē-ā'.

Dostoievsky, or Dostoyevsky dŏs-tō-yĕf'-skĭ.

Dotheboys Hall . . . . dō'-thē-boiz hôl.

Douai, or Douay . . . dōō-ā'.

Douaumont . . . . . dōō-ō-mŏṅ'.

Doubs . . . . dōō.

Doulton . . . . . . dōl'-tŏn.

Douma, see Duma . . . dōō'-mä.

Douro . . . . dōō'-rō.

Douw, or Dow . . . . dow.

Drachenfels . . . . . drăk'-ĕn-fĕlz.
  Ger. drä'-ċhen-fĕlz.

Draconian . . . . . . drà-kō'-nĭ-àn.

Draconic . . . . . . drä-kŏn'-ĭk.

Drakenberg (Mts.) . . . drä'-kĕn-bĕrċh.

Drave . . . . drä'-vĕ.

Drdla . . . . dērd'-lä.

Dreibund . . . . . . drī'-bŏont.

Dreiser . . . . drī'-sĕr.

Dreux . . . . drẽ.

Dreyfus . . . . drä-füs'.

Drina . . . . drē'-nä.

Drogheda . . . . . . drŏċh'-ĕ-dä, drŏ'-'hĕd-à.

Dromio . . . . drō'-mĭ-ō.

Drouet . . . . drōō-ā'.

Droz	drō.
Druid	drū′-ĭd.
Druidian	drū-ĭd′-ĭ-an.
Druidic	drū-ĭd′-ĭk.
Druses	drōōz′-ĕz.
Dryburgh	drī′-bŭr-ŭ.
Dryope	drī′-ō-pē.
Dry Tortugas	drī tôr-tōō′-gȧz.
Du Barry	dü băr-ē′.
Dubois	*Fr.* dü-bwä′.
Du Bois-Reymond	dü bwä-rā-môn′.
Duc	*Fr.* dük.
Duca	dōō′-kä.
Ducange, or Du Cange	dü-känzh′.
Duccio di Buoninsegna	dōōch′-ō dē bōō=ōn″-ēn-sän′-yä
Du Chaillu	dü shä-yü′.
Du Châtelet	dü shät-lā′.
Duchesne	dü-shän′.
Duchessa	*It.* dōō-kĕs′-sä.
Duchesse	*Fr.* dü-shĕs′.
Ducrot	dü-krō′.
Dudevant	düd-vän′.
Duero	dōō-ā′-rō
Du Guesclin, or Duguesclin	dü gä-klăn′.
Dukas	dü-kä′.
Dukhobori	dōō-ĉhū-bō′-rē.
Dulcamara	dōōl-kä-mä′-rä.
Dulcinea del Toboso . .	dŭl-sĭn′-ē-ä dĕl tō-bō′-sō *Sp.* dōōl-thē-nä′-ä dāl tō-bō′-sō.
Dulwich	dŭl′-ĭch.
Duma, see Douma . . .	dōō′-mä.
Dumas	dūmä. *Fr.* dü-mä′.
Du Maurier	dü mō rē=ā′.
Dumbarton	dŭm-bär′-tŏn
Dumfries	dŭm-frēz′.

Dumouriez. . . . . . dü-mōō-rē=ā'.
Dünaburg . . . . . . dü'-nä-bōōrċh.
Dunajecs . . . . . . dōō-nä-yĕts'.
Dunbar . . . . . . dŭn-bär'.
Dundee . . . . . . dŭn-dē'.
Dunedin . . . . . . dŭn-ē'-dĭn, dŭn-ĕd'-ĭn.
Dunes . . . . dūnz.
Dunfermline . . . . . dŭn-fĕrm'-lĭn.
Dunkeld . . . . . . dŭn-kĕld'.
Dunois . . . . dü-nwä'.
Dunsany . . . . . . dŭn-sā'-nĭ.
Dunsinane. . . . . . dŭn'-sĭ-nān, dŭn-sĭn'-ān.
Duomo . . . . . . dōō=ō'-mō.
Dupaty . . . . . . dü-pä-tē'.
Du Paty de Clam . . . dü pä-tē' dŭ klän'.
Duplessis . . . . . . dü-plĕ-sē'.
Duplessis-Mornay . . . düplĕ-sē'-mōr-nä'.
Duprat . . . . dü-prä'.
Dupré . . . . dü-prä'.
Duprétis . . . . . . dōō-prä-tēs'.
Dupuy . . . . . . dü-pwē'.
Duquesne . . . . . . dü-kān'.
Duquesnoy . . . . . dü-kä-nwä'.
Duran, Carolus . . . . kä-rō-lüs' dü-rän'.
Durandarte . . . . . dōō-rän-där'-tä.
Durango . . . . . . dōō-rän'-gō.
Durazzo . . . . . . dōō-rät'-sō.
Durban, or D'Urban . . dĕr'-bŭn.
Durbar . . . . . . dŭr'-bär.
Durbunga, see Darbhangah dŭr-bŭn'-gä.
Dürer . . . . dü'-rĕr.
Durham . . . . . . dŭr'-ȧm.
Duroc . . . . dü-rōk'.
Duruy . . . . dü-rü=ē'.
Durward . . . . . . dĕr'-wȧrd.
Duse . . . . dōō'-sĕ, dōō'-sā. *It.* dōō'-zä.
Dussek . . . . dōō'-shĕk.

Düsseldorf . . . . . düs′-ĕl-dôrf.
Dvinsk . . . . dvĭnsk.
Dvořák, Anton . . . . än′-tōn dvōr-zhäk′.
Dyak . . . . dī′-ăk.
Dyea . . . . dī′-ā.
Dynow . . . . dē′-nŏv.

E

Eadred . . . . ĕd′-rĕd.
Eadric (Edric) . . . . ĕd′-rĭk.
Eames (Emma) . . . . āmz.
Eau de Cologne . . . . ō dŭ kō-lōn′.
         Fr. kō-lōn′=yŭ.
Ebal . . . . ē′-băl.
Eberhard . . . . . . ā′-bĕr-härt.
Ebers, Georg . . . . gā=ōrch′ ā′-bĕrs.
Ebert . . . . ā′-bârt.
Eblis, see Iblis . . . . ĕb′-lĭs.
Eboli . . . . ā′-bō-lē.
Eboracum, see Eburacum. ē-bŏr′-à-kŭm,
         ĕb-ō-rā′-kŭm.
Ebro . . . . ē′-bro. *Sp.* ā′-brō.
Eburacum, see Eboracum ē-bŭr′-à-kŭm,
         ĕb-ōō-rā′-kŭm.
Ecbatana . . . . . . ĕk-băt′-à-nà.
Ecce Homo . . . . . ĕk′-sē hŏ′-mŏ.
Eccelino da Romano, see
 Ezzelino . . . . . ĕch-ā-lē′-nō dä rō-mä′-nō.
Ecclefechan . . . . . ĕk-l-fĕch′-ăn, ĕk-l-fĕk′-ăn.
Ecclesiastes . . . . . ĕk-klē″-zĭ-ăs′-tēz.
Echague . . . . . . ā-chä′-gā.
Echegaray . . . . . ā″-chā-gä-rä′=ē.
Echeverría . . . . . ā-chā-vĕr-ē′-ä.
Echo . . . . ĕk′-ō, ē′-kō.
École des Beaux Arts, L′ . lā-kōl′ dā bō-zär′.
École des Femmes, L′ . . lā-kōl′ dā făm′.

École des Maris, L' . .	lā-kōl′ dā mǎ-rē′.
École Polytechnique . .	ā-kōl′ pō-lē-těk-nēk′.
Écorcheurs, Les . . .	lā zā-kǒr-shēr′.
Ecuador	ěk-wȧ-dōr′. *Sp.* ā-kwä-dōr′.
Edam	ē′-dǎm. *D.* ā-dǎm′.
Eden	ē′-dn.
Edfu	ěd-fōō′.
Edgecote	ědj′-kōt.
Edinburgh	ěd′-ĭn-bŭr″-ō,
	ěd′-ĭn-bŭr″-ŭ.
Edmond	*Fr.* ěd-môṅ′.
Edom	ē′-dǒm.
Édouard	ā-dōō-är′.
Edrei	ěd′-rē-ī.
Eckhoud Georges . . .	zhôrzh āk′-howt.
Eecloo	ā-klō′.
Égalité, Philippe . . .	fē-lēp′ ā-gǎl-ē-tā′.
Egean, see Aegean . .	ē-jē′-ȧn.
Eger	ā′-gěr.
Egeria, see Aegeria . .	ē-jē′-rĭ-ȧ.
Egeus	ē-jē′-ŭs.
Eginhard, see Einhard .	ā′-gĭn-härt.
Eglamour	ěg′-lȧ-mōōr.
Eglantine	ěg′-lȧn-tīn.
Eguren, José	hō-sā′ ā-gōō′-rěn.
Ehrenbreitstein	ā-rěn-brīt′-stīn.
Ehrenfels	ā′-rěn-fělz.
Eichberg	īch′-běrċh.
Eiffel	ī′-fěl. *Fr.* ě-fěl′.
Eikon Basilike	ī′-kōn bǎ-sĭl′-ĭ-kē.
Eikonoclastes	ī-kǒn″-ō-klǎs′-tēz.
Eimbeck, or Einbeck . .	īm′-běk, īn′-běk.
Einhard, see Eginhard .	īn′-härt.
Einstein	īn′-stīn.
Eisenach	ī′-zā-näċh.
Eisleben	īs′-lā-běn.
Eisner, Kurt	kōōrt īs′-něr.

Eisteddfod	ī-stĕth′-vōd.
Eitel	ī′-tĕl.
Ekaterinburg, see Yeka-	
terinburg	ĕ-kä″-tĕ-rēn-bōōrg′.
Ekber, see Akbar . . .	ĕk′-bēr. *Hind.* ŭk′-bĕr.
Elagabalus, see Helioga-	
balus	ē-là-găb′-à-lŭs,
	ĕl″-à-găb′-à-lŭs,
	ĕl″-ā-gā-bā′-lŭs.
Elamite	ē′-làm′-īt.
Elandslaagte	ā-lănts-läċh′-tĕ.
Elbe	ĕlb. *Ger.* ĕl′-bŭ.
Elberfeld	ĕl′-bĕr-fĕlt.
Elbrooz, Elbruz	ĕl-brōōz′.
El Camino Real	ĕl kä″-mē′-no rā-äl′
El Campeador	āl käm″-pā-ä-dōr′.
El Caney	āl kä-nā′=ē.
Elchingen	ĕlċh′-ĭng-ĕn.
El Dorado	ĕl dō-rä′-dō. *Sp.* ĕl dō-rä′-dō
Eleanor	ĕl′-ē-ā-nôr″, ĕl′-à-nēr.
Eleanora d'Este . . .	ā″-lā-ō-nō′-rä dās′-tĕ.
Eleatic	ĕl-ē-ăt′-ĭk.
Eleazar	ĕl-ē′-zàr, ē-lē′-ā-zär.
Eleusinia	ĕl ū-sĭn′-ĭ-à.
Eleusis	ĕ-lū′-sĭs.
Eleuthera	ĕ-lū′-thĕ-rà.
Elgin	ĕl′-jĭn.
Elia	ē′-lĭ-à.
Eliab	ē-lī′-ăb.
Eliakim	ē-lī′-à-kĭm.
Elias	ĕ-lī′-às.
Elidure	ĕl′-ĭ-dūr.
Élie de Beaumont . . .	ā-lē′ dŭ bō-môn′.
Eliezer	ĕl-ĭ-ē′-zēr.
Elihu	ĕ-lī′-hū.
Elihu (Root)	ĕl′-ĭ-hū.
Elimelech	ĕ-lim′-ĕ-lĕk.

Elío (Gen.) . . . . . ā-lē′-ō.

Eliodoro . . . . . . ā″-lē-ō-dō′-rō.

Eliphalet . . . . . . ĕ-lĭf′-à-lĕt.

Élise . . . . ā-lēz′.

Elisir d'amore, L' . . . lä-lē-zēr′ dä-mō′-rä.

Elizabethan . . . . . ē-lĭz′-ā-bĕth″-ăn, or
ē-lĭz″-ā-bĕth′-àn.

Elkanah . . . . . . ĕl-kā′-nä, ĕl′-kā-nä.

Ellichpur . . . . . . ĕl-ĭch-poōr′.

El Mahdi, see Mahdi . . āl mä′-dē.

Elmire . . . . ĕl-mēr′.

Elman, Mischa . . . . mĭsh′-ä ĕl′-män.

El Obeid . . . . . . ĕl ŏb-ād′.

Elohim . . . . ē-lō′-hĭm, ĕl′-ō-hĭm.

El Paso del Norte . . . ĕl pă′-sō dĕl nōr′-tĕ.

El Puerto . . . . . . āl pwârt′-tō, poō=âr′-tō.

Elsass . . . . āl′-zäs.

Elsass-Lothringen . . . āl′-zäs-lōt′-rĭng-ĕn.

Elsinore . . . . . . ĕl-sĭ-nōr′.

Elssler . . . . ĕls′-lēr.

Eltekeh . . . . ĕl′-tĕ-kē.

Elul . . . . ē′-lŭl.

Élysée . . . . ā-lē-zā′.

Elysian . . . . . . ē-lĭz′-ĭ-ăn, ē-lĭzh′-ē-an,
ē-lĭzh′-ăn.

Elysium . . . . . . ē-lĭz′-ĭ-ŭm, ē-lĭzh′-ĭ=ŭm,
ē-lizh′-ŭm.

Elzevir . . . . ĕl′-zĕ-vēr, ĕl′-zē-vēr.

Emanuele, Vittorio . . vēt-tō′-rē-ō ā-mä-noō-ā′lä.

Emeer, see Emir . . . ē-mēr′.

Émigrés, Les . . . . . lā zä-mē-grä′.

Emil . . . . ā′-mēl.

Émile . . . . ā-mēl′.

Emilian . . . . . . ē-mĭl′-ĭ-an.

Éminence Grise, L' . . lä-mē-nŏṅs′ grēz.

Emin Pacha (or Bey) . . ā′-mēn păsh-ô′ (bā),
pä-shä′, päsh′-à̇.

Emir, see Emeer . . . ē-mēr, ē-mēr'.
Emmaus . . . . . . ĕ-mā'-ŭs, ĕm'-mā-ŭs.
Empedocles . . . . ĕm-pĕd'-ō-klēz.
Ems . . . . ĕms.
Énault (Louis) . . . ā-nō'.
Enceladus . . . . ĕn-sĕl'-à-dŭs.
Encina . . . . . . ĕn-sē'-nà. *Sp.* ān-thē'-nà.
Encke . . . . . . ĕng'-kŭ.
Encyclopédie . . . . ŏn-sē-klō-pā-dē'.
Endymion . . . . . ĕn-dĭm'-ĭ-ŏn.
Eneas, see Aeneas . . . ē-nē'-às.
Eneid . . . . . . ē-nē'-ĭd, ē'-nē-ĭd.
Enemessar . . . . ĕn-ē-mĕs'-sàr.
Enfant Prodigue, L' . . lôn-fän' prō-dēg'.
Engadine . . . . . ĕn-gä-dēn'.
Engaño . . . . . . ĕn-gän'-yō.
Engedi . . . . . . ĕn-gē'-dī, ĕn'-gē-dī.
Enghien, Duc d' . . . . dük dän-gē=än', dän-gän'.
England . . . . . ĭng'-glànd.
English . . . . . ĭng'-glĭsh.
Enid . . . . . . ē'-nĭd.
Enobarbus . . . . ĕn-ō-bär'-bŭs.
Enseñada . . . . ĕn-sĕn-yä'-dà.
Entente . . . . . ôn-tônt'.
Entraigues, Henrietta d',
  see Antraigues . . . ŏn-rē-ĕt' dôn-trāg'.
Eolian, see Aeolian . . ē-ō'-lĭ-àn.
Eolic, see Aeolic . . . ē-ŏl'-ĭk.
Eolis, see Aeolis . . . ē'-ō-lĭs.
Eothen . . . . . . ē-ō'-thĕn.
Epaminondas . . . . ē-păm"-ĭn-ŏn'-dăs.
Epaphroditus . . . . ē-păf"-rō-dī'-tŭs.
Epeiros, see Epirus . . ē-pī'-rŭs.
Épernay . . . . . ā-pĕr-nā'.
Épernon, d' . . . . dā-pĕr-nŏn'.
Epes . . . . . . ĕps.
Ephesians . . . . . ē-fē'-zhànz.

Ephesus . . . . . . ĕf'-ĕ-sŭs.
Ephraim . . . . . . ē'-frā-ĭm.
Ephrata . . . . . . ĕf'-rā-tä, ĕf'-ra̍-ta̍.
Epicœne . . . . . . ĕp'-ĭ-sēn.
Epictetus . . . . . . ĕp-ĭk-tē'-tŭs.
Epicurean . . . . . . ĕp″-ĭ-kū-rē'-a̍n,
　　　　　　　　　　ĕp-ĭ-kū'-rē-a̍n.
Epicureanism . . . . ĕp″-ĭ-kū-rē'-ăn-ĭzm,
　　　　　　　　　　ĕp-ĭ-kū'-rē-ăn-ĭzm″.
Epicurus . . . . . . ĕp-ĭ-kū'-rŭs.
Épidaurus . . . . . ĕp-ĭ-dôr'-ŭs.
Épinay, d' . . . . . dā-pē-nā'.
Epipsychidion . . . . ĕp″-ĭ-sī-kĭd'-ĭ-ŏn.
Epirot . . . . ĕ-pī'-rŏt.
Epirote . . . . . . ĕ-pī'-rōt.
Epirus, see Epeiros . . ē-pī'-rŭs.
Epithalamium . . . . ĕp″-ĭ-thā-lā'-mĭ-ŭm.
Érard . . . . ā-rär'.
Erasmus . . . . . . ē-răz'-mŭs.
Eraste . . . . ā-răst'.
Erastianism . . . . . ē-răst'-yăn-ĭzm.
Erato . . . . ĕr'-ā-tō.
Erastosthenes . . . . ĕr-ā-tŏs'-thē-nēz.
Ercilla . . . . ĕr-sēl'-ya̍.
Erckmann-Chatrian . . ĕrk'-män-shä-trē-äṅ'.
Erebus . . . . . . ĕr'-ē-bŭs.
Erechtheum . . . . . ĕr-ĕk-thē'-ŭm,
　　　　　　　　　　ē-rĕk-thē'-ŭm.
Eretria . . . . ĕ-rē'-trĭ-a̍.
Eretrian . . . . . . ĕ-rē'-trĭ-an.
Erfurt . . . . ĕr'-fo͞ort.
Eric, see Erik . . . . ĕr'-ĭk, ē'-rĭk.
Ericsson . . . . . . ĕr'-ĭk-sŏn.
Erigena . . . . . . ĕ-rĭj'-ē-nä, ĕr-ĭj'-ĕ-na̍,
　　　　　　　　　　ĕr-ĭ-jē'-na̍.
Erik, see Eric . . . . ĕr'-ik, ē'-rĭk. *Sw.* ā'-rĭk.
Erin . . . . ĕ'-rĭn.

Erinnyes, or Erinyes, or
    Erinnys . . . . . ĕr-ĭn'-ĭ-ēz, ē-rĭn'-ĭ-ēz,
                   ĕr-ĭn'-ēz, ē-rĭn'-ēz.
Erivan . . . . . . ĕr-ĭ-vän'.
Erlangen . . . . . . ĕr'-läng-ĕn.
Erl-King, or Ger. Erl-König ērl'-kĭng. Ger. ĕrl kē'-nĭch.
Ernani . . . . âr-nä'-nē.
Eroica . . . . ā-rō'-ē-kä.
Eros . . . . ē'-rŏs.
Erostratus . . . . . ē-rŏs'-trā-tŭs.
Erskine . . . . . . ĕrs'-kĭn.
Ervine, St. John . . . sĭn'-jŭn ĕr'-vīn.
Erzerum . . . . . . ĕrz-rōōm'.
Esaias . . . . ē-zā'-yȧs.
Escadrille, Lafayette . . lä-fā-yĕt' ĕs-kä-drē'=yŭ.
Escalus . . . . . . ĕs'-kȧ-lŭs.
Escamillo . . . . . . ĕs-kä-mēl'-yō
Eschenbach, Wolfram von vŏlf'-räm fŏn ēsh'-ĕn-bäch.
Escholier . . . . . . ĕs-kŏl-ē=ā'.
Escholtzia . . . . . . ĕsh-ŏltz'-ē-ȧ.
Escorial, or . . . . . ĕs-kō'-rĭ-ȧl. Sp. ĕs-kō-rē-äl'.
Escurial . . . . . . ĕs-kū'-rĭ-ȧl.
Esdraelon . . . . . . ĕs-drā-ē'-lŏn, ĕs-drā'-e-lŏn.
Eskimo, see Esquimaux . ĕs'-kĭ-mō.
Esneh . . . . ĕs'-nĕ.
Esop, see Aesop . . . ē'-sŏp.
España . . . . ĕs-pän'-yä.
Española . . . . . . ĕs-pän-yō'-lä.
Esperey, Franchet d' . . fräṅ-shä' dĕs-pĕ-rā'.
Espinasse, de l', see Les-
    pinasse . . . . . . dŭ lā-pē-näs'.
Espiritu Santo . . . . ās-pē'-rē-tōō sän'-tō.
Esprémesnil, or Épréménil ā-prā-mä-nēl'.
Esquiline . . . . . . ĕs-kē-lēn', ĕs'-kwĭ-lĭn.
Esquimaux, or Eskimo . ĕs-kē-mō'.
Esquirol . . . . . . ĕs-kē-rōl'.
Essenes . . . . . . ĕs-sēnz', ĕs'-sē-nēz.

Essipoff	ĕs-ē-pŏf'.
Estaing, d'	dĕs-tăṅ'.
Estaires	ĕs-târ'.
Estaunié	ĕs-tōn-yā'.
Estcourt	ĕst'-kōrt.
Este	ās'-tĕ.
Esterhazy, see Estzerházy	ĕs'-tĕr-hä-zĭ, ĕstĕr-hä'-zē.
	Fr. ās-târ-ä-zē'.
Esther	ĕs'-tĕr.
Esthonia	ĕs-thō'-nĭ-à.
Estienne, see Étienne	ā-tē=ĕn'.
Estrées, Gabrielle d'	gä-brē-ĕl' dā-trā'.
Estrella, La	lä ĕs-trāl'-yä.
Estramadura	ĕsh″-trā-mä-dōō'-rä.
Estzerházy, see Esterhazy	ĕs'-ter-hä-zĭ, ĕs-tĕr-hä'-zē.
	Fr. ās-târ-ä-zē'.
Etah	ē'-tà.
Etampes	ā-täṅp'.
Etesian	ē-tē'-zhĭ-àn, ē-tē'-zhàn.
Ethelbert, see Aethelberht	ĕth'-ĕl-bērt.
Ethiopic	ĕ-thĭ-ŏp'-ĭk, ē-thĭ-ō'-pĭk.
Étienne, see Estienne	ā-tē=ĕn'.
Eu	ē.
Eubœa	ū-bē'-ä.
Eucken	oi'-kĕn.
Eudes	ēd.
Eudoxia	ū-dŏk'-sĭ-à.
Euergetes	ū-ēr'-jĕ-tēz.
Eugen	*Ger.* oi-gän'.
Eugene	ū-jēn'.
Eugène	*Fr.* ē-zhĕn'.
Eugène de Beauharnais	ē-zhĕn' dŭ bō-är-nā'.
Eugénie de Montijo	ē-zhā-nē' dŭ môn-tē-ċhō'.
	Sp. dā môn-tē'-ċhō.
Eugénie Grandet	ē-zhā-nē' gräṅ-dā'.
Eulalia	ā=ōō-lä'-lē-ä.
Eulalie	ē-lä-lē'.

Eulate	ā=ōō-lä′-tā.
Eulenspiegel	oi′-lĕn-shpē″-gĕl.
Euler	oi′-lĕr.
Eumenes	ū′-mē-nēz.
Eumenidæ	ū-mĕn′-ĭ-dē.
Eumenides	ū-mĕn′-ĭ-dēz.
Eunice	ū′-nĭs, ū-nī′-sē.
Euphrates	ū-frā′-tēz.
Euphrosyne	ū-frŏs′-ĭn-ē.
Euphues	ū′-fū-cz.
Eurasia	ū-rā′-shĭ-à, ū-rā′-zhĭ-à.
Eurasian	ū-rā′-shĭ=àn, ū-rā′-zhĭ=àn.
Eure	ĕr.
Eure-et-Loire	ĕr-ā-lwär′.
Euridice	Fr. ĕr-ē-dēs′.
	It. ā=ōō-rē′-dē-chē.
Euripides	ū-rĭp′-ĭ-dēz.
Euroclydon	ū-rŏk′-lĭ-dŏn.
Europa, or	ū-rō′-pä.
Europe	ū′-rŏp, Class. ū-rō′-pē.
European	ū-rō-pē′-àn.
Euryanthe	ū-rĭ-ăn′-thē.
Eurydice	ū-rĭd′-ĭs-ē.
Eusenada Honda . . .	ā″=ōō-sa-nä′-dä ōn′-dä.
Eustache, St.	săn-tēs-tăsh′.
Eustachian	ūs-tā′-kĭ-àn.
Eustachio	ā=ōōs-tä′-kē-o.
Eustachius	ūs-tā′-kĭ-ŭs.
Euterpe	ū-tĕr′-pē.
Euterpean	ū-tĕr′-pē-àn.
Euxine	yūks′-ĭn.
Evangeline	ē-văn′-jĕ-līn, ē-văn′-jĕ-lēn.
Evelina	ĕv-ē-lī′-nà, ĕv-ĕ-lē′-nà.
Evesham	ēvz′- hăm, ēvz′-ăm,
	ĕv′-shăm.
Évreux	āv-rē′.
Ewart	ū′-àrt.

Excalibar (—bur) . . . ĕks-kăl′-ĭ-bàr.
Exeter . . . . ĕks′-ĕ-tẽr.
Eyck, van . . . . . . văn īk.
Eylau . . . . ī′-low.
Eyre . . . . âr.
Eytinge . . . . ĕt′-tĭng.
Ezekias . . . . . ĕz-ĕ-kī′-ás.
Ezekiel . . . . . . ē-zē′-kĭ-ĕl.
Ezra . . . . ĕz′-rä.
Ezzelino da Romano, see
    Eccelino . . . . . ĕt-zā-lē′-nō dä rō-mä′-nō.

F

Fabian . . . . fā′-bĭ-àn.
Fabliau . . . . fă-blē-ō′.
Fabliaux . . . . . . fă-blē-ō′.
Fabre . . . . făbr.
Fabriano . . . . . fä-brē-ä′-nō.
Faenza . . . . fä-ĕn′-dzä.
Fagin . . . . fā′-gĭn.
Fahrenheit . . . . fä′-rĕn-hīt.
Faidherbe . . . . . fä-dârb′.
Failly . . . . fä-yē′.
Fainéants, Les Rois . . lā rwä fā-nā-äṅ′.
Faizabad, see Fyzabad . fī-zä-bäd′.
Fajardo, see Faxardo . . Sp. fä-ċhär′-dō.
Falaise . . . . fä-lĕz′.
Falconbridge . . . . fôk′-àn-brĭj.
Falernian . . . . . . fȧ-lẽr′-nĭ-àn.
Falieri . . . . fä-lē-ä′-rē.
Falkenhayn . . . . fäl′-kĕn-hīn.
Falkland . . . . . . fôk′-lànd.
Faneuil . . . . făn′-ĕl.   pop. fŭn′-ĕl.
Fantine . . . . . . fäṅ-tēn′.
Fantin-Latour . . . fän-tăṅ′ lä-tōōr′.
Faraday . . . . . . făr′-ȧ-dā.

Farallones . . . . . fä-räl-yō'-nĕs.
Faridpur, see Furidpur . fŭr-ēd-pōōr'.
Farnese . . . . . . fär-nēz'. *It.* fär-nā'-zĕ.
Faro, or Faroe . . . . fā'-rō, fā'-rōō=ĕ.
Farquhar . . . . . . fär'-kwär, fär'-kär.
Farrakhabad, see Farruk-
    habad . . . . . . fŭr-rŭk-ä-bäd'.
Farrar (Canon) . . . . fär'-àr.
Farrar (Geraldine) . . . fàr-är'.
Farrukhabad, see Farrak-
    habad . . . . . . fŭr-rŭk-ä-bäd'.
Fascisti , , ... fä-ɛhōɒ' tō.
Fashoda . . . . . . fä-shō'-dä.
Fata Morgana . . . . fā'-tà mȯr-gā'-nà,
                           fä'-tä mȯr-gä'-nä.
Fathipur, see Futtehpur . fŭt-ē-pōōr'.
Fatima . . . . fä'-tē-mä. *pop.* făt'-ĭ-mà.
Fatimites . . . . . . făt'-ĭ-mīts.
Faubourg St. Antoine . . fō-bōōr' săṅ-täṅ-twäṅ'.
Foubourg St. Germain . fō-bōōr' săn zhâr-măn'.
Fauntleroy . . . . . fȯnt'-lēr-oi.
Faure, Félix . . . . . fä-lēks' fōr'.
Fauresmith . . . . . fȯr'-ɛmĭth.
Faust . . . . fowɛt.
Faustina . . . . . . fȯs-tī'-nà.
Faustus . . . . . . fȯs'-tŭs. *Ger.* fows'-toȯs.
Favre . . . . făvr.
Faxardo, see Fajardo . . fä-ċhär'-dō.
Fayal . . . . fī-ôl'. *Port.* fī-äl'.
Fayoum, Fayum . . . fī-ōōm'.
February . . . . . . fĕb'-rōō-ā"-rĭ.
Fechter . . . . . . fĕċh'-tĕr, fĕsh'-tēr.
Fédora . . . . fä-dō'-rä.
Fedotoff (—ov) . . . . fĕ-dŏ'-tŏf.
Feejee, see Fiji . . . . fē'-jē.
Feejeean, see Fijian . . fē-jē'-àn.
Felahie . . . . fä-lä-hē'.

Felice	*It.* fā-lē'-chā.
Félice	*Fr.* fā-lēs'.
Félicité	fā-lēs-ē-tā'.
Felipe	fā-lē'-pā.
Felix	fē'-lĭks.
Félix	*Fr.* fā- lēks'.
Femme de Trente Ans	făm dŭ trŏnt än.
Fénelon	fĕn'-ĕ-lŭn. *Fr.* fā=nŭ-lôn'.
Fenian	fēn'-yȧn.
Feodor	fā'-ō-dōr.
Feodosia	fā-ō-dŏ'-sē-ȧ.
Fère-en-Tardenois . . .	fĕr-ôn-tärd-nwä'.
Ferichta, Feirshta, Ferischta, see Firishtah	fĕr'-ĭsh-tä.
Fernandez	fĕr-năn'-dēz. *Sp.* fĕr-nän'-dĕth.
Fernandina	fĕr-năn-dē'-nȧ. *Sp.* fĕr-nän-dē'-nä
Fernando, San	săn fĕr-năn'-dō, sän fĕr-nän'-dō.
Ferney or Fernex . . .	fâr-nā'.
Ferozepore, see Firozpur	fē-rōz-pōr'.
Ferrand	fĕ-rän'.
Ferrara	fĕr-rä'-rä.
Ferrero, Guglielmo . .	gōōl-yäl'-mō fär-rā'-rō.
Ferrières	fĕr-ē=âr'.
Ferrol, El	āl fĕr-rōl'.
Ferronnière, La Belle . .	lä bĕl fĕr-rŏn-ē=âr'.
Ferry, Jules	zhül fĕ-rē'.
Fesole, see Fiesole . . .	fā'-zō-lä.
Festubert	fĕs-ü-bĕr'.
Fétis	fā-tēs'.
Feuerbach	foi'-ĕr-bäċh.
Feuillet, Octave	ōk-täv' fĕ-yä'.
Feydeau	fā-dō'.
Feyjoo y Montenegro . .	fā=ē-hō' ē mōn-tā-nä'-grō.
Fezzan	fĕz-zän'.

Ffrangcon-Davies . . .	frăng'-kŏn-dā'-vēz.
Fichte	fĭċh'-tŭ.
Fidelio	fē-dā'-lē-o.
Fierabras	fē=ä-rä-brä'.
Fiesole	fē=ä'-zō-lä.
Figaro	fē-gä-rō'.
Figueroa	fĭg-ĕr-ō'-å.
Fiji, see Feejee	fē'-jē.
Fijian, see Feejeean . .	fē-jē'-ȧn.
Filarete	fē-lä-rā'-tĕ.
Filipina	fĭl-ĭ-pē'-nȧ, *Sp.* fē-lē-pē'-nä
Filipino	fĭl-ĭ-pē'-nō. *Sp.* fē-lē-pē'-nō
Filippo	fē-lēp'-pō.
Fille du Régiment, La . .	lä fē dü rä-zhē-môṅ'.
Filomena (St.)	fĭl-ō-mē'-nȧ.
Finistère (—terre) . . .	fĭn-ĭs-tĕr'.
Fiorentino	fē-ō-rän-tē'-nō.
Firenze	fē-rän'-dzä.
Firishtah, see Ferichta .	fē'-rēsh-tä.
Firmin Didot	fēr-măṅ' dē-dō'.
Firozpur, see Ferozepore .	fē-rōz-pōōr'.
Fismettes	fē-mĕt'.
Fiume	fē-ōō'-mä.
Flagellants	flăj'-ĕl-ȧnts.
Flameng	flä-môṅ'.
Flaminian	flȧ-mĭn'-ĭ-ȧn.
Flammarion	flä-mä-rē-ôṅ'.
Flandrin	fläṅ-drăṅ'.
Flaubert	flō-bâr'.
Fleance	flē'-ȧns.
Fleurus	flē-rüs'.
Fleury	flē-rē'.
Fliegende Holländer, Der	dĕr flē'-gĕn-dŭ hŏl'-ēn-dĕr.
Flodden	flŏd'-ĕn.
Flonzaley	flôṅ-ză'-lä.
Floréal	flō-rā-ăl'.
Florentine	flŏr'-ĕn-tĭn, flŏr'-ĕn-tīn.

Flores . . . . flō'-rĕs.
Florizel . . . . flŏr'-ĭzĕl.
Flotow, von . . . . . fŏn flō'-tō, *Ger.* flō'-tōv.
Flourens . . . . flōō-rŏn'.
Foch . . . . fŏsh.
Focsani . . . . . . fŏk'-shä-nē.
Fogazzaro . . . . . . fō-gäts-sä'-rō.
Foggia . . . . fŏd'-jä.
Foix . . . . fwä.
Fokien, see Fu-kien . . fō-kē-ĕn'.
Folies Bergères, Les . . lä fŏ-lē' bĕr-zhĕr'.
Foligno, see Fuligno . . fō-lēn'-yō.
Folkestone. . . . . . fōk'-stŭn.
Folkething . . . . . fōl'-kē-tĭng.
Fomalhaut . . . . . fō-mäl-ō'.
Fond du Lac . . . . . fŏn dŭ lăk.
Fonseca . . . . . . fōn-sā'-kä.
Fontainebleau . . . . fŏn-tān-blō'.
Fontenoy . . . . . . fŏnt'-ĕ-noi. *Fr.* fôn̂t-nwä'.
Fontevrault . . . . . fôn̂=tĕ-vrō'.
Foochow, see Fu-chau . fōō-chow'.
Forlì . . . . fŏr-lē'.
Formosa . . . . . . fôr-mō'-sä.
Formosan . . . . . . fôr-mō'-sàn.
Fornarina, La . . . . lä fôr-nä-rē'-nä,
Forres . . . . fŏr'-ĕs.
Fors Clavigera . . . fôrz klă-vĭj'-ēr-à.
Fort de France . . . . fōr dŭ fräns.
Fortescue . . . . . . fôr'-tĕs-kū.
Fortinbras . . . . . . fŏr'-tĭn-brăs.
Fortunatus . . . . . fŏr-tū-nā'-tūs.
Fortuny . . . . . . fŏr-tōō'-nē.
Forza del Destino, La . lä fōr-dzä däl däs-tē'-nō.
Foscari . . . . fŏs'-kä-rē.
Foscarini . . . . . . fōs-kä-rē'-nē.
Foscolo . . . . . . fŏs'-kō-lō.
Fotheringay . . . . . fŏth'-ēr-ĭn-gā.

Foucault	fōō-kō′.
Fouché	fōō-shā′.
Foucquet	fōō-kä′.
Foulques	fōōk.
Fouqué	fōō-kä′.
Fourier	fōō-rē̅=ā′.
Fourierism	fōō′-rĭ-ēr-ĭzm″.
Fournet, du	dü fōōr-nä′.
Fournier	fōōr-nē̅=ā′.
Fra Angelico	frä än-jäl′-ē-ko.
Fra Bartolommeo . . .	frä bär-to-lōm-mä′-ō.
Fracasse, Capitaine . .	kä-pē-tĕn′ frä-käs′.
Fra Diavolo	frä dē̅=ä′-vō-lō.
Fraermann	frâr′-män.
Fragiacomo, Pietro . . .	pē-ä′-trō frä-jä′-kō-mō.
Fragonard	fră-gō-när′.
France	frăns. *Fr.* fräns.
France, Anatole	ä-nä-tōl′ fräns.
France, Île de	ēl dŭ fräns′.
Francesca da Rimini . .	frăn-sĕs′-kȧ dä rē′-mē-nē. *It.* frän-chĕs′-kä dä-rē′-mē-nē.
Francesco	frăn-sĕs′-kō. *It.* frän-chĕs′-kō.
Franche-Comté	fränsh kôn-tā′.
Francia	frän′-chä.
Francisco	frăn-sĭs′-kō. *Sp.* frän thōs′-kō.
Francis de Sales	frăn′-sĭs dŭ sälz. *Fr.* săl.
Franck, César	sä-zär′ fränk.
François	frän-swä′.
Françoise	frän-swäz′.
Franconian	frăng-kō′-nĭ-ȧn.
Frangipani	frăn-jĭ-păn′-ĭ. *It.* frän-jĕ-pä′-nē.
Franz	frănts.
Franz-Josef	frănts′ yō′-zĕf.

Frari . . . . frä'-rē.
Frascati . . . . . . fräs-kä'-tē.
Fraunhofer . . . . . frown'-hō-fĕr.
Frédégonde . . . . . frā-dā-gōńd'.
Freiberg . . . . . . frī'-bĕrċh.
Freiburg, see Fribourg . frī'-bōōrċh.
Freiligrath . . . . . frī'-lĭg-rät.
Freischütz, Der . . . . dĕr frī'-shüts.
Freitag, see Freytag . . frī'-täċh.
Frelinghuysen . . . . frē'-lĭng-hī"-zĕn.
Frémiet . . . . . . frā-mē=ā'.
Fréminet . . . . . . frā-mē-nā'.
Frémont (Gen.) . . . . frā-mŏnt'. *pop.* frē'-mŏnt.
Fremont (Ohio) . . . . frē-mŏnt', frē'-mŏnt.
Fremstad . . . . . . frĕm'-städ.
Freneau . . . . . . frĕ-nō'.
Frere . . . . frēr.
Frère . . . . frâr.
Frescobaldi . . . . . frĕs-kō-bäl'-dē.
Freud . . . . froit.
Freudian . . . . . . froi'-dĭ-ȧn.
Frey . . . . frī.
Freya . . . . frī'-ä.
Freycinet . . . . . . frā-sē-nā'.
Freytag, see Freitag . . frī'-täċh.
Friant . . . . frē-äń'.
Fribourg, see Freiburg . frē-bōōr'.
Fridthiof, see Frithjof . . frēt'-yŏf.
Friedland . . . . . . frēd'-länt.
Friedrichsbau . . . . frēd'-rĭċhs-bow.
Friedrichshafen . . . . frēd'-rĭċhs-hä'-fĕn.
Friesian, see Frisian . . frez'-yȧn, frēzh'-yȧn.
Frimaire . . . . . . frē-mâr'.
Frisian, see Friesian . . frĭz'-ĭ=ȧn, frĭzh'-yȧn.
Frithjof, see Fridthiof . . frēt'-yŏf.
Fritz, Der Alte . . . . dĕr äl'-tŭ frĭts.
Fritz, Unser . . . . . ōōn'-zĕr frĭts.

Friuli	frē'-ōō-lē.
Fröbel, or Froebel . . .	frē'-bĕl.
Frobisher	frō'-bĭsh-ēr.
Froissart	froi'-särt. *Fr.* frwä-sär'.
Frollo, Claude	clōd frō-lō'.
Fromentin	frō-mŏn-tăn'.
Fronde	frŏnd. *Fr.* frônd.
Front de Bœuf	frôn dŭ bēf.
Frontenac	frônt-näk'.
Frossard	frŏs-sär'.
Froude	frōōd.
Frou-Frou	froo'-froo'.
Fructidor	frük-tē-dōr'.
Frydek	frē'-dĕk.
Fu-chau, see Foochow .	fōō-chow'.
Fuji-san, or	fōō'-jē-sän'.
Fuji-yama	fōō'-jē-yä'-mä.
Fu-kien, see Fokien . .	fōō-kē-ĕn'.
Fulc, see Fulk	fōōlk.
Fulda	fōōl'-dä.
Fulham	fŭl'-ȧm.
Fuligno, see Foligno . .	fōō-lĕn'-yō.
Fulk, see Fulc	fōōlk.
Furidpur, see Faridpur .	fŭr-ēd-pōōr'.
Furca (-ka)	fōōr'-kä.
Furness	fēr'-nĕs.
Furor	fū'-rôr'. *Sp.* fōō-rōr'.
Fürst	fürst.
Fürstin	fürst'-ĭn.
Fusan	fōō-sän'.
Fust	fōōst.
Fuszki	fōōs'-kē.
Futtehpur, see Fathipur .	fŭt-tĕ-pōōr'.
Fyne, Loch	lŏċh fīn.
Fyt, Jan	yăn fīt.
Fyzabad, see Faizabad .	fī-zä-bäd'.

G

Gabael	găb'-ā-ĕl, gā'-bā-ĕl.
Gaberones	găb-ĕ-rō'-nĕs.
Gaboriau, Émile . . .	ā-mĕl' gä-bō-rē=ō'.
Gabriel	gā'-brĭ-ĕl.
Gabriele	gä-brē-ā'-lĕ.
Gabrielle	Fr. gă-brē-ĕl'.
Gabrielli	gä-brē-ĕl'-lē.
Gabrilowitch	gä-brĭl-ō'-vĭch.
Gaby DesLys	gă-bē' dä-lēs'.
Gadarenes	găd-ā-rēnz'.
Gaddi, Gaddo	gäd'dō gäd'-dē.
Gade	gä'-dĕ.
Gadeira, or	gă-dī'-rä.
Gades	gā'-dēz.
Gadhelic	găd-ĕl'-ĭk, găd'-ĕl-ĭk.
Gadite	gā'-dīt.
Gæa, see Ge	jē'-à.
Gaekwar, see Gaikwar .	gīk'-wär.
Gael	gāl.
Gaelic	gā'-lĭk.
Gaeta	gä-ā'-tä.
Gaikwar, see Gaekwar .	gīk'-wär.
Gainsborough	gānz'-bŭr-ŭ, gānz'-bŭr-ō, gānz'-brō.
Gaiseric	gī'-zĕr-ĭk.
Gakutei	gä-kōō-tä'-ē.
Galahad	găl'-à-hăd.
Galapagos (Is.)	găl-à-pā'-gōs.
	Sp. gä-lä'-pä-gōs.
Galashiels	găl-à-shēlz'.
Galatea	găl-à-tē'-à.
Galatians	gà-lā'-shĭ=àns.
Galdos, Pérez	pā'-rĕth gäl'-dōs.
Galen	gā'-lĕn.
Galignani	gä-lĕn-yä'-nē.

Galilean . . . . . . găl-ĭ-lē'-ăn.
Galilee . . . . găl'-ĭ-lē.
Galilei, Galileo . . . . gä-lē-lā'-o gä-lē-lā'-ē.
Galitzin, see Gallitzin . . gä-lēts'-ĕn.
Gallait . . . . gäl-lā'.
Gallatin . . . . . găl'-à-tĭn.
Gallaudet . . . . . găl-ô-dĕt'.
Gallegos . . . . . gäl-yā'-gŏs.
Gallicism . . . . . găl'-ĭ-sĭzm.
Galli-Curci . . . . . gäl'-lē kōōr'-chē.
Gallinéi . . . . . . găl-yū-ụē'.
Gallienus . . . . . . găl-ĭ-ē'-nŭs.
Gallifet, de . . . . . dŭ gäl-ē-fā'.
Gallipoli . . . . . găl-lĭp'-ō-lĭ. *Il.* gäl-lēp'-ō-lē.
Gallitzin, see Galitzin . . gä-lēts'-ēn.
Galsworthy . . . . . gôlz-wĕr-ŧhĭ.
Galuppi . . . . . gä-lōōp'-pē.
Galvani . . . . . . gäl-vä'-nē.
Galveston . . . . . găl'-vĕs-tŭn.
Galway . . . . . . gôl'-wā.
Gama, da . . . . . . dä gä'-mä.
Gamaliel . . . . . gă-mā'-lĭ-ĕl..
Gambetta . . . . . . găm-bĕt'-tä.
        Fr. gän-bĕt-tä'.
Gambia . . . . . . găm'-bĭ-ä.
Gananoque . . . . . gä-nä-nōk'.
Gand, see Ghent . . . gän.
Gandercleugh . . . . găn'-dĕr-klūċh.
Gandhi . . . . gänd'-hē.
Gando . . . . . . gän'-dō.
Ganga, or . . . . . . *Hind.* gŭng'-gä.
Ganges . . . . găn'-jēz.
Ganjam . . . . . gän-jäm'.
Ganymede . . . . găn'-ĭ-mēd.
Ganymedes . . . . găn-ĭ-mē'-dēz.
Garagantua, see Gargantua gär-à-găn'-tū-ä.
        Fr. gär-ä-gän-tü-ä'.

Garay . . . . gä-rä′=ē.
Garbieh, see Gharbieh . gär-bē′-yĕ.
García, or . . . . . . gär′-shĭ=a. *Sp.* gär-thē′-ä.
Garcías, see Garzía . . gär-thē′-äs.
Garcilaso . . . . . . gär-thē-lä′-sō.
Gard . . . . gär.
Gardafui, see Guardafui . gär-dä-fwē′.
Gargantua, see Garagantua gär-gän′tū-ä.
     Fr. gär-gän-tü-ä′.
Garguille . . . . . . gär-gē′=yŭ.
Garhwal, see Gurhwal . gŭr-wäl′.
Garibaldi . . . . . . gär-ĭ-bäl′-dĭ.
     It. gä-rē-bäl′-dē.
Garigliano . . . . . . gä-rēl-yä′-nō.
Garnier . . . . . . gär-nē=ä′.
Garnier-Pagès . . . . gär-nē=ä′-pä-zhĕz′.
Garofalo . . . . . . gä-rō′-fä-lō.
Garonne . . . . . . gä-rŏn′. *Fr.* gä-rŏn′.
Garshin . . . . . . gär′-shēn.
Garzía, see García . . . gär-thē′-ä.
Gascogne . . . . . . gäs-kōn′=yŭ.
Gascony . . . . . . găs′-kō-nĭ.
Gassend . . . . . . gäs-sŏn′.
Gassendi . . . . . . gäs-sen′-dē. *Fr.* gä-săn-dē′.
Gastein . . . . . . gäs′-tīn.
Gaston de Foix . . . . gäs-tôn′ dŭ fwä.
Gaston d'Orléans . . . gäs-tôn′ dōr-lä-än′.
Gatacre . . . . . . găt′-à-kĕr.
Gatshina . . . . . . gä′-chē-nä.
Gatti-Casazza . . . . găt′-tē-kä-zäts′-sä.
Gatun . . . . gä-tōōn′.
Gauchet . . . . . . gō-shä′.
Gaudenzio . . . . . gow-dĕn′-dzē-ō.
Gaudissart . . . . . gō-dē-sär′.
Gauguin . . . . . . gō-găn′.
Gautama, see Gotama . gô′-tà-mà.
     Hind. gow′-tä-mä.

Gautier, Théophile . . tä-ō-fēl′ gō-tē=ā′.
Gavan . . . . gắv′-án.
Gaveston . . . . . . gắv′-ĕs-tŭn. *Fr.* gă-vĕs-tŏṅ′
Gavin . . . . gắv′-ĭn.
Gaviota . . . . . . gä-vē-ō′-tȧ.
Gavroche . . . . . . gä-vrŏsh′.
Gawain, or Gawayne . . gä′-wān.
Gay-Lussac . . . . . gā-lüs-săk′.
Gaza . . . . gā′-zȧ.
Gazaland . . . . . . gä′-zä-länd.
Ge, see Gæa . . . . . gē.
Geber . . . . gū′-bĕr.
Gebir . . . . gā′-bēr.
Geddes. . . . . . . gĕd′-ĕs.
Gefleborg . . . . . yāf′-lĕ-bōrg.
Gehenna . . . . . . gē-hĕn′-ä.
Geierstein. . . . . . gī′-ĕr-stīn.
Geikie . . . . gē′-kĭ.
Gelée, Claude . . . . klōd zhē-lā′.
Gellert . . . . gĕl′-lĕrt.
Gemini. . . . . . . jĕm′-ĭ-nī.
Geminiani . . . . . . jäm″-ē-nē-ä′-nē.
Gemmi . . . . gĕm′-ē.
Genée . . . . zhĕ-nā′.
Genesareth, see Gennesa-
   ret . . . . gĕ-nĕs′-ȧ-rĕth.
Genesis . . . . . . jĕn′-ĕ-sĭs.
Geneva . . . . . . jĕ-nē′-vä.
Geneviève, Ste. . . . . sắṅt zhĕn-vē=ĕv′.
Genevra . . . . . . jĕn-ĕv′-rȧ.
Genghis Khan, see Jenghiz jĕn′-gĭs khän.
Genlis, de . . . . . . dŭ zhŏṅ-lēs′.
Gennesaret, see Genesa-
   reth . . . . gĕn-nĕs′-ȧ-rĕt, jĕ-nĕs′-ȧ-rĕt
Genoa . . . . jĕn′-ō-ä.
Genoese . . . . . . jĕn-ō-ēz′, jĕn-ō-ēs′.
Genova . . . . jän′-ō-vä.

Genovefa . . . . . . gā-nō-fä′-fä.
Genseric . . . . . . jĕn′-sĕr-ĭk.
Gentiles . . . . . . jĕn′-tīlz.
Geoffrey . . . . . . jĕf′-rĭ.
Geoffrin . . . . . . zhō-frăn′.
Geoffroy . . . . . . zhō-frwä′.
Georg . . . . *Ger.* gā=ōrċh′. *Sw.*
　　　　　　　　　yā-ôrċh′.
Georges . . . . . . zhôrzh.
Georgics . . . . . . jôr′-jĭks.
Georgievsk . . . . . gē=ôr′-gē-ĕfsk,
　　　　　　　　　dyôr′-dyĕfsk.
Geraint . . . . gĕ-rānt′.
Gérard . . . . *Fr.* zhā-rär′.
Gerardy (Jean) . . . . zhē-rär-dē′.
Gergesenes . . . . . gĕr-gē-sēnz′.
Gerhardt . . . . . . *Fr.* zhā-rär′. *Ger.* gâr′-härt.
Géricault . . . . . . zhā-rē-kō′.
Gericke . . . . . . gâr′-ĭ-kŭ.
Gerizim . . . . . . gĕr′-ĭz-ĭm.
Germain . . . . . . jĕr-mān′. *Fr.* zhâr-măn′.
Germania . . . . . . jĕr-mā′-nĭ-à.
　　　　　　　　　Ger. gĕr-mä′-nē-ä.
Germanicus . . . . . jĕr-măn′-ĭ-kŭs.
Germinal . . . . . . zhâr-mē-năl′.
Gernszheim . . . . . gĕrns′-hīm.
Gérôme . . . . . . zhā-rōm′.
Gerona, see Jerona, Xerona *Sp.* ċhā-rō′-nä.
Geronimo, Chief . . . jĕ-rŏn′-ĭ-mō.　　　.
　　　　　　　　　Sp. chā-rŏn′-ē-mō.
Géronte . . . . . . zhā-rônt′.
Gerould (Mrs. K. F.) . . jĕr-ō′.
Gerry . . . . gĕr′-ĭ.
Gers . . . . zhâr.
Gerster . . . . . . gĕrs′-tĕr.
Gervais . . . . . . zhĕr-vā′.
Gervaise . . . . . . zhĕr-vĕz′.

Gervase . . . . . . jĕr'-vās, jĕr-vāz'.
Gervex . . . . . . zhâr-vā'.
Gerville-Réache . . . . zhâr-vēl'-rā-äsh'.
Gervinus . . . . . gĕr-vē'-nŏŏs.
Geryon . . . . . . jĕ'-rĭ-ŏn.
Geryones . . . . . jē-rī'-ō-nēz.
Gesenius . . . . . gĕ-sē'-nĭ-ŭs. *Ger.*
                    gā-zā'-nē-ŏŏs.
Gessart, see Gossaert . . gĕs'-ärt.
Gesta Romanorum . . jĕs'-tä rō-mā-nō'-rŭm.
Gethsemane . . . . . gĕth-sĕm'-à-nĕ.
Geulincx . . . . . . chĕ'-lĭnks. *Fr.* zhē-lănks'.
Gezer . . . . gē'-zĕr.
Gharbieh, see Garbieh . gär-bē'-yĕ.
Ghats, Ghaunts . . . . gôts.
Ghazipur . . . . . gä-zē-pōōr'.
Ghent, see Gand . . . gĕnt.
Gherardesca, Ugolina della ōō-gō-lē'-nō dĕl'-lä
                    gā-rär-dĕs'-kä.
Ghetto . . . . . . gĕt'-tō.
Ghibellines . . . . . gĭb'-ĕ-lĭnz.
Ghiberti . . . . . gē-bĕr'-tē.
Ghil, René . . . . . rē-nā'gēl.
Ghirlandajo . . . . . gĕr-län-dä'-yŏ.
Ghizeh, see Gizeh . . . gē'-zĕ.
Ghoorkas, see Goorkhas,
  or Ghurkas . . . . gōōr'-käs.
Giacomo . . . . . jä'-kō-mō.
Gian Galeazzo Visconti . jän gä-lā-ätz'-ō vĭs-kōn'-tē.
Gibara . . . . . . ċhē-bä'-rä.
Gibeah . . . . . . gĭb'-ē-ä.
Gibra . . . . . . ċhē'-brä.
Gibraltar . . . . . jĭb-rôl'-tàr.
Giers . . . . . . gērs.
Giessbach . . . . . gēs'-bäċk.
Gil . . . . *Fr.* zhēl. *Sp.* 'hēl.
Gila . . . . hē'-lä. *Sp.* ċhē'-lä.

Gil Blas de Santillane,	*Fr.* zhēl blăs dŭ säṅtēl-ăn'.
Sp. Santillana	*Sp.* 'hēl bläs dā
	sän-tēl-yä'-nȧ.
Gilboa	gĭl-bō'-ä, gĭl'-bō-ä.
Gilda	*Fr.* zhēl-dä', *It.* jēl'-dä.
Gilead	gĭl'-ē-ăd.
Giles	jīlz.
Gilgal	gĭl'-găl.
Gilibert	zhēl-ē-bĕr'.
Ginchy	zhăṅ-shē'.
Ginevra	gĭ-nĕv'-rä, jē-nĕv'-rȧ.
Gioconda, La	lä jŏ-kōn'-dä.
Giocondo	jō-kŏn'-dō.
Gioja del Colle, or Gioia .	jō'-yä dāl kŏl'-lĕ.
Giordano Bruno	jōr-dä'-nō brōō'-nō.
Giorgio	jŏr'-jō.
Giorgione	jŏr-jō'-nĕ.
Giotto	jŏt'-tō.
Giovanni	jō-vän'-nē.
Girardin	zhē-rär-dăṅ'.
Giraudoux	zhē-rō-dōō'.
Girgeh	jēr'-jĕ.
Girgenti	jēr-jĕn'-tē.
Girolamo	jē-rō'-lä-mō.
Gironde	jĭ-rŏnd'. *Fr.* zhē-rôṅd'.
Girondins	jĭ-rŏṅ'-dĭnz.
	Fr. zhē-rôṅ-dăṅ'.
Girondists	jĭ-rŏn'-dĭsts.
Gisors	zhē-zŏr'.
Gittite	gĭt'-īt.
Giulia	jōōl'-yä.
Giuliano	jōō-lē=ä'-nō.
Giulietta	jōō-lē-ät'-tä.
Giulio di Pietro di Filippo	jōō'-lē=ō dē
	pē=ä'-trō dē fē-lēp'-pō.
Giulio Romano	jōō'-lē=ō rō-mä'-nō.
Giuseppe	jōō-sĕp'-pĕ.

Giustiniani	jōōs″-tē-nē-ä′-nē.
Givenchy	zhē-vôṅ-shē′.
Gizeh, see Ghizeh . .	gē′-zŭ.
Gladstone	glăd′-stŭn, glăd′-stōn.
Glamis, or Glammis . .	glämz.
Glamorgan	glă-môr′-găn
Glasgow	glăs′-gō.
Glaucus	glô′-kŭs.
Glazounoff (-ow), or	
Glazunov (-ow) . . .	glă-zōō-nŏf′.
Glendower	glĕn-dow′-ẽr, glĕn′-dōōr.
Glière	glē-ĕr′.
Godard, Benjamin. . .	bŏṅ-zhă-maṅ′ gō-där′.
Gloriana	glō-rĭ-ä′-nä.
Gloster, or Gloucester .	glŏs′-tẽr.
Glück	glük.
Glumdalclitch	glŭm-dăl′-klĭch.
Glycera	glĭs′-ĕ-rä.
Glyptotheca	glĭp-tō-thē′-kȧ.
Glyptothek	glĭp-tō-tāk′.
Gneist	g=nīst.
Gnostics	nŏs′-tĭks.
Goa	gō′-ä.
Goajira, see Guajira . .	gō=ä-'hō′-rü, gwä-'hē′-rä.
Goalpara	gō-äl-pä′-rä.
Gobelin	gŏb-lăṅ′.
Gobi, see Cobi	gō′-bē.
Gobseck	gŏb-sĕk′.
Godavari	gō-dä′-vä-rē.
Godebski	gō-dĕb′-skĭ.
Godefroy de Bouillon . .	*Fr.* gō=dŭ-frwä′ dŭ bōō-yôṅ′.
Godfrey of Bouillon . .	gŏd′-frĭ ov bōō-yôṅ′.
Godiva	gō-dĭ′-vȧ.
Godolphin	gŏ-dŏl′-fĭn.
Godowsky	gō-dŏf′-skĭ.
Godoy	gō′-doi. *Sp.* gō-dō′=ē.

Godounoff (Godunov),
 Boris . . . . bō-rēs' gō-dōō-nŏf'.
Goebel (Wm.) . . . . gō'-bĕl.
Goeben . . . . . . gē'-bĕn.
Goessler, see Gössler . . gĕs'-lĕr.
Goethals . . . . . gō'-thȧlz.
Goethe, see Göthe . . gē'-tŭ.
Goetz von Berlichingen,
 see Götz . . . . . gētz fŏn bȧr'-lĭċh-ĭng"-ĕn.
Gogol . . . . gŏ̄-gŏl'.
Goldoni . . . . . . gōl-dō'-nē.
Golgotha . . . . . . gŏl'-gō-thȧ.
Goliath . . . . gō-lī'-ăth.
Golitzin . . . . . . gō-lĭts'-ĭn.
Gomara . . . . . . gō-mä'-rä.
Gomez . . . . gō'-mĕz. *Sp.* gō'-mĕth.
Gomorrah . . . . . . gŏ-mŏr'-ä.
Gompers . . . . . . gŏm'-pērs.
Gonaive, La . . . . . lä gō-nä-ēv'.
Gonaives, Les . . . . lā gō-nä-ēv'.
Goncharoff (-ov) . . . gŏn-chär'-ŏf.
Goncourt, de . . . . . dŭ gôn̄-kōōr'.
Gonda . . . . gŏn'-dä.
Goneril . . . . gŏn'-ēr-ĭl.
Gonfaloniere . . . . . gōn"-fä-lō-nē-ā'-rĕ.
Góngora . . . . . . gŏn'-gō-rȧ.
Gonsalvo de Cordova . . gōn-säl'-vō dĕ kŏr'-dō-vä.
Gonse . . . . gŏn'-sĕ.
Gonzaga . . . . . gŏn-zä'-gä. *Sp.* gōn-thä'-gä.
   It. gōn-dzä'-gä.
Gonzales . . . . . . *Sp.* gōn-thä'-lĕs.
Gonzalez . . . . . . gōn-thä'-lĕth.
Gonzalo de Córdoba . . gōn-thä'-lō dā kŏr'-dō-bä.
Goorkhas, see Ghoorkas . gōōr'-käz.
Gorakhpur, see Goruckpur gŏ-rŭk-pōōr'.
Gorboduc . . . . . . gôr'-bō-dŭk.
Gordian, or Gordianus . . gôr'-dĭ-ȧn, gôr-dĭ-ā'-nŭs.

Görgei, or Görgey . . . gēr'-gĕ-ĭ.
Gorgias . . . . . . gôr'-jĭ-ȧs.
Goriot, Père . . . . . pâr gō-rē-ō'.
Gorizia . . . . gō-rēdz'-ē-ä.
Gorki (-ky) . . . . . gôr'-kĭ.
Görlitz . . . . gēr'-lĭts.
Gortchakoff, or -kow, or
  -kov . . . . gŏr-chä-kŏf'.
Goruckpur, see Gorakhpur gŏ-rŭk-pōōr'.
Görz . . . . gērts.
Goshenland . . . . . gō'-shĕn-lånd.
Gossaert, see Gessart . . gŏs'-ärt.
Cossé, or Cossoo . . . gŏs-sā', gŏ-sĕk'
Gössler, see Goessler . . gēs'-lĕr.
Got . . . . gō.
Gotama, see Gautama . gô'-tȧ-mȧ.
Göteborg, see Gothenburg yē'-tĕ-bŏrch.
Goth . . . . gŏth.
Gotha (duchy) . . . . gō'-thä.   Ger. gō'-tä.
Götha (canal) . . . . gē'-tä.   Sw. yē'-tä
Gotham . . . . . . gō'-thȧm.
Göthe, see Goethe . . . gē'-tŭ.
Gothenburg, see Gotten-
  burg, Göteborg . . . gŏt'-ĕn-bōōrch.
Gothic . . . . gŏth'-ĭk.
Gothland, or . . . . . gŏth'-lånd.
Gotland, Sw. . . . . . gōt'-länd.
Gotland (I.) . . . . . gōt'-länd.
Gottenburg, see Gothen-
  burg . . . . gŏt'-ĕn-bōōrch.
Götterdämmerung, Die . dē gēt-tĕr-dȧm'-mĕ-rōōng.
Göttingen . . . . . . gēt'-tĭng-ĕn.
Gottschalk . . . . . gŏt'-shälk.
Götz von Berlichingen, see
  Goetz . . . . . . gēts fŏn bâr'-lĭch-ĭng"-ĕn.
Gough . . . . gŏf.
Goujon . . . . gōō-zhôn'.

Gounod . . . . . . gōō-nō′.

Gouraud . . . . . . gōō-rō′.

Gouverneur . . . . . gōōv′-ēr-nēr.
              Fr. gōō-vĕr-nēr′.

Gouvion- Saint-Cyr . . gōō-vĭ=ôṅ′-săṅ-sēr′.

Gower . . . . gow′-ēr.

Goya y Lucientes . . . gō′-yä ē lōō-thē=ĕn′-tĕs.

Goyaz . . . . gō-yäz′.

Gozo, or Gozzo . . . . gŏd′-zō, gŏt′-sō.

Gozzoli, Benozzo . . . bä-nŏt′-sō gŏts′-ō-lē.

Graal, see Grail, Grael . grāl.

Gracias á Dios . . . . grä′-thē=äs ä dē-ōs′.

Gradiska . . . . . . grä-dĭs′-kä.

Graefe, Gräfe, von . . . fōn grå′-fŭ.

Grael, see Grail, Graal . grāl.

Graeme . . . . . . grām.

Graf . . . . gräf.

Gräfin . . . . grå′-fĭn.

Graham . . . . . . grā-àm, grām.

Grail, see Grael, Graal . grāl.

Gramont . . . . . . grä-môṅ′.

Granada . . . . . . gră-nä′-dä.

Grande Anse du Diamante gräṅ däṅs dü dē-ä-mäṅt′.

Grande Mademoiselle, La lä gräṅd mäd-mwä-zĕl′-ŭ.

Grande-Terre . . . . gräṅd-tår′.

Grandet, Eugénie . . . ē-zhä-nē′ gräṅ-dā′.

Grand Monarque, Le . . lē gräṅ mō-närk′.

Grandpré . . . . . . gräṅ-prā′.

Grand Prix, Le . . . . lē gräṅ prē.

Granier de Cassagnac . . grä-nē=ā′ dü käs-sän-yăk′.

Gratiano . . . . . . grä-shĭ-ä′-nō.
              It. grä-tē=ä′-nō.

Gratz, see Graz . . . . gräts.

Gravelines, or . . . . gräv-lēn′.

Gravelingen, or . . . . *Ger.* grä′-vĕ=lǐng″-ĕn.

Gravelinghe . . . . . *Fl.* grä′-vĕ-lǐng″-ĕ.

Gravelotte . . . . . . gräv-lōt′.

Graveure . . . . . . gră-vĕr'.
Graz, see Gratz . . . . gräts.
Grechaninoff (-ov) . . grĕch-ä-nē'-nŏf.
Greenough . . . . . grēn'-ŏ.
Greenwich . . . . . *Eng.* grĭn'-ĭj.
Gregory Nazianzen . . grĕg'-ō-rĭ năz-ĭ-ăn'-zĕn.
Greig . . . . grĕg.
Gremio . . . . grē'-mĭ-ō.
Grenada . . . . . . grĕn-ā'-dä.
Grenoble . . . . . . grĕ-nō'-bl.
Greta . . . . grō' tà.
Gretchen . . . . . . grĕch'-ĕn. *Ger.* grāt'-ċhĕn.
Gretel . . . . . grā'-tĕl.
Grétry . . . . . . grā-trē'.
Greuze . . . . . . grēz.
Grève . . . . grĕv.
Greville . . . . . . grĕv'-ĭl.
Gréville . . . . . . *Fr.* grā-vēl'.
Grévy . . . . grā-vē'.
Griboyédoff . . . . . grē-bō-yā'-dŏf.
Gridley . . . . grĭd'-lĭ.
Grieg . . . . grēg.
Grillparzer . . . . . grĭl'-pärt-zĕr.
Grindelwald . . . . . grĭn'-dĕl-vält.
Griqualand . . . . . grē'-kwà-lănd.
Crisi . . . . grē'-zĕ.
Grisons . . . . . . grē-zôn'.
Grodno . . . . grŏd'-nō.
Grolier . . . . grō'-lē=ā. *Fr.* grō-lē=ā'.
Groningen, or . . . . *D.* ċhrō'-nĭng-ċhĕn.
Gröningen, Ger. . . . . grē'-nĭng-ĕn.
Groot . . . . grōt.
Groote Kerke . . . . grō'-tĕ kĕr'-kĕ.
Gros . . . . grō.
Grossi . . . . grŏs'-sē.
Grosvenor . . . . . . grōv'-nĕr, grō'-vĕ-nĕr.
Grote . . . . grōt.

Grotius . . . . grō'-shǐ-ŭs.
Grouchy, de . . . . . dǔ groō-shē'.
Grütli, see Rütli . . . . grüt'-lǐ.
Gruyère, Gruyères . . grü-yâr'.
Guadalajara . . . . . gwä″-dä-lä-ċhä'-rä.
Guadalquivir . . . . . gô-dăl-kwǐv'-ēr.
　　　　　　　　　　 Sp. gwä″-däl-kē-vēr'.
Guadalupe . . . . . gô-dä-loōp'.
　　　　　　　　　　 Sp. gwä-dä-loō'-pā.
Guadeloupe . . . . . gô-dĕ-loōp'. Fr. gäd-loōp'.
Guahan, Sp. Guajan . . gwä-hän'.
Guaira, La, see La Guayra lä gwī'-rȧ, lä gī'-rȧ.
　　　　　　　　　　 Sp. lä gwä'=ē-rä.
Guajan, see Guahan . . Sp. gwä-'hän'.
Guajira, see Goajira . . gwä-'hē'-rä.
Gualfonda . . . . . . gwäl-fŏn'-dä.
Guam . . . . gwăm. Sp. gwäm.
Guanabacoa . . . . . gwä″-nä-bä-kō'-ä.
Guanahani . . . . . gwä-nä-ä-nē'.
Guanaja . . . . . . gwä-nä'-'hä.
Guanajay . . . . . . gwä-nä-ċhä'=ē.
Guanica . . . . . . gwä-nē'-kä.
Guantanamo . . . . gwän-tä-nä'-mō.
Guap, see Yap . . . . gwäp.
Guardafui, see Gardafui . gwär-dä-foō=ē'.
Guarico . . . . . . gwä'-rē-kō.
Guarneri, or . . . . . gwär-nä'-rē.
Guarnerius . . . . . gwär-nē'-rǐ-ŭs.
Guatemala . . . . . gô-tē-mä'-lä.
　　　　　　　　　　 Sp. gwä-tä-mä'-lä.
Guayaquil . . . . . . gī-ȧ-kēl'. Sp. gwī-ä-kēl'.
Guaymas . . . . . . gwī'-mäs. Mex. wī'-mȧs.
Guayra, La, see La Guaira lä gwī'rä, lä gī'rȧ.
　　　　　　　　　　 Sp. lä gwä'=ē-rä.
Gudrun . . . . . . goō-droōn'.
Guébriant . . . . . . gä-brē-äṅ'.
Guelfs, Guelphs . . . . gwĕlfs.

Guendolen	gwĕn'-dŏ-lĕn.
Guenevere	gwĕn'-ĕ-vēr.
Guercino	gwĕr-chē'-nō.
Guérin	gā r̤ăṅ'.
Guernsey	gĕrn'-zĭ.
Guerrero	gĕr-âr'-ō.
Guerrière, La . . .	lä gâr-rē=âr'.
Gueux	gē.
Guglielmo	gōōl-ē=ĕl'-mo.
Gui, see Guy	*Fr.* gē.
Guiana, see Guyana . .	gū-ü'-nä.
Guicciardini	gwē-chär-dē'-nē.
Guiccioli	gwē'-chō-lē.
Guichard	gē-shär'.
Guiderius	gwĭ-dē'-rĭ-ŭs.
Guidi, Casa	kä'-zä gwē'-dē.
Guido Aretino . . .	gwē'-dō ä-rä-tē'-nō.
Guido d'Arezzo . . .	gwē'-dō dä-rĕt'-sō.
Guido Franceschini . .	gwē'-dō frän-chĕs-kē'-nē.
Guido of Lusignan, see	
Guy de	gwē'-dō ŭv lü-zēn-yäṅ'.
Guido Reni	gwē'-dō rä'-nē.
Guilbert, Yvette . . .	ē-vĕt' gĕl-bĕr'.
Guillaume	gē-yom'=ŭ.
Guillaumet	gē-yŏ-mä'.
Guillemont	gēl-môṅ'.
Guillotin	gē-yō-tăṅ'.
Guilmant	gĕl-mäṅ'.
Guimarás	gē-mä-räs'.
Guines	gēn.
Guinever, Guinevere . .	gwĭn-ĕ-vēr'.
Guion	gī'-ŏn. *Fr.* gē-ôṅ'.
Guiscard	gēs-kär'.
Guise, de	dŭ gēz.
Guitry, Sacha . . .	săsh-ä' gē-trē'.
Guizot	gē-zō'.
Gujranwala	gŭzh-răn-wä'-lä.

Gujrat . . . . gŭzh-rät'.
Gula . . . . gōō'-lä.
Gulistan . . . . . . gōō-lĭs-tän'.
Günther, Guenther . . gün'-tĕr.
Gurdaspur . . . . . gōō-däs-pōōr'.
Gurhwal, see Garhwal . gŭr-wäl'.
Gurkhas, see Ghoorkas . gōōr'-käz.
Gustavus Adolphus . . gŭs-tā'-vŭs ä-dŏl'-fŭs.
                                    Ger. gōōs-tä'-vōōs
                                    ä-dōl-fōōs. [vä'-sä.
Gustavus Vasa . . . . gŭs-tā'-vŭs, gōōs-tä'-vōōs
Gutenberg . . . . . gōō'-tĕn-bĕrg.
                                    Ger. gōō'-tĕn-bĕrċh.
Gutiérrez Nájera . . . gōō-tē-ĕr'-ĕs näċh'-ā-rä.
Gutzkow . . . . . . gōōts'-kō.
Guy, see Gui . . . . gī. Fr. gē.
Guyana, see Guiana . . gē-ä'-nä.
Guyandotte . . . . . gī-ăn-dŏt'.
Guy de Lusignan, see Guido
  of Lusignan . . . . gē dŭ lü-zēn-yäṅ'.
Guyon . . . . gī'-ŏn. Fr. gē-ôṅ'.
Guyot . . . . gē-ō'.
Guzman . . . . . . gōōth-män'.
Gwalior . . . . . . gwä'-lē-ôr.
Gyges . . . . gī'-jēz.

H

Haag, Den, see The Hague dĕn häċh.
Haakon . . . . . . hô'-kŏn.
Haas . . . . häs.
Habakkuk . . . . . hă-băk'-ŭk, hăb'-å-kŭk.
Habana, see Havana . . ä-bä'-nä.
Habsburg, see Hapsburg . häps'-bōōrċh.
Hadad . . . . hā'-dăd.
Haden . . . . hā'-dn.
Hades . . . . hā'-dēz.

Hading (Jane) . . . . ă-dăn'.
Hadrian, see Adrian . . hā'-drĭ-an.
Haeckel . . . . . . hĕk'-l. *Ger.* hâk'ĕl.
Hafiz . . . . *Pers.* hô-fīz'.
Hagar . . . . hā'-gär.
Hagedorn, von . . . . fōn hä'-gā-dôrn.
Hagen . . . . *Ger.* hä'-gĕn.
Haggai, or Haggi . . . hăg'-i.
Hagiographa . . . . . hā-jĭ-ŏg'-rà-fà,
                          hăg-ĭ-ŏg'-rä-fä.

Hague (The), see Den
    Haag, La Haye . . . hāg.
Hahnemann . . . . . hä'-nā-män.
Haidarabad, see Hydera-
    bad . . . . hī″-dä-rà-bäd'.
Haidar-Ali, see Hyder Ali hī'-där ä'-lē.
Haidee . . . . hī-dē'.
Haiduks, see Hayduks . hī'-dōōks.
Hainan . . . . hī-nän'.
Hainault, or Hainaut . . hā-nō'. *Fr.* ā-nō'.
Haiti, see Hayti . . . hā'-tĭ. *Fr.* ä-ē-tē'.
Hakluyt . . . . . . hăk'-lōōt.
Hakodate . . . . . hä-kō-dä'-tā.
Halberstadt . . . . . häl'-bĕr-stät.
Halcyone, see Alcyone . häl-sī'-ō-nē.
Haldane . . . . . . häl'-dān.
Haldeman . . . . . hôl'-dĕ-män.
Halévy . . . . ă-lā-vō'.
Halicarnassus . . . . häl'-ĭ-kär-năs'-ŭs.
Halicz . . . . hä'-lĭch.
Halle . . . . häl'-lŭ.
Haller, von . . . . . fŏn häl'-lĕr.
Hals . . . . häls.
Ham (Fort) . . . . . äm.
Hamah, or Hamath . . hä'-mä, hā'-măth.
Hamburg . . . . . . hăm'-bĕrg.
                          Ger. häm'-bōōrch.

Hamelin, or Hameln . . hä'-mŭ-lĭn, hä'-mĕln.
Hamerling . . . . . hä'-mĕr-lĭng.
Hamerton . . . . . . hăm'-ēr-tŭn.
Hamilcar Barca . . . . hă-mĭl'-kär bär'-ka.
Hamitic . . . . . . hăm-ĭt'-ĭk.
Hamsun, Knut . . . . knüt häm'-sōōn.
Hanabusa . . . . . hä'-nä'-bōō'-sä'.
Hanau . . . . hä'-now.
Händel, Handel . . . . hăn'-dĕl. Ger. hân'-dĕl.
Hang-chau, or Hangchow häng'-chow.
Hangshan . . . . . häng'-shän.
Han Hok . . . . . . hän' hōk.
Han-Kow, or Hankow, or
Han-kau . . . . . hän-kow'.
Hannover, see Hanover . hän-nō'-vĕr.
Hanoi . . . . hä-no'-ĭ.
Hanover, see Hannover . hăn'-ō-vĕr.
Hanotaux . . . . . . än-ō-tō'.
Hans . . . . hänts.
Hansa . . . . hän'-sä.
Hanseatic . . . . . . hăn-sē-ăt'-ĭk.
Hänsel and Gretel . . . hĕn'-zĕl ŏŏnt grä'-tĕl.
Hanyang . . . . . . hän-yäng'.
Hapsburg, see Habsburg . hăps'-bĕrg.
Ger. häps'-bōōrċh.
Harbin . . . . här'-bēn.
Hardanger Fjord . . . här'-däng-ĕr fyôrd.
Hardecourt . . . . . ärd-kōōr'.
Hardelot, Guy d' . . . gē där=dē-lō'.
Harderwijk . . . . . här'-dĕr-wĭk.
Hardicanute . . . . . här''-dĭ-kā-nūt'.
Hardoi . . . . hŭr'-dō-ē.
Harfleur . . . . . . är-flĕr'.
Harleian . . . . . . här'-lē-ȧn.
Harlequin . . . . . . här'-lē-kwĭn, här'-lē-kĭn.
Haro, Luis de . . . . lōō-ēs' dä ä'-rō.

Haroun al Raschid, see
Harun . . . . . . hä-rōōn' äl răsh'-ĭd,
                  hä-rōōn' äl rä-shēd'.
Harpagon . . . . . . är-pä-gôn'.
Harpagus . . . . . . här'-pā-gŭs.
Harpignies . . . . . är-pēn-yē'.
Harpocrates . . . . . här-pŏk'-rȧ-tēz.
Hartmann von Aue . . härt'-män fŏn ow'-ŭ.
Harun al Rashid, see
Haroun . . . . . . hä-rōōn' äl răsh'-ĭd, *or*
                  rä-shēd'.
Harwich . . . . . . hăr'-ĭch, hăr'-ĭj.
Harz . . . . härts.
Hasan, see Hassan . . hä'-sȧn.
Hasdrubal, see Asdrubal . hăs'-drōō-băl.
Hassan, see Hasan . . häs'-sȧn.
Hauch, (J. C.), von . . . fŏn howch.
Hauck (Minnie) . . . hôk.
Haupt . . . . howpt.
Hauptmann, Gerhart . . gâr'-härt howpt'-män.
Hauser, Caspar . . . . käs'-pär how'-zĕr.
Haussman (Baron) . . . ōs-män'.
Haute-Garonne . . . . ōt-gä-rŏn'.
Haute-Loire . . . . . ōt-lwär'.
Haute-Marne . . . . ōt-marn'.
Hautes-Alpes . . . . ōt-zälp'.
Haute-Saône . . . . ōt-sōn'.
Haute-Savoie . . . . ōt-sä-vwä'.
Hautes-Pyrénées . . . ōt-pē-rā-nā'.
Haute-Vienne . . . . ōt-vē-ĕn'.
Haüy, Abbé . . . . . äb-ā' ä-wē', ä-ü=ē'.
Havana, see Habana . . hă-văn'-ȧ.
Havel . . . . hä'-fĕl.
Haverhill . . . . . *Am.* hā'-vēr-ĭl.
               Eng. hăv'ēr-ĭl.
Havilah . . . . . . hăv'-ĭl-ȧ.
Havre-de-Grace . . . ä'-vr-dŭ-grȧs'.

Hawaii . . . . hä-wǐ'-ē.
Hawaiian . . . . . . hä-wǐ'-yän.
Hawarden . . . . . . hôr'-dn, här'-děn.
Haweis . . . . hois.
Hayakawa, Sessue . . sās'-ōō'-ä hä'-yä'-kä'-wä'.
Haydée . . . . . . ä-dä'.
Haydn . . . . hä'-dn. *Ger.* hī'-dn.
Hayduks, see Haiduks . hī'-dōōks.
Haye, La, see The Hague,
Den Haag . . . . lä ä.
Hayti, see Haiti . . . hä'-tǐ. *Fr.* ä-ē-tē'.
Hazael . . . . hǎz'-ā-ěl, hā'-zä-ěl.
Hazaribagh . . . . . hä-zä-rē-bô'.
Hazebrouck . . . . . ǎz'-brŏŏk.
Hazlitt . . . . hǎz'-lǐt.
Hebe . . . . hē'-bē.
Hébert . . . . ä-bâr'.
Hebraist . . . . . . hē'-brä-ǐst.
Hebrides . . . . . . hěb'-rǐ-dēz.
Hebron . . . . hē'-brŏn.
Hecate . . . . hěk'-ä-tē, hěk'-āt.
Hecuba . . . . . . hěk'-yū-bȧ.
Hedin, Sven . . . . . svǐn hǐ-dēn'.
Hedone . . . . . . hěd'-ō-nē.
Hédouin . . . . . . ä-dōō-äṅ'.
Hegel . . . . hä'-gěl.
Hegelian . . . . . . hē-gē'-lǐ-ȧn.
Hegira, see Hejira . . . hē-jǐ'-rȧ, hěj'-ǐ-rȧ.
Heidelberg . . . . . hī'-děl-bērg.
                     Ger. hī'-děl-běrċh.
Heidenmauer . . . . hī'-děn-mow"-ěr.
Heijn (Admiral) . . . . hīn.
Heilbronn . . . . . . hǐl'-brŏn.
Heimskringla . . . . hǐms'-krǐng-lä.
Heine . . . . hī'-nǔ.
Heinrich . . . . . . hīn'-rǐċh.
Hejira, see Hegira . . . hē-jǐ'-rȧ, hěj'-ǐr-ȧ.

Helen . . . . hĕl'-ĕn.
Helena . . . . hĕl'-ĕ-nȧ.
Helena (Montana) . . . hĕl'-ĕ-nȧ.
Helena, St. (I.) . . . . sċnt hĕl-ē'-nȧ.
Helenus . . . . . . hĕl'-ĕ-nŭs.
Helgoland, see Heligo-
land . . . . . . hĕl'-gō-länd.
Helicanus . . . . . . hĕl-ĭ-kā'-nŭs.
Helicon . . . . . . hĕl'-ĭ-kŏn.
Heligoland, see Helgo-
land . . . . . . hĕl'-ĭ-gō-länd".
Heliodorus . . . . . hē"-lĭ-ō-dō'-rŭs.
Heliogabalus, see Elagaba-
lus . . . . hē"-lĭ-ō-găb'-ā-lŭs,
hē"-lĭ-ō-gā-bā'-lŭs.
Heliopolis . . . . . . hē-lĭ-ŏp'-ō-lĭs.
Helios . . . . hē'-lĭ-ŏs.
Hellas . . . . hĕl'-ȧs.
Hellenes . . . . . . hĕl-lē'-nēz, hĕl'-ēnz,
Hellenic . . . . . . hĕl-lē'-nĭk, hĕl-lĕn'-ĭk.
Hellespont . . . . . hĕl'-lĕs-pŏnt.
Hellevoetsluis, see Hel-
voetsluis . . . . . hĕl-lĕ-vōōt-slois'.
Héloïse . . . . . . ā-lō-ēz'.
Helots . . . . hĕl'-ŏts, hē'-lŏts.
Helsingfors . . . . . hĕl'-sĭng-fŏrs.
Helsinki . . . . . . hĕl'-sĭnk-kĭ.
Helvetia . . . . . . hĕl-vē'-shĭ=ȧ.
Helvétius . . . . . . hĕl-vē'-shĭ-ŭs.
Fr. ĕl-vā-sē-üs'.
Helvoetsluis . . . . . hĕl-vōōt-slois'.
Hemans (Mrs.) . . . . hĕm'-ȧnz. pop. hē'-mȧnz.
Hengist . . . . . . hĕng'-gĭst.
Hengstenberg . . . . hĕng'-stĕn-bĕrċh.
Henlopen . . . . . . hĕn-lō'-pĕn.
Hennepin . . . . . . hĕn'-ĕ-pĭn. Fr. ĕn-păṅ'.
Hennequin . . . . . hĕn'-nĕ-kwĭn. Fr. ĕn-kăṅ'.

Henri	ŏn̊-rē′.
Henriade	ŏn̊-rē-yăd′.
Henrici	hān-rēt′-sē.
Henri de Bourbon . . .	ŏn̊-rē′ dŭ bōōr-bôn̊′.
Henriette	hĕn-rĭ-ĕt′. *Fr.* ôn̊-rē-ĕt′.
Henri Quatre	ôn-rē′ kätr′.
Henriquez	ān-rē′-kĕth.
Henry (Col.)	ôn̊-rē′.
Hephæstion	hē-fĕs′-tĭ-ŏn.
Hephæstus, or	hĕ-fĕs′-tŭs.
Hephaistos	hē-fīs′-tŏs.
Heptameron	hēp-tăm′-ĕ-rŏn.
Heptarchy	hĕp′-tär-kĭ.
Heptateuch	hĕp′-tȧ-tūk.
Hera	hē′-rä.
Heraclean	hĕr-ȧ-klē′-ȧn.
Heracles	hĕr′-ȧ-klēz.
Heraclidæ	hĕr-ā-klĭ′-dē.
Heraclitus	hĕr-ā-klĭ′-tŭs.
Herat	hĕr-ät′.
Hérault	ā-rō′.
Herculaneum	hĕr-kū-lä′-nē-ŭm.
Herculean	hĕr-kū′-lē-ȧn.
Hercules	hĕr′-kū-lēz.
Here	hē′-rē.
Heredia	*Sp.* ā-rä′-dē-ä.
Hérédia	*Fr.* ā-rä-dē-ä′.
Hereford	hĕr′-ĕ-fŭrd.
Hereward	hĕr′-ĕ-wȧrd.
Hergesheimer	hĕr′-gĕs-hī-mẽr.
Héricourt	ā-rē-kōōr′.
Heristal, or Heristall, see	
Herstal	hĕr′-ĭs-täl.
Hermann	hĕr′-män.
Hermant	âr-män′.
Hermaphroditus . . .	hĕr-măf″-rō-dī′-tŭs.
Hermes	hĕr′-mĕz.

Hermione	hēer-mī'-ō-nē.
Hermogenes	hĕr-moj'-ĕ-nēz.
Hermosillo	hĕr-mō-sēl'-yō.
Hernandez	ār-nän'-dĕth.
Hernani	ār-nä'-nē.
Herod	hĕr'-ŏd.
Hérodiade	ā-rō-dē-ăd'.
Herodian	hē-rō'-dĭ-àn.
Herodias	hē-rō'-dĭ-às.
Herodotus	hē-rŏd'-ō-tŭs.
Hérold	a-rōld'.
Herrera	ār-rā'-rä.
Herreros	ār-rā'-rōs.
Herschel	hĕr'-shĕl.
Herstal, see Heristal . .	hĕr'-stäl.
Hertford	hĕrt'-fôrd, här'-fôrd.
Heruli	hĕr'-ōō-lī
Hervé Riel	âr-vā' rē-ĕl'.
Hervieu, Paul	pōl âr-vē=ē'.
Herzegovina	hĕrt"-sĕ-gō-vē'-nä.
Herzog	hĕrt'-zōċh.
Herzogin	hĕrt'-zō-gĭn.
Heshvan, see Hesvan . .	hĕsh'-văn.
Hesiod	hē'-sĭ-ŏd, hē'-shĭ-ŏd.
Hesiodus	hē-sī'-ō-dŭs.
Hesione	hē-sī-ō-nē.
Hesperides	hĕs-pĕr'-ĭ-dēz.
Hesse	hĕs.
Hesse-Cassel	hĕs-kăs'-ĕl.
Hessen	hĕs'-sĕn.
Hesse-Nassau	hĕs-năs'-ô.
Hessian	hĕsh'-ĭ-àn.
Hestia	hĕs'-tĭ-à.
Hesvan, see Heshvan . .	hĕs'-văn.
Heureaux, Ulisse . . .	ü-lēs' ĕr-ō'.
Heyne	hī'-nŭ.
Heyse	hī'-zŭ.

Hexö . . . . hĕx'-ē.
Hiawatha . . . . . . hī-à-wô'-thȧ, hĭ-à-wô'-tȧ.
Hibernia . . . . . . hī-bēr'-nĭ=ȧ.
Hidalgo . . . . . . ē-dȧl'-gō.
Hiero . . . . hī'-ĕ-rō.
Hieron . . . . hĭ'-ĕ-rŏn.
Hieronymus . . . . hĭ-ē-rŏn'-ĭ-mŭs.
Hilary . . . . hĭl'-à-rĭ.
Hildebrandslied . . . hĭl'-dā-bränts-lēt.
Hilo . . . . hē'-lō.
Himalaya . . . . . . hĭm-ä'-lā-yȧ, hĭm-ā-lā'-yä.
Himilco . . . . . . hĭ-mĭl'-kō.
Hindenburg . . . . . hĭn'-dĕn-bōōrċh.
Hindoo, see Hindu . . hĭn'-dōō, hĭn-dōō'.
Hindoostan, see Hindustan hĭn-dōō-stän'.
Hindoostanee, see Hindu-
stani . . . . hĭn-dōō-stän'-ē.
Hindostan, see Hindoo-
stan, Hindustan . . . hĭn-dō-stän', hĭn-dō-stăn'.
Hindu, see Hindoo . . hĭn'-dōō, hĭn-dōō'.
Hindu Kush . . . . . hĭn'-dōō kōōsh.
Hindustan, see Hindoostan hĭn-dōō-stän'.
Hindustani, see Hindoo-
stanee . . . . . . hĭn-dōō-stăn'-ē.
Hiogo . . . . hē-ō'-gō.
Hippocrates . . . . hĭp-pŏk'-rä-tēz.
Hippocrene . . . . hĭp'-ō-krēn, hĭp-ō-krē'-nē.
Hippolita, or Hippolyta . hĭ-pol'-ĭ-tä.
Hippolyte . . . . . . hĭ-pŏl'-ĭ-tē. Fr. ē-pō-lēt'.
Hippolytus . . . . . hĭ-pŏl'-ĭ·tŭs.
Hiren . . . . hĭ'-rĕn.
Hiroshige . . . . . . hē'-rō'-shē'-gä'.
Hiroshima . . . . . hē'-rō'-shē'-mä'.
Hirsch . . . . hērsh.
Hishikawa Moronobu . . hē'-shē'-kä'-wä'
                       mō'-rō'-nō'-bŭ'.
Hispania . . . . . . hĭs-pā'-nĭ=ȧ.

Hispaniola	hǐs″-păn-ǐ=ō′-lȧ.
	Sp. ēs″-pä-nē=ōō′-lä.
Hissar	hǐs-sär′.
Hittite	hǐt′-īt.
Hivite	hī′-vīt.
Hlangwane (Hill) . . .	hlăng-wä′-nŭ.
Hoang-ho, see Hwang-ho	hwäng′-hō.
Hobbema	hŏb′-bĕ-mä.
Hobbes	hŏbz.
Hobbesian	hŏb′-zǐ-ȧn.
Hobbididence	hŏb′ ĭ dǐ″-dĕns.
Hoboken	hō′-bo-kĕn, hō-bō′-kĕn.
Hoche (Gen.)	ŏsh.
Hochkirch	hōćh′-kērćh.
Höchst	hēćhst.
Höchstädt	hēćh′-stĕt.
Hogolen, or Hogolin . .	hō′-gō-lĕn, hō′-gō-lǐn.
Hogolu, or Hogolou . .	hō′-gō-lōō.
Hohenlinden	hō-ĕn-lǐn′-dĕn.
Hohenlohe	hō-ĕn-lō′-ŭ.
Hohenlohe-Schillingsfürst	hō-ĕn-lō′-ŭ shǐl′-lǐngs-fürst
Hohenstaufen, or -stauffen	hō′-ĕn-stow-fĕn.
Hohenzollern	hō′-ĕn-tsŏl-ĕrn.
Hohenzollern-Sigmaringen	hō′-ĕn-tsŏl-lĕrn
	zēg′-mä-rǐng″-ĕn.
Hokkaido	hŏk′-kī′-dō′.
Hokusai	ho′-kōō′-sä′=ē′.
Holbein	hōl′-bīn, hŏl′-bīn.
Holberg	hŏl′-bĕrćh.
Holborn	hō′-bŭrn.
Holger Danske	hōl′-gĕr däns′-kĕ.
Holguin	hŏl-gēn′, ŏl-gēn′.
Holinshed	hŏl′-ǐnz-hĕd.
Holmes	hōmz
Holmès (Augusta) . .	ōl-mĕs′.
Holofernes	hŏl-ō-fĕr′-nēz.
Holstein	hōl′-stīn.

Holyhead . . . . . . hŏl-ĭ-hĕd′, hŏl′-ĭ-hĕd.
Holyoke . . . . . . hōl′-yōk.
Holyrood . . . . . . hŏl′-ĭ-rōōd, hōl′-ĭ-rōōd.
Hombourg, or . . . . ōm-bōōrg′.
Homburg . . . . . . hōm-bōōrċh.
Homer . . . . hō′-mĕr.
Homeric . . . . . . hō-mĕr′-ĭk.
Homildon Hill . . . hŏm′-l-dŏn hĭl.
Hondekoeter . . . . . hŏn′-dĕ-kōō″-tĕr.
Honduras . . . . . . hŏn-dōō′-rȧs.
Hong-Kong . . . . . hŏng′-kŏng′.
Honiton . . . . . . hŭn′-ĭ-tŭn.
Honolulu . . . . . . hō-nō-lōō′-lōō.
Honoré . . . . ō-nō-rā′.
Hooge . . . . *D.* hô′-ghĕ.   *Fr.* ŏzh.
Hooghly, see Hugli . . hōōg′-lē.
Hoogvliet . . . . . . hōċh′-vlēt.
Hoopstad . . . . . . hōp′-stăt.
Hoorn (Count), see Horn hōrn.
Hoozier . . . . . . hōō′-zhĕr.
Horace . . . . . . hŏr′-ȧs.
Horæ . . . . hō′-rē.
Horatii . . . . . . hō-rā′-shĭ-ī.
Horatio . . . . . . hō-rā′-shĭ-ō.
Horatius Cocles . . . . hō-rā′-shĭ-ŭs kō′-klēz.
Horn (Count), see Hoorn hōrn.
Horsa . . . . hôr′-sȧ.
Hortense . . . . . . ôr-täṅs′.
Hortensio . . . . . . hôr-tĕn′-shĭ-ō.
Hortensius . . . . . hôr-tĕn′-shĭ-ŭs.
Hortus Inclusus . . . . hôr′-tŭs ĭn-klū′-sŭs.
Hosea, see Hoshea . . hō-zē′-ȧ.
Hoshangabad, see Hu-
  shangabad . . . . . hō-shŭng′-ä-bäd.
Hoshea, see Hosea . . hō-shē′-ȧ.
Hôtel de Cluny . . . . ō-tĕl′ dŭ klü-nē′.
Hôtel de Rambouillet . . ō-tĕl′ dŭ räṅ-bōō-ē=ā′.

Hôtel des Invalides . .	ō-tĕl′ dā zăṅ-vä-lēd′.
Hôtel de Ville	ō-tĕl′ dŭ vēl.
Hôtel Dieu	ō-tĕl′ dē-ē′.
Hötzendorf	hĕtz′-ĕn-dŏrf.
Houdin	ōō-dăṅ′.
Houdon	ōō-dôṅ′.
Houssain, see Hussain, and Hussein	ʻhōō′-sīn, ʻhōō-sīn′, ʻhōō′-sän.
Houssaye, Arsène . . .	är-sĕn′ ōō-sä′.
Houston (Tex.)	hūs′-tŏn.
Houyhnhnms	hōō′-ĭn-ĭn-mz.
Hsüan-tung	shü′-än-tōōng′.
Hubert de Burgh . . .	hū′-bĕrt dŭ bĕrg, bōōrg.
Hudibras	hū′-dĭ-brăs.
Hué, or	hōō-ā′, hwä.
Hué-fu	hōō-ā′-fōō′.
Huerta, Victoriano . .	vĭk-tō-rē-ä′-nō wĕr′-tȧ.
Hugh Capet	hū kā′-pĕt. *Fr.* üg kä-pā′.
Hugli, see Hooghly . .	hōōg′-lē.
Hugo, Victor	hū′-gō. *Fr.* ü-gō′.
Huguenots	hū′-gĕ-nŏts.
Huguenots, Les	lā üg=ŭ-nō′.
Huis ten Bosch	hois tĕn bŏsćh′.
Humacao	ōō-mä-kä′-ō.
Humboldt	hŭm′-bōlt. *Ger.* hŏŏm′-bōlt.
Humperdinck	hoom′-pĕr-dĭnk.
Humphrey	hŭm′-frĭ.
Huneker	hŭn′-ĕ-kĕr.
Hungarian	hŭng-gȧ′-rĭ-ȧn.
Hungary	hŭng′-gā-rĭ.
Hunyady János	hōōn′-yä-dē yä′-nōsh.
Hus, see Huss	hŭs. *Ger.* hŏŏs.
Hushangabad, see Ho-shangabad	hŭsh-ŭng′-ä-bäd.
Huss, see Hus	hŭs. *Ger.* hŏŏs.

Hussain, see Houssain, or
   Hussein . . . . . .   'hōō'-sĭn, 'hōō-sĭn',
                    'hōō'-sän.

Hussan . . . . . .   'hōō'-sän.

Huygens, or Huyghens .   hī'-gĕnz.   D. hoi'-ċhĕns.

Huysmans . . . . .   D. hois'-mäns.
                    Fr. wēs-mäṅ.

Huysmans, J. K. . . .   wēs-mäṅs'.

Huysum, Jan van . . .   yăn văn hoi'-sŭm.

Hwang-ho, see Hoang-ho   hwăn'-hō.

Hyacinthe, Père . . . .   pår ē-ä-săṅt'.

Hyacinthus . . . . .   hī-à-sĭn'-thŭs.

Hyades . . . . . .   hī'-ā-dēz.

Hybla . . . .   hī'-blä.

Hyblæan (-blean) . . .   hī-blē'-àn.

Hyderabad, see Haidara-
   bad . . . .   hī″-dĕr-à-bäd'.

Hyder Ali, see Haidar Ali .   hī'-dĕr ä'-lē.

Hydra . . . .   hī'-drà.

Hyères . . . .   ē-âr'.

Hygeia . . . .   hī-jē'-à.

Hyksos . . . .   hĭk'-sŏs, hĭk'-sōz.

Hymen . . . .   hī -mĕn.

Hymettos (-tus) . . . .   hī-mĕt'-ŭs.

Hypatia . . . . . .   hī-pā'-shĭ=à.

Hyperboreans . . . .   hī-pĕr-bō'-rē-ànz.

Hypereides, Hyperides .   hī-pĕr-ī'-dēz.

Hyperion . . . . . .   hī-pē'-rĭ-ŏn, hī-pĕr-ī'-ŏn.

Hyppolite . . . . . .   ē-pō-lēt'.

Hyrcanian . . . . . .   hĕr-kā'-nĭ-àn.

Hyrcanus . . . . . .   hĕr-kā'-nŭs.

I

Iachimo	yăk'-ĭm-ō, ī-ăk'-ĭ-mō.
Iago	ē=ä'-gō.
Ian	ī'-ȧn *or* ē'-ȧn.
Iapetus	ī-ăp'-ē-tŭs.
Ibañez, Vicente Blasco .	vē-thĕn'-tĕ bläs'-kō ē-bän'-yĕth.
Ibea	ī-bē'-ȧ.
Iberia	ī-bē'-rĭ-ȧ.
Ibiza, see Ivica	ē'-bō-thä.
Iblis, see Eblis	ĭb'-lĭs.
Ibo, see Igbo	ē'-bō. *Port.* ē'-bōō.
Ibrahim Pasha	ĭb-rä-hēm' păsh-ô', pȧ-shä', päsh'-ȧ.
Ibsen	ĭb'-sĕn.
Icarian	ī-kā'-rĭ-ȧn.
Icarus	ĭk'-ȧ-rŭs, ĭk'-ā-rŭs.
Ichabod	ĭk'-ȧ-bŏd.
Ichang	ē-chäng'.
Icolmkill	ī-kōm-kĭl'.
Ictinus	ĭk-tī'-nŭs.
Ides	īdz.
Iditarod	ī-dĭt'-ȧ-rŏd.
Idumæa, Idumea . .	ī-dū-mē'-ȧ, ĭd-ū-mē'-ȧ.
Idumæan, Idumean . .	ī-dū-mē'-ȧn.
Idzo	ēd'-zō.
If, Château d'	shä-tō' dēf'.
Ifugao	ēf-ōō-gä'=o.
Igbo, see Ibo	ēg'-bō.
Igdrasil, see Yggdrasil .	ĭg'-drȧ-sĭl.
Igerna, or	ĭ-gẽr'-nȧ.
Igerne, see Yguerne . .	ĭ-gẽrn'.
I Gioelli della Madonna .	ē jō-yāl'-lē dĕl'-lä mä-dŏn'-nä.
Ignatieff	ĭg-nät'-yĕf.
Ignatius	ĭg-nā'-shĭ=ŭs.

Igorrote . . . . ē-gōr-rō′-tä.
Ik Marvel . . . . . . īk mär′-vĕl.
Il Barbiere di Seviglia . ēl bär-bē-à′-rä dē sä-vēl′-yä.
Ile-de-France . . . . ēl-dŭ-fräns′.
Ile de la Tortue . . . . ēl dŭ lä tôr-tü′.
Il Flauto Magico . . . ēl flä′=ōō-tō mä′-jē-kō.
Illinois . . . . ĭl-ĭ-noi′, ĭl-ĭ-noĭz′.
Illuminati . . . . . . ēl-lōō-mē-nä′-tē.
Illusions Perdues, Les . lä zē-lü-zē=ôṅ′ pâr-dü′.
Ilocos . . . . ē-lō′-kōs.
Iloilo . . . . ĭ′-lō-ĭ′-lō. *Sp.* ē-lō-ē′-lō.
Ilori, or Ilorin . . . . ē-lō′-rē, ē-lō′-rēn.
Il Penseroso . . . . . ĭl pĕn-sĕ-rō′-sō.
Il Pensiero . . . . . ēl pān-sē=ā′-rō.
Il Segreto di Susanna . . ēl sä-grä′-tō dē sōō-zän′-nä.
Imber . . . . ăṅ-bâr′.
Imbert de Saint-Amand . ăṅ-bâr′ dŭ săṅ-tä-män′.
Immelmann . . . . . ĭm′-ĕl-män.
Imogen . . . . ĭm′-ō-jĕn.
Imola . . . . ē′-mō-lä.
Imus . . . . ē′-mōōs.
Inca . . . . ĭng′-kä.
Indy, d' . . . . . . däṅ-dē′.
Indore . . . . ĭn′-dōr.
Indre-et-Loire . . . . ăṅdr-ā-lwär′.
Ines . . . . ē-nĕs′.
Inez . . . . ĭ′-nĕz. *Port.* ē-nĕs′.
Iñez . . . . *Sp.* ēn′-yeth.
Infanta . . . . ĭn-făn′-tà. *Sp.* ĭn-fän′-tä.
Infante . . . . ĭn-făn′-tĕ. *Sp.* ĭn-fän′-tä.
Inferno . . . . ĭn-fĕr′-nō. *It.* ēn-fĕr′-nō.
Ingelow, Jean . . . . jēn ĭn′-jĕ-lō.
Ingres . . . . ăṅg′-r.
Inigo . . . . ĭn′-ĭ-gō.
Injalbert . . . . . . ăṅ-zhăl-bĕr′.
Inkerman . . . . . . ĭnk′-ĕr-màn.
　　　　　　　　　Russ. ĭngk-ĕr-män′.

In Montibus Sanctis . .	ĭn mŏn'-tĭ-bŭs sănk'-tĭs.
Innsbruck, or Innspruck .	ĭns'-brŏŏk, ĭns'-prŏŏk.
Intelligentsia	ĭn-tĕl-ĭ-gĕnt'-sĭ-à.
Interlachen, or	ĭn'-tĕr-läċh-ĕn.
Interlaken	ĭn'-tēr-lä-kĕn.
Intombi	ĭn-tŏm'-bĭ.
Invalides, Hôtel des . .	ō-tĕl' dä-zăṅ-văl-ēd'.
Inverness	ĭn-vēr-nĕs'.
Io	ī'-ō.
Iolanthe	ī-ō-lăn'-thē.
Ion	ī'-ŏn.
Iona	ī-ō'-nä.
Ionia	ī-ō'-nĭ=à.
Ionian	ī-ō'-nĭ=àn.
Ionic	ī-ŏn'-ĭk.
Iowa	ī'-ō-wä.
I Pagliacci	ē päl-yä'-chē.
Iphigeneia, or Iphigenia .	ĭf"-ĭ-jē-nī'-à.
Iphigenie auf Tauris . .	ĭf-ē'-gä'-nē-ŭ owf tow'-rĭs.
Iphigénie en Aulide . .	ĭf-ē-zhä-nē' ôn=nō-lēd'.
Ippolitoff-Ivanoff . . .	ĭp-ō-lē'-tŏf-ē-vä'-nŏf.
Ipswich	ĭps'-wĭch.
I Puritani	ē pōō-rē-tä'-nē.
Iquique	ē-kē'-kä.
Iran	ē-rän'.
Iras	ī'-ràs.
Irawadi, see Irrawaddy .	ĭr-à-wăd'-ĭ.
Irenæus	ī-rē-nē'-ŭs.
Irene	ī-rē'-nē. pop. ī-rēn'.
Irène	Fr. ē-rĕ'n'.
Iriarte, see Yriarte . . .	ē-rē-är'-tä.
Irigoyen	ē-rē-gō'-yĕn.
Iris	ī'-rĭs.
Irkutsk, Irkootsk, Irkoutsk	ĭr-kōōtsk'.
Iroquois	ĭr-ō-kwoī'. Fr. ĭr-o-kwä'.
Irrawaddy, see Irawadi .	ĭr-à-wăd'-ĭ.
Isaacs, Jorge	ċhōr'-ċhä ē-zäk'.

Isabela . . . . ēs-ä-bā'-lä.
Isabey . . . . ēz-ä-bā'.
Isaiah . . . . ĭ-zā'-yä, ĭ-zä'=ĭ-à.
Isandlana, or Isandula . ē-sänd-lä'-nä, ē-sän-dōō'-lä
Isar (R.) . . . . . . ē'-zär.
Ischia . . . . ēs'-kē-ä.
Ischl . . . . ēshl.
Isengrim . . . . . . ĭs'-ĕn-grĭm.
Iser . . . . ē'-zēr.
Iseult, see Isolde, Yseult . ĭ-sōōlt', ē-sēlt'.
Isfahan, see Ispahan . . ĭs-fä-hän'.
Isham . . . . ĭ'-shăm.
Ishbosheth . . . . . ĭsh-bō'-shĕth.
Ishii . . . . ēsh'-ē-ē.
Ishmael . . . . . . ĭsh'-mä-ĕl.
Ishmaelite . . . . . ĭsh'-mä-ĕl-īt".
Isis . . . . ĭ'-sĭs.
Isla, see Islay . . . . *Sp.* ēs'-lä.   *Sc.* ĭ'-lä.
Isla de Pinos . . . . . ēs'-lä dä pē'-nōs.
Islam . . . . ĭs'-lăm.
Islamic . . . . ĭs-lăm'-ĭk.
Islamite . . . . . . ĭs' lăm-īt.
Islas Filipinas . . . . ēs'-läs fē-lē-pē'-näs.
Islay, see Isla . . . . ĭ'-lä.
Islington . . . . . . ĭs'-lĭng-tŭn.
Islip . . . . ĭs'-lĭp.
Ismail Pasha . . . . . ĭs-mä-ēl' păsh-ô', pà-shä',
                          päsh'-ä.
Ismailia . . . . . . ĭs-mä'-lĭ=à.
                  Turk. ĭs-mä-ē'-lē-ä.
Isocrates . . . . . . ĭ-sŏk'-rà-tēz.
Isola Bella . . . . . ē'-zō-lä bĕl'-lä.
Isolde, see Iseult, Yseult . ĭ-sōld'.   *Ger.* ē-zōl'-dŭ.
Isonzo . . . . ē-zōn'-dzō.
Isoude, see Ysoude . . ē-sōōd'.
Ispahan, see Isfahan . . ĭs-pà-hän'.
Israel . . . . ĭs'-rä-ĕl.

Israelitic	ĭz″rä-ĕl-ĭt′-ĭk.
Israelitish	ĭz″-rä-ĕl-ĭt′-ĭsh.
Israels, Josef	yō′-sĕf ĭz′-rä-ĕls.
	D. ēz-rä-äls′.
Israfil, Israfel, Israfeel	ĭz-rä-fēl′, ĭs′-rä-fēl,
	ĭz′-rä-fēl.
Issachar	ĭs′-à-kär.
Istamboul, or Istambul	ēs-täm-bōōl′.
Isthmian	ĭs′-mĭ-àn.
Istria	ĭs′-trĭ-à.
Italia Irredenta . . .	ē-tä′-lē-ä ēr-rä-dän′-tä.
Italian	ĭ-tăl′-yàn.
Italianate	ĭ-tăl′-yăn-āt.
Italiens, Boulevard des	bōōl-vär′ dä zē-tăl-yĕn′
Ithaca	ĭth′-à-kà.
Ithuriel	ĭ-thōō′-rĭ-ĕl.
Ito	ē′-tō.
Ituræa	ĭ-tū-rē′-ä.
Iturbide	ē-tōōr-bē′-dä.
Iulus	ĭ-ū′-lŭs.
Ivan	ĭ-văn. Russ. ē-vän′.
Ivanhoe	ĭ′-văn-hō.
Ivan Ivanovitch	ē-vän′ ē-vän′-ō-vĭch.
Iviça, or Iviza, see Ibiza	ē′-bē-thä.
Ivry-la-Bataille . . .	ēv-rē′-lä-bä-tä′=yŭ.
Ivry-sur-Seine	ēv-rē′-sür-sĕn′.
Ixion	ĭks-ĭ′-ŏn.
Ixtaccihuatl, see Iztacci-	
huatl	ēs-täk-sē′-hwätl.
Ixtlilxochitl	ĭst-tlĭl-shō′-chĭtl.
Iyar	ē′-är.
Izdubar	ĭz-dōō-bär′.
Iztaccihuatl, see Ixtacci-	
huatl	ēs-täk-sē′-hwätl.

J

Jabalpur, see Jubbulpore . jŭb-ăl-pōōr'.
Jablonica . . . . . . yä-blō-nē'-kä.
Jablunka (Pass) . . . yäb-lōōn'-kä.
Jacmel . . . . zhäk-mĕl'.
Jacob . . . . jā'-kŏb. *Ger.* yä'-kōp.
Jacobean, Jacobian . . jăk-ō-bē'-àn, jà-kō'-bē-àn.
Jacobi . . . . jă-kō'-bĭ. *Ger.* yä-kō'-bē.
Jacobins . . . . . . jăk'-ō-bĭnz.
Jacobites . . . . . . jăk'-ō-bīts.
Jacòbo . . . . 'hä-kō'-bō.
Jacobsdal . . . . . . yä'-kŏps-dăl.
Jacopo . . . . yä'-kō-pō.
Jacquard . . . . . . jäk'-ärd. *Fr.* zhä-kär'.
Jacqueline . . . . . zhäk-lēn'.
Jacquerie . . . . . . zhäk-rē', zhäk=ēr-ē'.
Jacques . . . . . . zhäk.
Jael . . . . jā'-ĕl.
Jaëll . . . . yä'-ĕl.
Jaen . . . . 'hä-ĕn'.
Jaffa, see Yafa, Japho, Heb. jăf'-fä, yäf'-fä.
Jagellons . . . . . . yä-gĕl'-ŏnz.
Jagow . . . . yä'-gŏf.
Jagua . . . . 'hä'-gwä.
Jah . . . . yä.
Jahveh . . . . yä'-vä, yä'-vĕ.
Jaime (Don.) . . . . 'hä'-ē-mä.
Jain . . . . jīn.
Jaipur, see Jeypore . . jī-pōōr'.
Jairus . . . . jī'-rus *in New Testament.*
jā'-ĭr-ŭs *in Apocrypha.*
Jakobäa . . . . . . yä-kō-bā'-ä.
Jakutsk, see Yakutsk . . yä-kōōtsk'.
Jalabert . . . . . . zhä-lä-bâr'.
Jalalabad, see Jalalabad . jăl-à-lä-bäd'.
Jalandhar, see Jullunder . jŭl'-àn-dhär.

Jalapa, see Xalaps . . . 'hä-lä'-pä.
Jalisco, see Xalisco . . . 'hä-lēs'-kō.
Jamaica . . . . . . jȧ-mā'-kȧ.
Jamblichus . . . . jăm'-blĭk-ŭs.
Jameson . . . . . . jā'-mĕ-sŭn.
Jammersberg . . . yăm'-ĕrs-bĕrċh.
Jammes, François . . . frän-swä' zhăm.
Jamont . . . . zhä-môṅ'.
Jan . . . . *D*. yăn.
Janauschek . . . . . yä'-now-shĕk.
Jane Eyre . . . . . . jān âr.
Janet, Paul . . . . . pōl zhä-nā'.
Janiculum . . . . . jăn-ĭk'-yū-lŭm.
Janin, Jules . . . . . zhül zhä-năṅ'.
Janina, see Yanina . . . yä'-nē-nä.
Jansen . . . . jăn'-sĕn. *D*. yän'-sĕn.
Jansenist . . . . . . jăn'-sĕn-ĭst.
Jansenius . . . . . . jăn-sē'-nĭ=ŭs.
January . . . . . . jăn'-ū-ā-rĭ.
Janus . . . . jā'-nŭs.
Japanese . . . . . . jăp-ăn-ēz' *or* -ēs'.
Japapa . . . . hä-pä'-pä.
Japheth, or Japhet . . . jā'-fĕth, jā'-fĕt.
Japho, Heb., see Jaffa, Yafa jä'-fō.
Jaquenetta . . . . . jăk-e-nĕt'-tä.
Jaques . . . . jāks, jäks. *Shakespeare*,
jā'-kwēz.

Jardar . . . . yär-dar'.
Jardin des Plantes . . . zhär-dăṅ' dä pläṅt.
Jardine . . . . jär-dēn'.
Jardines . . . . . . *Sp.* 'här-dē'-nĕs.
Jardinière, La Belle . . lä bĕl zhär-dēn-ē=âr'.
Jardinillos . . . . . . 'här-dē-nēl'-yōs.
Jared . . . . jā'-rĕd.
Jarnac . . . . zhär-näk'.
Jarndyce . . . . . . järn'-dĭs.
Jaroslaff, see Yaroslaff . yä-rō-släf'.

Jaruco . . . . 'hä-rōō'-kō.

Jasher . . . . jā'-shẽr.

Jason . . . . jā'-sŭn.

Jaudenes . . . . . . 'hä=ōō-dā'-nĕs.

Jauja, see Xauxa . . . 'how'-ċhä.

Jaunpur, see Jounpoor . jown-pōōr'.

Jaurès . . . . zhō-rĕz'.

Java . . . . jä'-vä.

Javan . . . . adj. jä'-vȧn. *Bib.* jā'-văn.

Javert . . . . zhȧ-vâr'.

Jean de Meun . . . . zhŏṅ dŭ mŭṅ'.

Jean Jacques Rousseau . zhŏṅ zhäk rōō-sō'.

Jeanne d'Albret . . . . zhän däl-brä'.

Jeanne d'Arc, or Darc . . zhän därk'.

Jean Paul . . . . . . zhŏṅ pōl.

Jebusite . . . . . . jĕb'-ū-zīt.

Jedburgh . . . . . . jĕd'-bŭr-ŭ.

Jeddo, see Yeddo . . . yĕd'-dō.

Jehoahaz . . . . . . jē-hō'-ȧ-hăz.

Jehoiachin . . . . . . jē-hoi'-ȧ-kĭn.

Jehoiada . . . . . . jē-hoi'-ȧ-dä.

Jehoiakim . . . . . . jē-hoi'-ȧ-kĭm.

Jehoram, see Joram . . jĕ-hō'-rȧm.

Jehoshaphat . . . . . jē-hŏsh'-ȧ-făt.

Jeisk, see Yeisk . . . . yā'-ĭsk.

Jekyll . . . . jē'-kĭl.

Jelalabad, see Jalalabad . jĕl″-ȧ-lä-bäd'.

Jellicoe . . . . jĕl'-ĭ-kō.

Jellyby . . . . jĕl'-ĭ-bĭ.

Jemappes, see Jemmapes. zhĕ-mäp'.

Jemima . . . . jē-mī'-mȧ. *Bib.* jē-mī'-mȧ,
                       jĕm'-ĭm-ȧ.

Jemmapes, see Jemappes zhĕ-mäp'.

Jena . . . . jĕn'-ȧ. *Ger.* yā'-nä.

Jenghiz Khan, see Genghis
  Khan, or Jinghis Khan . jĕn'-gĭs khän.

Jenner . . . . jĕn'-ẽr.

Jephthah . . . . . . jĕf'-thä.
Jeremiah . . . . . . jĕr-ĕ-mī'-ȧ.
Jeremy . . . . jĕr'-ĕ-mĭ
Jeres, see Xeres, or . . 'hä'-rĕs.
Jerex de la Frontera, see
  Xerez de la Frontera . 'hä-rĕth' dä lä frŏn-tä'-rä.
Jerome . . . . jĕ-rōm', jĕr'-ōm.
Jérôme Bonaparte . . . zhä-rŏm' bō-nä-pärt'.
Jerona, see Gerona, Xerona 'hä-rō'-nä.
Jerrold . . . . jĕr'-ŏld.
Jerusalem . . . . . . jĕ-rōō'-sȧ-lĕm.
Jessica . . . . jĕs'-ĭ-kȧ.
Jesso, see Yesso . . . yĕs'-sō.
Jessor, or Jessore . . . jĕs-sōr'.
Jesu . . . . jē'-zōō, yä -sōō.
Jesuit . . . . jĕs'-yū-ĭt.
Jesus . . . . jē'-zŭs. _Sp._ 'hä-sōōs.
Jethro . . . . jĕth'-rō, jē'-thro.
Jeunesse Dorée . . . . zhē-nĕs' dō-rä'.
Jevons . . . . jĕv'-ŏnz.
Jeypore, see Jaipur . . jī-pōr'.
Jezebel . . . . jĕz'-ĕ-bĕl.
Jezreel . . . . jĕz'-rē-ĕl.
Jhansi . . . . jän'-sē.
Jiguani . . . . 'he-gwa'-ne.
Jimena, see Ximena . . 'hē-mĕn'-ä.
Jimenez, see Ximenez . 'hē-mĕn'-ĕth.
Jinghis Khan, see Jenghiz
  Khan, Genghis Khan . jĭn'-gĭs khän.
Jitomir, see Zhitomir . . zhĭt-ōm'-ēr.
Joachim . . . . . . jō'-ȧ-kĭm.
                    Ger. yō'-ȧċh'-ĭm.
Joan of Arc . . . . . jōn, _or_ jō-ăn', _or_ jō'-ȧn ŏv
                    ärk.
João . . . . _Port._ zhō-owṅ'.
Joaquin . . . . . . 'hō=ä-kēn'.
Jodhpur . . . . . . jōd-pōōr'.

Joffre . . . . zhŏfr.

Johann . . . . yō'-hän.

Johannes . . . . . . jō-hăn'-ēz.
　　　　　　　　　Ger. yō-hän'-nĕs.

Johannisberg . . . . jō-hăn'-nĭs-bĕrg.
　　　　　　　　　D. yō-hăn'-nĭs-bĕrċh.

John o' Groat's . . . . jŏn ō grôts.

Joinville . . . . . zhwăṅ-vēl'.

Jókai . . . . yō'-kä=ĭ.

Joló, see Sooloo . . . . 'hō-lō'.

Jomelli, see Jommelli . . yō-mĕl'-lē.

Jomini . . . . zhō-mē-nē'.

Jommelli, see Jomelli . . yŏm-mĕl'-lē.

Jonescu, Take . . . . tä'-kē yō-nĕs'-kŭ.

Jongleur . . . . . . zhôṅ-glēr'.

Joram, see Jehoram . . jō'-rȧm.

Jordaens . . . . . . yŏr'-däns.

Jordanes, or . . . . . jôr-dā'-nēz.

Jordanis, see Jornandes . jôr-dā'-nĭs.

Jorge . . . . *Sp.* 'hōr'-ċhā.

Jorilla . . . . 'hō-rēl'-yä.

Jornandes, see Jordanes . jôr-năn'-dēz.

Jorullo, see Xorullo . . 'hō-rōōl'-yō.

José . . . . *Sp.* 'hō-sā'. *Port.* zhō-zhā'.

Joseffy . . . . yō-sĕf'-ĭ.

Josephus . . . . . . jō-sē'-fŭs.

Josiah . . . . jō-sī'-ä.

Josquin Desprez . . . zhŏs-kăṅ' dā-prā'.

Jost . . . . yōst.

Jotham . . . . jō'-thȧm.

Jötunheim . . . . . . yĕ'-tōōn-hīm.

Jouaust . . . . . . zhōō-ō'.

Joubert, Fr. . . . . . zhōō-bâr'.

Joubert, D. . . . . . yow'-bĕrt.

Joule . . . . jowl.

Jounpoor, see Jaunpur . jown-pōōr'.

Jourdain . . . . . . zhōōr-dăṅ'.

Jourdan . . . . . . zhōōr-dän′.
Journal des Débats . . zhōōr-năl′ dä dä-bä′.
Jouvenet, Jean . . . . zhän zhōōv-nä′.
Jouy . . . . zhōō-ē′.
Jowett . . . . jow′-ĕt.
Joyeuse Garde, La . . . lä zhwä-yēz′ gärd.
Juan . . . . ‘hōō=än′.
Juana, see Juanna . . . ‘hōō-ä′-nä.
Juan Diaz . . . . . . ‘hōō-än′ dē′-äth.
Juan Fernandez . . . . jōō′-àn fĕr-năn′-dēz.
    Sp. ‘hōō-än′
    fĕr-nän′-dĕth.
Juanna, see Juana . . . ‘hōō-än′-nä.
Juarez . . . . ‘hōō-ä′-rĕth.
Juba . . . . jōō′-bä.
Jubbulpore, see Jubalpur . jŭb-bŭl-pōr′.
Jubilate . . . . . . jū-bĭl-ä′-tē, jū-bĭl-ä′-tē
Júcar, see Xúcar . . . ‘hōō′-kär.
Júcaro . . . . ‘hōō′-kä-rō.
Judaic . . . . jū-dä′-ĭk.
Judas Maccabeus . . . jōō′-dàs măk-à-bē′-ŭs.
Judic . . . . zhü-dēk′.
Juggernaut . . . . . jŭg′-ēr-nôt.
Jugurtha . . . . . . jōō-gēr′-thä.
Juif Errant, Le . . . . lē zhü=ēf′ ″r-rän′.
Juillard . . . . . . zhwē-yär′.
Jules . . . . zhül.
Jülich, see Juliers . . yü′-lĭċh.
Julie . . . . Fr. zhü-lē′.
Julien . . . . Fr. zhü-lē=ĕn′.
Juliers, see Jülich . . . Fr. zhü-lē=ä′.
Juliet . . . . jū′-lĭ=ĕt.
Julliot . . . . zhü-lĭ-ō′.
Jullunder, see Jalandhar . jŭl′-lŭn-dĕr.
Jumel . . . . zhū-mĕl′.
Jumièges . . . . . . zhü-mē=ĕzh′.
Juneau . . . . jū-nō′.

Jungfrau . . . . . . yŏŏng'-frow.
Juniata (R.) . . . . . jōō-nǐ-ăt'-ä.
Junkers . . . . . . yŏŏng'-kĕrz.
Junot . . . . zhü-nō'.
Junta . . . . jŭn'-tä.
Jupiter . . . . jōō'-pǐ-tĕr.
Jura (I. and Mts.) . . . jōō'-rä.
Jura . . . . *Fr.* zhü-rä'.
Jurassic . . . . . . jū-răs'-ǐk.
Jurgensen . . . . . . yōōr'-gĕn-sĕn.
Jusserand . . . . . . zhüs-räṅ'.
Jussieu, de . . . . . dŭ jŭs-sū'.
               Fr. dŭ zhü-sē=ē'.
Justine . . . . jŭs-tēn'. *Fr.* zhüs-tēn'。
Justinian . . . . . . jŭs-tǐn-ǐ-ȧn.
Jutes . . . . jōōts.
Juvenal . . . . . . jōō'-vĕ-nȧl.

K

Kaaba, see Caaba . . . kä'-bä, kā'-ȧ-bȧ.
Kaaterskill . . . . . kä'-tĕrs-kǐl.
Kabail, see Kabyle . . kȧ-bīl'.
Kabbala, see Cabala . . kăb'-ȧ-lä.
Kabul, see Cabul . . . kä-bōōl'.
Kabyle, see Kabail . . . kȧ-bīl'.
Kadapa, see Cuddapah . kŭd'-ä-pä.
Kadesh Barnea . . . . kā'-dĕsh bär'-nē-ä。
Kaffa . . . . käf'-fä.
Kaffir, see Kafir, Caffre,
   Kaffre . . . . . . käf'-ĕr.
Kaffraria . . . . . . kăf-frâr'-ǐ-ȧ.
Kaffre, see Kafir, Caffre . kăf'-ĕr.
Kafir, see Kaffir, Caffre,
   Kaffre . . . . . . kăf'-ĕr.
Kaifeng, or . . . . . kī-fĕng'.
Kai-fung . . . . . . kī-fŭng'.

Kaiser . . . . kī'-zĕr.
Kaiser Friedrich. . . . kī'-zĕr frēd'-rĭċh.
Kaiserin . . . . . . kī'-zĕr-ĭn.
Kaiserin Augusta . . . kī'-zĕr-ĭn ow-gōos'-tä.
Kaiser Wilhelm . . . . kī'-zĕr vĭl'-hĕlm.
Kalakaua . . . . . . kăl-à-kow'-ä.
Kalevala, or Kalewala . . kä-lĕ-vä'-lä.
Kalid Bahr . . . . . kä'-lēd bär.
Kalidasa . . . . . . kä-lĭ-dä'-sà.
Kalmar, see Calmar . . käl'-mär.
Kálnoky . . . . . . käl'-nŏ-kĭ.
Kaluga . . . . kä-lōō'-gä.
Kamchatka, see Kamt-
    chatka . . . . . . käm-chät'-kä.
Kamehameha . . . . kä-mā"-hä-mā'-hä.
Kamerun, see Cameroon. kä-mĕ-rōōn'.
Kamimura . . . . . kä'-mē'-mōō'-rä'.
Kamtchatka, Fr., see Kam-
    chatka . . . . . . käm-chät'-kä.
Kanakas . . . . . . kă-năk'-àz.
Kanaris, see Canaris . . kä-nä'-rĭs.
Kanawha . . . . . . kà-nô'-wà.
Kanazawa . . . . . . kä-nä-zä'-wä.
Kanchanjanga, see Kun-
    chainjunga, Kinchinjinga kän-chän-jäng'-gä.
Kandahar, Candahar, or . kän-dä-här', kăn-dà-här'.
Kandehar . . . . . . kän-dĕ-här', kăn-dĕ-här'.
Kang-Kao, see Cancao . käng-kow'.
Kang-Wu-Wei . . . . käng'-wōo-wä'.
Kano Masanobu . . . kä'-nō' mä'-sä'-nō'-bŭ'.
Kansas . . . . kăn'-zàs.
Kan-su . . . . kän-sōo'.
Kant . . . . känt.
Kantian . . . . . . kăn'-tĭ-àn.
Kanuck, see Canuck . . kă-nŭk'.
Kara Bagh, or Karabagh,
    see Carabagh . . . . kä-rä-bäg'.

Kara-Hissar . . . . . kä″-rä-hĭs-sär′.
Kara Mustapah, see Cara
Mustafa . . . . . kä′-rä mŏŏs′-tä-fä, kä′-rä′
                    mŏŏs′-tä-fä.
Karénina, Anna . . . . än′-nä kä-rä′-nē-nä.
Karnak . . . . kär′-năk.
Karlovingian, see Carlo-
vingian . . . . . . kär-lo-vĭn′-jĭ-àn.
Karlowitz, see Carlowitz . kär′-lō-vĭts.
Karlsbad, see Carlsbad . kärlz′-bät.
Karlsruhe, see Carlsruhe . kärlz′-rōō-ū.
Kartoum, Kartum, see
Khartoum . . . . . kär-tōōm′, ćhär-tōōm′.
Karwina . . . . . . kär-vē′-nä.
Kasan, see Kazan . . . kä-zän′.
Kashgar . . . . . . kăsh′-gär. *Turk.* käsh-gär′.
Kashmere, Kashmir, see
Cashmere . . . . . kăsh-mēr′.
Kassai, (R.) . . . . . kä-sī′.
Katahdin, see Ktaadn . . kà-tä′-dĭn.
Katak, see Cattack, Cuttack kà-täk′.
Kathiawar, see Kattywar kät″-ē-ä-wär′.
Kathlamba, see Quath-
lamba . . . . . . kät-läm′-bä.
Katrine, Loch . . . . lŏćh kăt′-rĭn.
Kattegat, see Cattegat . kăt′-ĕ-gät.
Kattywar, see Kathiawar . kät-ē-wär′.
Kauai (I.) . . . . . . kow-ī′.
Kauffman . . . . . . kowf′-män.
Kaulbach . . . . . . kowl′-bäćh.
Kaun . . . . kown.
Kaunitz . . . . . . kow′-nĭts.
Kavanagh . . . . . . kăv′-ă-nä.
Kay . . . . kā. *Ger.* kī.
Kayor, see Cayor . . . kī-ōr′.
Kazak . . . . kä-zäk′.
Kazan, see Kasan . . . kä-zän′.

Keang-Se, see Kiang-si . kē=äng′-sē′.
Keang-Soo, see Kiang-su . kē-äng′-sōō′.
Kearney . . . . . . kär′-nĭ.
Kearsarge . . . . . . kēr′-särj.
Keble . . . . kē′-bl.
Kedleston . . . . . . kĕd′-l-stŭn, kĕl′-sŭn.
Kedron, see Cedron, Kid-
ron . . . . kŏ′-drŏn.
Kehama . . . . . . kē-hä′-mä.
Kei (R.) . . . . . . kā.
Keighley, or Keithley . . kēth′-lĭ.
Kekrops, see Cecrops . . kē′-krŏps.
Kelat, see Khelat . . . kĕ-lät′.
Kelts, see Celts . . . . kĕlts.
Kempis, (Thomas) à . . ä kĕm′-pĭs.
Kenai . . . . kē′-ni.
Kenelm Chillingly . . kĕn′-ĕlm chĭl -ĭng-lĭ.
Kenilworth . . . . . kĕn′-l-wērth.
Kennebec . . . . . . kĕn-ē-bĕk′.
Kensington . . . . . kĕn′-zĭng-tŭn.
Keokuk . . . . . . kē′-ō-kŭk.
Kerensky . . . . . . kēr-ĕn′-skĭ.
Kerguelen . . . . . kĕr′-gĕl-ĕn. *Fr.*
kĕr-gā-lôṅ′.

Kerman, see Kirman . . kēr-män′.
Kéroualle, see Quérouaille kā-rōō-äl′.
Keshab Chandra Sen . . kĕ-shŭb′ chăn′-drà sān.
Kesho . . . . kĕsh′-ō.
Keswick . . . . . . kĕz′-ĭk.
Ketshwayo, see Cettiwayo kāch-wä′-yō.
Khafra . . . . khăf′-rä.
Khalif, see Calif, Caliph kä-lēf′, kā′-lĭf.
Khalifa, or . . . . . kä-lē′-fä.
Khaliff . . . . kä-lēf′.
Khan . . . . kôn, kän, kăn.
Khandesh, see Candeish . khän-dĕsh′.
Khania, see Canea . . . kä-nē′-ä.

Khartoum, or Khartum,
see Kartoum . . . . kär-tōōm', char-tōōm'.
Khedive . . . . . . kä-dēv', kē'-dĭv, kĕ-dēv',
kä-dē'-vä.
Khelat, see Kelat . . . kĕ-lät'.
Kherson . . . . . . chĕr-sōn'.
Khiva . . . . kē'-vä, chē'-vä.
Khorasan, or Khorassan . chō-rä-sän'.
Khorsabad . . . . . khōr-sä-bäd'.
Khosru, or . . . . . kŏs-rōō'.
Khusrau . . . . . . khŭs-row'.
Khyber . . . . chĭ'-bĕr.
Kiang-si, see Keang-Se . kē-äng'-sē'.
Kiang-su, see Keang-Soo. kē-äng'-sōō'.
Kiao-chau . . . . . . kĭ-ä'=ō-chow'.
Kichinef, Kichenev, see
Kishineff . . . . kĭsh-ĭ-nĕf'.
Kidron, see Cedron . . kĭd'-rŏn.
Kieff, see Kiev . . . . kē'-ĕf, kē-ĕf'.
Kiel . . . . kēl.
Kiev, or Kiew, see Kieff . kē'-ĕv, kē-ĕf'.
Kilauea . . . . . . kē-low-ā'-ä.
Kilimane, see Quilimane . kē-lē-mä'-nä.
Kimry, Kymry, see Cymry kĭm'-rĭ.
Kincardine . . . . . kĭn-kär'-dĭn.
Kinchinjinga, see Kanchan-
janga, Kunchain-Junga kĭn-chĭn-jĭng'-gä.
King-te-chen . . . . . kĭng-tĕ-chĕn'.
Kioto, see Kyoto . . . kē-ō'-tō.
Kirchhoff . . . . . . kērch'-hŏf.
Kirchner . . . . . . kērch'-nĕr.
Kirghiz . . . . kĭr-gēz'.
Kirkcaldy . . . . . . kĕr-kô'-dĭ.
Kirkcudbright . . . . kĕr-kōō'-brĭ.
Kirman, see Kerman . kēr-män'.
Kishineff, Kichenev, Kis-
chenew, see Kichinef . kēsh-ē-nĕf'.

Kishlangov, or	kēsh-län-gŏv'.
Kishlanou	kēsh-lä-nō'.
Kiskelim	kĭs-kē'-lĭm.
Kissingen	kĭs'-sĭng-ĕn.
Kittim, see Chittim . .	kĭt'-ĭm.
Kiung-chau	kē-ōōng'-chow.
Kiusiu	kyōō'-syōō'.
Kiyomine	kē'-yo'-mē'-nā'.
Kiyonaga	kē'-yo'-nä'-gä'.
Kizil-Irmak (R.) . . .	kĭz'-ĭl ĭr-mäk'.
Klamath	klä'-măt.
Klaus	klows.
Kléber	klē'-bĕr, klä'-bâr.
	Fr. klä-bâr'.
Klephts	klĕfts.
Klindworth	klĭnt'-vŏrt.
Kluck, von	fŏn klŏŏk.
Knaus	k=nows'.
Knecht Ruprecht . . .	k=nĕċht rōō'-prĕċht.
Kneisel.	k=nī'-zĕl.
Kneller	nĕl'-ēr.
Knollys	nōlz.
Knut, see Canute . . .	k=nōōt. Dan. künt.
Kobe	kō'-bĕ.
Koch	kŏċh.
Kochanowski	kō-chän-ŏf'-skĭ.
Kochian	kōch'-ē-än.
Koedoesberg, see Koo-	
doesberg	kōō-dōōs'-bĕrch.
Koedoes Rand, see Koo-	
doos Rand	kōō-dōōs' rănt.
Koerner, see Körner . .	kĕr'-nĕr.
Koffyfontein	kŏf''-fī-fŏn'-tīn.
Koh-i-nur, Kohinoor . .	kō-ē-nōōr'.
Köhler	kē'-lĕr.
Koimbatur, see Coimbatore	kō-ĭm''-bà-tōōr'.
Kokstadt	kŏk'-stăt.

Kolapoor, Kolapur, Kol-
hapur, see Colapur . . kō-lä-poōr'.
Kolchak . . . . . . kōl-chäk'.
Kolmar, see Colmar . . kōl-mär'.
Köln . . . . kēln.
Kolokol . . . . . kŏl-ō-kŏl'.
Komorn . . . . . . kō'-mŏrn.
Koniah, or . . . . kō'-nē-ä.
Konieh . . . . kō'-nē-ĕ.
König . . . . kĕ'-nĭćh.
Königgrätz . . . . . kĕ'-nēg-grâtz.
Königin . . . . . . kĕ'-nē-gĭn. [kĕ'-nĭćhs-bĕrch
Königsberg . . . . . kēn'-ĭgz-bĕrg. Ger.
Koodoesberg, see Koe-
doesberg . . . . . koō-doōs'-bĕrch.
Koodoes Rand, see Koe-
does Rand . . . . . koō-doōs' rănt.
Koordistan, see Kurdistan koōr-dĭs-tän'.
Koords, see Kurds . . koōrdz.
Kooril, see Kurile . . . koō'-rĭl.
Koran . . . . kō'-răn, kō-rän'.
Kordofan . . . . . kŏr-dō-fän'.
Korea, see Corea . . . kō-rē'-ä.
Korean, see Corean . . kō-rē'-ȧn.
Körner, see Koerner . . kĕr'-nĕr.
Korn Spruit . . . . kŏrn sproit.
Korniloff . . . . . kôr-nē'-lŏf.
Korolenko . . . . . kō-rō-lĕn'-kō.
Korsakoff . . . . . kŏr-sä'-kŏf.
Kosciusko, or . . . kŏs-sĭ-ŭs'-kō.
Kosciuszko . . . . kŏsh-choō'-skō. [kŏsh'-oōt.
Kossuth . . . . . kŏs-soōth'. Hung.
Kotzebue (von) . . . kŏt'-sĕ-boō, kŏt'-sē-boō.
Koutouzof, see Kutusoff . koō-toō'-zŏf.
Kouyunjik . . . . . koō'-ŭn-jĭk.
Kraaft, or Krafft, or Kraft kräft.
Krag-Jörgensen . . . . kräg'-yĕr'-gĕn-sĕn.

Kragujevatz . . . . . krä'-gwē-yā-väts.

Krakau, or . . . . . krä'-kō, krä'-kow, *or*

Krakow, see Cracow . . *Pol.* krä'-kŏf.

Kramskoy. . . . . . kräm-skō'-ē.

Kranach, see Cranach . . krăn'-åk. *Ger.* krä'-näċh.

Krapf . . . . kräpf.

Krapotkin . . . . . . krä-pŏt'-kĭn.

Krasnik . . . . . . kräs'-nēk.

Krasnoi, or . . . . . kräs-noi'.

Krasnyi Jar . . . . . kräs-noi' yär.

Kraszewki. . . . . . krä-shĕf'-skĭ.

Krause . . . . krow'-zŭ.

Kreisler . . . . . . krīs'-lĕr.

Kremlin . . . . . . krĕm'-lĭn.

Kreutzer, Kreuzer . . . kroit'-zĕr.

Kriemhild, see Chriemhild krēm'-hĭlt.

Kronos, see Cronus . . krŏn'-ŏs.   [krōn'-stät.

Kronstadt, see Cronstadt. krŏn'-stät. *Russ.*

Kroonstad . . . . . . krōn'-stät.

Kruger . . . . krü'-gĕr.

Krugersdorp . . . . . krü'-gĕrs-dŏrp.

Krupp . . . . krōŏp.

Ktaadn, see Katahdin . . k=tä'-dn.

Kuanza, see Coanza,
  Quanza . . . . . . kwän'-zä.

Kubelik . . . . . . kōō'-bā-lēk.

Kubla Khan, or . . . . kōōb'-lä khän.

Kublai Khan . . . . . kōōb'-lī khän.

Ku-Klux-Klan . . . . kū'-klŭks-klăn.

Kuku-Khoto . . . . . kōō'-kōō-kō'-tō.

Kuli Khan . . . . . . kōō'-lē khän.

Kulmbach, see Culmbach kŏŏlm'-bäċh.

Kumassi, see Coomassie . kōō-mäs'-sē.

Kunchain-Junga, or . . kŭn-chīn-jŭng'-gå.

Kunchin-Ginga, or . . . kōōn-chĭn-jĭng'-gå.

Kunchin-Junga, see Kan-
  chanjanga . . . . . kōōn-chĭn-jŭng'-gå.

Kunersdorf . . . . . kōō'-nĕrs-dŏrf.

Kunisada . . . . . . kōō'-nē'-säd'-t̄hä'.

Kuniyoshi . . . . . . kōō'-nē'-yō'-shē'.

Kurdistan, see Koordistan kōōr-dĭs-tän'.

Kurds, see Koords . . . kōōrdz.

Kurfürst . . . . . . kōōr'-fürst.

Kurile, see Kooril . . . kōō'-rĭl.

Kuroki . . . . kōō'-rō'-kē'.

Kuropatkin . . . . . kōō-rō-pät'-kēn.

Kursk . . . . kōōrsk.

Kurukshetra . . . . . kōō-rōōk-shä'-trȧ.

Kurwenal . . . . . . kōōr'-vä-näl.

Küstrin, see Cüstrin . . küs-trēn'.

Kutais . . . . kōō-tīs'.

Kut-el-Amara . . . . kōōt-ĕl-ä-mä'-rä.

Kutusoff, or Kutuzoff, see
    Koutouzof . . . . . kōō-tōō'-zŏf.

Kuychau, see Kweichow . kwī-chow'.

Kuyp, see Cuyp . . . . koip.

Kwangsi, see Quangsi . . kwäng-sē'.

Kwang Su . . . . . . kwäng-sōō'.

Kwangtung, see Quang-
    tong . . . . kwäng-tōōng'.

Kweichow, see Kuy-chau kwī-chow'.

Kwhichpak . . . . . kwĭk-päk'.

Kymry, see Cymry . . . kĭm'-rĭ.

Kyoto, see Kioto . . . kē-ō'-tō.

Kyrie eleïson . . . . . kĭr'-ĭ-ĕ ĕ-lä'-ĭ-sŏn.

L

La Antigua . . . . . lä än-tē'-gwä.

Labanoff de Rostoff . . lä-bä'-nŏf dŭ rŏs'-tŏf.

La Bassée . . . . . . lä bȧs-sä'.

Labienus . . . . . . lä-bĭ-ē'-nŭs.

Lablache, Luigi . . . . lōō-ē'-jē lä-bläsh'.

La Bohème . . . . . lä bō-ĕm'.

Labori, Maître . . . . mātr lä-bō-rē'.
Labouchere . . . . . lä-bōō-shâr'.
Laboulaye . . . . . . lä-bōō-lä'.
Labrador . . . . . . lăb-rȧ-dôr'.
La Bruyère . . . . . lä brü-yâr'.
Labuan . . . . lä-bōō-än'.
La Cabaña . . . . . lä-kä-bän'-yä.
La Caille, or Lacaille . . lä kä'-yŭ.
La Caimanera . . . . lä kä"=ē-mä-nä'-rä.
Laccadive, see Lakkadiv . lăk'-ȧ-dīv.
Laccdæmon . . . . . lăs-ē-dē'-mön.
Lacépède . . . . . . lä-sä-pĕd'.
Lachaise, or La Chaise . lä shĕz'.
Lachesis . . . . . . lăk'-ē-sĭs.
Lachine . . . . lä-shēn'.
Lachme, see Lakme . . lăk'-mē.
La Cieca . . . . . . lä chē-ä'-kä.
Laconia . . . . lā-kō'-nĭ-ȧ.
Lacroix . . . . lä-krwä'.
Ladikieh, see Latakia . . lä-dē-kē'-ĕ.
Ladislaus . . . . . . lăd'-ĭs-lôs.
Ladoga . . . . lä'-dō-gä.
Ladrone (Is.) . . . . . lä-drōn'.
Ladrones . . . . . . lä-drōnz'. *Sp.* lä-drō'-nĕs.
Ladybrand . . . . . . lā'-dĭ-brănd.
Laeken . . . . lä'-kĕn.
Laennec . . . . lĕn-nĕk'.
Laertes . . . . lā-ēr'-tēz.
La Estrella . . . . . lä ĕs-trāl'-yä.
La Farge . . . . . . lä färj. *Fr.* färzh.
La Favorita . . . . . lä fä-vō-rē'-tä.
Lafayette, De . . . . dŭ lä-fä-ĕt'.
La Fère . . . . lä fâr.
La Ferrière . . . . . lä fĕr-rē=âr'.
Lafeu . . . . lä-fē'.
Laffitte . . . . lä-fēt'.   [dŭ lä fŏṅ-tĕn'.
La Fontaine, de . . . . dŭ lä fŏn'-tān. *Fr.*

La Forêt Bleu	lä fō-rĕ′ blē.
La Fourche	lä fōōrsh′.
L'Africaine	lä-frē-kĕn′.
Lagado	lä-gä′-dō.
La Gazza Ladra	lä gät′-zä lä′-drä.
Lagerlöf	lä′-gĕr-lēv.
La Gioconda	lä jō-kŏn′-dä.
La Gloire	lä glwär′.
Lagos	*Af.* lä′-gŏs. *Port.* lä′-gōōs.
Lagrange, de	dŭ lä gränzh′.
La Granja	lä grän′-ċhä.
Lagthing	läg′-tĭng.
La Guaira, or La Guayra .	lä gwī′ -rä *or* gī′-rȧ.
	Sp. lä gwä′=ē=rä.
Laguna de Bay	lä-gōō′-nä dä bä′=ē.
La Habanera	lä ä-bä-nä′-rȧ.
La Haye, see The Hague	lä ä′.
Lahor, or Lahore . . .	lä-hōr′.
Laibach, see Laybach . .	lī′-bäċh.
L'Aiglon	lä-glôṅ′.
Laing's Nek	längz nĕk.
Lajeunesse	lä-zhēn-ĕs′.
La Jolla	lä hō′-yȧ.
La Juive	lä zhwēv.
Lakhimpur, see Luckimpur	lŭk-ĭm-pōōr′.
Lakhnau, see Lucknow .	lŭk′-now. *pop.* lŭk′-nō.
Lakkadiv, see Laccadive .	läk′-ȧ-dīv.
Lakme, see Lachmi . .	läk′-mē.
Lakshmi, or Lakchmi . .	läksh′-mē.
Lalage	läl′-ā-jē.
La Liberté	lä lē-bĕr-tä′.
Lalitpur, see Lullitpur . .	lŭl-lĭt-pōōr′
Lalla Rookh	lä′-lä-rōōk.
L'Allegro	lä-lä′-grō.
Lamartine	lä-mär-tēn′.
Lamballe, Princesse du .	präṅ-sĕs′ dŭ läṅ-bäl′.
Lambert, Louis	lōō-ē′ läṅ-bâr′.

Lamech	lā'-mĕk.
Lamennais	lä-mĕ=nâ'.
Lamia	lā'-mĭ-à.
La Miranao	lä mē-rä-nä'-ō.
Lammermoor, or . . .	lăm-mēr-mōōr'.
Lammermuir	lăm-mēr-mūr'.
L'Amore di tre Re . . .	lä-mō'-rä dē-trä rä.
Lamoricière	lä-mō-rē-sē=âr'.
La Motte-Fouqué . . .	lä mŏt'-fōō-kā'.
Lamoureux	lä-mōō rō'.
Lanark	lăn'-ärk.
La Navidad	lä nä-vē-däd'.
Lancaster	lăng'-kăs-tēr.
Lancelot du Lac	lăn'-sē-lŏt dū lăk.
Lan-chau	län-chow'.
Lanciani	län-chä'-nē.
Lancret	län-krĕ'.
Landes (The)	länd.
Landgraf	länt'-gräf.
Landgravine	länt'-grä-vēn.
Landsthing	läns'-tĭng.
Landtag	länt'-täċh.
Landwehr	länt'-vâr.
Lanfranc	lăn'-frăngk. _Fr._ läṅ-fräṅ'.
Lange	läng'-ŭ.
Langres	längr.
Languedoc, or Langue d'Oc	lăng'-gwē-dŏk.
	_Fr._ läṅ=gŭ-dŏk'.
Langue d'Oil	läṅ dō=ēl'.
Lanier	lă-nēr'.
Lanjuinais	läṅ-zhwē-nä'.
Lannes	lăn. _Fr._ län.
La Noue	lä nōō'.
Lanson, Gustave . . .	güs-tăv' läṅ-sôṅ'.
Laocoön	lā-ŏk'-ō-ŏn.
Laodameia, or Laodamia .	lā"-ŏd-ā-mī'-à.
Laodicea	lā"-ŏd-ĭs-ē'-à.

Laomedon . . . . . . lā-ŏm'-ē-dŏn.
Laon . . . . lŏṅ.
Laos . . . . lä'-ōs.
Lao-tsze . . . . . . lä'-ō-tsĕ'.
La Paloma . . . . . lä pä-lō'-má.
La Patrie . . . . . . lä pä-trē'.
La Paz . . . . lä päz. *Sp.* lä päth.
Lapham . . . . . . lăp'-ȧm.
Lapithæ . . . . . . lăp'-ĭ-thē.
La Place, de . . . . . dŭ lä plăs.
La Plata . . . . . . lä plä'-tä.
La Princesse Lointaine . lä prăṅ-sĕs' lwăṅ-tĕn'.
Laputa . . . . lȧ-pū'-tȧ.
Lara . . . . lä'-rä.
La Rábida . . . . . lä rä'-bē-dä.
Laramie . . . . . . lăr'-ȧ-mĭ.
La Reine de Saba . . . lä rĕn dē sä-bä'.
Lares . . . . lā'-rēz.
Largellière . . . . . lär-zhĕl-yâr'.
Larisa, or Larissa . . . lä-rēs'-ȧ.
L'Arlésienne . . . . . lär-lä-zē=ĕn'.
La Rochefoucault . . . lä rōsh-fōō-kō'.
La Rochejacquelein . . lä rōsh-zhäk-lăṅ'.
La Rochelle . . . . . lä rō-shĕl'.
Larrey . . . . lä-rä'.
Larroumet . . . . . . lär-rōō-mä'.
La Saisiaz . . . . . . lä sâ-zē-äss'.
La Salle . . . . . . lä săl. *Fr.* lä säl.
La Scala . . . . . . lä skä'-lä.
Lascaris . . . . . . läs'-kä-rĭs.
Las Casas, de . . . . dä läs kä'-säs.
Las Cases, de . . . . *Fr.* dŭ läs käz.
Las Guasimas . . . . läs gwä-sē'-mäs.
La Socapa . . . . . lä sō-kä'-pä.
La Sorbonne . . . . . lä sōr-bŏn'.
Laspiñas . . . . . . läs-pēn'-yäs.
Lassalle . . . . . . lä-säl'.

Lassen . . . . läs'-sĕn.
Lassigny . . . . . . lăs-ēn-yē'.
Latakia, or Latakiyah, see
  Ladikieh . . . . . lä-tä-kē'-ȧ.
Lateran . . . . . . lăt'-ēr-ăn.
Latium . . . . lā'-shŭm.
Latour d'Auvergne . . . lä-tōōr' dō-vârn'=yŭ.
La Trappe . . . . . . lä träp.
Latreille . . . . . . lä-trä'=yŭ.
Laud . . . . lôd.
Laudon, see Loudon . . low'-dŏn.
Lauenburg . . . . . low'-ĕn-bōōrȯh.
Launfal . . . . . . lôn'-fȧl.
Laura . . . . lô'-rȧ.   It. lä'=ōō-rä.
Laurent . . . . . . lō-rôṅ'.
Laurier . . . . lō'-rē=ā.
Lausanne . . . . . . lō-zän'.
La Vallière . . . . . lä väl-lē=âr'.
Lavater . . . . . . lä'-vä-tēr.   Ger. lä-fä'-tĕr.
                    Fr. lä-vä-târ'.
Lavedan . . . . . . lä=vŭ-däṅ'.
Laveleye . . . . . . läv-lä'.
La Vendée . . . . . lä vôṅ-dā'.
Lavengro . . . . . . lăv-ȯn'-grō.
Lavigerie . . . . . . la-vezh-rē'.
Lavoisier . . . . . . lä-vwä-zē=ā'.
Laweman, or . . . . . lô'-măn.
Layamon . . . . . . lä'-yȧ-mŏn.
Layard . . . . lā'-ȧrd.
Laybach, see Laibach . . lī'-bäȯh.
Leah . . . . lē'-ä.
Leamington Spa . . . . lĕm'-ĭng-tŏn spä.
Leander . . . . . . lē-ăn'-dēr
Léandre . . . . . . lä-äṅdr'.
Le Cateau . . . . . . lĕ kă-tō'.
Lebbaeus, or Lebbeus . . lĕl-bē'-ŭs.
Leboeuf . . . . . . lē-bēf'.

Lebrun, see Vigée-Lebrun   lĕ-brŭṅ'.
Lecce . . . .   lĕch'-ĕ.
Leclerc, or Le Clerc . .   lĕ-klâr'.
Leconte de Lisle . . .   lĕ-kôṅt' dŭ lĕl'.
Lecouvreur, Adrienne . .   ä-drē-ĕn' lĕ-kōōv-rĕr'.
Le Creusot . . . . .   lĕ krē-so'.
Leda . . . .   lē'-dȧ.
Lederer . . . . . .   lā'-dĕr-ĕr.
Ledru-Rollin . . . .   lĕ-drü'-rōl-lăṅ'.
Leeds . . . .   lēdz.
Leeuwarden . . . . .   lā'-vär-dĕn.
Leeuwenhoek, see Leuwen-
  hoek . . . .   lā'-vĕn-hōōk.
Leeward . . . . . .   lē'-wȧrd, lē'-ärd, lū'-ärd.
Lefebre, or Lefèvre . .   lĕ-fĕvr'.
Legaré (H. S.) . . .   lŭ-grē'.
Legaspi, or . . . . .   lā-gäs'-pē.
Legazpe . . . . . .   lā-gäth'-pä.
Legendre . . . . . .   lĕ-zhŏṅdr'.
Leghorn . . . . . .   lĕg'-hôrn, lĕg-ôrn'.
Legnago . . . . . .   lān-yä'-gō.
Legouvé . . . . . .   lĕ-gōō-vä'.
Le Grand Monarque . .   lĕ gräṅ mō-närk'.
Lehar . . . .   lĕ-är'.
Lehman, Lisa . . . .   lĕ'-zȧ lā'-män.
Leibl . . . .   lībl.
Leibnitz, or Leibniz . .   līb'-nĭtz.
Leicester . . . . . .   lĕs'-tĕr.
Leiden, see Leyden . .   lī'-dĕn.
Leigh . . . .   lē.
Leighton . . . . . .   lā'-tŭn.
Leila . . . .   lē'-lȧ.
Leilah . . . .   lā-lä'.
Leinster . . . . . .   lēn'-stĕr, lĭn'-stĕr.
Leipsic, or . . . . . .   līp'-sĭk.
Leipzig . . . .   līp'-tsĭch.
Leith . . . .   lēth.

Le Jongleur de Notre
   Dame . . . . . . lē zhŏṅ-glēr' dē Nōtr dăm.
Le Journal des Débats . lē zhōōr-näl' dä dä-bä'.
Lely (Sir Peter) . . . . lē'-lĭ.
Lemaître . . . . . . lē-mĕtr'.
Léman . . . . lä-mäṅ'.
Le Mans . . . . . . lē mäṅ.
Lemberg . . . . . . lĕm'-bĕrch.
Lemercier . . . . . . lē-mâr-sē=ā'.
Lemerre . . . . . . lē-mĕr.'
Lemonnier, Camille . . kä-mēl'lē-mŏn-ē=ā'.
Le Moyne . . . . . . lē moin'. Fr. lē mwăn'.
Lemprière . . . . . . lĕm-prēr', lĕm'-prē-ēr.
                    Fr. lŏṅ-prē-âr'.
Lena (R.) . . . . . . lyĕ'-nȧ.
Lenape . . . . lĕn'-ă-pē.
Lenbach . . . . . . lĕn'-bäch.
Lenclos, Ninon de, or
   L'Enclos . . . . nē-nôṅ' dŭ lŏṅ-klō.'
L'Enfant Prodigue . . . lôṅ-fäṅ' prō-dēg'.
Lenglen, Suzanne . . . sü-zăṅ' lôṅ-glôṅ'.
Lenin . . . . lĕ-nēn'.
Lenni-Lenape . . . . lĕn'-nĭ-lĕn'-ă-pē.
Lenore . . . . lĕ-nōr'.
Lenôtre . . . . . . lĕ-nŏtr'.
Lens . . . . läṅ.
Leo . . . . lē'-ō. It. lä'-ō.
Leofric . . . . lĕ-ŏf'-rĭk.
Leofwine . . . . . . lĕ-ŏf'-wĭn-ĕ.
Leominster . . . . . lĕm'-ĭn-stēr.
Leon . . . . lē'-ōn. Sp. lä-ōn'.
Léon . . . . Fr. lä-ôṅ'.
Leonardo da Vinci . . . lä-ō-när'-dō dä vēn'-chē.
Leonato . . . . . . lē-ō-nä'-tō.
Leoncavallo, Ruggiero . roŏdzh'-ā-rō
                    lä″-ōn-kä-väl'-lō.
Leonidas . . . . . . lē-ŏn'-ĭ-dăs.

Leonora . . . . . . *It.* lä-ō-nō'-rä.
Léonore . . . . . . lä-ō-nōr'.
Leontes . . . . . . lē-ŏn'-tēz.
Leopardi . . . . . . lä-ō-pär'-dē.
Lepage, Bastien . . . . bäs-tē-ĕṅ'-lē-pǎzh'.
Lepando . . . . . . lä-pän'-dō.
Lepanto . . . . . . lĕ-pǎn'-tō, lä-pän'-tō.
Le Prophète . . . . . lē prō-fĕt'.
Le Nozze di Figaro . . lä nŏts-sä dē fē'-gä-rō.
Lérida . . . . lĕr'-ē-dä.
Lérins, Îles de . . . . ēl dē lä-rǎn'.
Lermontoff, Lermontov . lĕr'-mŏn-tŏf.
Leroux . . . . lē-rōō'.
Leroy-Beaulieu . . . . lē-rwä'-bō-lē=ē'.
Le Sage, or Lesage . . lē sǎzh'.
Leschetizki . . . . . lĕsh-ĕ-tĭts'-kĭ.
Les Contes d'Hoffman . lä-kōṅt dŏf-män'.
Lesdiguières . . . . . lä-dē-gē=âr'.
Les Huguenots . . . . lä üg-nō'.
Les Italiens . . . . . lä zē-tä-lē=ĕṅ'.
Lespinasse, de, see Espi-
nasse . . . . . . dŭ lä-pē-näs'.
Les Rougon-Macquart . lä rōō-gôṅ'-mäk-är'.
Lesseps, de . . . . . dŭ lĕs'-ĕps.
                    Fr. dŭ lē-sĕps'.
Lessing . . . . lĕs'-sĭng.
Le Sueur, or Lesueur . lē-sü-ēr'.
Leszczynski, Stanislaus . stǎn'-ĭs-läs lĕsh-chĭn'-skē.
Le Temps . . . . . . lē tôṅ.
Lethe . . . . lē'-thē.
Lethean . . . . . . lē-thē'-ȧn.
Letitia . . . . lē-tĭsh'-ȧ.
L'Étoile . . . . . . lä-twäl'.
Leucophryne . . . . . lū-kō-frī'-nē.
Leucothea . . . . . . lū-kō'-thē-ä.
Leuctra . . . . lūk'-trä.
Leuk . . . . loik.

Leuthen . . . . . . loi'-tĕn.
Leutze . . . . loit'-zŭ.
Leuwenhoek, see Leeu-
 wenhoek . . . . . lĕ'-vĕn-hōōk.
Lévan . . . . lä-vän'.
Levant . . . . lĕ-vänt', lē-vänt'.
Levantine . . . . . . lĕ-văn'-tĭn.
Leven, Loch . . . . . lŏch lēvn.
Lever, Chas. . . . . . lē'-vēr.
Leverrier, or Le Verrier . lŭ-vĕr'-ĭ-ēr. Fr. lĕ-vĕ-rē=ā'.
Leveson-Gower . . . . lū'-sŭn-gōr'.
Levitan . . . . lä-vē'-tän.
Levite . . . . lē'-vīt.
Levitic . . . . lē-vĭt'-ĭk.
Leviticus . . . . . . lĕ-vĭt'-ĭ-kŭs.
Lévy (Émile) . . . . . lä-vē'.
Lewes . . . . lū'-ĕs.
Leyden, see Leiden . . lī'-dĕn.
Leyds . . . . līts.
Leyra (Antonio), de . . dä lä'=ē-rä.
Leys . . . . līs, lä.
Leyte . . . . lä'-tä. Sp. lä'-ē-tä.
L'hermitte . . . . . lĕr-mēt'.
L'Hôpital, or L'Hospital . lō-pē-tăl'.
Liadow . . . . lē-ä'-dŏf.
Liaotung, Liantung . . lē=ow-tŏń'.
Liapounoff (-ov) . . . lē-ä-pōō'-nŏf.
Libanius . . . . . . lĭ-bä'-nĭ=ŭs.
Libanus . . . . . . lĭb'-ä-nŭs.
Libau . . . . lē'-bow.
Liber . . . . lī'-bēr.
Liberi . . . . lē'-bä-rē.
Liberia . . . . lī-bē'-rī-à.
Libra . . . . lī'-brä.
Libya . . . . lĭb'-ĭ-à.
Lichas . . . . lī'-kàs.
Lichnowsky . . . . . lĭch-nŏv'-skĭ.

Lichtenstein . . . . . lĭċh′-tĕn-stīn.
Licinian . . . . . . lĭ-sĭn′-ĭ-àn.
Liddell . . . . lĭd′-ĕl.
Lie (Jonas) . . . . . lē.
Lieber . . . . lē′-bĕr.
Liebig . . . . lē′-bĭċh.
Lieder ohne Worte . . lē′-dĕr ō′-nŭ vŏr′-tŭ.
Liège . . . . *Fr.* lē-ĕzh′.
Liegnitz . . . . . . lēg′-nĭtz. *Ger.* lēċh′-nĭtz.
Ligea, or Ligeia . . . . lĭ-jē′-ä.
Ligne, de . . . . . . dŭ lēn′=yŭ.
Ligny . . . . lēn′-yĭ. *Fr.* lēn-yē′.
Ligonier . . . . . . lĭg-ō-nēr′.
Liguori . . . . lē-gwō′-rē.
Li Hung Chang . . . . lē hōōng chông.
Lilis . . . . lĭ′-lĭs.
Lilith . . . . lĭ′-lĭth, lĭl′-ĭth.
Liliuokalani . . . . . lē″-lē-wō-kä-lä′-nē.
Lille . . . . lēl.
Lillibullero . . . . . lĭl″-lĭ-bŏŏl-lâ′-rō.
Lima . . . . lĭ′-mà. *Sp.* lē′-mä.
Limerick . . . . . . lĭm′-ĕ-rĭk.
Limoges, see Lymoges . lē-mŏzh′.
Limousin . . . . . . lē-mōō-zăṅ′.
Limpopo . . . . . . lĭm-pō′-pō.
Linares . . . . lē-nä′-rĕs.
Lincoln . . . . lĭng′-kŭn.
Lingayen . . . . . . lēn-gä-yĕn′.
Linlithgow . . . . . lĭn-lĭth′-gō.
Linnankoski . . . . . lĭn-än-kŏs′-kĭ.
Linnæan, see Linnean . lĭn-nē′-àn.
Linnæus . . . . . . lĭn-nē′-ŭs.
Linnean, see Linnæan . lĭn-nē′-àn.
Linz . . . . lĭnts.
Liotard . . . . lē=ō-tär′.
Lipari . . . . lĭp′-ä-rē.
Lippe . . . . lĭp′-pŭ.

Lippi, Lippo	lēp′-pō lēp′-pē.
Lisboa, or	*Port. and Sp.* lēs-bō′-ä.
Lisbon	lĭz′-bŏn.
Lisieux	lē-zē̆=ĕ̆′.
Lisle, Leconte de . . .	lē-kŏṅt′ dĕ lēl′.
L'Isle, Rouget de . . .	rōō-zhä′ dĕ lēl′.
Liszt	lĭst.
Littorale	lēt-tō-rä′-lä.
Littré	lē-trä′.
Litvinof	lĭt-vē′-nŏf.
Liu Kiu, see Loo Choo,	
Lieou Khieou, and . .	lē-ōō′ kē-ōō′.
Liu Tchou	lē-ōō′ chōō.
Liutprand, see Luitprand .	lĭ-ōōt′-prånd.
Livenza	lē-vän′-dzä.
Livonia	lĭ-vō′-nĭ=ä.
Livorna, see Leghorn . .	lē-vōr′-nō.
Li Yuan-Lung	lē-yōō-än-hôṅ′.
Llanberis	ċhlăn-bĕr′-ĭs.
Llandaff	ċhlăn-dăf′.
Llangollen	ċhlăn-gŏċh′-lĕn.
Llanos	*Sp.* l-yä′-nōs.
Llewelyn ap Gruffydd, or	
Llywelyn ap Gruffydd .	ċhlōō-ĕl′-ĭn ăp grü′-fĕ̆ťh.
Loanda	lō-än′-dä.
Loanda, São Paulo de . .	säṅ pow′-lōō dĕ lō-än′-dä.
Loango	lō-äng′-gō.
Loangwa	lō-ăng′-wä.
Lobengula	lō-bĕng-gōō′-lä.
Lochaber	lŏċh-ä′-bēr.
Loches	lŏsh.
Lochiel	lŏċh-ēl′.
Lochinvar	lŏċh-ĭn-vär′.
Loch Katrine	lŏċh kăt′-rĭn.
Lochleven	lŏċh-lĕv′-n, lŏċh-lē′-vn.
Loch Lomond	lŏċh lō′-mŭnd.
Lockroy	*Fr.* lōk-rwä′.

Lodi	lō'-dē.
Lodovico	lō-dō-vē'-kō.
Lódz	lōdz.
Loew	lĕv.
Loffoden, or Lofoden, or .	lŏf-fō'-dĕn.
Lofoten	lō-fō'-tĕn.
Loggia dei Lanzi . . .	lōj'-jä dä'-ē länd'-zē.
Logroño	lō-grōn'-yō.
Lohardaga, or	lō-här-dä'-gä.
Lohardugga	lō-här-dŭg'-gä.
Lohengrin	lō'-ĕn-grĭn.
Loire	lwär.
Loire, Haute	ōt-lwär'.
Loire-Inférieure	lwär'-ăṅ-fā-rē=ĕr'.
Loiret	lwä-rā'.
Loir-et-Cher	lwär'-ā-shâr'.
Lokal-Anzeiger	lō-käl'-än'-tsī-gĕr.
Loke, or Loki	lō'-kĕ.
Lola Montez	lō'-lä mŏn'-tĕz.
Lombard's Kop	lŏm'-bärts kŏp.
Lombardy	lŏm'-bär-dĭ.
Lombroso	lōm-brō'-zō.
Lome	lō'-mä.
Lomonosoff	lō-mō-nō'-sŏf.
Lomza	lŏm'-zhä.
Longchamp	lôṅ-shäṅ'.
Longimanus	lŏn-jĭm'-ā-nŭs.
Longinus	lŏn-jī'-nŭs.
Longjumeau	lôṅ-zhü-mō'.
Longueville, de	dŭ lôṅg-vēl'.
Longwy	lŏṅ-vē'.
Loo Choo, Liu Tchou, see Liu Kiu, and Lieou Khieou	lōō chōō.
Loos	lŏ-ŏs'.
Lope de Vega	lō'-pā dā vā'-gä.
Lopez	lō'-pĕth.

Lopez (C. A., Pres. Para-
guay) . . . . . . lō'-pĕth, *locally* lō'-pĕz.
Lorbrulgrud . . . . . lŏr-brŭl'-grŭd.
Lorelei, or Loreley, see
Lurlei . . . . . . lō'-rā-lī.
Lorenzetti . . . . . lō-rĕnd-zĕt'-tē.
Lorenzo . . . . . . lō-rĕn'-zō. *It.* lō-rĕnd'-zō.
Sp. lō-rĕn'-thō.
Lorenzo de' Medici . . lō-rĕnd'-zō dā mā'-dē-chē.
Lorenzo Marques, see
Lourenço Marques . . lō-rcn'-sō mär'-kĕs.
Port. lṳ-rṳṅ'-sŏō
mär'-kĕs.
Loreto, or . . . . . . lō-rā'-tō.
Loretto . . . . . . lō-rĕt'-tō.
Lorraine . . . . . . lŏr-rān'. *Fr.* lō-rĕn'.
Los Angeles . . . . . lōs ăn'-gĕl-ĕs.
Sp. lōs äng'-ċhā-lās.
Lot-et-Garonne . . . lō-tā-gä-rŏn'.
Lothario . . . . . . lō-thā'-rē-ō.
Lothringen . . . . . lōt'-rĭng-ĕn.
Loti, Pierre . . . . pē̄=âr' lū-tē'.
Lotophagi . . . . . lō-tŏf'-ā-jī.
Lotto, Lorenzo . . . lō-rĕnd'-zō lŏt'-tō.
Lotze . . . . lōt'-sŭ.
Loubet . . . . lōō-bā'.
Loucheur . . . . . . lōō-shĕr'.
Loudon, see Laudon . . low'-dŏn.
Loudun . . . . . . lōō-dŭṅ'.
Louis . . . . lōō'-ĭs. *Fr.* lōō-ē'.
Louisiana . . . . . lōō"-ē̄-zē̄-ä'-nä,
lōō"-ē̄-zē̄-ăn'-ä.
Louis Lambert . . . . lōō-ē' läṅ-bâr'.
Louis Philippe . . . . lōō-ē' fē-lēp'.
Louis Quatorze . . . . lōō-ē' kă-tôrz'.
Louis Quinze . . . . . lōō-ē' kăṅz.
Louis Seize . . . . . lōō-ē' sĕz.

Louis Treize . . . . . loͦo-ē′ trēz.
Louisville . . . . . . loͦo′-ĭ-vĭl, loͦo′-ĭs-vĭl.
Lourdes . . . . . . loͦord.
Lourenço Marques,   see
  Lorenzo Marques . . lō-rĕn′-sō mär′-kĕs.
                       Port. loͦo-răṅ′-soͦo
                       mär′-kĕs.
Louvain . . . . . . loͦo-văṅ′.
Louverture, Toussaint, or
  L'Ouverture . . . . toͦo-săṅ′ loͦo-vĕr-tür′.
Louvre . . . . . . loͦovr.
Louÿs, Pierre . . . pē=âr′ loͦo-ēs′.
Lowestoft . . . . . lō′-stŏft, lō′-ĕ-stŏft.
Loyola . . . . . . loi-ō′-lä. *Sp.* lō-yō′-lä.
Lozère . . . . . . lō-zâr′.
Lo Zingaro . . . . lō dzēn′-gä-rō.
Lualaba . . . . . loͦo-ä-lä′-bä.
Luapula . . . . . loͦo-ä-poͦo′-lä.
Lübeck . . . . . . lü′-bĕk.
Lübke . . . . . . lüb′-kŭ.
Lublin . . . . . . loͦo′-blĭn.
Lucan . . . . . . lū′-kȧn.
Lucania . . . . . lū-kā′-nĭ=ȧ.
Lucaya . . . . . . loͦo-kī′-ä.
Lucayos . . . . . loͦo-kī′-ōs.
Lucca, Bagni di . . . bän′-yē dē loͦok′-ä.
Lucchese . . . . . lŭk-ēz′, lŭk-ēs′.
Lucerne, see Luzern . lū-sērn′. *Fr.* lü-sârn′
Lucia di Lammermoor . loͦo-chē′-ä dē
                       läm-mĕr-moͦor′
Lucian . . . . . . lū′-shĭ-ȧn.
Luciana . . . . . loͦo-shi-ā′-nä.
Lucina . . . . . . lū-sī′-nä.
Lucinda . . . . . lū-sĭn′-dȧ.
Lucinde . . . . . lü-săṅd′.
Luckimpur, see Lakhimpur lŭk-ĭm-poͦor′.
Lucknow, see Lakhnau . lŭk′-now. *pop.* lŭk-nō.

Luçon, see Luzon . . . loo-zōn'.   *Sp.* loo-thōn'.
Lucrece . . . . . . lū'-krēs, lū-krēs'.
Lucretius . . . . . lū-krē'-shĭ-ūs.
Lucrezia Borgia . . . loo-krād'-zē-ä bōr'-jä.
Lucullus . . . . . . lū-kŭl'-ŭs.
Ludendorf . . . . . loo'-dĕn-dŏrf.
Ludhiana . . . . . . loo-dē-ä'-nä.
Ludovisi Ares . . . loo-dō-vē'-zē ä'-rēz.
Ludwig . . . . . . lood'-vĭċh.
Lugano . . . . . . loo-gä'-nō.
Lugo . . . . loo'-gō.
Luigi . . . . loo-ē'-je.
Luini . . . . loo-ē'-nē.
Luis . . . . loo-ēs'.
Luise . . . . *Ger.* loo'-ē'-zŭ.
Luitpold . . . . . . loo'-ĭt-pōlt.
Luitprand, see Liutprand . loo-ĭt'-pränd.
Luiz . . . . *Port.* loo-ēth'.
Lulli . . . . lool'-lē.
Lullitpur, see Lalitpur . . lŭl-lĭt-poor'.
Lüneburg . . . . . lü'-nĕ-boorċh.
Lunéville . . . . . lü-nä-vēl'.
Lupercal . . . . . lū'-pĕr-kăl, lū-pĕr'-kăl.
Lupercalia . . . . . lū-pĕr-kä'-lĭ=à.
Luria . . . . loo'-rē-ä.
Luristan . . . . . loo-rĭs-tän'.
Lurlei, see Lorelei . . loor'-lī.
Lusiad . . . . . . lū'-sĭ-ăd.
Lusignan . . . . . lü-zēn-yäṅ'.
Lusitania . . . . . lū-sĭ-tā'-nĭ-à.
Lutetia . . . . . . lū-tē'-shĭ-à.
Luther . . . . . . lū'-thĕr.   *Ger.* loo'-tĕr.
Lützen . . . . . . lüt'-zĕn.
Luxembourg . . . . lüks-än-boor'.
Luxemburg . . . . lŭk'-sĕm-bērg.
        D. lük'-sĕm-bŭrċh.
Luxor . . . . lŭks'-ôr, looks'-ôr.

Luynes, de . . . . . dŭ lü=ēn'.
Luzern, see Lucerne . . lōō-tsĕrn'.
Luzon, see Luçon . . . lōō-zōn'. *Sp.* lōō-thōn'.
Lvoff . . . . l-vŏf'.
Lyautey . . . . . . lē-ō-tā'.
Lycaon . . . . lĭ-kā'-ŏn.
Lycaonia . . . . . . lĭk-ä-ō'-nĭ=ȧ.
Lyceum . . . . . . lĭ-sē'-ŭm.
Lycidas . . . . lĭs'-ĭ-dȧs.
Lydenburg . . . . . lĭ'dĕn-bŭrċh.
Lyell . . . . lĭ'-ĕl.
Lyly (John) . . . . . lĭl'-ĭ.
Lymoges, see Limoges . lē-mŏzh'.
Lyonesse . . . . . . lĭ-ŏn-ĕs'.
Lyonnais . . . . . . lĕ-ŏn-â'.
Lyonnaise . . . . . . lē-ŏn-ĕz'.
Lyons . . . . lĭ'-ŏnz. *Fr.* lē-ôṅ'.
Lys dans la Vallée, Le . lē lēs däṅ lä väl-ā'.
Lysias . . . . lĭs'-ĭ-ȧs.
Lysimachus . . . . . lĭ-sĭm'-ȧ-kŭs.
Lysippus . . . . . . lĭ-sĭp'-ŭs.
Lystra . . . . lĭs'-trȧ.
Lytton . . . . lĭt'-ŭn.

M

Maartens, Maarten . . mär'-tĕn mär'-tĕnz.
Maas, see Meuse . . . mäs.
Maastricht, see Maestricht,
  Mastricht . . . . . mäs'-trĭċht.
Mabillon . . . . . . mä-bē-yôṅ'.
Mabinogion (The) . . . mäb-ĭ-nō'-gĭ-ŏn.
Mabuse, see Maubeuge . mä-büz'.
Macao . . . . mä-kä'=ō, mä-kow'.
Macbeth . . . . . . mǎk-bĕth'.
Maccabaeus . . . . . mǎk-ȧ-bē'-ŭs.
Maccabean . . . . . mǎk-ȧ-bē'-ȧn.

Maccabees . . . . . măk'-á-bēz.
Macchiavelli, see Machia-
velli . . . . . . măk''-ĭ-á-věl'-lĭ.
    It. mä''-kē-ä-väl'-lē.
Macedonia . . . . măs-ē-dō'-nĭ-á.
Maceo . . . . . . mä-thä'-ō.
Macerata . . . . . mä-chä-rä'-tä.
Machado . . . . . mä-chäd-t̄hō.
Machiavel . . . . . măk'-ĭ-á-věl''.
Machiavelian . . . măk''-ĭ-á-vēl'-yán,
    măk''-ĭ-á-vē'-lĭ-án.
Machiavelism . . . măk'-ĭ-á-věl-ĭz''-m.
Machiavelli, see Macchia-
velli . . . . . . măk''-ĭ-á-věl'-lĭ.
    It. mä''-kē-ä-väl'-lē.
Machpelah . . . . măk-pē'-lä.
Macias . . . . . . mä-thē'-äs.
MacIvor . . . . . măk-ē'-vôr.
Mackay (Charles) . . măk-ī', măk-ā', măk'-ĭ.
Mackaye (Percy) . . mă-kī'.
Mackensen . . . . mäk-ĕn'-zĕn.
Maclaren, Ian . . . ē'-án, ī'-ăn má-klă'-rĕn,
    măk-lä'-rĕn.
Maclise . . . . . . má-klēs', măk-lēs'.
MacMahon . . . . măk-mä'-ŏn.
    Fr. mäk-mä-ôṅ'.
MacMonnies . . . . măk-mŭn'-ĭz.
Mâcon . . . . . . Fr. mä-kôṅ'.
Macon (Ga.) . . . . mä'-kŏn.
Macready . . . . . má-krē'-dĭ, măk-rē'-dĭ.
Mactan . . . . . . măk-tän'.
Madame Bovary . . mă-dăm' bō-vä-rē'.
Madeira (R.) . . . . mä-dä'=ē-rä.
Madeira (I.) . . . . mă-dē'-rä.
    Port. mä-dä'=ē-rä.
Madeleine (Church) . . mäd-lĕn'.
Mademoiselle de Maupin mäd-mwä-zĕl' dŭ mō-păṅ'.

Mademoiselle, La Grande	lä gränd mäd-mwä-zĕl'.
Madonna	mă-dŏn'-à. *It.* mä-dōn'-nä.
Madras	mă'-dràs, măd-răs'.
Madrazo	mä-drä'-thō.
Madrid.	mà-drĭd'. *Sp.* mä-drēd'.
Madruga	mä-drōō'-gä.
Madura	mä-dōō'-rä.
Mæcenas	mē-sē'-nàs.
Mænad	mē'-năd.
Maestricht, see Maas-	
tricht, Mastricht . . .	mäs'-trĭċht.
Maeterlinck	mĕt'-ēr-lĭngk.
	D. mä'-tĕr-lĭngk.
Mafeking	mä-fä-kĭng'.
Maffei	mäf-fä'-ē.
Maffia, or Mafia . . .	mä-fē'-ä.
Magalhães, see Magellan	*Port.* mä-gäl-yä'=ĕńs
Magaliesberg	măg'-ă-lēs-bĕrċh.
Magallanes, see Magellan	mä-gäl-yä'-nĕs.
Magdala	(Abyssinia) mäg-dä'-là
	Bib. măg'-dà-lä.
Magdalen	măg'-dà-lĕn. *Eng. college,*
	môd'-lĭn.
Magdalene	măg-dä-lē'-nĕ, măg'-dä-lēn.
Magdeburg	măg'-dĕ-bŭrg.
	Ger. mäċh'-dä-bōōrċh.
Magellan, see Magalhães,	
Maghellanes	mà-jĕl'-àn.
	Sp. mä-gĕl-yän'.
Magellanic	măj-ĕl-lăn'-ĭk.
Magendie	mà-jĕn'-dĭ.
	Fr. mä-zhŏn-dē'.
Magenta	ınä-jĕn'-tä.
Magersfontein	mä"-ċhĕrs-fŏn'-tīn.
Maggiore	mäd-jō'-rĕ.
Maghellanes, see Magel-	
lan	mä-gĕl-lä'-nās.

Magi . . . . mā'-jī.
Magian . . . . . . mā'-jĭ-àn.
Magna Carta, or Magna
  Charta . . . . . . măg'-nä kär'-tä.
                  pop. chär'-tà.
Magnard . . . . . . măn-yär'.
Magnusson . . . . . mäg'-nōōs-sŏn.
Maguindanao, see Min-
  danao . . . . . . mä-gēn"-dä-nä'-ō.
Magog . . . . mā'-gŏg.
Magyar . . . . . . mŏd'-yŏr, mă-jär'.
Mahabarata, or Mahablia-
  rata . . . . mä"-hä-bä'-rä-tä.
Mahableshwur . . . . mä"-hä-blĕsh-wŭr'.
Mahalaleel . . . . . mà-hä'-là-lē"-ĕl,
                  mà-hăl'-à-lē"-ĕl.
Mahan . . . . mà-hăn'.
Maharajah . . . . . mä-hä-rä'-jä.
Mahdi, see El Mahdi . . mä-dē.
Mahdist . . . . . . mä'-dĭst.
Mahican, see Mohican . mä-hĭk'-àn.
Mahmud . . . . . . mä-mōōd'.
Mahomet, see Mohammed mä-hŏm'-ĕt, mä'-hō-mĕt,
                  mä'-hō-mĕt.
Mahon . . . . mà-hon'.
Mahony . . . . . . mà-hŏ'-nĭ, mä'-hŏ-nĭ.
Mahopac . . . . . . mä'-ō-păk.
Mahound . . . . . . mă-hownd', mä'-hownd.
Mahrattas, see Marhattas mă-răt'-äz, mä-rä'-tàz.
Mahu . . . . mä'-hōō, mà-hōō'.
Maia . . . . mā'-yà.
Mailand, *Ger.* for Milan . mī'-länt.
Maillol . . . . mä=ē-yŏl'.
Maimansinh, see My-
  mensing . . . . . mī-män-sĭn'.
Maimonides . . . . . mĭ-mŏn'-ĭ-dēz.
Main (R.) . . . . . . mān. *Ger.* mīn.

Maindron	măn̈-drôn̈'.
Maine-et-Loire	mān'-ā-lwär'.
Mainpuri, see Mynpuri	mīn-pōō'-rē.
Maintenon, de	dŭ măn̈=tŭ-nôn̈'.
Mainz, see Mayence . .	mīnts.
Maison Vauquer . . .	mä-zôn̈' vō-kā'.
Maistre, Xavier de . .	zăv'-ĭ-ēr. *Fr.* zăv-ē-ā' dŭ mä=tr.
Maisur, see Mysore . .	mī-sōōr'.
Maiwand	mī-wänd'.
Majano	mä-yä'-nō.
Majorca, see Mallorca .	mȧ-jôr'-kä.
Majuba	mä-jōō'-bä.
Makart	mäk'-ärt, mä-kärt'.
Makua	mä-kōō'-ä.
Malabar	măl-ȧ-bär'.
Malacca	mȧ-lăk'-ä.
Malachi	măl'-ȧ-kī.
Malaga	măl'ȧ-gȧ. *Sp.* mä'-lä-gä.
Malate	mä-lä'-tä.
Malay	mä-lā'.
Malayan	mä-lā'-ȧn.
Malaysia	mä-lā'-shĭ=ȧ. mä-lā'-zhĭ=ȧ.
Malaprop (Mrs.) . . .	măl'-ȧ-prŏp.
Malbrook, or	măl-brŏŏk'.
Malbrough	mäl-brōŏk'.
Malczewski	măl-chĕf'-skĭ.
Maldive	măl'-dīv.
Male-bolge	mä-lĕ-bōl'-jĕ.
Malebranche	măl-brän̈sh'.
Malesherbes, de . . .	dŭ măl-zârb'.
Malet, Lucas	lū'-kȧs măl-ā'.
Malherbe	măl-ârb'.
Malibon	mä-lē-bōn'.
Malibran	mä-lē-brän̈'.
Malignants	mȧ-lĭg'-nȧnts.

Malines, see Mechlin . mă-lēn'.
Mallarmé, Stéphane . . stā-făn' măl-är-mā'.
Mallorca, see Majorca . mäl-yŏr'-kä.
Mallory, see Malory . . măl'-lŏ-rĭ.
Malmaison . . . . . mäl-mā-zôn'.
Malmesbury . . . . . mämz'-bĕr-ĭ.
Malmö . . . . mäl'-mē.
Malmsey . . . . . . mäm'-zĭ.
Malolos . . . . . . mä-lō'-lōs.
Malory, see Mallory . . măl'-ō-rĭ.
Malot, Hector . . . . ĕk-tōr' mä-lō'.
Malpighi . . . . . . mäl-pē'-ge.
Malpighian . . . . . măl-pē'-gĭ=àn,
                        măl-pĭg'-ĭ-àn.
Malplaquet . . . . . măl-plă-kā'.
Malta, or . . . . . . môl'-tà. It. mäl'-tä.
Malte, Fr. . . . . . . mält='ŭ.
Maltese . . . . . . môl-tēz', môl-tēs'.
Malthus . . . . . . măl'-thŭs.
Malthusianism . . . . măl-thū'-sĭ-ăn-ĭzm", or
                        măl-thū'-zhăn-ĭzm.
Malvern (Ark.) . . . . măl'-vĕrn.
Malvern (Eng.) . . . . mô'-vĕrn.
Malvoisy . . . . . . măl-vwä-zē'.
Malvolio . . . . . . măl-vō'-lĭ-ō.
Malyavin . . . . . . mäl-yä-vĭn'.
Mambrino . . . . . mäm-brē'-nō.
Mambrinus . . . . . măm-brĭ'-nŭs.
Mambulao . . . . . mäm-bōō-lä'-ō.
Mamelukes . . . . . măm'-ĕ-lūks.
Mamertine . . . . . măm'-ĕr-tĭn, măm'-ĕr-tēn.
Mamertines, or . . . . măm-ĕr-tīnz.
Mamertini . . . . . măm-ĕr-tī'-nĭ.
Mamiani della Rovere . mä-mē-ä'-nē dĕl'-lä
                        rō'-vä-rä.
Mamre . . . . măm'-rē.
Manaos . . . . . . mä-nä'-ōs.

Manasseh . . . . . . măn-ăs'-ŭ.
Manbhoom, Manbhum . män'-bhōōm.
Mancha, La . . . . . lä män'-chä.
Manchester . . . . . măn'-chĕs-tẽr.
Manchoos, see Manchus . măn-chōōz'.
Manchuria, see Mantchuria măn-chōō'-rĭ-à.
Manchus, see Manchoos . măn-chōōz'.
Mancinelli . . . . . män-chē-nāl'-lē.
Mancini . . . . . . män-chē'-nē.
     _Fr._ män-sē-nē'.
Mandalay, or . . . . măn'-dà-lā.
Mandelay . . . . . . măn'-dĕ-lā.
Manet . . . . mä-nā'.
Manetho . . . . . . măn'-ĕ-thō.
Mangalore, or . . . . măng-gà-lōr'.
Mangalur . . . . . . măng-gà-lōōr'.
Mangin . . . . män-zhăṅ'.
Manichæans, or Mani-
 cheans . . . . . . măn-ĭ-kē'-ànz.
Manichee . . . . . . măn'-ĭ-kē.
Manila, Manilla . . . . mà-nĭl'-à. _Sp._ mä-nē'-lä.
Manin . . . . mä-nēn'.
Manipur, see Mannipur . măn-ĭ-pōōr'.
Manito, see Manitou . . măn'-ĭ-tō.
Manitoba . . . . . . măn-ĭ-tō-bä', măn-ĭ-tō'-bà.
Manitou, see Manito . . măn'-ĭ-tōō.
Mannheim . . . . . . män'-hīm.
Mannipur, see Manipur . măn-ĭ-pōōr'.
Manoah . . . . mà-nō'-ä.
Manon Lescaut . . . . mä-nôṅ' lĕs-kō'.
Manrico . . . . . . män-rē'-kō.
Manrique, Gómez . . . gō-mĕth män-rē'-kä.
Mans, Le . . . . . . lĕ mäṅ.
Mansard, or Mansart . . män-sär'.
    Anglicized, măn'-särd.
Mansfeld . . . . . . mäns'-fĕlt.
Mansour, or Mansur, Al . äl män-sōōr'.

Mantalini . . . . . . măn-tȧ-lē′-nē.
Mantchuria, see Manchuria măn-chōō′-rĭ-ȧ.
Mantegna . . . . . . män-tān′-yä.
Mantelli . . . . . . măn-tāl′-lē.
Manteuffel . . . . . män′-toif-fĕl.
Mantinea, or . . . . . măn-tĭ-nē′-ȧ.
Mantineia . . . . . . măn-tĭ-nī′-ä.
Mantova, or . . . . . *It.* män′-tō-vä.
Mantua . . . . . . măn′-tū-ȧ.
Mantuan . . . . . . măn′-tū-ȧn.
Manutius . . . . . . mă-nū′-shĭ=ŭs.
Manzanares . . . . . män-thä-nä′-rĕs.
Manzanilla . . . . . män-·hä-nēl′-yä.
Manzanillo . . . . . män-thä-nēl′-yō.
Manzoni . . . . . . män-dzō′-nē.
Maori . . . . mä′=ō-rĭ, mow′-rĭ.
Maoris . . . . mä′-ō-rĭz, mow′-rĭz.
Map (Walter), or . . . măp.
Mapes (Walter) . . . . māps.
Maracaibo, or Maracaybo mä-rä-kī′-bō.
Marah . . . . mā′-rä.
Marais, Le . . . . . lē mă-rā′.
Maran, René . . . . . rē-nä′ mă-räṅ′.
Marat . . . . mä-rä′.
Marathon . . . . . . măr′-ȧ-thŏn.
Maratta, or . . . . . mä-rät′-tä.
Maratti . . . . mä-rät′-tē.
Marceau . . . . . . mär-sō′.
Marchesa . . . . . . mär-kā′-zä.
Marchese . . . . . . mär-kā′-zĕ.
Marchesi . . . . . . mär-kā′-zē.
Marcke, von . . . . . fŏn mär′-kŭ.
Marconi . . . . . . mär-kō′-nē.
Marcus Aurelius Antoninus mär′-kŭs′- ô-rē′-lĭ=ŭs
　　　　　　　　　ăn-tō-nī′-nŭs.
Mardi Gras . . . . . mär′-dē grä′.
Marengo . . . . . . mä-rĕng′-gō.

Mareotis . . . . . . mā-rē-ō'-tĭs, mä-rē-ō'-tĭs.
Mareuil, Villebois- . . . vēl-bwä'-mä-rē'=yŭ.
Margarethe . . . . . mär-gä-rä'-tŭ.
Margot, La Reine . . . lä rĕn mär-gō'.
Margrave . . . . . . mär'-grāv.
Margravine . . . . . mär'-grä-vēn.
Marguérite . . . . . mär-gä-rēt'.
Margueritte, Paul . . . pōl mär-gē-rĭt'.
Marhattas, see Mahrattas mä-rä'-tȧz, mă-răt'-äz.
Maria de' Medici, see
   Marie de Médicis . . mä-rē'-ä dä mä'-dē-chē.
Maria Feodorovna . . . mä-rē'-ä fä-ō-dōr'-ŏv-nä.
Maria-Hérédia, José de . ċhō-sä' dä mä-rē'-ä-
                ä-rä-dē-ä'.
Mariamne . . . . . . mä-rĭ-ăm'-nē.
Marian (Maid) . . . . mȧr'-ĭ-ȧn.
Mariana (Is.) . . . . mä-rē-ä'-nä.
Mariana (Mason's) . . mä-rĭ-ä'-nȧ.
Mariana (Shak.) . . . mä-rĭ-ăn'-ȧ, mă-rē-ä'-nä.
Marianao . . . . . . mä"-rē-ä-nä'-ō.
Marianne, La . . . . lä mär-ē̇=än'.
Maria Theresa . . . . mä-rī'-ȧ tē-rē'-sȧ.
                Ger. mä-rē'-ä tä-rä'-zä.
Mariazell . . . . . . mä-re"-ä-tsĕl'.
Marie Amélie . . . . mä-rē' ă-mä-lē'.
Marie Antoinnette . . . mȧr'-ĭ ăn-toi-nĕt'.
                Fr. mä-rē' äntwä-nĕt'.
Marie de Médicis, see
   Maria de' Medici . . mä-rē' dŭ mä-dē-sēs'.
Marie Galante . . . . mä-rē' gä-länt'.
Marienburg . . . . . mä'-rē-ĕn-bōōrċh".
Marignano, see Melegnano mä-rēn-yä'-nō.
Marilhat . . . . . . mär-ē-lä'. [mä-rē'-nä.
Marina . . . . Shak. mȧ-rī'-nȧ. Sp.
Marinduque . . . . . mä-rēn-dōō'-kä.
Marini, or . . . . . . mä-rē'-nē.
Marino . . . . mä-rē'-nō.

Marino Faliero	mä-rē′-nō fä-lē=ā′-rō.
Mario	mä′-rē-ō.
Mariolatry	mâr′-ĭ-ŏl′-à-trĭ.
Marion Delorme . . .	mă-rē-ôṅ′ dŭ-lôrm′.
Mariotte	mă-rē=ŏt′.
Maris	mär′-ēs.
Maritzburg	mär′-ĭts-bōōrċh.
Marius	mā′-rĭ-ŭs.
Marivaux	mä-rē-vō′.
Mariveles	mä-rē-vä′-lĕs.
Marjoribanks	märsh′-bănks.
Markgraf	märk′-gräf.
Marlboro, or Marlborough	*Am.* märl′-bŭr-ō, môl′-brō.
Marlborough (Duke) . .	môl′-brō, môl′-bŭr-ŭ.
Mármaros-Sziget . . .	mär′-mŏ-rŏsh-sĭg′-ĕt.
Marmont	mär-môṅ′.
Marmontel	mär-môṅ-tĕl′.
Marmora (Sea) . . .	mär′-mō-rà.
Marne	märn.
Marni	mär-nē′.
Marochetti	mä-rō-kāt′-tē.
Maronite	mȧr′-ō-nīt.
Marot, Clément . . .	klä-môṅ′ mă-rō′.
Marquesas (Is.)	mär-kä′-säs.
Marquette	mär-kĕt′.
Marquis	mär′-kwĭs. *orig.* mär′-kis.
	Fr. mär-kē′.
Marquise	mär-kēz′.
Marryat	mȧr′-ĭ-ăt.
Marseillaise, La	lä mär-sĕl-āz′. *Fr.* lä
	mär-sä-yĕz′.
Marseille, *Fr.* or . . .	mär-sä′-yŭ.
Marseilles	mär-sälz′.
Marshalsea	mär′-shăl-sē.
Mars-la-Tour	märs-lä-tōōr′.
Marsyas	mär′-sĭ-ȧs.
Marszalkowska	mär-shäl-kŏv′-skä.

Martel de Janville . . . mär-tĕl′ dŭ zhŏṅ-vēl′.
Martin, Henri . . . . ôṅ-rē′ mär-tăṅ′.
Martineau . . . . . . mär′-tĭ-nō.
Martinez Campos . . . mär-tē′-nĕth käm′-pōs.
Martini-Henry . . . . mär-tē′-nē-hĕn′-rĭ.
Martini, Simone . . . sē-mō′-nä mär-tē′-nē.
Martinique . . . . . mär-tĭ-nēk′.
Martinist . . . . . . mär′-tĭn-ĭst.
Martius . . . . . . mär′-shĭ-ŭs.
Marullus . . . . . . mä-rŭl′-ŭs.
Marylebone . . . . . mä′-rĭ-lĕ-bōn″, mär′-lĕ-bŭn,
                      mär′-ĭ-bŭn.
Masaccio . . . . . . mä-sät′-chō.
Masaniello . . . . . mä-sä-nē=äl′-lō.
Masaryk . . . . . . mä′-sä-rīk.
Masbate . . . . . . mäs-bä′-tä.
Mascagni . . . . . . mäs-kän′-yē.
Mascarene . . . . . mäs-kȧ-rēn′.
Mascarille . . . . . mäs-kä-rēl′.
Masefield . . . . . . māz′-fēld.
Maseru . . . . . . māz′-ēr-ōō.
Mashonaland . . . mä-shō′-nä-lănd,
                  mä-shō′-nä-lănd.
Maskelyne . . . . . măs′-kĕ-lĭn, măs′-kĕ-līn.
Masolino da Panicale . . mä-zō-lē′-nō dä
                        pä-nē-kä′-lĕ.
Maspéro . . . . . . măs-pä-rō′.
Massada . . . . . . mäs-sä′-dä.
Massasoit . . . . . . măs′-ȧ-soit.
Masséna . . . . . . mä-sä′-nä. *Fr.* mä-sā-nä′.
Massenet . . . . . . măs-nä′.
Massillon . . . . . . *U. S.* măs′-ĭl-ŏn.
                      Fr. mä-sē-yôṅ′.
Massimo . . . . . . mäs′-ē-mō.
Massinger . . . . . . măs′-ĭn-jĕr.
Masso . . . . mäs′-sō.
Massuccio, see Masuccio mä-sŏŏt′-chō.

Massys, see Matsys and
  Metsys . . . . . .   mäs-sīs'.
Mastricht, see Maastricht
  and Maestricht . . .   mäs'-trĭċht.
Masuccio di Salerno, see
  Massuccio . . . . .   mä-zōōt'-chō dē sä-lĕr'-nō.
Masurenland . . . . .   mä-zōō'-rĕn-länt.
Masurian, see Mazurian .   mă-sŭ'-rĭ-àn.
Mataafa . . . . . .   mà-tä'-fà.
Matabele, see Matabeli
  and Matebeli . . . .   mä-tä-bā'-lĕ.
Matabeleland . . . .   mä-tä-hä'-lĕ-länd.
Matabeli, see Matabele
  and Matebele . . . .   mä-tä-bā'-lē.
Matanzas . . . . . .   mă-tăn'-zàs.
                Sp. mä-tän'-thäs.
Matapan (Cape) . . . .   mà-tä-pän'.
                pop. măt-à-păn'.
Matebele, see Matabele .   mä-tĕ-bā'-lĕ.
Matejko . . . . . .   mä-tā'-kō.
Mater Dolorosa . . . .   mä'-tĕr dŏl-ō-rō'-sä,
                mä'-tĕr dō-lō-rō'-zä.
Materna . . . . . .   mà-tĕr'-nä.
                Ger. mä-tĕr'-nä.
Mather (Cotton) . . .   măth'-ĕr.
Mathieu . . . . . .   mä-tċ=ċ'.
Mathilde . . . . . .   mä-tēld'.
Matisse . . . . . .   mă-tēs'.
Matsys, Quentin, **see**
  Massys and Metsys .   kwĕn'-tĭn mät-sīs'.
Mattei, Tito . . . . .   tē'-tō mät-tä'-ē.
Matthias . . . . . .   mà-thī'-às. *Ger.* mät-tē'-äs.
Matthias Corvinus . .   mà-thī'-às kôr-vī'-nŭs.
Maturin . . . . . .   măt'-ū-rĭn.
Matzenauer . . . . .   mäts'-ĕn-ow-ĕr.
Maubeuge, see Mabuse .   mō-bēzh'.
Mauch Chunk . . . .   môk chŭngk'.

Maugham . . . . . . môm.
Maui (I.) . . . . . . mow'-ē.
Mauna Kea . . . . . mow'-nä kā'-ä.
Mauna Loa . . . . . mow'-nä lō'-ä.
Maundy . . . . . . môn'-dĭ.
Maupassant . . . . . mō-pä-säṅ'.
Maupertuis . . . . . mō-pâr-twē'.
Maupin, Mlle. de . . . mäd-mwä-zĕl' dŭ mō-păŭ.
Mauprat . . . . . . mō-prä'.
Maurel . . . . mō-rĕl'.
Maurepas . . . . . . mō=rē-pä'.
Maurice . . . . . . *Fr.* mō-rēs'.
Mauritius . . . . . . mô-rĭsh'-ĭ=ŭs.
Maurocordatos, see Mav-
rocordatos . . . . mäv"-rō-kŏr-dä'-tŏs.
Mauser . . . . . . mow'-zĕr.
Mausolus . . . . . . mô-sō'-lŭs.
Mauve . . . . mōv.
Mavrocordatos, see Mau-
rocordatos . . . . mäv"-rō-kŏr-dä'-tŏs.
Maximilian . . . . . măks-ĭ-mĭl'-yȧn.
                                    Ger. mäks-ē-mē'-lē-än.
Maximin . . . . . . măks'-ĭ-mĭn.
Maya . . . . mä'-yä, mī'-ä.
Mayaguez . . . . . . mī-ä-gwĕth'.
Maybun . . . . . . mä=ē-bōōn'.
Mayence, see Mainz . . *Fr.* mä-yŏṅs'.
Mayenne . . . . . . mī-ĕn', mä-yĕn'.
Mayer . . . . mā'-ēr. *Ger.* mī'-ĕr.
Maysi . . . . mä-ē'-sē.
Maytsouye . . . . . māt-sōō'-yĕ.
Mazagan . . . . . . mȧz-ȧ-gän'.
Mazanderan . . . . . mä"-zȧn-dĕ-rän'.
Mazarin . . . . . . măz'-ȧ-rĭn, măz-ȧr-ēn'.
                                    Fr. mă-zä-răṅ'.
Mazarini . . . . . . mäd-zär-ē'-nē.
Mazurian, see Masurian . mä-tsōō-rē'-än.

Mazzini	mät-sē'-nē.
Mazzuola	mät-zōō-ō'-lä.
Meagher	mä'-ċhĕr, mä'-'hĕr.
Meaux	mō.
Mechlin, see Malines . .	mĕk'-lĭn. *D.* mĕċh'-lĭn.
Mechoacan, see Michoacan	mā-chō"-ä-kän'.
Mecklenburg-Schwerin .	mĕk-lĕn-bōōrċh-shvā-rēn'.
Mecklenburg-Strelitz . .	mĕk'-lĕn-bōōrċh-strā'-lĭts.
Medea	mē-dē'-ä.
Médée	mā-dā'.
Media	mē'-dĭ-à.
Medici, de'	dā mä'-dĕ-chĕ.
Médicis, de	dŭ mā-dē-sēs'.
Medina	*Sp.* mā-dē'-nä.
	U. S. mē-dī'-nà.
Medina-Celi	mā-dē'-nä-thā'-lē.
Medina-Sidonia	mā-dē'-nä-sē-dō'-nē-ä.
Medjidi	mĕ-jēd'-ē.
Médoc	mā-dŏk'.
Medusa	mĕ-dū'-sä.
Meerkatsfontein . . .	mâr'-kăts-fŏn'-tīn.
Meerut, see Mirat . . .	mē'-rŭt.
Mefistofele	mā-fēs-tō'-fä-lä.
Megæra	mĕ-gē'-rà.
Megara	mĕg'-à-rä.
Megiddo	mĕ-gĭd'-ō.
Mehemet Ali, see Moham-	
med Ali	mā'-hĕ-mĕt ä'-lē.
Méhul	mā-ül'.
Meilhac	mā-yäk'.
Meissen	mī'-sĕn.
Meissonier	mā-sō-nē=ā'.
Meistersinger von Nürn-	
berg, Die	dē mīs'-tĕr-zĭng"-ĕr fŏn
	nürn'-bĕrċh.
Mejnoun	mĕj-nōōn'.
Mekhong, or Mekong . .	mā-kŏng'.

Melanchthon, or . . . . mē-lăngk'-thŏn.
         Ger. mä-längċh'-tōn.
Melanthon . . . . . mě-lăn'-thŏn.
Melba . . . . měl'-bä.
Melchisedec, or Melchize-
  dek . . . . měl-kĭz'-ĕ-děk.
Meleager . . . . . . měl-ē-ā'-jĕr, mē-lē-ā'-jĕr,
         mē-lē'-ā-jĕr.
Melegnano, see Marignano mä-län-yä'-nō.
Melibœus . . . . . . měl-ĭ-bē'-ŭs.
Melilla . . . . *Sp. Af.* mä-lēl'-yả.
Méline . . . . mä-lēn'.
Melita . . . . měl'-ĭt-à.
Mello (José de) . . . . mä'-lōō.
Melos, see Milo . . . mē'-lŏs.
Melozzo da Forlì . . . mä-lŏt'-zō dä fŏr-lē'.
Melpomene . . . . . měl-pŏm'-ĕ-nē.
Melton Mowbray . . . měl'-tŭn mō'-brä, mō'-brĕ.
Melusina . . . . . . měl-ōō-sī'-nä.
Mélusine, *Fr.* . . . . mä-lü-zēn'.
Memling . . . . . . měm'-lĭng.
Menabrea . . . . . . mä-nä-brä'-ä.
Menahem . . . . . . měn'-à-hěm.
Menai . . . . měn'-ī. *pop.* měn'-ā *or*
         měn'-ĕ.
Ménard, René . . . . rē-nä' mä-när'.
Mencayan . . . . . . män-kä-yän'.
Menchikoff, see Menshi-
  koff . . . . měn'-shē-kŏf.
Mencius . . . . . . měn'-shĭ-ŭs.
Mendelssohn-Bartholdy . měn'-děl-sōn-bär-tōl'-dē.
Mendès, Catulle . . . . kä-tül' môṅ-děz'.
Mendocino . . . . . měn-dō-sē'-nō.
Mendoza . . . . . . měn-dō'-thä.
Menelaus . . . . . . měn-ĕ-lā'-ŭs.
Menendez de Aviles . . mä-nän'-děth dä äbē'-lěs.
Ménippée, Satire . . . sä-tēr' mä-nē-pā'.

Menocal	mā-nō-käl'.
Menorca, *Sp.* for Minorca	mā-nōr'-kä.
Menpes, Mortimer . .	měm'-pěs.
Menshikoff, see Menchi-	
koff	měn'-shē-kǒf.
Menton, or	môṅ-tǒṅ'.
Mentone	měn-tō'-ně.
Menzel	měnt'·zěl.
Mephibosheth	mě-fĭb'-ō-shěth.
	Heb. měf-ĭ-bō'-shěth.
Mephistophelcan . . .	měf''-ĭs-tō-fē'-lē-ȧn.
Mephistopheles	měf-ĭs-tǒf'-ě-lēz.
Mercator	měr-kā'-tẽr.
	D. měr-kä'-tǒr.
Mercédes	měr-thā'-děs.
Mercia	měr'-shĭ=à.
Mercié	měr-sē=ā'.
Mercier	mȧr-sē=ā'.
Mercurius	měr-kū'-rĭ-ŭs.
Mercutio	měr-kū'-shĭ=ō.
Merejkowski . . ; . .	měr-ězh-kǒv'-skē.
Mergui	měr-gē'.
Mérimée	mā-rē-mā'.
Merindol	mě-răṅ'-dōl'.
Merle (Maj.)	měrl.
Merle d'Aubigné . . .	měrl dō-bēn-yā'.
Merlin	měr'-lĭn.
Merodach	měr' ō dǎk.
Meroë	měr'-ō-ē.
Merom	mē'-rǒm.
Merope	měr'-ō-pē.
Merovingians	měr-ō-vĭn'-jĭ-ȧnz.
Merowig, see Merwig . .	měr'-ō-wĭg.
Merrilies	měr'-ĭ-lēz.
Merry del Val	měr-ē' děl väl.
Mersey	měr'-sĭ.
Merwig, see Merowig . .	měr'-wĭg.

Méry . . . . mā-rē′.
Mesa, or . . . . . . mē′-zä. *Sp.* mā′-sä.
Mesha . . . . mē′-shä.
Meshach . . . . . mē′-shăk.
Mesmer . . . . . . mĕs′-mēr.
Mesolonghi, see Misso-
  longhi . . . . . . mā-sō-lŏng′-gē.
Mesolongion, *mod. Gr.* . mā-zō-lŏng′-gē-ŏn.
Mesopotamia . . . . . mĕs″-ō-pō-tā′-mĭ-à.
Messalina, or Messallina . mĕs-ă-lī′-nä.
Messianic . . . . . mĕs-sĭ-ăn′-ĭk.
Messidor . . . . . . mĕs-ē-dōr′.
Messina, Antonello da . än-tō-nāl′-lō dä mĕs-sē′-nä.
Messines . . . . . . mĕs-ēn′.
Mestrovich . . . . . mĕs′-trō-vĭch.
Mesurado (Cape) . . . mā-soō-rä′-dō.
Metastasio . . . . . mā-täs-tä′-zē-ō.
Météren . . . . . . mā-tā-rôṅ′.
Methuen (Gen.) . . . mĕth′-ŭ-ĕn.
Methuen (U. S.) . . . mĕ-thū′-ĕn.
Methuselah . . . . . mĕ-thū′-sĕ-lä.
Metsu, see Metzu . . . mĕt′-sü.
Metsys, see Massys and
  Matsys . . . . . . mĕt-sīs′.
Metternich-Winneburg . mĕt-tĕr-nĭch-
                          vĭn′-nĕ-boōrch.
Metz . . . . *Fr.* mĕz. *Ger.* mĕts.
Metzu, see Metsu . . . mĕt′-zü.
Meudon . . . . . . mĕ-dŏṅ′.
Meung, Jean de . . . zhäṅ dū mŭṅ.
Meunier . . . . . . mĕ-nē=ā′.
Meurthe-et-Moselle . . mĕrt′-ā-mō-zĕl′.
Meuse, see D. Maas . . mūz. *Fr.* mĕz.
Mexicali . . . . . . mĕks-ĭ-kä′-lĭ.
Meyerbeer . . . . . mī′-ĕr-bār.
Meynell . . . . . . mā′-nĕl.
Meyrick . . . . . . mī′-rĭk.

Mézières	mā-zē=âr'.
Mezzofanti	mĕt-zō-fän'-tē.
Miako	mē-ä'-kō.
Miami	mī-äm'-ē, mī-äm'-ĭ.
Miantonomoh . . .	mĭ-ăn"-tō-nō'-mō.
Micaela	mĭ-kä'-ā-lä.
Micah	mī'-kä.
Mi-Carême	mē-kă-rĕm'.
Micawber	mĭ-kô'-bẽr.
Michael	mī'-kĕl, mī'-kā=ēl.
Michael Angelo . . .	mī'-kā=ĕl ăn'-jē-lō.
Michaelis	mē-kā'-lēs.
Michael Nicolaevitch (Grand Duke) . . .	mī'-kĕl nē-kō-lā'-ĕ-vĭch.
Michaelmas	mĭk'-ĕl-mȧs.
Michal	mī'-kȧl.
Michel	Fr. mē-shĕl'.
Michelagnolo, or . . .	mē-kĕl-än'-yō-lō.
Michelangelo . . .	mī-kĕl-ȧn'-jĕ-lō.
	It. mē-kĕl-än'-jä-lō.
Michelet	mēsh-lā'.
Michelis	mē-ċhä'-lĭs.
Michelozzo Michelozzi .	mē-kĕ-lŏt'-zō mē-kĕ-lŏt'-zē.
Michetti, Paolo	pä'-ō-lō mē-kät'-tē.
Michoacan, see Mechoacan	mē-chō-ä-kän'.
Mickiewicz	mĭts-kē-ĕv'-ĭch.
Micronesia	mī-krō-nē'-shĭ-ȧ.
Micronesian	mĭ-krō-nē'-shĭ=ȧn, mĭk-rō-nē'-shĭ=ȧn.
Midas	mī'-dȧs.
Midgard	mĭd'-gärd.
Midianites	mĭd'-ĭ-ăn-īts".
Midnapur	mĭd-nȧ-pōōr'.
Mierevelt	mē'-rĕ-vĕlt.
Mieris	mē'-rĭs.
Mieroslawski	mē=ä-rō-släv'-skē.
Mignard	mēn-yär'.

Mignet . . . . . . mēn-yā'.
Mignon . . . . . . mēn-yôṅ'.
Miguel . . . . mē-gĕl'.
Mikado . . . . . . mǐ-kä'-dō.
Milan (City) . . . . . mǐl'-ăn, mǐ-lăn'.
Milan (King of Servia) . mǐl'-än.
Milanese . . . . . mǐl-ăn-ēz', or ēs'.
Milano, see Milan . . . mē-lä'-nō.
Milazzo . . . . . . mē-läts'-sō.
Milesian (Irish) . . . . mǐ-lē'-shǐ=àn, mǐ-lē'-zhàn.
Miliukoff (-kow, -kov) . mǐl'-yū-kŏf.
Millais . . . . mǐl-lā'.
Millerand . . . . . mēl-räṅ'.
Millet . . . . *Eng.* mǐl'-lĕt. *Fr.* mē-yā'.
  pop. mē-lä'.
Millevoye . . . . . . mēl-vwä'.
Millot . . . . mē-yō'.
Milne-Edwards . . . mǐln-ĕd'-wàrdz.
  Fr. mēl-nā-dōō-är', *or*
  mēl-nā-dōō-ärs'.
Milnes . . . . mǐlnz.
Milo, see Melos . . . mē-lō'.
Miloradovitch . . . mē-lō-rä'-dō-vǐch.
Miltiades . . . . . . mǐl-tī'-ă-dēz.
Mimi . . . . mē-mē'.
Mimir . . . . mē'-mǐr.
Mincio . . . . mǐn'-chō.
Mindanao, see Maguin-
  danao . . . . . . mǐn-dä-nä'-ō.
Mindoro . . . . . . mǐn-dō'-rō.
Minerva . . . . . . mǐn-ēr'-và.
Ming . . . . mēng.
Minho, *Port.,* see Miño . mēn'-yōō.
Minié . . . . mǐn'-ĕ. *Fr.* mē-nē=ā'.
Minna von Barnhelm . . mǐn'-ä fŏn bärn'-hĕlm.
Minnegerode . . . . mǐn'-ĕ-gä-rōd.
Minnewit, see Minnuit . mǐn'-ĕ-wǐt.

Miño, *Sp.*, see **Minho** . . mēn'-yō.
Mino da Fiesole . . . . mē'-nō dä fē-ä'-zō-lä.
Minorca, see **Menorca** . mĭ-nōr'-kä.
Minos . . . . mī'-nŏs.
Minotaur . . . . . mĭn'-ō-tôr.
Minnuit, see **Minnewit** . mĭn'-ū-ĭt.
Mir . . . . mēr.
Mirabeau . . . . . mĭr'-ă-bō.   *Fr.* mē-rä-bō'.
Miraflores . . . . mē-rà-flō'-rĕs.
Miragoane . . . . . mĭ-rà-gōn'.
      Fr. mē-rä-gwän'.
Miramon . . . . . . mē-rä-mōn'.
Miranao, La . . . . . lä mē-rä-nä'-ō.
Miranda . . . . . . *Shak.* mĭ-răn'-dà.
      Sp. mē-rän'-dä.
Mirandola, Pico della . . pē'-kō däl'-lä mē-rän'-dō-lä.
Mirat, or . . . . . . mē'-ràt.
Mirath, see **Meerut** . . mē'-räth.
Mirbeau, Octave . . . ōk-tăv' mer-bō'.
Mirbel . . . . mĕr-bĕl'.
Mirebalais . . . . mē=rĕ-bä-lā'.
Mirecourt . . . . . mŏr-kōōr'.
Miron, Diaz . . . . dē'-äs mē-rōn'.
Mirouét, Ursule . . . ür-sül' mē-rōō-ā'.
Mirs (Bay) . . . . . mērs.
Mirzapur . . . . . mēr-zä-pōōr'.
Mirza-Schaffy . . . mēr'-zä-shäf-fē'.
Misamis . . . . . . mē-säm'-ēs.
Misanthrope, Le . . . lē mē-zän-trŏp'. [äm-ē-ôn'.
Mise of Amiens . . . mīz ŏv ăm'-ĭ-ĕns.   *Fr.*
Misérables, Les . . . . lä mē-zā-rä'-bl.
Miserere . . . . . . mē-zā-rā'-rä.
Misericordia . . . . . mē"-zā-rē-kōr'-dē-ä.
Miskólcz . . . . . . mĭsh-kŏlts.
Missolonghi, see **Mesolon-**
   ghi, mod. Gr. **Mesolon-**
   gion . . . . mĭs-sō-lŏng'-gē.

Missouri . . . . . . mĭs-sōō'-rĭ, mĭ-zōō'-rĭ.
             pop. mĭz-ōō'-rȧ.
Misterosa . . . . . . mēs-tā-rō'-sȧ.
Mistral . . . . mēs-träl'.
Mitau . . . . mē'-tow.
Mithradates, see Mithri-
  dates . . . . mĭth-rȧ-dā'-tēz.
Mithridate . . . . . *Fr.* mēt-rē-dät'.
Mithridates, see Mithra-
  dates . . . . mĭth-rĭ-dā'-tēz.
Mithridatic . . . . . mĭth-rĭ-dăt'-ĭk.
Mitre, Bartolomé . . . bär-tō-lō-mä' mē'-trä.
Mitsuoki . . . . . . mēts'-ōō'-ō'-kē'.
Mitylene, see Mytilene . mĭt-ĭ-lē'-nē.
Mivart . . . . mĭv'-ärt.
Mizraim . . . . . . mĭz-rā'-ĭm, mĭz'-rā-ĭm.
Mlava . . . . mlä'-vä.
Mnemosyne . . . . . nē-mŏs'-ĭn-ē.
Moa . . . . mō'-ä.
Moab . . . . mō'-ăb.
Mobangi . . . . . . mō-bäng'-gē.
Mobile . . . . mō-bēl'.
Mocenigo . . . . . . mō-chä-nē'-gō.
Mocha . . . . mō'-kä. *Arab.* mō'-ċhä.
Modder . . . . . . mŏd'-ĕr.
Modder's Spruit . . . mŏd'-ĕrs sproit.
Modena . . . . . . mō'-dĕ-nä. *It.* mō'-dā-nä.
Modeste Mignon . . . mō-dĕst' mēn-yôṅ'.
Modjeska . . . . . . mŏd-jĕs'-kȧ.
Modred, see Mordred . mō'-drĕd, mŏd'-rĕd.
Moeris (L.) . . . . . mē'-rĭs.
Moewe . . . . mē'-vŭ.
Mogador . . . . . . mŏg-ȧ-dōr'.
Mogilef, see Mohileff . mō-gē-lĕf'.
Moguls, see Mughals . . mō-gŭlz'.
Mohács . . . . . . mō-häch'.
Mohammed, see Mahomet mō-hăm'-ĕd.

Mohammed Ali, see Mehemet Ali	mō-hăm'-ĕd ä'-lē.
Mohave, see Mojave . .	mō-hä'-vā.
Mohican, see Mahican .	mō-hĭk'-àn.
Mohileff, see Mogilef . .	mō-ċhē-lĕf'.
Mohun	mō'-hŭn.
Moiseiwitsch	mō-ē-sē'-vĭch.
Moldavia	mōl-dā'-vĭ-à.
Moivre	mwävr.
Mojave, see Mohave . .	mō-'hä'-vā.
Moldau	mŏl'-dow.
Molech, see Moloch . .	mō'-lĕk.
Molenbeek-Saint-Jean .	mŏ-lŏn-bāk'-săn-zhän'.
Molière	mō-lē=âr'.
Molina	mō-lē'-nä.
Molinists	mō'-lĭ-nĭsts.
Molinos	mō-lē'-nōs.
Mollwitz, see Molwitz .	mŏl'-vĭts.
Moloch, see Molech . .	mō'-lŏk.
Molokai	mō-lō-kī'.
Molokani	mō-lō-kä'-nē.
Moltke, von	fŏn mŏlt'-kŭ.
	Ger. mŏlt'-kŭ.
Moluccas	mō-lŭk'-àz.
Molwitz, see Mollwitz .	mŏl'-vĭts.
Molyneux	mŭl'-ĭ-nŏŏks, —nū.
Mombas, or	mŏm-bäs'.
Mombasa, or	mŏm-bä'-sä.
Mombaz	mŏm-bäs'.
Mombuttu, see Monbuttu	mŏm-bōōt'-tōō.
Mommsen	mŏm'-zĕn.
Momus	mō'-mŭs.
Monaco	mŏn'-ä-kō.
Mona Lisa	mō'-nä lē'-zä.
Monarque, Le Grand . .	lē grän mō-närk'.
Monastir	mō-näs-tēr'.
Monbuttu, see Mombuttu	mŏn-bōōt'-tōō.

Moncey . . . . . . môṅ-sā'.
Mondidier . . . . . . mŏṅ-dē-dē=ā'.
Monet . . . . mō-nā'.
Monfalcone . . . . mōn-fäl-kō'-nä.
Monge . . . . mŏṅzh.
Monghir, or Monghyr, see
    Mungir . . . . . . mŏn-gēr'.
Mongol . . . . . . mŏng'-gŏl, mŏn'-gŏl.
Mongolian . . . . mŏn-gō'-lĭ-ȧn.
Monmouth . . . . mŏn'-mŭth, mŭn'-mŭth.
Monna Vanna . . . mōn'-nä vän'-nä.
Monreale . . . . . mŏn-rā-ä'-lĕ.
Monroe . . . . . . mŭn'-rō.
Mons . . . . môṅs.
Monseigneur . . . . môṅ-sān-yĕr'.
Mons-en-Pévêle . . . môṅs'-ŏṅ-pā-vĕl'.
Monserrat, see Montserrat mōn-sĕr-rät'.
Monsieur . . . . . mŏ-sē=ē'.
Monson . . . . . . mŭn'-sŭn.
Montagu, or Montague . mŏnt'-ȧ-gū.
Montaigne . . . . mŏn-tān'.
          Fr. môṅ-tān'=yŭ.
Montalembert . . . môṅ-tä-lŏṅ-bâr'.
Montalvan . . . . . mōn-täl-bän'.
Montana . . . . . mŏn-tä'-nä.
Montargis . . . . . môṅt-är-zhē'.
Montauban . . . . môṅ-tō-bäṅ'.
Montauk (Point) . . . mŏn-tôk'.
Mont Blanc, see Mount
    Blanc . . . . . . *Fr.* môṅ bläṅ.
Montcalm Gozon de Saint-
    Véran . . . . . . mŏnt-käm'.
          Fr. môṅ-kälm' gōzôṅ'
          dŭ säṅ-vä-räṅ'.
Mont Cenis . . . . . môṅ sĕ-nē'.
Montebello . . . . mōn-tā-bāl'-lō.
Monte Cristo . . . . mŏn'-tĕ krĭs'-tō.

Montecucoli, or . . . . mŏn-tĕ-kōō'-kō-lē.
Montecuculi . . . . . mŏn-tĕ-kōō'-kōō-lē.
Montefiore . . . . . mŏn-tĕ-fē=ō'-rĕ.
Montego (Bay) . . . . mŏn-tē'-gō.
Monte Grappa . . . . mōn'-tä gräp'-pä.
Montejo . . . . . . mōn-tä'-ċhō.
Montemezze . . . . . mōn-tä-mäts'-sä.
Montenegro . . . . . *pop.* mŏn-tĕ-nē'-gro.
                      It. mōn-tä-nä'-grō.
Montereau . . . . . mô̂n̈=tĕ-rō'.
Monterey (Cal.) . . . . mŏn-tĕ-rā'.
Monterey (Mexico) . . mōn-tä-rä'=ē.
Montero Rios . . . . mon-ta'-ro re'-ōs.
Montes, Lola, see Montez lō'-lä mōn'-tĕs.
Montespan . . . . . mŏn-tĕs-păn'.
                      Fr. mô̂n̈-tĕs-päṅ'.
Montesquieu . . . . . mŏn-tĕs-kū'.
                      Fr. mô̂n̈-tĕs-kē=ē'.
Montessori . . . . . mōn-täs-sō'-rē.
Monte Testaccio . . . mōn'-tĕ tĕs-tä'-chō.
Monteverde . . . . . *It.* mōn-tĕ-vâr'-dĕ.
                      Sp. mōn-tä-vĕr'-t̯hä.
Montevideo . . . . . mŏn-tĕ-vĭd'-ē-ō.
                      Sp. mōn''-tä-vē-ä'-t̯hō.
Montez, Lola, see Montes lō'-lä mōn'-tĕs.
Montfaucon . . . . . mô̂n̈-fō-kôn̈'.
Montfleury . . . . . mô̂n̈-flē-rē'.
Montfort . . . . . . mŏnt'-fôrt. *Fr.* mô̂n̈-fōr'.
Montgolfier . . . . . mŏnt-gŏl'-fĭ-êr.
                      Fr. mô̂n̈-gōl-fē=ä'.
Montholon . . . . . mô̂n̈-tō-lôn̈'.
Monti, Vincenzo . . . vēn-chänd'-zō mŏn'-tē.
Monticello . . . . . mŏn-tē-sĕl'-lō.
                      It. mōn-tē-chäl'-lō.
Montijo . . . . . . *Sp.* mōn-tē'-ċhō.
Montijo, Eugénie de . . *Fr.* ē-zhä-nē' dŭ
                      mô̂n̈-tē-zhō'.

Montjoie . . . . . . môṅ-zhwä'.
Montluc . . . . . . môṅ-lük'.
Montmartre . . . . . môṅ-mär'=tr.
Montmirail . . . . . môṅ-mē-rä'=yŭ.
Montmorenci, or . . . mŏnt-mō-rĕn'-sē.
Montmorency . . . . Fr. môṅ-mō-rôṅ-sē'.
Montojo . . . . . . mōnt-ō'-ċhō.
Montpelier . . . . . mŏnt-pēl'-yĕr.
Montpellier . . . . . Fr. môṅ-pĕl-lē=ā'.
Montpensier . . . . . môṅ-pôṅ-sē=ā'.
Montreal . . . . . . mŏn-trē-äl'.
                      Fr. môṅ-rä-äl'.
Montreuil-sous-Bois . . môṅ-trē'=yŭ-sōō-bwä'.
Montserrat, see Monserrat mônt-sĕr-rät',
                      mônt-sĕ-ràt'.
Montserrat (I.) . . . . mŏnt-sĕ-rǎt'.
Monza . . . . mōn'-zä.
Moodkee, see Mudki . . mōōd'-kē.
Mooi . . . . mō'-ē.
Mooltan, see Multan . . mōōl-tän'.
Moore (Thomas) . . . mōōr, mōr.
Moorshedabad, see Mur-
   shidabad . . . . . mōōr"-shĕ-dä-bäd'.
Moraczewski . . . . . mō-rä-chĕv'-skĭ.
Moradabad, see Murad-
   abad . . . . . . mō"-räd-ä-bäd'.
Morales . . . . . . mō-rä'-lĕs.
Moran (Thomas) . . . mō-rǎn'.
Moray . . . . mŭr'-ĭ, mŭr'-ā.
Mordecai . . . . . . môr'-dĕ-kī, môr'-dē-kā.
Mordred, see Modred . môr'-drĕd.
Morea . . . . mō-rē'-ä.
Moreau . . . . . . mō-rō'.
Morelos . . . . . . mō-rä'-lŏs.
Moren . . . . mō-rän'.
Morghen . . . . . . mōr'-gĕn.
Morgue . . . . . . môrg. Fr. mōrg.

Moriah . . . .   mō-rī'-ä.
Morillo . . . .   mō-rēl'-yō.
Morisot, Berthe . . . .   bĕrt mō-rē-sō'.
Moritz . . . .   mō'-rĭts.
Mornay, Duplessis . .   dü-plä-sē' mōr-nä'.
Morny . . . .   mōr-nē'.
Moro (Castle), see Morro   mŏr'-rō.   *Sp.* mōr'-rō.
Moroko . . . . . .   mō-rō'-kō.
Moron de la Frontera . .   mō-rōn' dā lä fron-tä'-rä.
Morosini . . . . . .   mō-rō-zē'-nē.
Morpheus . . . . . .   mŏr'-fē-ŭs, mŏr'-fūs.
Morrisania . . . . .   mŏr-rĭs-ā'-nĭ=à.
Morro (Castle), see Moro   mŏr'-rō.   *Sp.* mōr'-rō.
Morte d'Arthur . . . .   môrt där-tür'.
Mort Homme . . . .   mōr-tŏm'.
Mortier . . . . . .   mōr-tē=ā'.
Mosaic . . . .   mō-zā'-ĭk.
Mosby . . . .   mōz'-bĭ.
Moscheles . . . . .   mōsh'-ĕ-lĕs.
Moscow . . . . . .   mŏs'-kō.
Mosel, or . . . . . .   mō-zĕl'.
Moselle . . . . . .   mō-zĕl'.
Mosenthal . . . . .   mō'-zĕn-täl.
Mosheim . . . . . .   mōs'-hīm.
Moskva . . . . . .   mŏsk-vä'.
Moslem . . . . . .   mŏs'-lĕm.
Mosquitia, or . . . .   mōs-kē-tē'-ä.
Mosquito . . . . . .   mōs-kē'-tō.
Mossoul, Mosul, see Mou-
   sul . . . .   mō'-sŭl.
Moszkowski . . . . .   mōs-kŏv'-skĭ.
Moukden, see Mukden .   mook-dĕn'.
Moulin Rouge . . .   moo-lăṅ' roozh. [moo'-trĭ.
Moultrie . . . . . .   mōl'-trĭ, mool'-trĭ,
Mounet Sully . . . .   moo-nä' sü-lē'.
Mount Blanc, see Mont
   Blanc . . . . . .   mownt blăngk.

Mount Desert . . . . mownt dĕ-zẽrt'

Mouquet . . . . . . mōō-kā'.

Mousqueton . . . . . mōōsk=ŭ=tôṅ'.

Moussorgsky . . . . . mōō-sôrg'-skĭ.

Mousul, see Mossoul . . mōō'-sŭl.

Mouton . . . . . . mōō-tôṅ'.

Mowbray . . . . . . mō'-brā.

Mozambique . . . . . mō-zăm-bēk'.

Mozarab . . . . . . mōz-âr'-ăb, mō-zä'-răb.

Mozart . . . . . . mō'-zärt. *Ger.* mō'-tsärt.

Mozuffergurh, see Mu-

  zaffargarh . . . . . mŭz-ŭf-ȧr-gōōr'.

Mozuffernugger, see Mu-

  zaffarnagar . . . . mŏz-ŭf-ẽr-nŭg'-gẽr.

Mozufferpore, see Muzaff-

  arpur . . . . . . mŏs-ŭf-ẽr-pōr'.

Msta . . . . mstä.

Mtesa . . . . mtā'-sä.

Mucha, Alphonse . . . mōōċh'-ȧ.

Mudie . . . . mōō'-dē.

Mudki, see Moodkee . . mōōd'-kē.

Muette de Portici, La . . lä mü-ĕt' dŭ pōr'-tē-chē.

Mughals, see Moguls . . mōō'-gȧlz.

Mühlbach . . . . . . mül'-bäċh.

Mühlhausen . . . . . mül'-how-zĕn.

Muir . . . . mūr.

Mukden, see Moukden . mōōk-dĕn'.

Müller (Max) . . . . mül'-ĕr.

Multan, see Mooltan . . mōōl-tän'. [mōōn'-kä-chē.

Muncaczy, see Munkácsy mōōn-kä'-chē,

Münchausen, see Münch-

  hausen . . . . . . *Eng.* mŭn-chô'-zĕn.

                 Ger. münċh-how'-zĕn.

München, see Munich . mün'-ċhĕn.

Münchhausen, see Mün-

  chausen . . . . . . *Eng.* mŭn-chô'-zĕn.

                 Ger. münċh-how'-zĕn.

Mungir, see Monghir . . mŭn-gēr'.
Munich, see München . mū'-nĭk.
Munkácsy, see Muncaczy moōn-kä'-chē,
moōn'-kä-chē.
Muñoz . . . . moōn-yōth'.
Münster . . . . . . mün'-ster.
Murad . . . . moō'-räd.
Muradabad, see Morada-
bad . . . . moō''-räd-ä-bäd'.
Murano . . . . . . moō-rä'-nō.
Murat . . . . mū-răt'. *Fr.* mü-rä'.
Muratore, Lucien . . . lü·ɑō ŏn' mü-rà-tōr'.
Muratori . . . . . . moō-rä-tō'-rē.
Muravieff . . . . . . moō-rä-vē=ĕf'.
Murcia . . . . mēr'-shĭ-à.
Sp. moōr'-thē-ä.
Murfreesboro, or Mur-
freesborough . . . . mēr'-frēz-bŭr''-ō.
Murger . . . . mür-zhâr'.
Murillo . . . . mū-rĭl'-ō. *Sp.* moō-rēl'-yō.
Muroy Salazar . . . . moō'-rō-ē sä-lä-thär'.
Murshidabad, see Moor-
shedabad . . . . . moōr''-shĭ-dä-bäd'.
Muscovite . . . . . . mŭs'-kō-vīt.
Muscovy . . . . . . mŭs'-kō-vĭ.
Musée des Thermes . . mü-zā dā târm'.
Musée du Louvre . . . mü-zā' dü loōvr'.
Musée du Luxembourg . mü-zā' dü lük-sŏn-boōr'.
Muskingum . . . . . mŭs-kĭng'-gŭm.
Musset . . . . müs-ā'.
Mussulman . . . . . mŭs'-sŭl-mán.
Mustafa, or Mustapha . moōs'-tä-fä.
Mustapha Kemal . . . moōs'-tä-fä kä-mäl'.
Mutra . . . . mŭt'-rä.
Mutsuhito . . . . . . moōt'-soōsh-tō.
Muzaffargarh, see Mozuff-
ergurh . . . . . . mŭz-ăf-ȧr-gär'.

Muzaffarnagar, see Mo-
zuffernugger . . . .   mŭz-ăf-ȧr-năg'-är.
Muzaffarpur, see Mozuff-
erpore . . . . .   mŭz-ăf-ȧr-pōōr'.
Muziano . . . . . .   mōōd-zē-ä'-nō.
Mycale . . . . . .   mĭk'-ā-lē.
Mycenæ . . . . . .   mī-sē'-nē, mĭ-kĕn'-ĭ.
Mymensing, see Mai-
mansinh . . . .   mī-mĕn-sĭng'.
Mynpuri, see Mainpuri .   mīn-pōō'-rē.
Myrmidons . . . .   mēr'-mĭ-dŏnz.
Myron . . . . . .   mī'-rŏn.
Mysia . . . . . .   mĭsh'-ĭ=ä.
Mysore, see Maisur . .   mī-sōr'.
Mytilene, see Mitylene .   mĭt-ĭ-lē'-nē.

N

Naaman . . . . . .   nä'-ȧ-màn.
Naauw Poort . . . . .   nä'=üv-pōrt.
Nabonidus . . . . .   năb-ō-nī'-dŭs.
Nadelman, Elie . . . .   ĕl-yĕ' nä'-dĕl-män.
Nadir Shah . . . . .   nä'-dĕr shä.
Nadiya, see Nuddea . .   nŭd'-ē-yä.
Nador . . . . . .   nä-dōr'.
Nagasaki, see Nangasaki   nä-gä-sä'-kē.
Nägeli . . . .   nȧ'-gĕ-lē.
Nagny-Várad . . . . .   nŏd'-yŭ-vä-räd.
Nagoya . . . . . .   nä-gō'-yä.
Nagpore, or . . . . .   näg-pōr'.
Nagpur . . . . . .   näg-pōōr'.
Nahant . . . . . .   nȧ-hänt', nȧ-hănt'.
Naiad . . . . . .   nä'-yȧd.
Nain . . . . . .   nä'-ĭn.
Nájara . . . . . .   nä'-ċhä-rä.
Nájera, Gutiérrez . . .   gōō-tē-ĕr'-ĕs näċh'-ä-rȧ.
Namaqualand . . . .   nä-mä'-kwä-länd.

Namur . . . . nā'-mōōr. *Fr.* nä-mür'.
Nana . . . . nä-nä'.
Nana Sahib . . . . . nä'-nä sä'-hĭb.
Nan-chang . . . . . nän-chäng'.
Nancy (France) . . . . năn'-sĭ. *Fr.* näṅ-sē'.
Nangasaki, see Nagasaki nän-gä-sä'-kē.
Nanking . . . . . . nän-kĭng'.
Nansen . . . . nän'-sĕn.
Nantes . . . . nănts. *Fr.* näṅt.
Nanteuil . . . . . . näṅ-tē'-yŭ.
Naomi . . . . . . ⁣ . nā-ō'-mī, nā'-ō-mē.
Naonabu . . . . . . nä'-ō' nō'-bë'.
Naphtali . . . . . . năf'-tȧ-lī, năf'-tä-lī.
Napier . . . . nā'-pĭ-ēr.
Napoleon . . . . . . nȧ-pō'-lē-ŏn.
Napoléon . . . . . . *Fr.* nä-pō-lä-ôṅ'.
Napoleone . . . . . . nä-pō-lä-ō'-nä.
Napravnik . . . . . . nä-präv'-nĭk.
Narbada, see Nerbudda . när-bä'-dä.
Narciso Lopez . . . . när-thē'-sō lō'-pĕs, *or*
                    lō'-pĕth.
Narcissus . . . . . . när-sĭs'-ŭs.
Narvaez . . . . . . när-bä'-ĕth.
Naseby . . . . nāz'-bĭ.
Nasik, see Nassick . . . nä'-sĭk.
Nasmyth . . . . . . nā'-smith.
Nasr-ed-Din, see Nassr-
  ed-Din . . . . . . näs'=r-ĕd-dēn'. [nä-sō'.
Nassau . . . . năs'-ô. *Ger.* näs'-ow. *Fr.*
Nassau (Is.) . . . . . năs'-ô.
Nassick, see Nasik . . . nä'-sĭk.
Nassr-ed-Din, see Nasr-
  ed-Din . . . . . . näs'=r-ĕd-dēn'.
Natal . . . . nȧ-tăl'. *Port.* nä-täl'.
Natalie, see Nathalie . . năt'-ȧ-lē. *Fr.* nä-tä-lē'.
Natchitoches . . . . . năk-ē-tŏsh',
                    năch-ĭ-tŏch'-ĕs.

Nathalie, see Natalie . . nǎth'-ȧ-lē.
National Zeitung . . . nät"-zē-ō-näl' tzī'-tŏŏng.
Naucydes . . . . . . nô-sī'-dēz.
Nauplia . . . . . . nô'-plĭ-ȧ.
Nausicaa . . . . . . nô-sĭk'-ā-ä, nô-sĭ-kā'-ä.
Nautch . . . . nôch.
Navajo . . . . nǎv'-ȧ-'hō.
Navarete, see Navarrette nä-vär-rā'-tä.
Navarino . . . . . . nä-vär-rę̄'-nō.
Navarra, Sp., or . . . . nä-vär'-rä.
Navarre . . . . . . nȧ-vär'. Fr. nä-vär'.
Navarrette, see Navarete nä-vär-rā'-tä.
Navarro . . . . . . nä-vär'-rō.
Nazarene . . . . . . nǎz-ȧ-rēn', nǎz'-ā-rēn.
Nazarite . . . . . . nǎz'-ȧ-rīt.
Naze . . . . Eng. nāz. Norw. nä'-zě.
Nazianzen . . . . . . nä"-zĭ-ǎn'-zěn.
Nazimof . . . . . . nä-zē'-mǒf.
Nazimova . . . . . . nä-zē'-mō-vä.
Nebuchadnezzar, or . . něb"-ū-kǎd-něz'-är.
Nebuchadrezzar . . . . něb"-ū-kǎd-rěz'-är.
Nebushazban . . . . něb-ū-shǎz'-bǎn.
Neckar (R.) . . . . . něk'-kär.
Necker (Jacques) . . . něk'-ēr. Fr. nā-kâr'.
Neerwinden . . . . . når'-vĭn-děn.
Negri, Ada . . . . . ä'-dä' nä'-grē.
Négrier . . . . nä-grē=ä'.
Negritos . . . . . . ně-grē'-tōs.
            Sp. nä-grē'-tōs.
Negropont . . . . . . něg'-rō-pǒnt.
Negros (Philippine I.) . . nä'-grōs.
Nekrasoff, or Nekrassoff . něk-rǎ'-sǒf.
Nellore, or . . . . . ně-lōr'.
Nellur . . . . ně-lōōr'.
Nemea (City) . . . nē'-mē-ȧ, ně-mē'-ȧ.
Nemea (Games) . . . ně-mē'-ȧ, nē'-mē-ȧ,
            něm'-ē-ȧ.

Nemean . . . . ně-mē'-àn, nē'-mē-àn.
Nemesis . . . . něm'-ě-sĭs.
Némours . . . . nā-mōōr'.
Neoptolemus . . . . nē-ŏp-tŏl'-ē-mŭs.
Nepal, or Nepaul, see Nipal ně-pôl'.
Nepissing, see Nipissing . něp'-ĭs-ĭng.
Nepomuk . . . . . . nā'-pō-mōōk.
Nepos . . . . nē'-pŏs.
Neptune . . . . . . něp'-tūn.
Nerbudda, or Nerbuddah,
    see Narbada . . . . něr-bŭd'-dä.
Nereids . . . . nē'-rē-ĭdz.
Nereus. . . . . nē'-rē-ŭs, nē'-rūs.
Nergalsharezer . . . . něr"-gäl-shă-rē'-zěr.
Neri . . . . nā'-rē.
Nerissa . . . . nē-rĭs'-sä.
Néron . . . . nā-rŏn'.
Néry . . . . nā-rē'.
Nesle . . . . nāl.
Neuchâtel. . . . . . ně-shä-těl'.
Neueste Nachrichten . . noi'-ěs-tŭ näċh'-rĭċh-těn.
Neuilly-sur-Seine . . . nē-yē"-sür-sěn'.
Neumann . . . . . . nū'-màn. Ger. noĭ'-män.
Neuss . . . . nois.
Neuve Chapelle . . . . něv shă-pěl'.
Neuvillette, Christian de . krĭs-tō̄=än' dŭ ně-věl-ět'.
Neuwied . . . . noĭ'-vēt.
Neva . . . . nē'-và. Russ. nyě'-vä.
Nevada. . . . . ně-vä'-dä.
Nevers . . . . ně-vâr'.
Nevis . . . . něv'-ĭs.
Nevskii Prospekt . . . něf'-skĭ=ĭ prŏs-pěkt'.
New-Chwang, see Niu-
    chuang . . . . . . nū-chwäng'.
Newfoundland . . . . *pop.* nū-fownd'-lànd,
                     loc. nū'-fŭnd-lănd,
                     nū-fŭnd-lănd'.

Newnham . . . . . . nūn'-ȧm.
New Orleans . . . . . nū ôr'-lē-ȧnz.
                  loc. nū ōr-lā-äṅ'.
Nexö . . . . nĕks'-ē.
Ney . . . . nā.
Nez Percé . . . . . . nā pĕr-sā'.
Ngan-hui, see Anhwei . . n-gän-hwē'.
Niam-Niam, see Nyam-
  Nyam . . . . . nĭ=ăm'-nĭ=ăm'.
Niassa, see Nyassa . . nē=äs'-sä.
Nibelungenlied, or Nibe-
  lungen Lied . . . . nē'-bĕ-lōŏng"-ĕn-lēt.
Nicæa . . . . . . nĭ-sē'-ä.
Nicaragua . . . . . . nĭk-ȧr-ä'-gwä.
                Sp. nē-kä-rä'-gwä.
Niccola Pisano, see Nicola nēk'-ō-lä pē-zä'-nō.
Niccolini . . . . . . nēk-kō-lē'-nē.
Niccolò, see Nicolò . . nē-kō-lō'.
Nice . . . . nēs.
Nicene . . . . nĭ'-sēn.
Nicias . . . . nĭs'-ĭ-ȧs, nĭsh'-ĭ-ȧs.
Nicola, Niccola . . . . *It.* nē-kō'-lä.
Nicolai . . . . nē'-kō-lī.
Nicolette . . . . . . nē-kō-lĕt.'
Nicolò de' Lapi, see Niccolò nē-kō-lō' dā lä'-pē.
Nicot . . . . nē-kō'.
Nictheroy, see Nitherohi . nē-tä-rō'-ē.
Niebuhr . . . . . . nē'-bōōr.
Niemen . . . . . . nē'-mĕn. *Pol.* nyĕm'-ĕn.
Niepce . . . . nyĕps.
Nietzsche . . . . . . nēt'-shŭ.
Nieuport, see Nieuwport . nē=ê-pōr'.
Nieuwe Kerke . . . . nē-êv'-ĕ kĕrk'-ĕ.
Nieuwport, see Nieuport . nē=êv'-pōrt.
Nieuwveld . . . . . nē=êv'-fĕlt.
Nièvre . . . . nē-ĕvr'.
Niflheim . . . . . . nĕf'-l-hīm.

Nigel	nī'-jĕl.
Niger	nī'-jēr.
Nigra	nē'-grä.
Niigata	nē-ē-gä'-tä.
Nijni-Novgorod, or Nij-niy-Novgorod, see Nizhni-Novgorod . . .	nēsh'-nĭ-nŏv'-gŏ-rŏd.
Nike Apteros	nī'-kē ăp'-tĕ-rŏs.
Nikisch	nē'-kĭsh.
Nikita	nē-kē'-tä.
Nikko	nēk'-kō.
Nikola	nē'-kō-lä.
Nilsson (Christine) . . .	nĭl'-sŏn.
Nimar	nē-mär'.
Nimeguen, see Nimwegen	nĭm'-ā-gĕn.
Nîmes, see Nimes . . .	nēm.
Nimwegen, see Nimeguen and Nymegen	nĭm'-wā-gĕn.
Niña, La	lä nēn'-yä.
Nineveh	nĭn'-ĕ-vŭ.
Ningpo, or	nĭng'-pō'.
Ningpo-fu	nĭng'-pō'-fōō'.
Niño	nēn'-yō.
Ninon de Lenclos, or L'En-clos	nē-nôṅ' dŭ lŏṅ-klō'.
Niobe	nī'-ō-bē.
Nipal, see Nepal . . .	nĭ-pôl'.
Niphon, see Nipon . . .	nĭf-ŏn'.
Nipissing, see Nepissing .	nĭp'-ĭs-sĭng.
Nipon, or	nĭp-ŏn'.
Nippon, see Niphon . .	nĭp-ŏn'.
Nirvana	nĭr-vä'-nä.
Nisan	nī'-săn.
Nisard	nē-zär'.
Nisch, or Nish, see Nissa	nēsh.
Nismes, see Nîmes . .	nēm.
Nissa, see Nisch . . .	nēs'-sä.

Nitherohi, see Nictheroy . nē-tā-rō'-ē.
Nitocris . . . . . . nĭ-to'-krĭs.
Nitti . . . . nēt'-tē.
Niu-chuang, see New-
    Chwang . . . . . nū-chwăṅ'.
Nivelle . . . . . . nē-věl'.
Nivernais . . . . . nē-věr-ně'.
Nivernaise . . . . nē-věr-něz'.
Nivôse . . . . . . nē-vŏz'.
Nizam . . . . . . nĭ-zăm', nī'-zăm.
Nizhni-Novgorod, see Nij-
    ni-Novgorod . . . nēzh'-nĭ-nŏv'-gŏ-rŏd.
Noachian . . . . . nō-ā'-kĭ-àn.
Noacolly, see Noakhali . nō-ă-kŏl'-ĭ.
Noailles . . . . . nō-ĭ', nō-ä'=yŭ.
Noakhali, see Noacolly . nō-äk-hä'-lē.
Nobel . . . . . . nō-běl'.
Noctes Ambrosianae . . nŏk'-tēz ămbrō"-zĭ-ā'-nē.
Nodier . . . . . . nō-dē=ā'.
Noël . . . . nō-ěl'.
Nogi . . . . nō'-gē'.
Noir Fainéant . . . nwär fā-nā-äṅ'.
Noli me tangere . . . nō'-lī mē tăn'-jě-rē.
Noll . . . . nŏl.
Nombre de Dios . . . nŏm'-brā dā dē'-ōs.
Nome . . . . . . nōm.
Nord . . . . . . *Fr.* nōr.
Nordau . . . . . . nōr'-dow.
Nordenskjöld . . . . nōō'-děn-shēlt.
Nordica . . . . . nôr'-dĭ-kä.
Nördlingen . . . . nērd'-lĭng-ěn.
Norn . . . . . . nôrn.
Northanger (Abbey) . . nôrth'-ān-jěr.
Norumbega . . . . nō-rŭm-bē'-gä.
Norwich . . . . . *Eng.* nŏr'-ĭch, nŏr'-ĭj.
                    Am. nôr'-wĭch.
Nôtre Dame . . . . nō'-tr dăm.

Nottingham . . . . . nŏt'-ĭng-àm.
Nourmahal . . . . . noōr-mà-häl'.
Novaes, Guiomar . . . gē-ō'-mär nō-vä'-ĕs.
Novalis . . . . . . nō-vä-'lĭs.
Novara . . . . . . nō-vä'-rä.
Nova Scotia . . . . nō'-và skō'-shĭ=à.
Novaya Zemlya, or . . Russ., nō'-vä-yä zĕm-lĭ=ä'.
Nova Zembla . . . . nō'-và zĕm'-blà.
Novgorod . . . . . nŏv'-gŏ-rŏd.
Novikoff . . . . . nŏv'-ĭ-kŏf.
Novó Bazar . . , , . nō-'vō' bä-zär'.
Novo Georgievsk . . . nō-vō' gē-ôr'-gē-efsk.
Nowanagar, or . . . . nō"-wä-nä-gär'.
Nowanuggur . . . . nō"-wä-nŭ-gŭr'.
Noyes . . . . . . noiz.
Noyon . . . . . . nwä-yōṅ'.
Nozze di Figaro, Le . . lā nŏt'-sĕ dē fē'-gä-rō.
Nuchingen, La Maison . lä mā-zôṅ' nü-säṅ-zhôṅ'.
Nuddea, see Nadiya . . nŭd'-ē-ä.
Nueva Andalucía . . . noō=ā'-vä
                        än"-dä-loō-thē'-ä.
Nueva Ecija . . . . . noō=ā'-vä ā'-thē-ćhä.
Nueva Galicia . . . . noō=ā'-vä gä-lē'-thē-ä.
Nueva Vizcaya . . . . noō='-vä bēth-kī'-ä.
Nuevitas . . . . . . noō=ā"-vē-täs'.
Nuevo Leon . . . . . noō=ā'-vō lā-ōn'.
Nuggur . . . . . . nŭg'-ŭr.
Nunce Dimittis . . . noŏnk dĭ-mĭt'tĭs.
Nundydroog . . . . . nŭn-dĭ-drōōg'.
Nuneaton . . . . . nŭn'-ē-tŭn.
Nuñez . . . . . . noōn'-yĕth.
Nuova Antologia . . . noō=ō'-vä än-tō-lō'-jä.
Nu-Pieds, Nu-pieds . . nü-pē-ā'.
Nyam-Nyam . . . . . n-yäm'-n-yäm'.
Nyanza . . . . . . n-yăn'-zä.
Nyassa, see Niassa . . nē=äs'-sä.
Nyassaland . . . . . nē=äs'-ä-lănd.

Nydia . . . . nĭd'-ĭ-ä.
Nyland . . . . nü'-länd.
Nymegan, see Nimwegen   nĭm'-ā-gĕn.
Nyoro . . . . n-yō'-rō.
Nystad . . . . nü'-städ.

O

Oahu . . . . ō-ä'-hoō, wä'-hoō.
Ob, see Obi . . . . . ŏb.
Obeid, El . . . . . . ĕl ō-bād', ĕl ō-bā'-ēd.
Ober Ammergau . . . ō'-bĕr äm'-mĕr-gow.
Oberland . . . . . . ō'-bĕr-länt.
Obermann. . . . . . ō-bĕr-män'.
Oberon . . . . ō'-bĕ-rŏn, ŏb'-ēr-ŏn.
Oberpfalz . . . . . . ō'-bĕr-pfälts.
Obi, see Ob . . . . . ō'-bē.
Obidicut . . . . . . ō-bĭd'-ĭ-cŭt.
Obispo, Calle . . . . käl'-yā ō-bĭs'-pō.
Obiter dicta . . . . . ō'-bĭ-tēr dĭk'-tä.
Obregon . . . . . . ō-brā-gōn'.
Obrenovitch . . . . . ō-brĕn'-ō-vĭch.
Ocaña . . . . ō-kän'-yä.
Ocantos . . . . . . ō-kän'-tōs.
Oceana . . . . ō-sē'-ȧ-nä, ō-shē-ä'-nȧ,
                       ō-shē-ä'-nȧ.
Oceania, or . . . . . ō-sē-ä'-nĭ-ȧ, ō-shē-ä'-nĭ-ȧ.
Oceanica . . . . . . ō-sē-ăn'-ĭ-kȧ,
                       ō-shē-ăn'-ĭk-ȧ.
Oceanides . . . . . . ō-sē-ăn'-ĭ-dēz.
Oceanus . . . . . . ō-sē'-ȧ-nŭs.
Ochiltree . . . . . . ōċh'-l-trē.
Ochoa y Acuña . . . . ō-chō'-ȧ ē ä-koōn'-yȧ.
Ocklawaha . . . . . ŏk-lä-wä'-hä.
Oconomowoc . . . . . ō-kō-nŏm'-ō-wŏk.
Octavian . . . . . . ŏk-tā'-vĭ-ȧn.
Odelsthing . . . . . ō'-dĕlz-tĭng.

Odéon . . . . ō-dē'-ŏn. *Fr.* ō-dā-ôṅ'.

Odessa . . . . ō-dĕs'-ä.

Odoacer, see Ottokar, or . ō-dō-ā'-sēr.

Odovaker . . . . . . ō-dō-vä'-kär.

Odysseus . . . . . . ō-dĭs'-ē-ŭs, ō-dĭs'-sūs.

Odyssey . . . . . . ŏd'-ĭs-ē.

Œdipe . . . . *Fr.* ē-dēp'.

Œdipus Coloneus . . . ĕd'-ĭ-pŭs kō-lō-nē'-ŭs,
       kō-lō'-nūs.

Œdipus Tyrannus . . . ĕd'-ĭ-pŭs tĭr-ăn'-ŭs.

Oehlenschläger, see Öhlenschläger . . . . . ē'-lĕn-shlā″-gĕr.

Oenone . . . . . . ĕ-nō'-nĕ.

Oersted, see Örsted . . ēr'-stĕd.

Oesterreich, see Österreich ēs'-tĕr-rīćh.

Offenbach, Jacques . . zhäk ŏf-ĕn-bäk'.
       Ger. ŏf-ĕn-bäćh'.

Ofterdingen . . . . . ŏf'-tĕr-dĭng″-ĕn.

Oggione, see Uggione . . ōj-jō'-nĕ.

Ogier . . . . ō'-jĭ-ēr.

Ogier de Danemarcke . . ō-zhē=ā' dŭ dăn-märk'.

Ogier le Danois . . . . ō-zhē=ä' lĕ dä-nwä'.

Ogoway, or Ogowé . . . ō-gō-wā'.

O'Higgins . . . . . . ō-hĭg'-ĭnz. *Sp.* ō-ē'-gēns.

Öhlenschläger, see Oehlenschläger . . . . . . ē'-lĕn-shlā″-gĕr.

Ohnet, Georges . . . . zhŏrzh zō-nā'.

Ohod, or . . . . . . ō-hŏd'.

Ohud . . . . ō-hōōd'.

Oileus . . . . ō-ĭl'-ē-ŭs, ō-ī'-lūs.

Oise . . . . wäz.

Ojeda . . . . ō-ćhā'-dä.

Ojetti . . . . ō-yāt'-tē.

Okayama . . . . . . ō'-kä'-yä'-mä'.

Okefinokee . . . . . ō″-kē-fī-nō'-kē.

Okhotsk Sea . . . . . ō-ćhtōsk', ō-hōtsk'.

Okinawa . . . . . . ō-kē-nä'-wä.

Oklahoma	ŏk-lä-hō′-mä.
Okuma	ō′-kōō′-mä′.
Okumura	ō′-kōō′-mōō′-rä′.
Olaf	ō′-läf.
Olaus (St.)	ō-lā′-ŭs.
Oldenbarneveldt, van . .	fän ōl″-dĕn-bär′-nĕ-vĕlt.
Ole	ō′-lā.
Oléron	ō-lā-rŏṅ′.
Olifaunt	ŏl′-ĭ-fȧnt.
Oliphant	ŏl′-ĭ-fȧnt.
Olitzka	ō′-lĭts-kä.
Oliva (Peace of)	ō-lē′-fä.
Olivarez	ō-lē-vä′-rĕth.
Olivia	ō-lĭv′-ĭ-ä.
Ollivier, Émile	ā-mēl′ ō-lē-vē=ā′.
Olmütz	ŏl′-mütz.
Olympe	*Fr.* ō-lăṅp′.
Olympiad	ō-lĭm′-pĭ-ăd.
Olympus	ō-lĭm′-pŭs.
Omaha	ō′-mȧ-hä.
Oman	ō-män′.
Omar Khayyam, see Umar Khaiyâm	ō′-mär khī-yäm′.
Omar Pasha, see Omer Pasha	ō′-mär păsh-ô′, pȧ-shä′, päsh′-ȧ.
Omega	ō′-mĕg-ä, ō-mĕg′-ȧ.
Omer Pasha, see Omar Pasha	ō-mēr pash-ô′, pȧ-shä′, päsh′-ȧ.
Omeyyades, see Ommiads	ō-mā′-yădz.
Ommaya	ŏm-mā′-yä.
Ommiads, see Omeyyades	ō-mī′-ădz.
Omphale	ŏm′-fȧ-lē.
Omsk	ŏmsk.
Oñate	ōn-yä′-tā.
Onega (L.)	ō-nē′-gȧ. *Russ.* ōn-yĕ′-gä.

Oneida	ō-nī′-dä.
Onesimus	ō-nĕs′-ĭ-mŭs.
Onesiphorus	ō-nē″-sĭf′-ō-rŭs.
Ongaro, Dall' . . .	däl ōng′-gä-rō.
Onias	ō-nī′-as.
Onions (Oliver) . . .	ō-nī′-ŭnz.
Onondaga	ŏn-ŏn-dô′-gȧ.
Oodeypoor, see Udaipur .	ōō-dī-pōōr′.
Oonalaska, see Unalaska	ōō-nȧ-lăs′-kȧ.
Ophelia	ō-fē′-lĭ-ȧ, ō-fēl′-yȧ.
Ophir	ō′-fēr.
Ophiucus	ō-fī-yū′-kŭs, ŏf-ĭ-ū′-kŭs.
Opie	ō′-pĭ.
Opigena	ō-pĭj′-ē-nȧ.
Oporto, Port, o. Porto . .	ō-pōr′-tō.
	Port. ōō-pōr′-tōō.
Oppenheim	ŏp′-ĕn-hīm.
Ops	ŏps.
Oran	ō-rän′. *Fr.* ō-räṅ′.
Orcagna	ōr-kän′-yä.
Oread	ō′-rē-ăd.
Orel	ō-rĕl′.
Orellana	ō-rāl-yä′-nä.
Orense	ō-rĕn′-sā.
Orestes	ō-rĕs′-tēz.
Orfeo ed Euridice . . .	ŏr-fā′-ō ĕd ā=ōō-rē-dē′-chĕ.
Oriana	ō-rĭ-ȧn′-ȧ.
Origen, or	ŏr′-ĭ-jĕn.
Origenes	ō-rĭj′-ē-nēz.
Orinoco	ō-rĭ-nō′-kō.
Orion	ō-rī′-ŏn.
Orissa	ō-rĭs′-ä.
Orizaba	ō-rē-thä′-bä.
Orlando	ôr-lăn′-dō. *It.* ōr-län′-dō.
Orlando Furioso . . .	ŏr-län′-dō fōō-rē-ō′-sō.
Orlando Innamorato . .	ŏr-län′-dō
	ēn-nä″-mō-rä′-to.

Orléanais, see Orléannais   ôr-lā-ä-nĕ'.
Orleanists . . . . . .   ôr'-lē-àn-ĭsts".
Orléannais, see Orléanais   ôr-lā-ä-nĕ'.
Orléans (Maid of) . . .   ôr'-lē-ànz. *Fr.* ôr-lā-äṅ'.
Orloff . . . .   ŏr-lŏf'.
Ormulum . . . . . .   ôr'-mū-lŭm.
Ormuzd . . . . . .   ôr'-mŭzd, ôr'-mŏŏzd.
Orne . . . .   ôrn.
Oronte . . . .   ō-rôṅt'.
Orontes . . . . . .   ō-rŏn'-tēz.
Orphée et Euridice . .   ôr-fā' ā ē-rē-dēs'.
Orphéon . . . . . .   ôr-fā-ôṅ'.
Orpheus . . . . . .   ôr'-fē-ŭs, ôr'-fūs.
Or San Michele . . . .   ōr sän mē-kā'-lā.
Orsay . . . .   ŏr-sā'.
Orsini . . . .   ōr-sē'-nē.
Orsino . . . .   ôr-sē'-nō. *It.* ōr-sē'-nō.
Orsova . . . .   ōr'-shō-và.
Örsted, see Oersted . .   ēr'-stĕd.
Ortega . . . .   ōr-tā'-gä.
Orthez, see D'Orthez . .   ōr-tĕss', ŏr-tĕz'.
Ortrud . . . .   ōr'-trōōt.
Oruba . . . .   ō-rōō'-bä.
Orvieto . . . .   ōr-vē=ā'-tō.
Osage . . . .   ō-sāj', ō'-sāj. *Fr.* ō-zäzh'.
Osaka, see Ozaka . .   ō-sä'-kä.
Osbaldistone . . . . .   ŏs-bôl'-dĭs-tŭn.
Osceola . . . . . .   ŏs-ē-ō'-lä.
Osiris . . . .   ō-sī'-rĭs.
Osman Digna . . . .   ŏs'-măn dĭg'-nä.
Osmanli . . . . . .   ŏs-măn'-lĭ.
Osnabrück . . . . .   ŏs'-nä-brük.
Ospedale degli Innocenti .   ōs-pā-dä'-lĕ dāl'-yē
                               ēn-nō-shān'-tē.
Osrick . . . .   ŏz'-rĭk.
Ossa . . . .   ŏs'-à.
Osserwatore Romano . .   ōs"-sĕr-vä-tō'-rä rō-mä'-nō.

Ossian	ŏsh'-àn, ŏsh'-ē=àn
Ossoli	ōs'-sō-lē.
Ostade	ŏs'-tä-dĕ.
Ostend	ŏs-tĕnd'.
Osterode (in Harz) . .	ŏs'-tĕ-rō''-dŭ.
Österreich, see Oesterreich	ēs'-tĕr-rīċh.
Ostrogoths	ŏs'-trō-gŏths.
Otaheite, or Otaheiti . .	ō-tä-hē'-tē.
Othello	ō-thĕl'-ō.
Othman	ŏth-män'.
Otho	ō'-thō.
Otranto	ō-trän'-tō.
Otricoli	ō-trē'-kŏ-lē.
Ottawa (Canada) . . .	ŏt'-à-wä.
Ottawa (Ohio)	ŏt'-à-wä.
Ottilie	ŏt'-tēl-yŭ.
Otto	ŏt'-tō.
Ottokar, see Odoacer . .	ŏt'-tō-kär.
Oude, see Oudh, Audh .	owd.
Oudenaarde, or Ouden- arde, see Audenarde .	ow'-dĕn-är''-dĕ.
Oudh, see Oude, Audh .	owd.
Oudinot	ōō-dē-nō'.
Ouida	ōō—ē'-dä, wē'-dä
Ourcq	ōōrk.
Ouse	ōōz.
Outram	ōō'-tràm.
Ovalle (Alfonso) de . .	dä ō-väl'-yä.
Overijssel, or Overyssel .	ō'-vĕr-īs''-sĕl.
Ovid	ŏv'-ĭd.
Oviedo	ō-vē-ā'-dō.
Owhyhee, or Owyhee . .	ō-wī'-hē.
Oxenstiern, or	ŏks'-ĕn-stērn.
Oxenstierna, or Oxen- stjerna, Sw.	ŏks'-ĕn-shâr''-nä.
Oxon	ŏks'-ŭn.
Oxonian	ŏks-ō'-nĭ=àn.

Oyama . . . . ō-yä′-mä.
Oyer . . . . ō′-yẽr.
Ozaka, see Osaka . . . ō-zä′-kä.
Ozaki . . . . ō′-zä′-kē′.
Ozias . . . . ō-zǐ′-ȧs.

P

Paardeberg . . . . . pär′-dĕ-bĕrċh.
Pablo . . . . *Sp.* päb′-lō.
Pabna . . . . päb′-nä.
Pacchiarotto . . . . . päk″-kē-är-ōt′-tō.
Pacha, see Pasha . . . pȧsh-ô′, pȧ-shä′, päsh′-ȧ.
Pacheco . . . . . . pä-chä′-kō.
Pachmann . . . . . . päċh′-män.
Pachuca . . . . . . pä-cho͞o′-kä.
Pactolus . . . . . . pǎk-tō′-lŭs.
Padan-aram . . . . . pä-dȧn-âr′-ȧm.
Paderewski . . . . . pä-dä-rĕv′-skē.
Padilla, Juan Lopez de . ċho͞o=än′ lō′-päth dä
pä-dēl′-yä.
Padishah . . . . . . pä-dē-shä′.
Padoue, *Fr.*, or . . . . pä-do͞o′.
Padova, *It.*, or . . . . pä′-dō-vä.
Padua . . . . pǎd′-yū-ȧ.
Paedobaptist, see Pedo-
baptist . . . . . . pē-dō-bǎp′-tǐst.
Paesiello, see Paissiello . pä″=ä-zē=ĕl′-lō.
Paestum . . . . . . pĕs′-tŭm.
Páez . . . . pä′-ĕs.
Paganini . . . . . . pä-gȧ-nǐn′-i.
It. pä-gä-nē′-nē.
Paget . . . . pǎj′-ĕt. *Fr.* pä-zhä′.
Pagliacci, I. . . . . . ē päl-yä′-chē.
Pago-Pago, see Pango-
Pango . . . . . . pän′-gō-pän′-gō.
Pailleron . . . . . . pä-yē-rôṅ′.

Painlevé . . . . . . păṅ-lē-vā'.
Paissiello, see Paesiello . pä"=ē-zē=āl'-lō.
Paiwar, see Peiwar . . pī-wär'.
Paix des Dames . . . pā dā dăm'.
Pajou . . . . pä-zhōō'.
Pakenham . . . . . păk'-ĕn-àm.
Pakhoi, see Peihai . . . päk-hoi'.
Pala d'Oro . . . . . pä'-lă dō'-rō.
Palaemon . . . . . . pà-lē'-mŏn, pă-lē'-mŏn.
Palaeologus . . . . . pā-lē-ŏl'-ō-gŭs.
Palais Bourbon . . . . pä-lä' bōōr-bôṅ'.
Palais de Justice . . . pä-lä' dē zhüs-tēs'.
Palais du Trocadéro . . pä-lä' dü trō-kä-dä-rō'.
Palais Royal . . . . . pä-lä' rwä-yăl'.
Palamedes . . . . . păl-ā-mē'-dēz.
Palamon and Arcite . . păl'-à-mŏn and är'-sīt.
Palaos . . . . pä-lä-ōs'.
Palatinate . . . . . . pă-lăt'-ĭ-nāt.
Palatine . . . . . . păl'-à-tīn, păl'-à-tĭn.
Palatinus . . . . . . păl-ā-tī'-nŭs.
Palau, see Pellew, Pelew pä-low'.
Paláwan . . . . . . pä-lä'-wän.
Palazzo Borghese . . . pä-lät'-sō bōr-gä'-zĕ.
Palazzo della Cancelleria pä-lät'-sō dĕl'-lä
                          kön" chĕl lā rō' ä.
Palazzo Doria . . . . pä-lät'-sō dō'-rĭ-ä.
Palazzo Farnese . . . . It. pä-lät'-sō fär-nā'-zĕ.
Palazzo Pandolfini . . . pä-lät'-sō pän-dōl-fē'-nē.
Palazzo Pitti . . . . . pä-lät'-sō pēt'-tē.
Palazzo Pubblico . . . pä-lät'-sō pŏŏb'-lē-kō.
Palazzo Reale . . . . pä-lät'-sō rā-ä'-lĕ.
Palazzo Vecchio . . . pä-lät'-sō vĕk'-kē-ō.
Palencia . . . . . . pä-lān'-thē-ä.
Palenque . . . . . . pä-lān'-kä.
Paleologus . . . . . pā-lē-ŏl'-ō-gŭs.
Palermo . . . . . . pà-lĕr'-mō. It. pä-lĕr'-mō.
Palestine . . . . . . păl'-ĕs-tīn.

Palestrina . . . . . . pä-lĕs-trē'-nä.
Palfrey . . . . . . pôl'-frĭ.
Palgrave . . . . . . pôl'-grāv.
Pali, see Pallee . . . . pä'-lē, pā'-lī.
Palikao . . . . pä-lē-kä'=ō.
Palinurus . . . . . . päl-ĭ-nū'-rŭs.
Palissy . . . . päl'-ĭs-ĭ. *Fr.* pä-lē-sē'.
Palitana . . . . . . pä-lē-tä'-nä.
Palladio . . . . . . päl-lä'-dē-ō.
Pallas . . . . päl'-ås.
Pallee, see Pali . . . pä'-lē.
Pall Mall . . . . . . pĕl mĕl.
Palma Giovine . . . . päl'-mä jō'-vē-nĕ.
Palma Vecchio . . . . päl'-mä vĕk'-kē-ō.
Palmerston . . . . . päm'-ēr-stŭn.
Palmyra . . . . . . päl-mī'-rå.
Palo Alto . . . . . . pä'-lō äl'-tō.
Palos . . . . pä-lōs', pä'-lōs.
Pameer, see Pamir . . pä-mēr'.
Pamela . . . . på-mē'-lå, päm'-ē-lå.
Pamir, see Pameer . . pä-mēr'.
Pamlico . . . . . . päm'-lĭ-kō.
Pampanga . . . . . . päm-pän'-gä.
Pampeluna, or . . . . päm-pä-lōō'-nä.
Pampelune, *Fr.*, or . . pŏṅp-lün'.
Pamplona . . . . . . päm-plō'-nä.
Panama . . . . pän-å-mä'. *Sp.* pä-nä-mä'.
Panathenæa . . . . . pän"-ăth-ē-nē'-å.
Panay . . . . pä-nä'=ē.
Panch Mahalz . . . . pånch må-hälz'.
Pandæan, see Pandean . pän-dē'-ån.
Pandarus . . . . . . pän'-då-rŭs.
Pandean, see Pandæan . pän-dē'-ån.
Pando . . . . pän'-dō.
Pandoor, see Pandour . pän-dōōr', pän'-dōōr.
Pandora . . . . . . pän-dō'-rä.
Pandour, see Pandoor . pän-dōōr', pän'-dōōr.

Pangani . . . . . . päng-gä′-nē.
Pangasinan . . . . . pän″-gä-sē-nän′.
Pango-Pango, see Pago-
   Pago . . . . . . pän′-gō-pän′-gō.
Panhard . . . . . . pän-är′.
Panizzi . . . . pä-nēt′-sē.
Panjab, see Punjab, Pen-
   jab . . . . pŭn-jäb′.
Panna, see Punnah . . pŭn′-ä.
Panslavic . . . . . . pän-släv′-ĭk.
Pantagruel . . . . . pän-tăg′-rōō-ĕl.
             Fr. pän-tä-grü-ĕl′.
Pantalon, or . . . . . pän′-tä-lŏn.
Pantalone . . . . . . pän-tä-lō′-nĕ.
Pantheon . . . . . . pän′-thē-ŏn, pän-thē′-ŏn.
Panthéon . . . . . . *Fr.* pän-tä-ôṅ′.
Panurge . . . . . . pän-ẽrj′. *Fr.* pä-nürzh′.
Panza, Sancho . . . . săn′-kō pän′-zä.
             Sp. sän′-chō pän′-thä.
Paola (Fra.) . . . . . pä′=ō-lä.
Paoli, di . . . . . . dē pä′=ō-lē.
Paolo Veronese . . . . pä′=ō-lō vä-rō-nä′-zĕ.
Pao-ting, see Pauting . . pä-ō-tĭng′.
Paphian . . . . . . pā′-fĭ-àn.
Paphos . . . . pā′-fŏs.
Papin . . . . pä-păṅ′.
Pappenheim . . . . . päp′-ĕn-hīm.
Papua . . . . păp′-ōō-à, pä′-pōō-à.
Pará . . . . pä-rä′.
Paracali, see Parakale . pä-rä-kä′-lē.
Paracelsus . . . . . păr-à-sĕl′-sŭs,
             păr-ā-sĕl′-sŭs.
Paraclet . . . . . . *Fr.* pä-rä-klĕ′.
Paraclete . . . . . . păr′-à-klēt.
Paradiso . . . . . . pä-rä-dē′-zō.
Paragoa . . . . . . pä-rä-gō′-ä.
Paragua . . . . . . pä-rä′-gwä.

Paraguay, or . . . . .   pär-à-gwī′, pä-rä-gwā′,
                    pär′-à-gwī.
Paraguaya, *Sp.* and *Port.*   pär-ä-gwī′-ä.
Parahiba, or Parahyba .   pä-rä-ē′-bä.
Parakale, see Paracali .   pä-rä-kä′-lä.
Paramaribo . . . . .   pär-à-mär′-ĭ-bō.
Paran . . . .   pā′-rȧn.
Paraná . . . .   pä-rä-nä′.
Parañaque . . . . .   pär-än-yä′-kä.
Parcae . . . .   pär′-sē, pär′-kē.
Parc-aux-Cerfs . . . .   pär-kō-sâr′.
Paré . . . .   pä-rä′.
Paredes . . . . . .   pä-rä′-dĕs.
Parepa-Rosa . . . . .   pä-rä′-pä-rō′-zä.
Paria . . . .   pä-rē-ä′, pä′-rē-ä.
Parian . . . .   pā′-rĭ-ȧn.
Paris . . . .   pär′-ĭs.   *Fr.* pär-ē′.
Paris, Comte de   . . .   kōṅt dŭ pär-ē′.
Parisian . . . . . .   pă-rĭz′-ĭ=ȧn, pā-rĭzh′-ȧn.
Parisien . . . . . .   pär-ēz-ē-ĕṅ′.
Parisienne . . . . .   pär-ēz-ē=ĕn′.
Parmegiano, see Parmigi-
   ano . . . .   pär-mä-jä′-nō.
Parmenides . . . . .   pär-mĕn′-ĭ-dēz.
Parmesan . . . . . .   pär-mē-zăn′.
Parmigiano, see Parme-
   giano . . . . . .   pär-mē-jä′-nō.
Parnassian . . . . .   pär-năs′-ĭ=ȧn.
Parnassus . . . . .   pär-năs′-ŭs.
Parnell . . . .   pär′-nĕl.
Parolles . . . . . .   pä-rŏl′-ĕs.
Paros . . . .   pā′-rŏs.
Parral . . . .   pär-räl′.
Parrhasius . . . . .   pă-rä′-shĭ=ŭs.
Parsee, or Parsi . . . .   pär′-sē.
Parsifal, or Parsival, see
   Ger. Parzival . . . .   pär′-sē-fäl.

Partabgarh, see Pertab-
gurh . . . . pŭr-täb-gŭr'.
Parthenon . . . . . . pär'-thĕ-nŏn.
Parthenope . . . . . pär-thĕn'-ō-pē.
Parthenopean . . . . pär-thĕn"-ō-pē'-án.
Parzival, see Parsifal . . pärt'-sē-fäl.
Pascal . . . . păs'-kăl. *Fr.* păs-kăl'.
Pasha, see Pacha . . . păsh-ô', pà-shä', päsh'-à.
Pasig . . . . pä-sēg'.
Pasini . . . . pä-sē'-nē.
Pasiphaë . . . . . . pā-sĭf'-ā-ē.
Pasquier . . . . . . păs-kē̄=ā'.
Passarowitz . . . . . päs-sä'-rō-vĭts.
Passau . . . . päs'-sow.
Passchendaele . . . . päs'-chĕn-dä-lĕ.
Passignano . . . . . päs-sēn-yä'-nō.
Passy . . . . pä-sē'.
Pasteur . . . . . . päs-tēr'.
Patchogue . . . . . păt-chōg', păt-chŏg'.
Pater (Walter) . . . . pā'-tēr.
Pater Patriæ . . . . pā'-tēr pā'-trĭ-ē.
Patiala . . . . pŭt-ē-ä'-lä.
Patna . . . . păt'-nä.
Paton . . . . pāt'-n.
Patrae, or . . . . . pā'-trē.
Patras . . . . pä-träs'.
Patroclus . . . . . pā-trō'-klŭs, pă-trō'-klŭs.
Patti (Adelina) . . . . păt'-ē.
Paty de Clam, du . . . dü pä-tē' dŭ-kläm.
Pau . . . . pō.
Pauer . . . . pow'-ĕr.
Paul . . . . pôl. *Fr.* pōl. *Ger.* powl.
Paulina . . . . . . pô-lē'-nà, pô-lī'-nä.
Pauline, adj. . . . . . pô'-līn, pô'-lĭn.
Pauline, n. . . . . . pôl-lēn'. *Fr.* pō-lēn'.
Paulo, see Polo . . . . pō'-lō. *It.* pä'=ōō-lō.
Pauncefote . . . . . pôns'-fŭt.

Paur	powr.
Pausanias	pô-sā′-nĭ-ás.
Pausilipo, see Posilipo	pow-zē-lē′-pō.
Pauting, see Paoting	pä=ō-tĭng′.
Pavia	pä-vē′-ä.
Pavlowa	päv′-lō-vä.
Pavlovsk	päv-lŏvsk′.
Pawnee	pô′-nē.
Paz, La	loc. lä-päz′. Sp. lä päth.
Pazzi	pät′-sē.
Peary (Robert E.)	pē′-rĭ.
Pecci, Gioachimo	jō-ä′-kē-mō pĕch′-ē.
Pe-chi-li, see Petchili	pĕ-chē-lē′.
Pedobaptist, see Paedo-baptist	pē-dō-băp′-tĭst.
Pedro	pē′-drō. Sp. pä′-drō.
Peer Gynt	pä′-ĕr günt, yünt.
Pegasean, Pegasian	pē-gā′-sĭ-án.
Pegasus	pĕg′-á-sŭs, pĕg′-ā-sŭs.
Pegu	pē-gōō′, pĕ-gōō′.
Péguy, Charles	shärl pä-gē′.
Peihai, see Peihoi, Pakhoi	pī-hī′.
Pei-ho	pä-hō′. pop. pī-hō′.
Peihoi, see Peihai, Pakhoi	pī-hoi′.
Peiræus, see Piræus	pī-rē′-ŭs.
Peirithous, see Pirithous	pī-rĭth′-ō-ŭs.
Peishwa, see Peshwa	pĕsh′-wä.
Peiwar, see Paiwar	pī-wär′.
Peixoto or Peixotto	pä-shō′-tōō.
Pekin (Ill.)	pē′-kĭn.
Pekin, or	pē-kĭn′.
Peking (China)	pē-kĭng′.
Pelagians	pē-lā′-jĭ-ánz.
Pelagius	pē-lā′-jĭ-ŭs.
Pelasgi	pē-lăs′-jī.
Pelayo	pä-lä′-yō.
Pele, or	pē′-lē.

Pelee, or	pē′-lē.
Pelée, Pointe	pwăṅt pĕ=la′.
Peleus	pē′-lē-ŭs, pē′-lŭs.
Pelew, see Pellew, Palau	pĕ-lōō′.
Pelion	pē′-lĭ-ŏn.
Pélissier	pā-lēs-ē=ā′.
Pelleas	pĕl′-ē-ăs.
Pelléas et Mélisande . .	pĕl-ā-ăs′ ā mā-lē-säṅd′.
Pellew, see Pelew, Palau	pĕ-lōō′.
Pellico, Silvio	sēl′-vē-ō pĕl′-lē-kō.
Pellieux (Gen.), Le . .	lē pĕl-ē-ē′.
Pelopid	pĕl′-ō-pĭd.
Pelopidas	pĕ-lŏp′-ĭ-dăs.
Peloponnesian	pĕl″-ō-pŏn-nē′-shĭ=ȧn,
	pĕl″-ō-pŏn-nē′-shȧn.
Peloponnesus	pĕl″-ō-pŏn-ē′-sŭs.
Pelops	pē′-lŏps.
Pemigewasset	pĕm″-ĭj-ē-wŏs′-ĭt.
Penang	pē-năng′.
Peñas	pĕn′-yäs.
Penates	pē-nā′-tēz.
Penelope	pē-nĕl′-ō-pē.
Peniel	pĕ-nī′-ĕl.
Penjab, see Panjab, Pun-	
jab	pĕn-jäb′.
Penrith	pĕn′-rĭth.
Penryn	pĕn-rĭn′.
Penseroso, Il	ĭl pĕn-sĕ-rō′-sō.
Pensiero, Il	ēl pān-sē-ā′-rō.
Pensieroso, Il	ēl pān-sē-ā-rō′-sō.
Pentateuch	pĕn′-tȧ-tūk, pĕn′-tā-tūk.
Pentecost	pĕn′-tē-kŏst, pĕn′-tĕ-kōst.
Pentelic	pĕn-tĕl′-ĭk.
Pentelican	pĕn-tĕl′-ĭ-cȧn.
Penthesilea	pĕn″-thē-sĭ-lē′-ȧ.
Pentheus	pĕn′-thē-ŭs, pĕn′-thūs.
Penuel	pĕ-nū′-ĕl.

Penza	pĕn′-zä.
Penzance	pĕn-zăns′.
Pepe	pā′-pĕ.
Pepin	pĕp′-ĭn.
Pépin le Bref . . .	pā-păn̍′ lē brĕf.
Pepys	pēps, pĕps, pĭps, pĕp′-ĭs.
Pera	pā′-rä.
Perak	pā-räk′.
Perceval, Percival . .	pĕr′-sĕ-val̇.
Percheron	pĕr=shĕ-rôn̍′.
Perdicaris	pĕr-dēk′-ä-rĕs.
Perdiccas	pĕr-dĭk′-ăs.
Perdita	pēr′-dĭ-tä.
Pereda, José Maria de .	ʻhō-sä′ má-rē′-ä dä pā-räd′-t̄hȧ.
Père Goriot	pâr gō-rē-yō′.
Père Lachaise . . .	pâr lä-shĕz′.
Peremysl	pĕr′-ĕ-mĭsl.
Perez (Antonio) . . .	pā′-räth.
Pergamos	pĕr′-gȧ-mŏs.
Pergamum	pĕr′-gȧ-mŭm.
Pergolese, or	pĕr-gō-lā′-zĕ.
Pergolesi	pĕr-gō-lā′-zē.
Peri	pē′-rĭ.
Peri (It. composer) . .	pā′-rē.
Periander	pĕr-ĭ-ăn′-dĕr.
Pericles	pĕr′-ĭ-klēz.
Périer, Casimir . . .	käz-ē-mēr′ pā-rē=ā′.
Périgord	pā-rē-gōr′.
Périgueux	pā-rē-gē′.
Periœci	pĕr-ĭ-ē′-sī.
Perizzites	pĕr′-ĭ-zīts.
Pernambuco	pĕr-nȧm-bū′-kō, pĕr-näm-boo͞′-kō. *Port.* pĕr-nän̍-boo͞′-koo͞.
Péronne	pā-rŏn′.
Perosi	pā-rō′-sē.

Perowne . . . . . . pĕ-rown'.
Perpignan . . . . . . pĕr-pēn-yän'.
Persephone . . . . . pĕr-sĕf'-ō-nē.
Perseus . . . . . . pĕr'-sē-ŭs, pĕr'-sūs.
Persia . . . . pĕr'-shĭ=à, pĕr'-shà,
            pĕr'-zhà.
Persian . . . . pĕr'-shàn, pĕr'-zhàn.
Pertabgurh,
   see Partabgarh . . . pĕr-täb-gŭr'.
Peru, or . . . . . . pĕ-rōo'.
Perú, Sp. . . . . . . pā-rōo'.
Perugia . . . . . . pā-rōo'-jä.
Perugino . . . . . . pā-rōo-jĕ'-nō.
Peruzzi, Baldassare . . bäl-däs-sä'-rā pā-rōōt'-sē.
Pesaro . . . . pā'-zä-rō.
Pescadores . . . . . pĕs-kä-dō'-rĕs.
Pescara . . . . . . pĕs-kä'-rä.
Peschiera . . . . . . pĕs-kē=ā'-rä.
Peshawar, or Peshawur . pĕsh-ow'-ēr.
Peshwa, see Peishwa . . pĕsh'-wä.
Pestalozzi . . . . . . pĕs-tä-lŏt'-sē.
Pesth . . . . pĕst.   Hung. pĕsht.
Pétain . . . . pā'-tăn'.
Petchili, see Pe-chi-li . . pĕ-chē-lē'.
Petchora . . . . . . pĕt-cho'-ra, pĕt'-cho-rä.
Péthion, or Pétion . . . pā-tē-ôn'.
Petit André . . . . . pē-tē' tän-drā'.
Petöfi . . . . pē'-tē-fĭ.
Petrarca, It., or . . . . pā-trär'-kä.
Petrarch . . . . . . pē'-trärk.
Petrine . . . . pĕ'-trīn, pē'-trĭn'.
Petrograd . . . . . . pĕt'-rō-gräd.
Petruccio . . . . . . pā-trōoch'-ō.
Petruchio . . . . . . pē-trū'-chĭ-ō.
            It. pā-trōo'-kē-ō.
Petschnikoff . . . . . pĕtsh'-nē-kŏf.
Peyrebrune . . . . . pâr-brün'.

Pfalz . . . . pfälts.
Phæacians . . . . . fē-ā'-shǐ-ánz.
Phædo, or . . . . . fē'-dō.
Phædon . . . . . . fē'-dŏn.
Phædra . . . . . . fē'-drä.
Phædrus . . . . . . fē'-drŭs.
Phæthon . . . . . . fā'-ĕ-thŏn.
Phalaris . . . . . . făl'-á-rǐs.
Phanariot . . . . . . fă-năr'-ǐ-ŏt.
Pharaoh . . . . . . fā'-rō, fā'-rā-ō.
Pharisee . . . . . . făr'-ǐ-sē.
Pharos . . . . fā'-rŏs, fä'-rŏs.
Pharpar . . . . . . fär'-pär.
Pharsalus . . . . . . fär-sā'-lŭs.
Phèdre . . . . fĕdr.
Phenice . . . . . . fē-nī'-sē.
Phenicia, see Phœnicia . fĕ-nǐsh'-ǐ=á.
Phidias . . . . . . fǐd'-ǐ-ás.
Philae . . . . fī'-lē.
Philemon . . . . . . fǐ-lē'-mŏn, fī-lē'-mŏn.
Philémon et Baucis . . fē-lā-mōn' ā bō-sēs'.
Philinte . . . . . . fē-lăṅt'.
Philippa . . . . . . fǐl-ǐp'-á.
Philippe Egalité . . . . fē-lēp' ā-găl-ē-tā'.
Philippi . . . . fǐ-lǐp'-ī.
Philippians . . . . . fǐ-lǐp'-ǐ-ánz.
Philippine (Is.) or . . . fǐl'-ǐp-ǐn.   pop. fǐl'-ǐ-pīn.
Philippines . . . . . fǐl'-ǐp-ǐnz.   pop. fǐl'-ǐ-pīnz.
Philistine . . . . . . fǐl-ís'-tǐn, fǐl'-ǐs-tǐn.
Philoctetes . . . . . fǐl-ŏk-tē'-tēz.
Philo Judæus . . . . fī'-lō jōō-dē'-ŭs.
Philomel . . . . . . fǐl'-ō-mĕl.
Philomela . . . . . . fǐl-ō-mē'-lä.
Phineas . . . . . . fǐn'-ē-ás.
Phlegethon . . . . . flĕj'-ĕ-thŏn, flĕj'-ē-thŏn.
Phlegyas . . . . . . flē'-jǐ-ás.
Phocæa . . . . . . fō-sē'-á.

Phocian . . . . . . fō'-shǐ=ȧn.
Phocion . . . . . . fō'-shǐ-ŏn.
Phocis . . . . fō'-sǐs.
Phœbus . . . . . . fē'-bŭs.
Phœnicia, see Phenicia . fē-nǐsh'-ǐ=ȧ.
Phorcys . . . . . . fôr'-sǐs, fôr'-kǐs.
Phrygia . . . . . . frǐj'-ǐ-ȧ.
Phryne . . . . frī'-nē.
Phthiotis . . . . . . thī-ō'-tǐs.
Piacenza . . . . . . pē-ä-chĕn'-zä.
Piauhí, or Piauhy . . . pē-ow-ē'.
Piave . . . . pē-ä'-vĕ.
Piazza del Gran Duca, or pē-ät'-sä dĕl grän dōō'-kä.
Piazza della Signoria . pē-ät'-sä dĕl'-lä
                          sēn-yō-rē'-ä.
Piazza del Popolo . . . pē-ät'-sä dĕl pō'-pō-lō.
Piazza di Spagna . . . pē-ät'-sä dē spän'-yä.
Picardy . . . . . . pǐk'-är-dǐ.
Picasso . . . . pē-kä-sō'.
Piccini . . . . pē-chē'-nē.
Picciola . . . . . . pē'-chō-lä.
Piccolomini . . . . . pēk-ō-lŏ'-mē-nē.
Pichegru . . . . . . pēsh-grōō'.
                          Fr, pēsh-grü',
Pichincha . . . . . . pē-chēn'-chä.
Pico della Mirandola . . pē'-kō dĕl'-lä
                          mē-rän'-dō-lä.
Pico, Giovanni . . . . jō-vän'-nē pē'-kō.
Picot . . . . pē-kō'.
Picquard . . . . . . pē-kär'.
Picquigny . . . . . . pē-kēn-yĕ'.
Piedmont, see Piémont,
    Piemonte . . . . . pēd'-mŏnt.
Piedres (R.) . . . . . pē-ä'-dräs.
Piémont, *Fr.*, see Piedmont pē=ä-môṅ'.
Piemonte, *It.*, see Piedmont pē-ä-mōn'-tĕ.
Pierian . . . . pī-ē'-rǐ-ȧn.

Pierné . . . . pēr-nā′.
Pierre . . . . pē=âr′.
Pierrefonds . . . . pē=âr-fôṅ′.
Pierrette . . . . . pē=âr-ĕt′.
Pierrot . . . . . . pē=ĕr-rō′.
Pietà . . . . pē-ā-tä′.
Pietermaritzburg . . . pē-tĕr-mär′-ĭts-bŭrċh.
Pietro . . . . pē=ā′-trō.
Pilate . . . . *Bib.* pī′-lāt.   *Fr.* pē-lät′.
Pilatus (Mt.) . . . . . pī-lā′-tŭs.   *It.* pē-lä′-tōōs.
Pilatus, Pontius . . . pŏn′-shĭ-ŭs pī-lā′-tŭs.
Piloty . . . . pē-lō′-tē, pē′-lō-tē.
Pilpay . . . . pĭl′-pī.
Pilsudski . . . . . . pĭl-soŏd′-skĭ.
Pinacotheca . . . . pĭn″-à-kō-thē′-kȧ.
Pinacothek . . . . pĭn′-à-kō-thĕk″.
                     Ger. pē-nä′-kō-tāk.
Pinar del Rio . . . pē-när′ dĕl rē′-ō.
Pinchot . . . . . . pĭn′-shō.
Pincian (Hill) . . . pĭn′-shĭ-ȧn, pĭn′-chȧn.
Pincio, Monte . . . mōn′-tĕ pēn′-chō.
Pindaric . . . . . . pĭn-dăr′-ĭk.
Pindarus . . . . . . pĭn′-dā-rŭs.
Pines, see Pinos, Isla de . pīnz.
Pinos, Isla de, see Pines . ēs′-lä dä pē′-nōs.
Pinta, La . . . . . . lä pēn′-tä.
Pinto, Aníbal . . . . ä-nē′-bäl pĭn′-tō.
Pinturicchio . . . . pēn-tōō-rēk′-kē=ō.
Pinzon . . . . *Sp.* pĭn-thōn′.
Piombo . . . . pē-ŏm′-bō.
Piotrkow . . . . . . pē-yŏtr′-kŏv.
Piozzi . . . . . . pĭ-ŏz′-ĭ.   *It.* pē-ŏt′-sē.
Pippa . . . . pĭp′-pä.
Piqua . . . . pĭk′-wä, pĭk′-wā.
Pique-Dame . . . . pēk-däm.
Piræeus, or . . . . . pī-rē′-yūs.
Piræus, see Peiræus . . pī-rē′-ŭs.

Pirithous, see Peirithous .	pī-rĭth'-ō-ŭs.
Piron	pē-rôn'.
Pisa	pī'-sà. *It.* pē'-zä.
Pisano, Niccolò	nē-kō-lō' pē-zä'-nō.
Piscataqua	pĭs-kăt'-à-kwä.
Pisces	pĭs'-ēz.
Pisgah	pĭz'-gä.
Pisistratidæ, or	pĭs-ĭs-trăt'-ĭ-dē.
Pisistratids	pĭs-ĭs'-trà-tĭds.
Pisistratus	pĭ-sĭs'-trà-tŭs,
	pī-sĭs'-trā-tŭs.
Pissarro	pē-sä-rō'.
Pistoia, or Pistoja . . .	pĭs-tō'-yä.
Pitcairn (I.)	pĭt'-kârn, pĭt-kârn'.
Pithom	pī'-thŏm.
Pittacus	pĭt'-à-kŭs.
Pitti	pĭt'-tē.
Pizarro	pĭ-zä'-rō. *Sp.* pē-thär'-rō.
Place de la Bastille . .	plăs dŭ lä bäs-tē'=yŭ.
Place de la Concorde . .	plăs dŭ lä kôn-kōrd'.
Place du Carrousel . .	plăs dü kä-rōō-zĕl'.
Place Vendôme	plăs vŏn-dōm'.
Plaideurs, Les	lā plā-dĕr'.
Planche	plänsh.
Planché	plän-shū'.
Planchette	plän-shĕt'.
Plançon, Pol	pōl plän-sôn'.
Plantagenet	plăn-tăj'-ĕ-nĕt.
Plantin, Musée	mü-zā' plän-tăn'.
Plassey, or Plassi . . .	pläs'-sĭ.
Plata, Rio de la, see Plate	rē'-ō dā lä plä'-tä.
Platæa, or	plă-tē'-à, plā-tē'-à.
Platææ	plă-tē'-ē.
Plate (R.), see Rio de la	
Plata	plāt, plät.
Platine	plä'-tĭn.
Plato	plä'-tō.

Platonic . . . . . . plā-tŏn'-ĭk.
Plautus . . . . . . plô'-tŭs.
Plava . . . . plä'-vä.
Pléiade, La . . . . . lä plā-yăd'.
Pleiades, or . . . . . plī'-à-dēz.
Pleiads . . . . plī'-ădz.
Plessis-les-Tours . . plĕ-sē'-lä-tōōr'.
Pleyel . . . . plī'-ĕl.
Pliny . . . . plĭn'-ĭ.
Plockhorst . . . . . plŏk'-hŏrst.
Ploërmel . . . . . . plō-ĕr-mĕl'.
Plombières . . . . . plôn-bē=âr'.
Plon-Plon . . . . . plŏn-plŏn.
Plotinus . . . . . . plō-tī'-nŭs.
Pluto . . . . plū'-tō.
Pluton . . . . *Fr.* plü-tōn'.
Plutus . . . . plū'-tŭs.
Pluviose . . . . . , . plü-vē-yŏz'.
Pnyx . . . . nĭks.
Pobyedonostsev . . . . pŏb"-yĕ-dŏ-nŏs'-tsĕf.
Pocono . . . . pō'-cŏ-nō.
Poděbrad, or Podiebrad . pŏd'-yĕ-bräd.
Podolia . . . . pō-dō'-lĭ-à.
Podolsk . . . . . . pō-dōlsk'.
Poictiers, see Poitiers . . poi-tērz'. *Fr.* pwä-tē=ā'.
Poincaré . . . . . . pwăn-kă-rā'.
Pointe Pelée, or . . . . *Fr.* pwănt pĕ-lä'.
(Point) Pelee, or Pele . . pē'-lē.
Poissy . . . . pwä-sē'.
Poitevin . . . . . . pwät-văn'.
Poitiers, see Poictiers . . poi-tērz'. *Fr.* pwä-tē=ā'.
Poitou . . . . pwä-tōō'.
Polaris . . . . pō-lā'-rĭs.
Polavieja, Camilo . . . kä-mē'-lō pō"-lä-vē=ĕċh'-ä.
Polignac . . . . . . pō-lēn-yäk'.
Polillo . . . . pō-lēl'-yō.
Politian . . . . . . pō-lĭsh'-ĭ-àn.

Polixenes	pŏ-lĭks'-ĕ-nēz.
Poliziano, It.	pō-lēd-zē-ä'-nō.
Polk	pōlk.
Pollaiuolo, or Pollajuolo .	pōl"-lä-yōō=ō'-lō.
Pollux	pŏl'-ŭks.
Polo, see Paulo	pō'-lō.
Polonius	pō-lō'-nĭ-ŭs.
Poltava, see Pultowa . .	pŏl-tä'-vä.
Polybius	pŏ-lĭb'-ĭ-ŭs.
Polycarp	pŏl'-ĭ-kärp.
Polycletus, or	pŏl-ĭ-klē'-tŭs.
Polyclitus	pŏl-ĭ-klĭ'-tŭs.
Polycrates	pŏ-lĭk'-rà-tēz,
	pō-lĭk'-rà-tēz.
Polyeucte	pō-lē-ēkt'.
Polygnotus	pŏl-ĭg-nō'-tŭs.
Polyhymnia, or	pŏl-ĭ-hĭm'-nĭ-à.
Polymnia	pō-lĭm'-nĭ-à.
Polynesia	pŏl-ĭ-nē'-shĭ=à.
Polyphemus	pŏl-ĭ-fē'-mŭs.
Pomerania	pŏm-ĕr-ā'-nĭ-à.
Pomfret, see Pontefract .	pŏm'-frĕt.
Pomœrium	pō-mē'-rĭ-ŭm.
Pomona	pō-mō'-nà.
Pompadour, de	dŭ pŏm'-pà-dōōr.
	Fr. dŭ pôṅ'-pä-dōōr'.
Pompeia	pŏm-pē'-yà.
Pompeian	pŏm-pē'-yàn.
Pompeii	pŏm-pā'-yē.
	Lat. pŏm-pē'-yī.
Pompeius	pŏm-pē'-yŭs.
Pompilia	pōm-pē'-lē-ä.
Ponape	pō'-nä-pā.
Ponce	pŏn'-sē. *Sp.* pōn'-thä.
Ponce de Leon	pŏns dŭ lē'-ŏn.
	Sp. pōn'-thä dä lä-ōn'.
Ponchielli	pōn-kē-ĕl'-lē.

Pondicherri, or
Pondicherry, or . . . . pŏn-dĭ-shĕr'-ĭ.
Pondichéry, Fr. . . . . pôṅ-dē-shä-rē'.
Pondoland . . . . . pŏn'-dō-lănd.
Poniatowski . . . . . pō-nē̄=ä-tŏv'-skē.
Pont-Aven . . . . . pŏṅ-tä-vôṅ'.
Pontchartrain . . . pŏn-chär-trän'.
                    Fr. pôṅ-shär-trăṅ'.
Pontefract, see Pomfret . pŏn'-tĭ-frăkt.
                    pop. pŏm'-frĕt.
Ponte Vecchio . . . . pŏn'-tĕ vĕk'-kē̄=ō.
Pontevedra . . . . . pōn-tä-vā'-drä.
Pontine . . . . . . pŏn'-tĭn, pŏn'-tīn.
Pontius . . . . . . pŏn'-shĭ-ŭs.
Pont Neuf . . . . . . pôṅ nēf.
Pont-Noyelles . . . pôṅ'-nwä-yĕl'.
Pontoise . . . . . . pŏnt-wäz'.
Poo Choo, see Pou Tchou,
    Pu Chu . . . . . poō choō'.
Poona, or Poonah . . . poō'-nä.
Pooree, see Puri . . . poō-rē'.
Pooshkin, see Pouschkin,
    Puschkin . . . . pŏŏsh'-kĭn, poōsh'-kĭn.
Popocatepetl . . . . pō-pō"-kä-tä-pĕt'-l,
                    pō-pō'-kä-tä-pĕt"-l.
Poppæa Sabina . . . pŏp-pē'-ä să-bī'-nä.
Pordenone . . . . . pōr-dä-nō'-nĕ.
Pornic . . . . pōr-nēk'.
Porpora . . . . . . pōr'-pō-rä.
Porsena, or . . . . . pôr'-sĕ-nȧ.
Porsenna . . . . . . pôr-sĕn'-nȧ.
Port Arthur . . . . . pōrt är'-thĕr.
Port-au-Prince . . . . pōrt'-ō-prĭns'.
                    Fr. pōr-tō-prăṅs'.
Porte (The) . . . . . pōrt.
Porteous . . . . . . pōr'-tē-ŭs.
Porte St.-Antoine . . . pōrt săṅ-tŏṅ-twăn'.

Porte St.-Denis . . . . pōrt săṅ-dē-nē'.
Porte St.-Martin . . . pōrt săṅ-mär-tăṅ'.
Porthos . . . . . . pōr-tōs'.
Portia . . . . pōr'-shĭ-à, pôr'-shĭ=à.
Portici . . . . pōr'-tē-chē.
Porto Bello, see Puerto
    Bello . . . . . . pōr'-tō bĕl'-lō.
        Port. pōr'-tōō bāl'-yō.
Porto Rico, see Puerto Rico   pōr'-tō rē'-kō.
Port Saïd . . . . . pōrt sä-ēd'. _pop._ sād.
Portugal . . . . . pōrt'-yū-gàl.
        Port. pōr-tōō-gäl'.
Portuguese . . . . pōrt-yū-gēz', pōr'-tū-gēz,
        _or_ gēs.
Poseidon, _or_ Posidon . . pō-sī'-dŏn.
Posilipo, see Pausilipo . pō-zē-lē'-pō.
Posthumus, Leonatus . . lē-ō-nā'-tŭs pŏst'-hū-mŭs,
        pŏs'-tū-mŭs.
Potchefstrom . . . . pŏ'-chĕf-strŏm.
Potemkin . . . . . pŏ-tĕm'-kĭn.
        Russ. pŏt-yŏm'-kĭn.
Potgieter . . . . . pŏt'-gē-tĕr.
Potinière, La . . . . . lä pō-tēn-yâr'.
Potocka . . . . . pŏ-tŏt'-skä.
Potocki . . . . . pŏ-tŏt'-skē.
Potomac . . . . . po-tó'-màk.
Potosí . . . . . . pō-tō'-sē. _Sp._ pō-tō-sē'.
Potsdam . . . . . pŏts'-dăm.
        Ger. pŏts'-däm.
Poughkeepsie . . . . pō-kĭp'-sĭ.
Pourbus . . . . . pōōr-büs'.
Pourceaugnac, de . . . dŭ pōōr-sōn-yäk'.
Pourtalès . . . . . pōōr-tä-lĕz'.
Pouschkin, _or_ Pouchekine,
    see Pushkin, Pooshkin,
    Puschkin . . . . pŏōsh'-kĭn, pōōsh'-kĭn.
Poussin . . . . . pōō-săṅ'.

Pou Tchou, see Poo Choo,
   Pu Chu . . . . . . poō choō'.
Powhatan . . . . . . pō-ăt-än', pow-hăt-ăn'.
Pozières . . . . . . pō-zē=âr'.
Pozzuoli, see Puteoli . . pōt-soō-ō'-lē.
Prado . . . . prä'-dō.
Praed . . . . präd.
Præmunire (Statute of) . prē-mū-nī'-rĕ.
Præterita . . . . . . prē-tēr'-ī-tä.
Prag . . . . präg.
Prague . . . . präg. *Fr.* präg.
Prairial . . . . . . prä-rē-ăl'.
Prairie de Chien . . . prä'-rē dū shēn.
                   Fr. prä-rē' dü shē-ĕṅ'.
Prakrit . . . . . . prä'-krĭt, prăk'-rĭt.
Prater . . . . prä'-tĕr.
Praxiteles . . . . . prăks-ĭt'-ĕ-lēz.
Pré aux Clercs (Le) . . prä ō klâr.
Pré Catalan . . . . prä kä-tä-läṅ'.
Précieuses Ridicules . . prä-sē-ēz' rē-dē-kül'.
Preciosa . . . . . prĕs-ĭ-ō'-sà.
                   Ger. prät-sē-ō'-zä.
Predis, Ambrogio de . . äm-brō'-jō dä prä'-dēs.
Prelude (The) . . . . prē'-lūd, prĕl'-ūd.
Presbyterian . . . . prĕz-bĭ-tē'-rĭ-ăn,
                   prĕs-bĭ-tē'-rĭ-ăn.
Presidio . . . . . . prä-sē'-dē-ō.
Pressensé . . . . . prĕs-sŏṅ-sä'.
Pretoria . . . . . . prē-tō'-rĭ-à.
Prévost-Paradol . . . . prä-vŏst'-pä-rä-dŏl'.
Priam . . . . prī'-ăm.
Priapus . . . . . . prī-ā'-pŭs.
Pribilof (-byloff) . . . prē-bē-lŏf'.
Priene . . . . prī-ē'-nē.
Prieska . . . . . . prēs'-kä.
Prigioni, Le Mie . . . lä mē'-ĕ prē-jō'-nē.
Prilep . . . . prē'-lĕp.

Prim (General)	prēm.
Prince	*Fr.* prăṅs.
Princesse de Clèves . .	prăṅ-sĕs′ dŭ klĕv.
Princesse Lointaine, La .	lä prăṅ-sĕs′ lwăṅ-tĕn′.
Principe	prēn′-chē-pĕ.
Principessa	prēn-chē-pĕs′-sä.
Prinz	prĭnts.
Prinzessin	prĭnts-ĕs′-ĭn.
Prinzivalle	prĭnts-ē-väl′-lē.
Priscian	prĭsh′-ĭ=ȧn.
Procne, see Progné . .	prŏk′-nē.
Procris	prŏk′-rĭs.
Procrustean	prō-krŭs′-tē-ȧn.
Proculeius	prō-kū-lē′-ŭs.
Procyon	prō′-sĭ-ŏn, prŏs′-ĭ-ŏn.
Profeta, Il, see Prophète,	
Le	ēl prō-fā′-tä.
Profillet	prō-fē-yā′.
Progné, see Procne . .	prŏg-nā′.
Prokofief	prō-kō′-fē-ĕf.
Promessi Sposi, I . . .	ē prō-mĕs′-sē spō′-zē.
Promethean	prō-mē′-thē-ȧn.
Prometheus	prō-mē′-thē-ŭs,
	prō-mē′-thŭs.
Prophète, Le, see Profeta,	
Il	lĕ prō-fĕt′.
Propylæa	prŏp-ĭ-lē′-ä.
Proserpina	prō-sēr′-pĭ-nȧ,
	prŏs-ēr-pī′-nä.
Proserpine	prŏs′-ēr-pīn, prŏs′-ēr-pĭn.
Protean	prō′-tē-ȧn, prō-tē′-ȧn.
Protesilaus	prō-tĕs″-ĭ-lā′-ŭs.
Protestancy	prŏt′-ĕs-tȧn-sī.
Protestant	prŏt′-ĕs-tȧnt.
Proteus	prō′-tē-ŭs, prō′-tūs.
Proudhon	prōō-dôṅ′.
Proust, Marcel	mär-sĕl′ prōōst.

Provençal . . . . . . prō-věn'-săl.
        Fr. prō-vŏn-săl'.
Provence . . . . . . prō-vôns'.
Pruḍhomme . . . . . prü-dŏm'.
Prud'hon (Pierre Paul) . prü-dôn'.
Prussia . . . . prŭsh'-à, prōŏsh'-ĭ=à.
Prussian . . . . . . prŭsh'-àn, prŭsh'-ĭ-àn,
        prōŏsh'-ĭ-àn.
Prytaneum . . . . . prĭt-ā-ně'-ŭm.
Przasnysz . . . . . . pshăs'-nĭsh.
Przemysl . . . . . . pshā'-mĭshl.
Psalms . . . . sämz.
Psammetichus . . . să-mět'-ĭ-kŭs.
Psichari . . . . . . psē-shă-rē'.
Pskoff . . . . pskŏf.
Psyche . . . . sī'-kē.
Ptah . . . . ptä.
Ptolemaic . . . . . . tŏl-ē-mā'-ĭk.
Ptolemais . . . . . . tŏl-ē-mā'-ĭs.
Ptolemy . . . . . . tŏl'-ē-mĭ.
Puccini . . . . pōō-chē'-nē.
Puccio . . . . . : . pōŏch'-ō.
Pucelle, La . . . . . lä pü-sĕl'.
Pu Chu, see Poo Choo,
 Pou Tchou . . . . . pōō chōō'.
Puebla . . . . pōō=ĕb'-lä.
Pueblo . . . . pōō=ĕb'-lō.
        Sp. pōō=ā'-blō.
Puerto, El . . . . . . äl pōō=âr'-tō.
Puerto Bello, see Porto
 Bello . . . . pōō=âr'-tō bĕl'-lō.
        Sp. pōō=âr'-tō bĕl'-yō.
Puerto Cabello . . . . pōō=âr'-tō kȧ-bĕl'-lō.
        Sp. pōō=âr'-tō kä-bĕl'-yō.
Puerto de Santa Maria . pōō=âr'-tō dä sän'-tä
        mä-rē'-ä.
Puerto d'España . . . pōō=âr'-tō dä spän'-yä.

Puerto Plata	pōō=âr'-tõ plä'-tä.
Puerto Princesa	pōō=âr'-tõ prēn-thä'-sä.
Puerto Príncipe	pōō-âr'-tõ prēn'-thē-pä.
Puerto Real	pōō=r'-tõ rä-äl'.
Puerto Rico, see Porto	
Rico	pōō=âr'-tõ rē'-kō.
Puget (Pierre)	pü-zhä'.
Puget (Sound)	pū'-jĕt.
Puglia	pōōl'-yä.
Pugno	pōōn'-yō.
Pujol, de	dẽ pü-zhŏl'.
Pulci	pōōl'-chē.
Pulcinella, or	pōōl-chē-nĕl'-lä.
Pulcinello	pōōl-chē-nĕl'-lō.
Pulkowa	pōōl'-kō-vä.
Pultava, see Poltava, or .	pōōl-tä'-vä.
Pultowa	pōōl-tō'-vä.
Pultusk	pōōl'-tōōsk, pōōl'-tōōsk.
Punchinello	pŭn-chĭ-nĕl'-ō.
Punic	pū'-nĭk.
Punjab, see Panjab, Pen-	
jab	pŭn-jäb'.
Punjaub	pŭn-jôb'.
Punnah, see Panna . .	pŭn'-ä.
Punta Gorda	pōōn'-tä gõr'-dä.
Puntilla	pōōn-tēl'-yä.
Purana	pōō-rä'-nà.
Purcell	pŭr'-sĕl.
Purgatorio	pōōr-gä-tō'-rē-ō.
Puri, see Pooree . . .	pōō-rē'.
Purim	pōō'-rĭm.
Puritani di Scozia, I . .	ē pōō-rē-tä'-nē dē skōd'-zē-ä.
Purneah, or	pēr'-nĕ-ä.
Purniah	pēr'-nĭ-ä.
Pusey	pū'-zĭ.
Puseyism	pū'-zĭ-ĭzm.

Pushkin, see Pouschkin,
   Pooshkin . . . . . poŏosh'-kĭn.
Puteoli, see Pozzuoli . . pū-tē'-ō-lī.
Putnik . . . . poŏot-nĭk'.
Puvis de Chavannes . . pü-vēs' dĕ shä-văn'.
Puy-de-Dôme . . . . pü=ē'-dŭ-dōm'.
Pyeshkov . . . . . . p-yĕsh'-kŏf.
Pylades . . . . . . pĭl'-à-dēz.
Pyramus . . . . . . pĭr'-à-mŭs.
Pyrenean . . . . . . pĭr-ē-nē'-àn.
Pyrenees, or . . . . pĭr'-ē-nēz.
Pyrénées, *Fr.* . . . . pē-rä-nā'.
Pyrrha . . . . pĭr'-à.
Pyrrhic . . . . pĭr'-ĭk.
Pyrrhus . . . . . . pĭr'-ŭs.
Pythagoras . . . . . pĭth-ăg'-ō-răs.
Pythagorean . . . . pĭth″-ā-gō'-rē-àn,
             pĭth″-à-gō-rē'-àn.
Pythia . . . . pĭth'-ĭ-à.
Pythian . . . . . . pĭth'-ĭ-àn.
Python . . . . pī'-thŏn.
Pythoness . . . . . pĭth'-ŏn-ĕs.

Q

Quadragesima . . . . kwäd-rä-jĕs'-ĭ-mä.
Quai d'Anjou . . . . kā dän-zhoŏo'.
Quai d'Orsay . . . . kā dôr-sā'.
Quangsi, see Kwangsi . kwäng-sē'.
Quangtong, see Kwangtung kwäng-toŏong'.
Quanza, see Coanza,
   Kuanza . . . . . . kwän'-zä.
Quasimodo . . . . . kwä-sĭ-mō'-dō.
           Fr. kä-zē-mō-dō'.
Quathlamba, see Kath-
   lamba . . . . . . kwät-läm'-bä.
Quatre-Bras . . . . kă'=tr-brä'.

Quatre-Vingt-Treize . .	kă'-tr-văṅ-trĕz'.
Quebec.	kwē-bĕk'. *Fr.* kĕ-bĕk'.
Queenston	kwēnz'-tŭn.
Queenstown	kwēnz'-town.
Queiros, see Quiros, de .	dā kā-ē-rŏs'.
Quelpaerd, or . . .	kwĕl'-pärd.
Quelpart, or Quelpaert .	kwĕl'-pärt.
Quentin	kwĕn'-tĭn. *Fr.* kôṅ-tăṅ'.
Quercia, della	dĕl'-lä kwĕr'-chä.
Querétaro	kā-rā'-tä-rō.
Querimba	kā-rēm'-bä.
Quérouaille (Louise Renée de) see Kéroualle . .	kā-rōō-ä'=yŭ.
Quesada, Ximenez de . .	zĭ-mē'-nēz.
	Sp. 'hē-mä'nāth dā kā-sä'-dä.
Quesnay	kā-nä'.
Quesnel	kā-nĕl'.
Quevedo y Villegas . .	kā-bā'-dō ē vēl-yā'-gäs.
Quiberon	kē-brôṅ'.
Quicherat	kē-shē=rä'.
Quijote, Don, see Quixote	dōn kē-'hō'-tä.
Quilimane, see Kilimane .	kē-lē-mä'-nä.
Quiller-Couch . . .	kwĭl'-ĕr-kōōch.
Quincy (Mass.)	kwĭn'-zĭ.
Quinet	kē-nä'.
Quiniluban	kē-nē-lōō-bän'.
Quinquagesima	kwĭn-kwȧ-jĕs'-ĭ-mȧ.
Quintas da Recreo . . .	kēn'-täs dä rā-krä'-ō.
Quintilian	kwĭn-tĭl'-ĭ-ăn.
Quirinal, or	kwĭr'-ĭ-năl.
Quirinale	kwē-rē-nä'-lä.
Quirinalis, Mons, *Lat.* .	mŏnz kwĭr-ĭ-nā'-lĭs.
Quirites	kwĭ-rī'-tēz.
Quiros, de, see Queiros .	dā kē'-rŏs.
Quito	kē'-tō.
Qui tollis	kwī tŏl'-ĭs.

Quixote, Don, see Quijote,
    Don . . . . *Eng.* dŏn kwĭks'-ōt.
                   Sp. dōn kē-'hō'-tā.
Quogue . . . . . . kwōg, kwŏg.
Quoniam . . . . . . kwō'-nĭ-ăm.

R

Raamah . . . . . . rā'-á-mä.
Rabelais . . . . . . răb-ĕ-lā'.
Rabelaisian . . . . răb-ĕ-lā'-zĭ-án.
Rabutin, Bussy . . . . büs-sē' rä-bü-tăṅ'.
Raca . . . . rā'-ká.
Rachel . . . . . . rā'-chĕl. *Fr.* rä-shĕl'.
Rachmaninoff . . . . räċh-mä-nē'-nŏf.
Racine . . . . . . ră-sēn'. *Fr.* rä-sēn'.
Radack, or Radak . . . rä'-däk.
Radetzki, or Radetzky . rä-dĕt'-skē.
Radom . . . . rä'-dōm.
Raemakers . . . . . rä'-mä-kĕrz.
Raffaelle, or . . . . . räf-fä-ĕl'.
Raffaello, see Raphael . räf-fä-ĕl'-lō.
Ragatz, or Ragaz . . . rä'-gäts.
Rages . . . . rā'-jēz.
Ragnar Lodbrok . . . räg'-när lōd'-brōk.
Ragnarök . . . . . . räg'-nä-rēk'.
Ragon, Félix . . . . . fä-lēks' rä-gôṅ'.
Ragusa . . . . rä-gōō'-zä.
Rahab . . . . rā'-hăb.
Rahway . . . . . . rô'-wä.
Rai Bareli, see Roy Ba-
    reilly . . . . . . rī bä-rā'-lē.
Raimondi, Marcantonio . märk-än-tō'-nē-ō
                  rä=ē-mōn'-dē.
Rainer . . . . rī'-nĕr.
Rainier (Mount) . . . rā'-nēr.
Raipur, or Raipoor . . . rī-pōōr'.

Rais, de, or Raiz . . .	dŭ rās.
Raisa	rä-ē'-sä.
Raisuli	rä-ē-sōō'-lē.
Rajah, or Raja	rä'-jä.
Rajeshaye, see Rajshahi .	rä-jĕ-shä'-ē.
Rajpeepla	räj-pē'-plä.
Rajpoor	räj-pōōr'.
Rajpootana, see Rajputana	räj-pōō-tä'-nä.
Rajpoots, see Rajputs . .	räj-pōōts'.
Rajputana, see Rajpootana	räj-pōō-tä'-nä.
Rajputs, see Rajpoots . .	räj-pōōts'.
Rajshahi, see Rajeshaye .	räj-shä'-hē.
Rákóczy	rä'-kōt-sē.
Rákos	rä'-kōsh.
Raleigh	rô'-lĭ, răl'-ĭ.
Ralick, Ralik	rä'-lĭk.
Rama	rā'-mȧ, rä'-mä.
Ramah	rā'-mä.
Ramapo	răm'-ȧ-pō, răm-ȧ-pō'.
Ramayana	rä-mä'-yä-nä,
	răm'-ä-yä''-nä.
Rambaud	rän-bō'.
Rambouillet, de	dŭ rän-bōō-yä'.
Rameau	rä-mō'.
Ramée, Pierre de la . .	pō̄-âr' dŭ lä rä-mä'.
Ramenghi	rä-mĕng'-gē.
Rameses, see Ramses .	răm'-ē-sēz, rä-mē'-sēz,
	răm'-ĕ-sēz.
Ramillies	răm'-ĭl-ēz. *Fr.* rä-mē-yē'.
Ramiro	rä-mē'-rō.
Rammohun Roy	räm-mō-hŭn' roi.
Ramona	rȧ-mō'-nȧ.
Rampur	räm-pōōr'.
Ramses, see Rameses .	răm'-sēz.
Ramus	rä-müs'.
Rancé	rän-sä'.
Rangoon, see Rangun . .	rän-gōōn'.

Rangpur, see Rungpoor . rŭng-pōōr'.
Rangun, see Rangoon . . rän-gōōn'.
Ranke, von . . . . . fŏn räng'-kŭ.
Ranz des Vaches . . . räṅ dā väsh.
Raoul . . . . rä=ōōl'.
Rapallo . . . . . . rä-päl'-lō.
Raphael, see Raffaelle . räf'-ā-ĕl, rä'-fä-ĕl, rā'-fā-ĕl.
Raphaelesque . . . . räf"-ā-ĕl-ĕsk'.
Raphaelite . . . . . räf'-ā-ĕl-īt".
Raphaelitism . . . . . räf'-ā-ĕl-ī-tizm".
Rapidan . . . . . . răp-ĭ-dăn'.
Ras-el-Abiad . . . . räs-ĕl-ä'-bē-äd.
Rasputin . . . . . . räs-pōōt'-ēn.
Rasselas . . . . . . răs'-ĕ-lăs.
Rata, see Rota . . . rä'-tä.
Rathenau . . . . . . rä'-tĕn-ow.
Ratisbon . . . . . . răt'-ĭs-bŏn.
Ratlam, see Rutlam . . rŭt'-läm.
Ratnagiri, see Rutnagherry rŭt-nȧ-gē'-rē.
Ratti . . . . rät'-tē.
Rauch . . . . rowċh.
Ravaillac . . . . . . rä-vä-yäk'.
Ravel . . . . rä-vĕl'.
Ravenna . . . . . . rȧ-vĕn'-ä.   *It.* rä-vĕn'-nä.
Rawal Pindi, or Rawul
  Pindee . . . . . rô'-ŭl pĭn'-dē.
Rayo . . . . rä'-yō.
Reay . . . . rā.
Ré, Ile de, see Rhé . . ēl dŭ rā.
Reading . . . . . . rĕd'-ĭng.
Réaumur, de . . . . dŭ-rā-ō-mür'.
Rebikoff . . . . . . rĕ-bē'-kŏf.
Récamier . . . . . . rā-kă-mē=ā'.
Rechab . . . . rē'-kăb.
Rechabites . . . . . rĕk'-ȧ-bīts, rē'-kăb-īts.
Recife . . . . rĕ-sē'-fĕ.
Reclus . . . . rĕ-klü'.

Recollet	rĕk'-ŏl-lĕt.
Reddersburg	rĕd'-dĕrs-bŭrċh.
Redon	rē-dŏṅ'.
Redriff	rĕd'-rĭf.
Regensburg	rā'-gĕns-bōōrċh.
Reger	rā'-gĕr.
Reggio	rĕd'-jō.
Regillus (L.)	rĕ-jĭl'-ŭs.
Regnard	rĕn-yär'.
Regnault	rĕn-yō'.
Régnier	rān-yā'.
Regulus	rĕg'-ū-lŭs
Rehan (Ada)	rē'-àn.
Rehoboam	rē-hō-bō'-àm.
Rehoboth	rĕ-hō'-bŏth.
Reichardt	rīċh'-ärt.
Reichenbach	rī-ċhĕn-bäċh.
Reichsrath	rīċhs'-rät.
Reichstadt	rīċh'-stät.
Reichstag	rīċhs'-täċh.
Reikiavik, see Reykjavik	rī'-kĭ=à-vĭk.
Reims, see Rheims	rēmz. *Fr.* răṅs.
Reina Mercedes	rā-ē'-nä mâr-thā'-dās.
Reine de Saba, La	lä rĕn dŭ sä-bä'.
Reine Margot, La	lä rĕn mär-gō'.
Reinhold	rīn'-hōlt.
Réjane	rā-zhăṅ'.
Religio Medici	rē-lĭj'-ĭ-ō mĕd'-ĭ-sī.
Rembrandt, or	rĕm'-brănt.
Rembrandt van Rijn, or	
Ryn	rĕm'-brănt făn rīn.
Remedios	rā-mā'-dē-ōs.
Remedius	rĕ-mē'-dĭ-ŭs.
Remenyi	rĕ-mān'-yē.
Remi, or	rĕ-mē'.
Remigius	rĕ-mĭj'-ĭ-ŭs.
Remus	rē'-mŭs.

Rémusat, de . . . . . dŭ rā-mü-zä′.
Renaissance . . . . . rē-nā-säṅs′, rĕ-nā′-säns.
Renan . . . . *Anglicized,*rē-năn′, rē′-năn.
           Fr. rē-näṅ′.
Renard, see Reynard . . *Fr.* rē-när′.
Renaud . . . . . . rē-nō′.
René, Renée . . . . . rē-nā′.
Renfrew . . . . . . rĕn′-frōō.
Reni, Guido . . . . . gwē′-dō rā′-nē.
Rennes . . . . rĕn.
Renouvier . . . . . . rē-nōō-vē=ā′.
Rensselaer . . . . . rĕn′-sē-lĕr.
Repin . . . . rā-pĕn′.
Repnin, Nikolai . . . . nē′-kō-lä=ē rĕp-nēn′.
Repplier . . . . . . rĕp′-lē-ĕr.
Resaca de Guerrero . . rā-sä′-kä dā gā-rā′-rō.
Resaca de la Palma . . rā-sä′-kä dā lä päl′-mä.
Reshid Pasha . . . . rĕ-shēd′ păsh-ô′, pȧ-shä′,
           pä′-shȧ.
Restigouche . . . . . rĕs-tē-gōōsh′.
Reske, de . . . . . . dŭ rĕsh′-kĕ.
Rethel . . . . rē-tĕl′.
Retté, Adolphe . . . . ä-dŏlf′ rēt-tā′.
Retz, see Rais, Raiz . . rĕz.
Reuchlin . . . . . . rōĭċh′-lĭn.
Réunion, Ile de la . . . rē-ūn′-yŭn.
           Fr. ēl· dŭ lä rā-ü-nē=ôṅ′.
Reuss . . . . rois.
Reuter . . . . roi′-tĕr.
Reutlingen . . . . . roit′-lĭng-ĕn.
Reval, or . . . . . . rĕv′-äl.
Revel . . . . rĕv′-ĕl.
Revue des Deux Mondes . rē-vü′ dā dē mōṅd.
Rewa, or Rewah . . . rā′-wä.
Reykjavik, see Reikiavik . rī′-kĭ=ä-vĭk.
Reynaldo . . . . . . rā-näl′-dō.   [*Fr.* rē-när′.
Reynard, see Renard . . rĕn′-ȧrd, rā′-närd, rĕn′-ärd.

Reynier	rā-nē=ā'.
Reynolds	rĕn'-ŭldz.
Rezonville	rē-zôn̄-vēl'.
Rhadamanthine, Rhada-	
mantin	răd-à-măn'-thĭn, -tĭn.
Rhadamanthus	răd-à-măn'-thŭs.
Rhaetian	rē'-shĭ=àn.
Rhé, Ile du, see Ré . .	ēl dŭ rā.
Rhea	rē'-ä.
Rheims, see Reims . .	rēmz. *Fr.* răn̄s.
Rheinberger	rīn'-bĕr-gĕr.
Rheingold, Das	däs rīn'-gōlt.
Rhenish	rĕn'-ĭsh.
Rhodes	rōdz.
Rhodesia	rōd'-zhĭ=à, rō-dē'-sĭ=à.
Rhodope	rŏd'-ō-pē.
Rhondda	rŏnd'-à.
Rhys	rēs.
Rialto	rē-äl'-tō.
Riazan, see Ryazan . .	rē-ä-zän'.
Ribault, or Ribaut . . .	rē-bō'.
Ribecourt	rēb-kōōr'.
Ribera	rē-bā'-rä.
Ribot	rē-bō'.
Ricardo	rĭ-kar'-dō, rē-kär'-dō.
Ricasoli	rē-kä'-sō-lē.
Ricci	rēt'-chē.
Ricciarelli	rēch-är-ĕl'-lē.
Riccio (David), see Rizzio	rēt'-chō.
Richelieu, de	dŭ rĭsh-ĕ-lū'.
	Fr. dŭ rēsh=ŭ-lē=ē'.
Richepin	rēsh-păn̄'.
Richier	rē-shē=ā'.
Richter	rĭch'-tĕr.
Ricimer	rĭs'-ĭ-mĕr.
Rickenbacker	rĭk'-ĕn-băk-ĕr.
Rictus, Jehan	zhän̄ rĭk-tüs'.

Ridel . . . . rē'-dĕl.
Riedesel (Gen.), von . . fŏn rēd'-ā″-zĕl.
Riego y Nuñez . . . . rē-ā'-gō ē nōōn'-yĕth.
Rienzi, Cola di, or . . . kō'-lä dē rē-ĕnd'-zē.
Rienzo . . . . rē-ĕnd'-zō.
Riesen-Gebirge . . . . rē'-zĕn-gä-bērg'-ŭ.
Riet (R.) . . . . . . rēt.
Riga . . . . rē'-gä.
Rigaud . . . . rē-gō'.
Rigault . . . . rē-gō'.
Righi, or Rigi . . . . rē'-gĭ.
Rigoletto . . . . . . rē-gō-lāt'-tō.
Rigsdag . . . . . . rĭgs'-dăg.
Rigveda . . . . . . rĭg-vā'-dä.
Riis . . . . rēs.
Rijks (Museum) . . . rīks.
Rijksdag . . . . . . rīks-dăćh.
Rimbault . . . . . . răṅ-bō'.
Rimini . . . . rē'-mē-nē.
Rimsky-Korsakov . . . rĭm″-ski-kōr-sä'-kŏf.
Rinaldo ed Armida . . rē-näl'-dō äd är-mē'-dä.
Rinehart . . . . . . rīn'-härt.
Ring der Nibelungen, Der dĕr rĭng dĕr
                         nē'-bĕ-lōōng″-ĕn.
Ring Strasse . . . . . rĭng'-shträ-sŭ.
Rio Bravo del Norte, see
   Rio Grande del Norte . rē'-ō brä'-vō dĕl nōr'-tä.
Rio de Janeiro . . . . *pop.* rē'-ō jà-nēr'-ō,
                jà-nī'-rō. *Port.* rē'-ō dä
                zhä-nä'-rō, zhä-nä'=ē-rō.
Rio de la Plata, see Plate . rē'-ō dä lä plä'-tä.
Rio Grande . . . . . rī'-ō grănd.
                Sp. rē'-ō grän'-dä.
Rio Grande de Cagayan . rē'-ō grän'-dä dä
                kä-gä-yän'.
Rio Grande de la Pampanga rē'-ō grän'-dä dä lä
                päm-păn'-gä.

Rio Grande del Norte, see
   Rio Bravo del Norte .   rē'-ō grän'-dā dĕl nōr'-tā.
Rio Grande de Santiago .   rē'-ō grän'-dā dā
          sän-tē̄=ä'-gō.
Rio Grande do Norte . . rē'-ō grän'-dā dōō nōr'-tĕ.
Rio Grande do Sul . . rē'-ō grän'-dā dōō sōōl.
Rio Negro . . . . . *Sp.* rē'-ō nā'-grō.
          Port. rē-ōō nā'-grōō.
Rio Negro, São José do . sowṅ zhō-zā' dōō
          rē'-ōō nā'-grōō.
Riordan . . . . . . rēr'-dȧn.
Ripon . . . . rĭp'-ŭn.
Ristori . . . . rē-stō'-rē.
Riviera . . . . rē-vē̄=ā'-rä.
Rivière, Duc de . . . . dük dŭ rē-vē̄-âr'.
Rivinus . . . . . rē-vē̄'-nŭs.
Rivoli, Rue de . . . . rü dŭ rē-vō-lē'.
Rizzio, see Riccio . . . rĭt'-sē̄-ō, rēt'-sē̄-ō.
Roanoke . . . . . rō-ȧ-nōk'.
Roatan, see Ruatan . . rō-ȧ-tän'.
Robbia, Luca della . . . lōō'-kä dĕl'-lä rōb'-bē̄-ä.
Robert-Fleury . . . rō-bâr'-flēr-ē'.
Robert Guiscard . . . rŏb'-ērt gēs-kär'.
          Fr. rō-bâr'.
Robert le Diable . . . rō-bâr' lĕ dē̄-ä'—bl.
Robespierre, de . . . . dŭ rō'-bĕs-pēr.
          Fr. dŭ rŏbs-pē̄=âr'.
Robsart (Amy) . . . . rŏb'-särt.
Robusti, Jacopo . . . . yä-kō'-pō rō-bōōs'-tē.
Roch, Saint . . . . . säṅ rōk.
Rochambeau, de . . . dŭ rō-shäṅ-bō'.
Rochefort . . . . . rŏsh-fōr'.
Rochefoucauld, La . . . lä rŏsh-fōō-kō'.
Rochejacquelein, La . . lä rŏsh-zhäk-lăṅ'.
Rochelle . . . . . rō-shĕl'.
Rochet . . . . . . rō-shā'.
Rochus . . . . . . rō'-kŭs.

Rockefeller . . . . . rŏk'-ĕ-fĕl-ēr.
Rockingham . . . . . rŏk'-ĭng-ȧm.
Rocroi . . . . rŏk-rwä'.
Rod, Édouard . . . . ä-dōō-är' rŏd.
Rode, Pierre . . . . . rŏd.
Rodenbach, Georges . . zhŏrzh rō-dĕn-bäċh'.
Roderick Dhu . . . . rŏd'-ēr-ĭk dū.
Roderigo . . . . . . rŏd-ēr-ē'-gō.
Rodin, Auguste . . . . ō-güst' rō-dȧṅ'.
Rodó, José . . . . . hō-sä' rō-dō'.
Rodrigo Diaz de Bivar . rōd-rē'-gō dē'-äth dä
                         bē-bär'.
Rodrigues, or . . . . *Fr.* rōd-rēg'.
Rodriguez (I.) . . . . rō-drē'-gĕs.
Rodríguez (José Joaquin) rōd-rē'-gĕth.
Rodzianko . . . . . rŏdz-yän'-kō.
Roelas, Juan de las . . 'hōō-än' dä läs rō-ä'-läs.
Roeselare, see Roulers,
   Rousselaere . . . . rōō-sĕ-lä'-rĕ.
Roeskilde, see Röskilde . rēs'-kēl-dĕ.
Rofreit . . . . rōf'-rīt.
Rogcro, see Ruggiero . . rō-jä'-rō.
Roget . . . . rō-zhä'.
Rohan, de . . . . . . dŭ rō-äṅ'.
Rohilcund, or Rohilkhand rō-hĭl-kŭnd'.
Rohtak . . . . rō-tŭk'.
Roi des Montagnes . . rwä dä môṅ-tän'-yŭ.
Roi d'Yvetot, Le . . . lĕ rwä dēv-tō'.
Roi s'Amuse, Le . . . lĕ rwä sä-müz'.
Rois Fainéants, Les . . lä rwä fä-nä-äṅ'.
Rojas-Zorilla, or Zorrilla . rō'-ċhäs-thōr-rēl'-yä.
Rokeby . . . . rōk'-bĭ.
Roland . . . . rō'-lȧnd. *Fr.* rō-läṅ'.
Roland, Chanson de . . shän-sôṅ' dŭ rō-läṅ'.
Roland de la Platière . . rō-läṅ' dŭ lä plä-tē=âr'.
Roland de Roncevaux . . rō-län' dŭ rôṅs-vō'.
Roldan . . . . rōl-dän'.

Rolf	rŏlf.
Rolland, Romain . . .	rō-mǎṅ′, rŏl-äṅ′.
Rollin	rŏl′-ĭn. *Fr.* rō-lǎṅ′.
Rollo	rŏl′-ō.
Romagna	rō-män′-yä.
Romaic	rō-mā′-ĭk.
Romance	rō-mǎns′.
Roman de la Rose . . .	rō-mäṅ′ dŭ lä rŏz.
Roman de Rou	rō-mäṅ′ dŭ rōō.
Romanes	rō-mä′-nēz.
Romanesque	rō-màn-ĕsk′.
Romano, Ezzelino da . .	ĕt-zä-lē′-nō dä rō-mä′-nō.
Romanof, or Romanoff .	rō-mä′-nŏf.
Romany, see Rommany .	rŏm′-à-nĭ.
Romeo	rō′-mē-ō.
Roméo et Juliette . . .	rō-mā-ō′ ā zhül-ē=ĕt′.
Romero (Matias) . . .	rō-mä′-rō.
Romilly	rŏm′-ĭ-lĭ.
Rommany, see Romany .	rŏm′-à-nĭ.
Romola	rŏm′-ō-là, rō-mō′-là.
Roncesvalles, or . . .	rŏn-sē-väl′-lĕs.
	Sp. rōn-thĕs-väl′-yĕs.
Roncevaux	*Fr.* rôṅs-vō′.
Ronda	rōn-dà.
Ronge	rŏng′-ṅ.
Ronsard (Pierre de) . .	rôṅ-sär′.
Röntgen	rĕnt′-gĕn.
Roodepoort	rō-dĕ-pōrt′.
Rooidam	rō-ē-dǎm′.
Roosevelt	rōs′-vĕlt, rō′-sĕ-vĕlt.
Roquefort	rŏk-fōr′.
Rosa, Salvator . . .	säl-vä′-tōr rō′-zä.
Rosalind	rŏz′-à-lĭnd.
Rosaline	rŏz′-à-lĭn.
Rosamond, Rosamund .	rŏz′-à-mŭnd.
Rosbach, see Rossbach .	rŏs′-bäċh.
Roscelin, or	*Fr.* rŏs=ĕl-ăṅ′.

Roscellin, or . . . . . rŏs'-ĕl-ĭn.
Roscellinus, see Rucelinus rŏs-ĕ-lī'-nŭs.
Roscius . . . . . . rŏsh'-ĭ-ŭs.
Roscommon . . . . . rŏs-kŏm'-ŭn.
Rosecrans . . . . . . rō'-zĕ-krănz.
Rosellini . . . . . . rō-zĕl-lē'-nē.
Rosenkranz . . . . . rō'-zĕn-kränts.
Rosetta . . . . . . rō-zĕt'-à.
Rosicrucian . . . . . rŏz-ĭ-krū'-shĭ=án,
  rōz-ĭ-krōō'-shĭ=án.
Rosinante, see Rozinante rŏz-ĭ-năn'-tē.
Röskilde, see Roeskilde . rĕs'-kēl'-dĕ.
Rosny (Léon de) . . . rŏs-nē'.
Rospigliosi, Palazzo . . pä-läts'-sō rō-spēl-yō'-sē.
Rossbach, see Rosbach . rŏs'-bäċh.
Rossellino . . . . . . rŏs-sĕl-lē'-nō.
Rossetti . . . . . . rŏs-sĕt'-tē.
Rossi . . . . rŏs'-sē.
Rossini . . . . rŏs-sē'-nē.
Rostand, Edmond . . . ĕd-môṅ' rōs-täṅ'.
Rostock . . . . . . rŏs'-tŏk.
Rostoff . . . . rŏs-tŏf'.
Rostoptchin . . . . . rŏs'-tŏp-chĭn,
  rŏs-tŏp-chēn'.
Rota, see Rata . . . . rō'-tä.
Rotherhithe . . . . . rŏṫh'-ēr-hīṫh.
Rothesay . . . . . . rŏth'-sā.
Rothschild . . . . . rŏths'-chīld, rōs'-chīld.
  Ger. rōt'-shĭlt.
Rotrou . . . . rō-trōō'.
Rotterdam . . . . . rŏt'-ēr-dăm.
  D. rŏt-tĕr-dăm'.
Roubaix . . . . . . rōō-bā'.
Roubillac . . . . . . rōō-bē-yäk'.
Rouen . . . . rōō'-ĕn. Fr. rōō-ôṅ'.
Rougé . . . . rōō-zhä'.
Rouget de Lisle, or l'Isle . rōō-zhä' dŭ lēl.

Rougon-Macquart, Les . lä rōō-gôn'-mä-kär'.
Roulers, see Roeselare,
Rousselaere . . . . rōō-lä'.
Roumania, see Rumania . rōō-mä'-nĭ-à.
Roumelia, see Rumelia . rōō-mē'-lĭ-à.
Rousseau . . . . . . rōō-sō'.
Rousselaere, see Roese-
lare, Roulers . . . . rōōs-lär'.
Roussillon. . . . . . *Fr.* rōō-sē-yôn',
rōō-sēl-yôn'.
Roustam, see Rustam . . rōōs'-tàm. *Pers.* rōōs-tĕm.
Rouxville . . . . . . rōō-vĕl'.
Rovere, della. . . . . dĕl-lä rō'-vä-rä.
Roveredo . . . . . . rō-vĕ-rä'-dō.
Rovereto . . . . . . rō-vä-rà'-tō.
Rovigo . . . . rō-vē'-gō.
Rowe . . . . rō.
Rowena . . . . . . rō-wē'-nà.
Rowland . . . . . . rō'-lànd.
Roxana, or . . . . . rŏks-ăn'-ä, rŏks-ä'-nä.
Roxane . . . . *Fr.* rōks-ăn'.
Roy, Rammohun . . . räm-mō-hŭn' roi.
Roy Bareilly, see Rai Bareli roi bä-rä'-lē.
Roye . . . . rwä.
Royer-Collard . . . . rwä-yä'-kŏl-lär'.
Rozinante, see Rosinante rŏʁ-ĭ-năn'-tō.
Ruatan, see Roatan . . rōō-ä-tän'.
Rubaiyat (The) . . . . rōō'-bĭ-yăt.
Rubens (Peter Paul) . . rōō'-bĕnz.
Rübezahl . . . . . . rü'-bĕ-tsäl.
Rubicon . . . . . . rōō'-bĭ-kŏn.
Rubinstein (Anton) . . rōō'-bĭn-stīn.
Rucelinus, see Roscelin . rōō-sĕ-lī'-nŭs.
Rucellai . . . . . . rōō-chĕl-lä'=ē.
Rückert . . . . . . rük'-ĕrt.
Rude . . . . rüd.
Rudesheim . . . . . rü'-dĕs-hĭm.

Rüdiger . . . . rü'-dĭ-gĕr.
Rue de la Paix . . . . rü dŭ lä pā.
Rue de Rivoli . . . . rü dŭ rē-vō-lē'.
Rueil . . . . rü-ā'=yŭ.
Rue St.-Antoine . . . . rü săṅ-täṅ-twăn'.
Rue St.-Denis . . . . rü săṅ-dē-nē'.
Rue St.-Honoré . . . . rü săṅ-tō-nō-rā'.
Ruffini . . . . ro͞of-fē'-nē.
Rufinus . . . . . . rōo-fī'-nŭs.
Rug . . . . rōog.
Rügen . . . . rü'-gĕn.
Ruggiero, see Rogero . . ro͞od-jā'-rō.
Ruhr . . . . rōor.
Ruisdaal, or Ruisdael, see
Ruysdael . . . . . rois'-däl.
Ruk (I.) . . . . . . rōok.
Rum (I.) . . . . . . rŭm.
Rumania, see Roumania . rōo-mā'-nĭ-à.
Rumelia, see Roumelia . rōo-mē'-lĭ-à.
Runeberg . . . . . . rōo'-nĕ-bĕrċh.
Rungpoor, see Rangpur . rŭng-pōor'.
Runjeet Singh . . . . rŭn-jēt' sĭngh.
Runnemede, or . . . . rŭn'-ĕ-mēd.
Runnimede, or Runny-
mede . . . . rŭn'-ĭ-mēd.
Rupert . . . . rōo'-pĕrt.
Ruprecht . . . . . . rōo'-prĕċht.
Rurik . . . . rōo'-rĭk.
Rus . . . . rŭs.
Ruscuk, see Rustchuk . rōos-chōok'.
Russ . . . . rŭs.
Russia . . . . rŭsh'-ĭ=à, ro͞osh'-ĭ=à.
Russian . . . . . . rŭsh'ĭ=àn, ro͞osh'-ĭ=àn.
Rustam, see Roustam and
Rustum . . . . . . rōos'-tàm. *Pers.*
rōos'-tăm'.

Rustchuk, see Ruscuk . rōos-chōok'.

Rustenburg . . . . . roŏs'-tĕn-boōrċh.
Rustum, see Roustam,
    Rustam . . . . . . roōs'-tŭm.
Rutherglen . . . . . rŭth'-ĕr-glĕn, rŭg'-lĕn.
Ruthven (Raid of) . . . rŭth'-vĕn. *loc.* rĭv'-ĕn.
Rutlam, see Ratlam . . rŭt'-làm.
Rütli, see Grütli . . . rüt'-lĭ.
Rutnagherry, see Ratnagiri rŭt-nà-gĕr'-ĭ.
Ruy Blas . . . . . . rü=ē' bläs.
Ruy Diaz . . . . . . roō'-ē dē'-äth.
Ruyghur . . . . . . rī-gŭr'.
Ruysdale, see Ruisdaal,
    Ruisdael . . . . . rois'-däl.
Ruyter . . . . rī'-tĕr. *D.* roi'-tĕr.
Ryazan, see Riazan . . rē-ä-zän'.
Rydal . . . . rī'-dàl.
Ryswick, or . . . . . rĭz'-wĭk.
Ryswijk . . . . . . *D.* rīs'-vīk.

S

Saadi, see Sadi . . . . sä'-dē, să-dē'.
Saale . . . . zä'-lŭ.
Saalfeld . . . . . . zäl'-fĕlt.
Oaar . . . . ᴌ̇äɪ.
Saarbrück, or . . . . zär'-brük.
Saarbrücken, see Sarre-
    bruck . . . . . . zär'-brük-ĕn.
Saarburg . . . . . . zär-bürg'.
Saardam, see Zaarrdam . sär-dăm'.
Saavedra (Cervantes) . sä-ä-vä'-drä.
Saba, see Sabea . . . sā'-bä.
Saba (I.) . . . . . . sä'-bä.
Sábana Grande . . . . sä'-bä-nä grän'-dä.
Sabaoth . . . . . . săb'-ā-ŏth, sā-bā'-ŏtʰ
Sabbatic . . . . . . săb-ăt'-ĭk.
Sabea, see Saba . . . să-bē'-ä.

Sabeans . . . . . . sā-bē'-ȧnz.
Sabine (Cross Roads) . . să-bēn'.
Sabine (Mts.) . . . . sā'-bīn.
Sabine (Sir Edward) . . săb'-ĭn.
Sabinella . . . . . . sä-bē-nĕl'-lä.
Sabines . . . . . . săb'-īnz, sā'-bīnz.
Sabini . . . . să-bī'-nī.
Sabrina . . . . . . să-brī'-nȧ, sā-brī'-nȧ.
Sacharissa . . . . . săk-ȧ-rĭs'-ȧ.
Sacheverell . . . . . să-shĕv'-ĕ-rĕl
Sachs (Hans) . . . . zäks.
Sachsen . . . . . . zäk'-zĕn.
Sachsen-Altenburg, see
  Saxe-Altenburg . . . zäk'-zĕn-äl'-tĕn-bōōrċh.
Sachsen-Coburg-Gotha,
  see Saxe-Coburg-Gotha zäk'-zĕn-kō'-bōōrċh-gō'-tä.
Sachsen-Meiningen, see
  Saxe-Meiningen . . zäk'-zĕn-mī'-ning-ĕn.
Sachsenspiegel . . . . zäk'-zĕn-spē"-gĕl.
Sachsen-Weimar-Eisenach,
  see Saxe-Weimar-Eise-   [näċh.
  nach . . . . zäk'-zĕn-vī'-mär-ī'-zĕ-
Sacile . . . . sä-chē'-lĕ.
Saco (R.) . . . . . . sô'-kō.
Saco (José Antonio) . . sä'-kō.
Sadducees . . . . . săd'-yū-sēz.
Sadi, see Saadi . . . . să-dē'.
Sadi-Carnot . . . . . să-dē'-kär-nŏ'.
Sadowa . . . . . . sä-dō'-vä, sä'-dō-vä.
Saenz Peña . . . . . sä'-änth pän'-yä.
Safed . . . . sä'-fĕd, sä-fĕd'.
Safed Koh, see Suffeed
  Koh . . . . sä'-fĕd kō.
Saffi, see Sufi, Sofi . . säf'-ĭ.
Saga Josoku . . . . . sä'-gä' zhä'-sō'-kĕ'.
Sagan . . . . zä'-gän. *Fr.* sä-gäṅ'.
Sagar, see Saugor, Saugur sä-gŭr'.

Sagasta (Praxedes Mateo) sä-gäs'-tä.
Sage, Le, see Lesage . . lē săzh'.
Saghalien, or Saghalin . sä-gä-lē'-ĕn, sä-gä-lēn'.
Sagittarius . . . . săj-ĭ-tā'-rĭ-ŭs.
Sagua La Grande . . . sä'-gwä lä grän'-dä.
Saguenay . . . . . . săg-ĕ-nā', sä-gĕn-ā'.
Sahara, see Zahara, Sahra,
Sahhra . . . . . să-hä'-rä, sä'-hȧ-rä.
Saharanpur, see Seharun-
poor . . . . sȧ-här-ȧn-pōōr'.
Sahhra, see Sahara, Zahara sä'-hrä.
Sahib . . . . sä'-hĭb.
Sahra, see Sahara, Zahara sä'-hrä.
Saïd (Port) . . . . sä-ēd'. pop. säd.
Saida . . . . sī'-dä.
Said Pasha . . . . sä-ēd', pop. säd, pȧsh-ô';
pȧ-shä', päsh'-ȧ.
Saigon . . . . sī-gōn'. Fr. sä-gôṅ'.
Saigo Takamori . . . sī'-gō tä-kä-mō'-rē.
Saikio . . . . . . sī-kē'-ō.
Sailly-Saillisel . . . sä-yē'-sä-yē-zĕl'.
St. Albans . . . . . sānt, sĕnt ôl'-bȧnz.
St.-Amand, or . . . săṅ-tä-mäṅ'.
St.-Amand-Montrond . . săṅ-tä-mäṅ'-môṅ-rôṅ'.
St.-Antoine, Faubourg . fō-bōōr' săṅ-täṅ-twäṅ'.
Saint-Arnaud . . . săṅ-tär-nō'.
St. Augustine . . . . sānt, sĕnt ô-gŭs'-tĭn,
ô'-gŭs-tīn.
St. Augustine (City) . . sānt, sĕnt ô'-gŭs-tēn.
St. Barthélemy . . . . Fr. săṅ bär-tāl-mē'.
St. Bernard . . . . . sānt, sĕnt bĕr-närd',
bĕr'-närd. Fr.
săṅ bĕr-när'.
St. Bernard de Menthon . săṅ bĕr-när' dŭ môṅ-tôṅ'.
St. Cecilia, see Santa
Cecilia . . . . . . sānt sē-sĭl'-ĭ-ȧ.
St. Chad . . . . . . sānt, sĕnt chăd.

St. Clair . . . . . .   sānt, sĕnt klår.
                   Eng. sĭng'-klår.
St. Cloud . . . . . .   sănt, sĕnt klowd'.
                   Fr. săṅ klōō'.
St. Croix, see Santa Cruz .   sānt kroi'.
St. Cyr . . . .   săṅ sēr'.
St. Denis . . . . . .   sānt, sĕnt dĕn'-ĭs.
                   Fr. săṅ dĕn-ē'.
Sainte-Aldegonde . . .   săṅt-äl-dē-gôṅd'.
Sainte-Beuve . . . .   săṅt-bēv'.
Sainte-Chapelle . . . .   săṅt-shä-pĕl'.
Sainte-Croix, see Santa
   Cruz . . . .   săṅt-krwä'.
Saint Dizier . . . .   săṅ dē-zē=ā'.
St. Eloi . . . . .   săṅ-tĕl-wä'.
St. Étienne du Mont . .   săṅ-tā-tē=ĕn' dü mŏṅ.
Ste. Geneviève . . .   săṅt zhĕn-vē=ĕv'.
Sainte-Gudule . . .   săṅt gü-dül'.
Sainte Lucie . . . .   săṅt lü-sē'.
Sainte Pélagie . . .   săṅt pā-lä-zhē'.
Saintes . . . . . .   săṅt.
St.-Étienne . . . .   săṅ-tā-tē=ĕn'.
St. Eustache . . . .   săṅ tēs-täsh'.
St. Eustatius . . . .   sānt, sĕnt ū-stā'-shĭ-ŭs.
Saint-Évremond . . .   săṅ-tāvr-môṅ'.
St. Francis Xavier . . .   sānt, sĕnt frăn'-sĭs
                   zăv'-ĕ-ĕr. *Sp.* ċhä-bē-âr'.
                   Fr. ksä-vē=ā'.
St. Gall, see Sankt Gallen   sānt gôl.   *Fr.* săṅ-gäl'.
Saint-Gaudens . . . .   sānt, sĕnt-gô'-dĕnz.
                   Fr. săṅ-gō-dôṅ'.
Saint-Germain . . . .   săṅ-zhĕr-măṅ'.
St.-Germain-des-Prés .   săṅ-zhĕr-măṅ'-dā-prā'.
St. Germain l'Auxerrois .   săṅ-zhĕr-măṅ' lōks-ĕr-wä'.
St. Gothard . . . . .   *Fr.* săṅ gō-tär'.
St. Gotthard . . . .   sānt, sĕnt gŏth'-ärd.
                   Ger. sänkt gŏt'-härt.

St. Helena (Mother of
Constantine) . . . . sānt hĕl'-ē-nȧ.
St. Helena (I.) . . . . sānt hĕ-lē'-nä.
Saint-Hilaire, Barthélemy bär-tāl-mē' săṅ-tē-lȧ̂r'.
Saint-Hilaire, Geoffroy . zhō-frwä' săṅ-tē-lȧ̂r'.
Saintine . . . . . . săṅ-tēn'.
Saint-Ives, see St. Yves . sānt, sĕnt īvz.
      Fr. săṅ-tēv'.
St. Jean d'Acre . . . . săṅ zhäṅ dä'=kr.
St.-Jean d'Angély . . . săṅ zhäṅ' däṅ-zhä-lē'.
St. John . . . . . . sānt, sĕnt jŏn'. *Eng.*
      sometimes sĭn' jŭn.
Saint Julien . . . . . săṅ zhü-lē=ĕṅ'.
Saint-Just . . . . . . săṅ zhüst'.
St. Leger . . . . . . sānt, sĕnt lĕj'-ēr. *Eng.*
      sometimes sĭl'-ĭn-jĕr.
St.-Leu . . . . săṅ-lē'.
St. Louis . . . . . . sānt, sĕnt loo'-ĭs, loo'-ĭ.
      Fr. săṅ loo-ē'.
St. Lucia (I.) see Santa
Lucia . . . . . . sānt, sĕnt loo'-shĭ=ȧ.
St. Malo . . . . . . *pop.* sānt măl'-ō.
      Fr. săṅ mä-lō'.
Saint Marceaux . . . . săṅ mär-sō'.
Saint-Mars . . . . . săṅ-mar'.
St. Martin . . . . . . sānt, sĕnt mär'-tĭn.
      Fr. săṅ-mär-tăṅ'.
St. Michael . . . . . sānt, sĕnt mī'-kĕl.
St. Michel . . . . . săṅ mē-shĕl'.
St. Mihiel . . . . . . săṅ mē-ĕl'.
St. Nicolas . . . . . *Fr.* săṅ nē-kō-lä'.
St. Olaus . . . . . . sānt, sĕnt ō-lä'-ŭs.
St. Omer . . . . . . săṅ tō-mȧ̂r'.
Saintonge . . . . . . săṅ-tôṅzh'.
St. Ouen . . . . . . săṅ-too-ŏṅ'.
Saint Pancras . . . sĕnt păn'-krȧs.
St. Paul de Loanda . . sānt, sĕnt pôl dĕ lō-än'-dä.

St. Pierre, de . . . . dŭ săṅ pē=âr'.
St. Pierre, Bernardin de . bĕr-när-dăn' dē săṅ pē=âr'.
St. Pol-de-Léon . . . . săṅ pōl-dŭ-lā-ôṅ'.
Saint-Preux . . . . . săṅ-prē'.
St. Quentin . . . . . sänt kwĕn'-tĭn.
                        Fr. săṅ kŏṅ-tăṅ'.
St. Roch . . . . . . săṅ rōk.
St. Roque, see São Roque,
  see San Roque . . . sänt, sĕnt rōk.
Saint-Saëns . . . . . săṅ-säṅs'.
St. Sebastian, see San Se-
  bastian . . . . . . sänt, sĕnt sĕ-băs'-tē=ȧn.
St. Simon, de . . . . dŭ sänt, sĕnt sī'-mŏn.
                        Fr. dŭ săṅ sē-môṅ'.
St. Sulpice . . . . . săṅ sül-pēs'.
St. Vincent de Paul . . sänt, sĕnt vĭn'-sĕnt dŭ pôl.
                        Fr. săṅ văṅ-sän' dŭ pōl.
Saint Yves, see St. Ives . săṅ tēv'.
Saïs . . . . sā'-ĭs.
Saisiaz, La . . . . . lä sĕ-zē-äs'.
Sakai . . . . sä'-kī.
Sakatal . . . . sä-kä-täl'.
Sakhalien . . . . . . sä́ch-ä-lēn'.
Sakuntala . . . . . sȧ-kōͦn'-tȧ-lȧ,
                        shȧ-kōͦn'-tȧ-lȧ.
Sala (G. A.) . . . . . sā'-lä, sä'-lȧ.
Saladin, see Salah-ed-Din săl'-ȧ-dĭn.
Salado de Tarifa . . . sä-lä'-dō dä tä-rē'-fä.
Salah-ed-Diu, see Saladin *Arab.* sä'-lä-ĕd-dēn'.
Salamanca . . . . . săl-ȧ-măn'-kȧ.
                        Sp. sä-lä-män'-kä.
Salamis . . . . . . săl'-ȧ-mĭs.
Salammbô . . . . . sä-läm-bō'.
Salanio, or . . . . . sȧ-lä'-nĭ-ō, sä-lä'-nē-ō.
Salarino . . . . . . sä-lȧ-rē'-nō, sä-lä-rē'-nō.
Saldanha . . . . . . säl-dän'-yä.
Salerno . . . . . . sȧ-lĕr'-nō.   *It.* sä-lĕr'-nō.

Sales (Francis of) . . . sālz. *Fr.* săl.
Saléza . . . . sä-lā'-zä.
Salian . . . . sā'-lĭ-àn.
Salic . . . . săl'-ĭk.
Salignac . . . . . . sä-lĕn-yăk'.
Salins . . . . să-lăṅ'.
Salisbury . . . . . . sôlz'-bŭ-rĭ.
Salle, De la . . . . . dŭ lä săl'.
Salmon (Falls) . . . . săm'-ŭn.
Salm-Salm . . . . . zälm-zälm.
Salome . . . . să-lō'-mĕ, sā-lō'-mē.
Salon (The) . . . . . sä-lôṅ'.
Salonica . . . . . . săl-ō-nē'-kà.
Saloniki . . . . . . sä-lō-nē'-kē.
Salpêtrière, La . . . . lä säl-pā-trē=âr'.
Salta . . . . säl'-tä.
Saltikoff, see Soltikoff . säl'-tē-kŏf.
Salvador . . . . . . säl-vä-dōr'.
Salvator Rosa . . . . säl-vä'-tōr rō'-zä.
Salvini . . . . säl-vē'-nē.
Salzburg . . . . . . zälts'-bōōrċh.
Salzkammergut . . . . zältz'-käm-ĕr-gōōt.
Samain, Albert . . . . äl-bâr' sä-măṅ'.
Samaná, Santa Barbara de sän'-tä bär'-bä-rä
                  dä sä-mä-näl'.
Samar . . . . sä-mär'.
Samara (City) . . . . *Russ.* sä-mä-rä'.
Samarang . . . . . . sä-mä-räng'.
Samarcand, or Samarkand säm-är-känd'.
Samaveda . . . . . . sä-mä-vä'-dä.
Sambalpur, see Sumbul-
  pur . . . . sŭm-bŭl-pōōr'.
Sambre (R.) . . . . . sŏṅ'=br.
Samminiato, see San Min-
  iato . . . . säm″-mĭn-ĭ-ä'-tō.
Samoa . . . . sä-mō'-à.
Samoan (Is.) . . . . . sä-mō'-àn, sä-mō'-än.

Samos . . . . sā'-mŏs.
Samoset . . . . . . săm'-ō-sĕt.
Samothrace . . . . . săm'-ō-thrās.
      Gr. săm-ō-thrā'-sē.
Samson et Dalila . . . săṅ-sôṅ' nä dä-lē-lä'.
Samurai . . . . . . sä'-mōō'-rä'-ē'.
San Ambrogio . . . . sän äm-brō'-jō.
San Antonio (City) . . sän ăn-tō'-nĭ-ō.
San Antonio (Cape) . . sän än-tō'-nē-ō.
Sanballat . . . . . . săn-băl'-àt.
Sancho Panza . . . . săng'-kō păn'-zä.
      Sp. sän'-chō pän'-thä.

San Clemente . . . . sän klä-mān'-tĕ.
San Cristóbal . . . . sän krēs-tō'-bäl.
Sand, George . . . . jôrj sănd. *Fr.* zhŏrzh säṅd.
Sandalphon . . . . . săn-dăl'-fŏn.
Sandeau . . . . . . säṅ-dō'.
Sandherr . . . . . . säṅ-dâr'.
San Diego . . . . . . sàn dē=ā'-gō.
San Domingo, see Santo
 Domingo . . . . . sän dō-mēng'-gō.
Sandoval . . . . . . sän-dō'-bäl.
Sandringham . . . . sănd'-rĭng-àm.
Sandys (Edwin) . . . . săn'-dĭs, săndz.
San Fernando . . . . sän fēr-nän'-dō.
Sangallo . . . . . . säng-gäl'-lō.
Sangar (Strait) . . . . sän-gär'.
San Giorgio . . . . . sän jŏr'-jō.
Sangir (Is.) . . . . . säng-gēr'.
Sangpo, see Sanpu . . săng-pō'.
Sangraal . . . . . . săng-grāl'.
Sangrado (Doctor) . . . sän-grä'-dō.
Sangreal . . . . . . săng'-grē-ăl.
Sanhedrim, or . . . . săn'-hē-drĭm.
Sanhedrin . . . . . . săn'-hē-drin.
San Jacinto . . . . . săn jà-sĭn'-tō.
      Sp. sän chä-thēn'-tō.

San Joaquin . . . . . sän chō-ä-kēn'.
San José . . . . . . sän chō-sā'.
San José de Buenavista . sän chō-sā' dä
  bōō=ä-nä-vēs'-tä.
San Juan . . . . . . sän chōō=än'.
San Juan Bautista . . . sän chōō=än' bä=ōō-tēs'-tä.
San Juan de Puerto Rico . sän chōō-än' dä
  pōō-ĕr'-tō rē'-kō.
San Juan de Ulloa . . . sän chōō-än'dä ōōl-yō'-ä.
Sankt Gallen, see Saint Gall sänkt gäl'-lĕn.
Sankt Goar . . . . . sänkt gō'-är.
Sankt Gotthard . . . . sänkt gŏt'-härt.
Sankt Jakob . . . . . sänkt yä'-kŏp.
Sankt Moritz . . . . sänkt mō-rĭts'.
San Luis de Apra . . . sän lōō-ēs' dä ä'-prä.
San Luis Potosí . . . . sän lōō-ēs' pō-tō-sē'.
San Marco . . . . . sän mär'-kō.
San Marino . . . . . sän mä-rē'-nō.
San Martin . . . . . sän mär-tēn'.
San Michele . . . . . sän mē-kä'-lä.
San Miguel . . . . . sän mē-gĕl'.
San Miniato, see Sammin-
  iato . . . . . . sän mē-nē=ä'-to',
  mĭn-ĭ-ä'-tō.
San Onofrio . . . . . sän ō-nō'-frē-ō.
San Pietro in Vincoli . . sän pē=ä'-trō ēn vēn'-kō-lē.
Sanpu, see Sangpo . . . sän-pōō'.
San Remo . . . . . . sän rä'-mō.
San Roque, see St. Roque,
  São Roque . . . . . sän rō'-kä.
San Salvador . . . . sän säl-väd-thō'.
Sanscrit, see Sanskrit . . săn'-skrĭt.
San Sebastian, see Saint
  Sebastian . . . . . sän sä-bäs"-tē-än'.
Sans Gêne, Madame . . mä-däm' säṅ zhĕn.
Sanskrit, see Sanscrit . . săn'-skrĭt.
Sansovino . . . . . . sän-sō-vē'-nō.

Sans Souçi . . . . .   *Fr.* sŏṅ sōō-sē'.
San Stefano . . . . .   sän stĕf'-ä-nō.
Santa Ana . . . . . .   sän'-tä ä'-nä.
Santa Cecilia, see St.
    Cecilia . . . . . .   sän'-tä chä-chĕl'-ē-ä.
Santa Croce sull' Arno   . sän'-tä krō'-chĕ sŏŏl är'-nō.
Santa Cruz, see Saint Croix sän'-tä krōōz.
Santa Cruz (Andres) . .   sän'-tä krōōth'.
Santa Cruz de la Palma . sän'-tä krōōth' dä lä
                             päl'-mä.
Santa Cruz de la Sierra . sän'-tä krōōth' dä lä
                             sē=ĕr'-rä.
Santa Cruz de Santiago . sän'-tä krōōth' dä
                             sän-tē=ä'-gō.
Santa Cruz de Tenerife . sän'-tä krōōth' dä
                             tä-nä-rē'-fä.
Santa Fé . . . . . .   sän'-tä fä.
Santal Parganas . . .   sän-täl' pär-gŭn'-ȧs.
Santa Lucia, see St. Lucia *It.* sän'-tä lōō-chē'-ä.
                             Sp. sän'-tä lōō-thē'-ä.
Santa Luzia . . . . .   sän'-tä lōō-zē'-ä.
Santa Maria, La . . .   lä sän'-tä mä-rē'-ä.
Santa Maria degli Angeli sän'-tä mä-rē'-ä däl'-yē
                             än'-jä-lē.
Santa Maria del Carmine . sän'-tä mä-rē'-ä dĕl
                             kär-mē'-nĕ.
Santa Maria del Popolo . sän'-tä mä-rē'-ä dĕl
                             pō'-pō-lō.
Santa Maria in Ara Coeli sän'-tä mä-rē'-äĭn ä'-rȧ
                             sē'-lī.
Santa Maria in Cosmedin sän'-tä mä-rē'-ä ĭn
                             kŏs'-mĕ-dĭn.
Santa Maria Maggiore . sän'-tä mä-rē'-ä
                             mäd-jō'-rĕ.
Santa Maria Novella . .   sän'-tä mä-rē'-ä nō-vĕl'-lä.
Santa Maria sopra Minerva sän'-tä mä-rē'-ä
                             sō'-prä mē-nĕr'-vä.

Santander . . . . . . sän-tăn-dâr'.
                       Sp. sän-tän-där'.
Sant' Angelo . . . . . *It.* sänt än'-jä-lō.
Santarem . . . . . . sän-tä-răṅ', sän-tä-rĕṅ'.
Santa Scala . . . . . sän'-tä skä'-lä.
Santayana . . . . . . sän-tä-yä'-nä.
Santerre . . . . . . säṅ-tĕr'.
Santillana . . . . . . sän-tēl-yä'-nä.
Santillane . . . . . . säṅ-tē-yăn'.
Santi, Raphael, see Ra-
  phael and Sanzio . . rä'-fä-ĕl sän'-tē.
Santiago . . . . . . săn-tē-ä'-gō.
                       Sp. sän-tē—ä'-go.
Santiago de Chile . . . sän-tē=ä'-gō dä chē'-lä.
Santiago de Compostela, or sän-tē=ä'-gō dä
                       kōm-pōs-tä'-lä.
Santiago de Compostella . sän-tē=ä'-gō dä
                       kōm-pōs-tĕl'-ä.
Santiago de Cuba . . . sän-tē=ä'-gō dä kōō'-bä.
                       Eng. kū'-bä.
Santiago de la Vegas . . sän-tē=ä'-gō dä läs
                       vä'-gäs.
Santiago del Estero . . sän-tē=ä'-gō dĕl ĕs-tä'-rō.
Santillana . . . . . . sän-tēl-yä'-nä.
Santo Domingo, see San
  Domingo . . . . . . săn'-tō dō-miṅg'-gō.
                       Sp. sän'-tō dō-mēng'-gō.
Santo Espíritu . . . . sän'-tō ĕs-pē'-rē-tōō.
Santoveneo . . . . . . sän"-tō-vä-nä'-ō.
Santuzza . . . . . . sän-tŏŏts'-sä.
San Yuste . . . . . . sän yōōs'-tä.
Sanzio, Raphael, see Ra-
  phael and Santi . . . rä'-fä-ĕl sänd'-zē-ō.
São Antão . . . . . . säṅ än-täṅ'.
São José do Rio Negro . säṅ zhō-zä' dōō rē'-ōō
                       nä'-grōō.
Saona . . . . sä-ō'-nä.

Saône . . . . sōn.
Saône-et-Loire . . . . sōn-ā-lwär'.
São Paulo de Loanda . . säṅ pow'-lōō dĕ lō-än'-dä.
São Roque, see Saint
    Roque . . . . . . säṅ rō'-kā.
Sapho . . . . sä-fō'.
Sapor, see Saphur and
    Shahpoor . . . . . sā'-pŏr.
Sapphic . . . . . . sǎf'-ĭk.
Sapphira . . . . . . sǎ-fī'-rȧ.
Sappho . . . . sǎf'-ō.
Saracen . . . . . . sǎr'-ȧ-sĕn.
Saracenic . . . . . . sǎr-ȧ-sĕn'-ĭk.
Saragossa, see *Sp.* Zaragoza sǎr-ȧ-gŏs'-ȧ.
Saran, see Sarun . . . sä-rŭn'.
Sarasate y Navascues . . sä-rä-sä'-tā ē
    nä-väs'-kōō=ĕs.
Saratoff . . . . . . sä-rä'-tŏf.
Sarawak . . . . . . sä-rä-wäk', sǎ-rȧ-wǎk'.
Sarcey, Francisque . . fräṅ-sēsk' sär-sā'.
Sardanapalus . . . sär"-dä-nä-pä'-lŭs.
Sardou . . . . sär-dōō'.
Sarpedon . . . . . . sär-pē'-dŏn.
Sarpi . . . . sär'-pē.
Sarrail . . . . sǎr-rä'=yŭ.
Sarrebruck, see Saarbrück sär-brük'.
Sartain . . . . sär-tän'.
Sarto . . . . sär'-tō.
Sartoris . . . . . . sär-tō'-rĭs.
Sartor Resartus . . . sär'-tôr rē-sär'-tŭs.
Sarum . . . . sȧr'-ŭm.
Sarun, see Saran . . . sä-rŭn'.
Saskatchewan . . . . sǎs-kǎch'-ĕ-wȧn.
Saskia . . . . säs'-kē-ä.
Sassari . . . . säs'-sä-rē.
Sassenach . . . . . . sǎs'-ĕ-nȧċh.
Sassoferrato . . . . . säs"-sō-fĕr-rä'-tō.

Satara, see Sattara . . . sä-tä′-rä.
Satire Ménippée, see
   Satyre Ménippée . . sä-tēr′ mā-nē-pā′.
Satolli . . . . sä-tŏl′-lē.
Satsuma . . . . . sät-sū′-mȧ, sät-sōo′-mä.
Sattara, see Satara . . . sä-tä′-rä.
Saturnalia . . . . . sät-ēr-nä′-lĭ=ä.
Satyre Ménippée, see
   Satire Ménippée . . sä-tēr′ mā-nē-pā̱′.
Saugor, or . . . . . sô-gōr′.
Saugur, see Sagar . . . sô-gŭr′.
Sault Sainte Marie . . sōo sänt mā′-rĭ.
                Fr. sō sȧnt mä-rē′.
Saumarez, see Sausmarez sō-mä-rĕs′.
Saumur . . . . . . sō-mür′.
Sausmarez, see Saumarez sō-mä-rĕs′.
Sauternes . . . . . . sō-târn′.
Savaii, see Sawaii . . . sä-vī′-ē.
Savana la Mar . . . . Sp. sä′-bä-nä lä mär.
Savary . . . . sä-vä-rē′.
Savigny . . . . . . sä-vēn-yē′.
Savile . . . . sȧv′-ĭl.
Savoie . . . . sä-vwä′.
Savoja . . . . sȧ vō′-yä.
Savonarola . . . . . sȧ″ vō nä-rō′-lä.
Savoy . . . . sȧ-voi′.
Savoyard . . . . . . sä-voi′-ärd.
Sawaii, see Savaii . . . sä-wī′-ē.
Sawantwari . . . . . sä-wŭnt-wä′-rē.
Saxe (Marshal de) . . . săks.
Saxe-Altenburg, see Sach-
   sen-Altenburg . . . săks-ăl′-tĕn-bĕrg.
Saxe-Coburg-Gotha, see
   Sachsen-Coburg-Gotha săks-kō′-bĕrg-gō′-tȧ.
Saxe-Lauenburg . . . săks-low′-ĕn-bōorċh.
Saxe-Meiningen, see Sach-
   sen-Meiningen . . . săks-mī′-nĭng-ĕn.

Saxe - Weimer - Eisenach,
  see   Sachsen-Weimar-
  Eisenach . . . . . săks-vī'-mär-ī'-zĕ-näċh.
Say, Léon . . . . . . lā-ôṅ' sā.
Say (Viscount), or Saye   sā.
Scæan (Gate) . . . . sē'-ȧn.
Scaevola, Mutius . . . mū'-shĭ-ŭs sĕv'-ō-lȧ.
Scafell, see Scawfell . . skä-fĕl'.
Scala, La . . . . . . lä skä'-lä.
Scala Santa . . . . . skä'-lä sän'-tä.
Scaliger . . . . . . skăl'-ĭ-jĕr.
Scamander . . . . . skā-măn'-dĕr.
Scanderbeg, see Skander-
  beg . . . . skăn'-dĕr-bĕg.
Scapa . . . . skä'-pä.
Scapin . . . . skä'-pĭn. *Fr.* skă-păṅ'.
Scapino . . . . . . *It.* skä-pē'-nō.
Scaramouche . . . . . skăr'-à-mowch. *Fr.*
               skä-rä-mōōsh'.
Scarborough . . . . . skär'-bŭ-rŭ.
Scaria (Emil) . . . . skä'-rē-ä.
Scarlatti . . . . . . skär-lät'-tē.
Scarron . . . . . . skä-rôṅ'.
Scawfell, see Scafell . . skô-fĕll'.
Sceaux . . . . sō.
Schadow . . . . . . shä'-dō.
Schaffhausen . . . . . shäf-how'-zĕn,
            shäf'-how-zĕn.
Scharwenka (Philipp) . . shär-vĕng'-kä.
Schaumburg-Lippe . . . showm'-bōōrċh-lĭp'-pŭ.
Schedone . . . . . . skä-dō'-nä.
Scheele (C. W.) . . . . shēl. *Sw.* shĭl'-ĕ.
Scheherezade, see She-
  herezade . . . . . shä-hä''-rä-zä'-dä,
            shĕ-hē'-rä-zäd.
Scheideck, or Scheidegg . shī'-dĕk.
Scheidemann . . . . shī'-dŭ-män.

Schelde, or . . . . . sċhĕl'-dĕ.
Scheldt . . . . skĕlt. *pop.* shĕlt.
Schelling, von . . . . fŏn shĕl'-lĭng.
Schenck . . . . . . skĕnk.
Schenectady . . . . . skĕn-ĕk'-tá-dĭ.
Schérer . . . . . . shā-rȧr'.
Scheurer-Kestner . . . shēr-ȧr'-kĕst-nȧr'.
Scheveningen . . . . sċhā'-vĕn-ĭng-ĕn.
Schiedam . . . . . . skē-dăm', skē'-dăm.
                       D. sċhē-dăm'.
Schichallion . . . . . shē-hăl'-yŭn.
Schiller, von . . . . . fŏn shĭl'-lĕr.
Schipka (Pass), see Shipka shĭp'-kä.
Schlegel, von . . . . fŏn shlä'-gĕl.
Schlei, see Schley . . . shlī.
Schleiermacher . . . . shlī'-ĕr-mäċh"-ĕr.
Schlemihl, Peter . . . *Ger.* pā'-tĕr shlä'-mēl.
Schleswig, see Sleswick,
   Slesvig . . . . . . shlĕz'-vĭċh, shlĕs'-vĭċh.
Schleswig-Holstein . . shlĕz'-vĭċh-hōl'-stīn.
Schley, see Schlei, Sley
   (Prussia) . . . . . shlī.
Schley (Winfield Scott) . slī.
Schliemann . . . . . shlē'-män.
Schlüter . . . . . . shlü'-tĕr.
Schmalkalden, see Smal-
   kald, Smalcald . . . shmäl'-käl-dĕn.
Schnorr von Karolsfeld . shnôr fŏn kär'-ŏls-fĕlt.
Schoeffer, see Schöffer . shĕf'-fĕr.
Schoelcher (Victor) . . *Fr.* skĕl-shȧr'. *Ger.*
                       shĕl'-ċhĕr.
Schöffer, see Schoeffer . shĕf'-fĕr.
Schoharie . . . . . . skō-hăr'-ĭ.
Schomberg, von . . . . fŏn shŏm'-bĕrg.
                       Fr. shôṅ-bȧr'.
Schömberg . . . . . shēm'-bĕrċh.
Schönberg-Cotta . . . shēn'-bĕrċh kŏt'-ä.

Schönbrunn	shēn'-brŏon.
Schönefeld	shē'-nĕ-fĕlt.
Schongauer (Martin) . .	shōn'-gow-ĕr.
Schönhausen	shēn-how-zĕn.
Schopenhauer	shō'-pĕn-how″-ĕr.
Schouler	skōō'-lĕr.
Schouvaloff, see Shuvaloff	shŏō-vä'-lŏf.
Schreiner (Olive) . . .	shrī'-nĕr.
Schreyer	shrī'-ĕr.
Schröder	shrē'-dĕr.
Schröder-Devrient . . .	shrē'-dĕr-dĕv-rē═ŏṅ'.
Schubert	shōō'-bĕrt.
Schumann	shōō'-män.
Schumann-Heink . . .	shōō'-män-hīnk'.
Schurz	shŏŏrts.
Schütt	shüt.
Schuyler	skī'-lĕr.
Schuylkill	skōōl'-kĭl.
Schwab (Chas.)	swäb.
Schwanthaler	shvän'-täl-ĕr.
Schwartzkoppen	shvärts'-kŏp-pĕn.
Schwarzenberg	shvärt'-zĕn-bĕrċh.
Schwarzwald	shvärts'-vält.
Schwerin	shvä-rēn'.
Schwob (Marcel) . . .	shvŏb.
Schwyz	shvĭts.
Schytte	shĭt'-ŭ.
Scilly (Is.)	sĭl'-ĭ.
Scinde, see Sind . . .	sĭnd.
Scio, see Chios	sī'-ō, shē'-ō.
Scipio	sĭp'-ĭ-ō.
Scituate	sĭt'-yū-āt.
Sclav	skläv, sklăv.
Scone	skōōn, skōn.
Scopas	skō'-pàs.
Scorpio	skôr'-pĭ-ō.
Scotti	skŏt'-tē.

Scriabine . . . . . . skrē-ä'-bĭn.

Scribe, Eugène . . . . ē-zhĕn' skrēb.

Scriblerus . . . . . . skrĭb-lē'-rŭs.

Scudéri, or Scudéry . . skü-dā-rē'.

Scuola di San Rocco . . skōō=ō'-lä dē sän rŏk'-kō.

Scurcolla, or . . . . . skōōr-kŏl'-lä.

Scurcula, or . . . . . skōōr-kōō'-lä.

Scurgola, see Scurcolla . skōōr-gō'-lä.

Scutari . . . . skōō'-tä-rē.

Scylla . . . . sĭl'-ä.

Sealkote, see Sialkot . . sē-äl-kōt'.

Scattle . . . . sē-ăt̓-l.

Sebastian . . . . . . sē-băs'-tĭ=ȧn. *Sp.*
            sä-bäs″-tē-än'.

Sebastiano del Piombo . sä-bäs-tē=ä'-nō dĕl
            pē=ŏm'-bō.

Sebastopol, see Sevastopol sĕb-'ăs-tō-pōl,
            sĕb-ăs-tō'-pōl.

Secchi (Angelo) . . . . sĕk'-ē.

Sechuen, see Szechuen,
   Se Tchuen . . . . . sä-chōō-ĕn'.

Sedalia . . . . sĕ-dā'-lĭ-ä.

Sedan . . . . sē-dăn'. *Fr.* sē-däṅ'.

Sedgemoor . . . . . sĕj'-mōōr.

Sedlitz, see Seidlitz . . sĕd'-lĭts.

Sée . . . . sā.

Seeland . . . . . . sē'-lănd.

Seetapoor, see Sitapur . sē-tä-pōōr'.

Segan-fu, see Singan Fu,
   Sian-fu . . . . . . sē-gän'-fōō.

Sego, see Segu . . . . sā'-gō.

Segovia . . . . . . sĕ-gō'-vĭ-ä. *Sp.*
            sä-gō'-vē-ä.

Segu, see Sego . . . . sā'-gōō.

Ségur, de . . . . . . dŭ sä-gür'.

Seharunpoor, see Saharan-
   pur . . . . sĕ-här-ŭn-pōōr'.

Seidl, Anton	än'-tŏn zī'-dl.
Seidlitz, see Sedlitz , .	zīd'-lĭts.
Seine (R.)	sān. *Fr.* sĕn.
Seine-et-Marne	sĕn'-ā-märn'.
Seine-et-Oise	sĕn'-ā-wäz'.
Seine-Inférieure . . .	sĕn'-ăṅ-fā-rē̄=ēr'.
Sejanus	sĕ-jā'-nŭs, sē-jā'-nŭs.
Sekiang, see Sikiang . .	sē-kē-äng'.
Seleucidae, or . . .	sē-lū'-sĭ-dē.
Seleucids	sē-lū'-sĭdz.
Seleucus	sē-lū'-kŭs.
Selim	sē'-lĭm, sē-lēm'.
Sélincourt (Hugh de) . .	sā-lăṅ-kōōr'.
Seljuks	sĕl-jōōks'.
Selle	sĕl.
Selous	sē'-lŭs.
Sembrich	zĕm'-brĭċh.
Semele	sĕm'-ĕ-lē.
Semering, see Semmering	zĕm'-ĕr-ĭng.
Seminole	sĕm'-ĭ-nōl.
Semiramide	sā-mē-rä'-mĭ-dĕ.
Semiramis	sĕ-mĭr'-à-mĭs,
	sē-mĭr'-ā-mĭs.
Semites	sĕm'-īts.
Semmering, see Semering	zĕm'-ĕr-ĭng.
Semonides, see Simonides	sĕ-mŏn'-ĭ-dēz.
Sempach	zĕm'-päċh.
Sempione, *It.* for Simplon	sĕm-pē̄=ō'-nĕ.
Senancour	sĕ-näṅ-kōōr'.
Sendai	sĕn-dī'.
Seneca	sĕn'-ĕ-kä, sĕn'-ē-kȧ.
Seneffe	sĕ-nĕf'. [sĕn'-ē-gȧl.
Senegal	*n.* sĕn-ē-gôl'. *adj. and n.*
Sénégal	*Fr.* sā-nā-gȧl'.
Senegambia	sĕn-ĕ-găm'-bĭ-ȧ.
Senekal	sĕn-ĕ-kȧl'.
Senigallia, see Sinigaglia .	sā-nē-gäl'-lē̄=ä.

Senlac	sĕn'-lăk.
Senlis	sôn-lē'.
Sennaar, see Sennar . .	sĕn-när'.
Sennacherif	sĕ-năk'-ĕ-rĭb, sĕn-à-kē'-rĭb.
Sennar, see Sennaar . .	sĕ-när'.
Señor	sān-yōr'.
Señora	sān-yō'-rä.
Sens	sŏns.
Seonee, or Seoni . . .	sē-ō'-nē.
Seoul, see Seul . . .	sē-ōōl'.
Sepoy, see Spahi . . .	sĕ-pô'-ē. *pop.* sē'-poi.
Septuagesima	sĕp''tū-à-jĕs'-ĭ-mà.
Septuagint	sĕp'-tū-à-jĭnt''.
Seraglio	sĕ-räl'-yō.
Serajevo	sū-rä'-yä-vō.
Serao, Matilde	mä-tēl'-dä sä-rä'-ō.
Serapeion, or	sĕr-à-pē'-ŏn.
Serapeium, or Serapeum .	sĕr-à-pē'-ŭm.
Séraphita	sä-rä-fē-tä'.
Serapion, see Serapeion .	sĕr-à-pē'-ŏn.
Serapis	sĕ-rä'-pĭs, sē-rä'-pĭs.
Seres	sĕr'-ĕs.
Sereth	sĕr-ĕt'.
Sergius	sĕr'-jĭ-ŭs.
Serinagur, see Srinagar .	sĕr''-ĭ-nà-gōōr'.
Seringapatam, see Sriran-	
gapatam	sē-rĭng''-gä-pä-tăm'.
Seringes	sĕr-ănzh'.
Serpukhoff	sĕr-pōō-ċhŏf'.
Serra, Junipero	'hōō-nĭp'-ā-rō sĕr'-ä.
Serrano y Dominguez . .	sĕr-rä'-nō ē dō-mĭn'-gäth.
Serre	sĕr.
Servetus	sĕr-vē'-tŭs.
Servius Tullius	sĕr'-vĭ-ŭs tŭl'-ĭ-ŭs.
Sesostris	sē-sŏs'-trĭs.
Se Tchuen, see Se Chuen,	
Szechuen	sä chōō-ĕn'.

Setebos . . . . . . sĕt'-ĕ-bŏs.
Seul, see Seoul . . . sē-ōōl'.
Seurat . . . . sĕr-ä'.
Sevastopol, see Sebastopol sĕv'-ăs'-tō-pōl.
       Russ. sĕv'-äs-tō'-pŏl.
Sevcik . . . . sĕv'-chĭk.
Severus (Lucius Septimius) sĕ-vē'-rŭs, sē-vē'-rus.
Sevier . . . . sĕ-vēr'.
Sévigné, de . . . . . dŭ sā-vēn-yā'.
Sevilla, *Sp.* . . . . . sā-vēl'-yä.
Séville, *Fr.* . . . . . sā-vēl'.
Sèville . . . . sĕv'-ĭl, sē-vĭl'.
Sèvres . . . . sĕvr.
Sexagesima . . . . . sĕks-ȧ-jĕs'-ĭ-mȧ.
Seychelles . . . . . sā-shĕl'.
Seydlitz . . . . . . zīd'-lĭts.
Sfakus, or . . . . . sfä'-kŭs.
Sfax . . . . sfäks.
Sforza . . . . sfōrd'-zä.
Sganarelle . . . . . sgä-nä-rĕl'.
'S Gravenhaage, see The
 Hague . . . . . . s-grä-vĕn-hä'-ċhĕ.
Shadrach . . . . . . shā'-drăk.
Shafalus . . . . . . shăf'-ȧ-lŭs.
Shah . . . . shä.
Shahabad . . . . . . shä-hä-bäd'.
Shah Jahan, or Jehan . . shä yȧ-hän', yĕ-hän'.
Shah Jehanpoor . . . . shä yĕ-hän-pōōr'.
Shahpoor, see Sapor, and
 Shapur . . . . . . shä-pōōr'.
Shakuntala . . . . . shă-kōōn'-tă-lä.
Shalmaneser . . . . . shăl-mȧ-nē'-zĕr.
Shalott . . . . shă-lŏt'.
Shanghai . . . . . . shăng-hī', shăng-hä'=ī.
Shanking . . . . . . shän-kĭng'.
Shansi . . . . shän-sē'.
Shantow, see Swatow . . shän-tow'.

Shan-tung	shän-tōōng'.
Shapur, see Sapor, Shah-	
poor	shä-pōōr'.
Sharezer	shă-rē'-zĕr.
Sharon	shâr'-ŏn.
Shawangunk	shŏng'-gŭm.
Shchedrin	shchĕd'-rĭn.
Shebat	shē-băt'.
Sheboygan	shĕ-boi'-gȧn.
Shebuyeff	shĕ-bōō'-yĕf.
Shcchem, see Sichem . .	shē'-kĕm.
Shechemite	shē'-kĕm-īt.
Shechinah, see Shekinah .	shē-kī'-nä.
Sheemogga, see Shimoga	shē-mŏg'-gä.
Sheeraz, see Shiraz . .	shē'-räz.
Sheherezade, see Sche-	
herezade	shā-hā''-rä-zä'-dä,
	shĕ-hē'-rä-zäd.
Sheik, or Sheikh . . .	shēk, shāk.
Sheila	shē'-lȧ.
Shekinah, or Shechinah .	shē-kī'-nä.
Shelley	shĕl'-ĭ.
Shenandoah	shĕn-ăn-dō'-ȧ.
Shen-si, Shen-See . . .	shĕn-sē'.
Sheol	shē̄ō' ōl.
Shcraton	shĕr'-ȧ-tŏn.
Sheriffmuir	shĕr-ĭf-mūr'.
Shiites	shē'-īts.
Shikarpur	shĭk-är-pōōr'.
Shikoku, see Sikoku . .	shē-kō'-kōō.
Shillaber	shĭl'-ȧ-bĕr.
Shiloh	shī'-lō.
Shimoga, see Sheemogga	shē-mō'-gä.
Shimonoseki, see Simo-	
noseki	shĭm-ō-nō-sĕk'-ē.
Shinar	shī'-när.
Shingking	shĭng-kĭng'.

Shinto . . . . shĭn'-tō.
Shintoism . . . . . . shĭn'-tō-ĭzm.
Shipka, see Schipka (Pass) shĭp'-kä.
Shiraz, see Sheeraz . . shē'-räz.
Shiré . . . . shē'-rā.
Shirvan . . . . . . shĭr-vän'.
Shiva, see Siva . . . shĭ'-và.
Shogun . . . . shō-gōōn'.
Shokwado . . . . . . shō'-kwä'-do'.
Sholapur . . . . . . shō-lä-pōōr'.
Shoshone . . . . . . shō-shō'-nē, shō-shō-nē'.
Shrewsbury . . . . . shrūz'-bĕr-ĭ.
Shcherbacheff . . . . shschĕr-bä-chĕf'.
Shuntien-fu . . . . . shōōn'-tē=ĕn'-fōō'.
Shushan . . . . . . shōō'-shăn.
Shuvaloff, see Schouvaloff shōō-vä'-lŏf.
Shylock . . . . . . shī'-lŏk.
Sialkot, see Sealkote . . sē-äl-kōt'.
Siam . . . . sĭ-ăm', sē-äm'.
Siamese . . . . . . sī-à-mēz', sī-à-mēs'.
Sian-fu, see Singan-fu, Se-
    gan-fu . . . . . . sē-än'-fōō.
Siasconset . . . . . sī-ăs-kŏn'-sĕt. *pop.*
                      'skŏn'-sĕt.
Sibelius . . . . . . sē-bā'-lē-ōōs.
Sibola, see Cibola . . . sē'-bō-lä.
Siboney . . . . . . sē-bō-nā'=ē.
Sibuyan . . . . . . sē-bōō-yän'.
Sibyl . . . . sĭb'-ĭl.
Sicard . . . . sē-kär'.
Sichem, see Shechem and
    Sychem . . . . . . sī'-kĕm.
Sicilian . . . . sĭ-sĭl'-ĭ=àn.
Sicily . . . . sĭs'-ĭ-lĭ.
Sickingen, von . . . . fŏn zĭk'-ĭng-ĕn.
Sicyon . . . . sĭsh'-ĭ-ŏn.
Siddhârta, or . . . . . sĭd-här'-tä.

Siddhartha . . . . . sǐ-dhär'-thä.
Sidon, see Zidon . . . sī'-dŏn.
Siegfried, see Sigfrid . . sēg'-frēd. *Ger.* zēg'-frēt.
Siemaradski . . . . . zē-mȧ-räd'-skǐ.
Siemering . . . . . . zē'-mä-rǐng.
Siena, see Sienna . . . sē-ĕn'-nä.
Sienese . . . . . . sē-ĕn-ēz', sē-ĕn-ĕs'.
Sienkiewicz . . . . . sē=ĕn-kē=ĕ'-vǐch.
Sienna, see Siena . . . sē-ĕn'-ä.
Sierra de los Ladrones . sē-ĕr'-rä dä lōs lä-drō'-nĕs.
Sierra Leone . . . . . sē-ĕr'-rä lē-ō'-nē. *loc.*
                      lē-ōn'. *Sp.* sē-ĕr'-rȧ
                      lä-ō'-nä.
Sierra Madre . . . . sē-ĕr'-rȧ mä'-drä.
Sierra Maestra . . . . sĕ-ĕr'-rä mä-äs'-trä.
Sierra Morena . . . . sē-ĕr'-rȧ mō-rä'-nä.
Sierra Nevada . . . . sē-er'-rȧ nĕ-vä'-dä.
                      Sp. sē-ĕr'-rä nä-vä'-dä.
Sieyès . . . . . . sē-yĕs', sē-ĕs', sē=ä-yĕs'.
Sigel, Franz . . . . . fräntz sē'-gĕl.
                      Ger. zē'-gĕl.
Sigfrid, see Siegfried . . sēg'-frēd. *Ger.* zēg'-frēt.
Sigismund (Emperor), see   [*Ger.* zē'-gǐs-mŏŏnt.
  Sigmund . . . . . sǐj'-ǐs-mŭnd.
Sigmaringen . . . . . zēg'-mä-rǐng"-ĕn,
Sigmund, see Sigismund . sǐg'-mŭnd. *Ger.* zēg'-mŏŏnt.
Signac . . . . sēn-yăk'.
Signora . . . . sēn-yō'-rä.
Signorelli . . . . . sēn-yō-rĕl'-lē.
Signoria . . . . . . sēn-yō-rē'-ä.
Signory . . . . . . sēn'-yō-rǐ.
Sigourney . . . . . . sǐg'-ēr-nǐ.
Sigurd . . . . zē'-gōōrd. *Fr.* sē-gür'.
Sikhs . . . . sēks.
Sikiang, see Sekiang . . sē-kē-äng'.
Sikoku, see Shikoku . . sē-kō'-kōō.
Silenus . . . . sī-lē'-nŭs.

Silesia . . . .   sĭl-ē'-shĭ=à.
Silhet, see Sylhet . . .   sĭl-hĕt'.
Siloah, or . . . . . .   sĭ-lō'-ä.
Siloam . . . .   sĭ-lō'-àm, sĭl-ō'-ăm.
Silva . . . .   sēl'-vä.
Silvanus . . . . . .   sĭl-vā'-nŭs.
Silvester . . . . . .   sēl-vĕs'=tr.
Silvio Pellico . . . .   sēl'-vē-ō pĕl'-lē-kō.
Simancas . . . . . .   sē-män'-käs.
Simbirsk . . . . . .   sĭm-bērsk'.
Simeon Stylites . . .   sĭm'-ē-ŏn stī-lī'-tēz.
Simla . . . .   sĭm'-là.
Simois . . . .   sĭm'-ō-ĭs.
Simon de Montfort . . .   sī'-mŏn dŭ mŏnt'-fōrt.
                            Fr. sē-môǹ' dŭ môǹ-fŏr'.
Simon, Jules . . . . .   zhül sē-môǹ'.
Simonides, see Semonides   sĭ-mŏn'-ĭ-dēz.
Simonoseki, see Shimono-
    seki . . . . . .   sĭm-ō-nō-sĕk'-ē.
Simplon, see Sempione .   sĭm'-plŏn. *Fr.* săǹ-plôǹ'.
Sinai (Mount) . . . .   sī'-nā, sī'-nā-ī, sī'-nī.
Sinaitic (Peninsula) . .   sī-ṅā-ĭt'-ĭk.
Sinclair . . . .   sĭn-klâr'. *Eng.* sĭng'-klâr.
Sind, or Sinde, or Sindh,
    see Scinde . . . . .   sĭnd.
Singan-fu, see Sian-fu,
    Segan-fu . . . . .   sēn-gän'-fōō.
Singapore . . . . . .   sĭng-gà-pōr', sĭn'-gà-pōr.
Singhalese . . . . .   sĭng-gà-lēz', *or* -lēs'.
Sinigaglia, see Senigallia   sē-nē-gäl'-yä.
Sinn Fein . . . . . .   shĭn fān.
Sinope, or . . . . . .   sĭ-nō'-pē.
Sinub, Turk. . . . . .   sē-nōōb'.
Sion, see Zion . . . .   sī'-ŏn.
Sioux . . . .   sōō.
Siraj-ud Daula, see Sura-
    jah Dowlah . . . .   sē-räj'-ōōd-dow'-lä.

Sirdar . . . . sẽr-där'.
Sirius . . . . sĭr'-ĭ-ŭs.
Sirsa . . . . sẽr'-sä.
Sisera . . . . sĭs'-ĕ-rä.
Sismondi, de . . . . . dŭ sĭs-mŏn'-dĭ.   *Fr.* dŭ
                                sẽs-môṅ-dē'.
Sissley . . . . sēs-lē'.
Sistine, see Sixtine . . sĭs'-tĭn.
Sisyphus . . . . . . sĭs'-ĭ-fŭs.
Sitapur, see Seetapoor . sẽ-tȧ-pōōr'.
Siut, see Assiut, Asyoot . sẽ-ōōt'.
Siva, see Shiva . . . . sẽ'-vȧ.
Sivan . . . . sĭv'-ȧn.
Siward . . . . sẽ'-wärd.
Siwash . . . . sẽ-väsh'.
Six, Jan . . . . . . yăn sẽks.
Sixtine (Chapel), see Sis-
  tine . . . . sĭks'-tĭn.
Sjögren . . . . . . shẽ'-grĕn.
Skager-Rack . . . . . skăg'-ẽr-răk', skăg'-ẽr-räk.
Skaguay . . . . . . skăg'-wā.
Skanderbeg, see Scander-
  beg . . . . skăn'-dẽr-bĕg.
Skaneateles (L.) . . . skăn'-ē-ăt'-lĕs.
Skeat . . . . skēt.
Skiddaw . . . . . . skĭd'-dô.
Skierniewice . . . . . skē=ẽr"-nē=ĕ-vēt'-sĕ.
Skobeleff . . . . . . skō'-bĕ-lĕf.
Skrzynecki, Jan Boncza . yän bŏn'-tsä
                                skrĭzh'-nĕt-skĭ.
Skupshtina . . . . . skōōpsh'-tĭ-nä.
Slav, or Slave . . . . släv, slăv.
Slavonic . . . . . . slä-vŏn'-ĭk.
Slesvig (Dan.), see Schles-
  wig . . . . slĕs'-vĭg.
Sleswick, see Schleswig . slĕs'-wĭk.
Sley, see Schlei . . . . slī.

Slidell . . . . slī-dĕl'.
Slowacki . . . . . . slō-väts'-kĭ.
Slovak . . . . slō-văk'.
Slovene . . . . . . slō-vēn'.
Sluis, or Sluys . . . . slois.
Smalcald, or Smalkald,
   see Schmalkalden . . smăl'-kăld.
Smalcaldic . . . . . smăl-kăl'-dĭk.
Smaldeel . . . . . . smălt'-āl.
Smectymnuus . . . . smĕk-tĭm'-nū-ŭs.
Smetana . . . . . . smĕ'-tä-nä.
Smillie . . . . smī'-lĭ.
Smith Cay . . . . . smĭth kä'=ē.
Smolensk . . . . . . smō-lĕnsk'.
Smuts . . . . smoŏts.
Sneyders, see Snyders . snī'-dĕrs.
Snorre, Snorri, or
   Snorro Sturleson . . snŏr'-rā, snŏr'-rē, or
                snŏr'-rō stōōr'-lā-sŏn.
Snowdon . . . . . . snō'-dŭn.
Snyders, see Sneyders . snī'-dĕrs.
Snyman (Gen.) . . . . snī'-măn.
Sobieski . . . . . . sō-bé=ĕs'-kē.
Sobranje . . . . . . sō-brän'-yĕ.
Socapa, La . . . . . lä sō-kä'-pä.
Socinian . . . . . . sō-sĭn'-ĭ-ȧn.
Socinus . . . . . . sō-sī'-nŭs.
Socrates . . . . . . sŏk'-rȧ-tēz.
Södermanland . . . . sē'-dĕr-män-länt".
Sodom . . . . sŏd'-ŏm.
Sodoma, or . . . . . sō-dō'-mä.
Sodona . . . . sō-dō'-nä.
Soerabaya, see Surabaya . sōō-rä-bī'-ä.
Sofala . . . . sō-fä'-lä.
Sofi, or Sophi, see Sufi,
   Saffi . . . . sō'-fĭ.
Sofia, see Sophia . . . sō-fē'-ä.

Soho (Square) . . . . sō'-hō.
Sohrab, see Suhrab . . *mod. Pers.* sōō-hrôb'.
                     Arab. sŏ-hrôb'.
Soignies . . . . . . swän-yē'.
Soissons . . . . . . swä-sôṅ'.
Sokoto . . . . . . sō-kō'-tō.
Sol . . . . sŏl.
Solace (The) . . . . sŏl'-ās.
Solario (Antonio) . . . sō-lä'-rē-ō.
Soldau . . . . . . zŏl'-dow.
Solebay . . . . . . sōl'-bā.
Solferino . . . . . sŏl-fä-rē'-nō.
Solinus . . . . . . sō-lĭ'-nŭs.
Soltikoff, see Saltikoff . . sŏl'-tē-kŏf.
Solyman, see Suleiman . sŏl'-ĭ-man.
Somaj . . . . . . sō-mäj'.
Somaliland . . . . . sō-mä'-lē-lǎnd.
Sombor, see Zombor . . sŏm'-bŏr.
Sombrero . . . . . sōm-brä'-rō.
Somme (R.) . . . . . sŏm.
Sömmering . . . . . zēm'-mĕr-ĭng.
Somosierra . . . . . sō"-mō-sĭ-ĕr'-ȧ.
Sonata Appassionata . . sō-nä'-tä
                     äp-päs"-sē-ō-nä'-tä.
Sonata Tragica . . . . sō-nä' tä trä' jō kä.
Sonderbund . . . . . zŏn'-dĕr-bŏont.
Sonnambula, La . . . lä sŏn-näm'-bōō-lä.
Sonnino . . . . . . sŏn-nē'-nō.
Sontag . . . . . . sŏn'-tǎg. *Ger.* zŏn'-täċh.
Soochow, see Su-chau . . sōō'-chow'.
Soodan, see Sudan, Soudan sōō-dän'.
Soodra, see Sudra . . sōō'-drä.
Sooloo, see Sulu, Joló . . sōō-lōō'.
Sopater . . . . . . sŏp'-ä-tẽr, sō'-pȧ-tẽr.
Sophia, see Sofia . . . sō-fĭ'-ä. *mosque,* sō-fē'-ä.
Sophia Dorothea . . . sō-fĭ'-ä dŏr-ō-thē'-ä
Sophrosyne . . . . . sō-frŏs'-ĭn-ē.

Sorbonne, La . . . . . lä sŏr-bŏn'.
Sorel, Agnès . . . . . än-yĕz' sō-rĕl'.
Soria . . . . sō'-rē-ä.
Soriano . . . . sō-rē-ä'-nō.
Sorolla . . . . sō-rŏl'-yȧ.
Sorosis . . . . sō-rō'-sĭs.
Sosigenes . . . . . . sō-sĭj'-ē-nēz.
Sotatsu . . . . sō'-täts'-ē'.
Soubise . . . . . . sōō-bēz'.
Soudan, see Sudan . . . sōō-dän'.
Souche . . . . sōōsh.
Souchez . . . . . . sōō-shä'.
Soudanese, see Sudanese sōō-dăn-ēz', sōō-dăn-ēs'.
Soufflot . . . . sōō-flō'.
Soulé . . . . sōō-lä'.
Soult . . . . sōōlt.
Sousa . . . . sōō'-zȧ.
Southey . . . . . . sow'-t͡hĭ, sŭt͡h'-ĭ.
Southampton (City) . . sowth-hămp'-tŏn, or
                         sŭt͡h-hămp'-tŏn.
Southampton (Earl of) . sŭt͡h-ămp'-tŏn, or
                         sŭt͡h-hămp'-tŏn.
Southwark . . . . . sŭt͡h'-ērk.
Souvaroff, see Suvaroff,
    Suwaroff . . . . . sōō-vä'-rŏf.
Souvestre, Émile . . . ā-mēl' sōō-vĕs'=tr.
Souvigny . . . . . . sōō-vēn-yē'.
Soviet . . . . sôv-yĕt'.
Spagnoletto, Il . . . ēl spän-yō-lĕt'-tō.
Spahee, or . . . . . spä'-ē, spä'-hē.
Spahi, see Sepoy . . . spä'-hĭ.
Spalato, or . . . . . spä-lä'-tō.
Spalatro . . . . . . spä-lä'-trō.
Spallanzani . . . . . späl-länd-zä'-nē.
Spandau . . . . . . spän'-dow.
Sparafucile . . . . . spä''-rä-fōō-chē'-lä.
Spartacus . . . . . . spär'-tȧ-kŭs.

Speichern, see Spicheren . . spī'-ċhĕrn.
Speier, see Speyer, Spire . spīr, spī'-ĕr.
Spencerian, or -serian . . spĕn-sē'-rĭ-an.
Speranski, or Speransky . spä-rän'-skē.
Spetzia, see Spezia . . . spĕt'-zē-ä.
Speyer, see Speier, Spires spī'-ĕr, spīr.
Speyerbach . . . . . spī'-ĕr-bäċh.
Spezia, or Spezzia, see
   Spetzia . . . . . . spĕt'-zē-ä.
Spica . . . . spī'-kä.
Spicheren, see Speichern . spē'-ċhĕr-ĕn.
Spielhagen . . . . . spēl'-hä-gĕn.
Spinola, de . . . . . dä spō'-nō-lä.
Spinoza . . . . . . spē-nō'-zä.
Spion Kop . . . . . . spē'-ŏn kŏp.
Spire, see Speier, Speyer . spēr.
Spires, see Speyer, Spire . spīrz.
Spiridon . . . . . . spĭ-rĭd'-ĭ-ŏn.
Spitalfields . . . . . spĭt'-ȧl-fēldz.
Spluga, or . . . . . . splōō'-gä.
Splügen . . . . . . splü'-gĕn.
Spohr (Louis) . . . . spōr.
Spokan, or . . . . . spō-kăn'.
Spokane . . . . . . spō-kān'.
Spoleto . . . . . . spō-lä'-tō.
Spontini . . . . . . spŏn-tē'-nē.
Sporades . . . . . . spŏr'-ä-dēz.
Spree . . . . sprä.
Spurgeon . . . . . . spŭr'-jŭn.
Spurzheim . . . . . spōōrts'-hīm.
Spuyten Duyvil . . . . spī'-tĕn dī'-vĭl.
Spytfontein . . . . . spīt'-fŏn-tīn.
Squarcione . . . . . skwär-chō'-nä.
Srinagar, see Serinagur . srĭ-nȧ-gär'.
Srirangapatam, see
   Seringapatam . . . . srĭ-răng″-gȧ-pȧ-tăm'.
Staal, de . . . . . . dŭ stäl.

Stabat Mater . . . . stā'-băt mā'-tĕr, stä'-bät
mä'-tĕr.

Stadtlohn . . . . . . stät-lōn'.

Stael-Holstein . . . . stä'-ĕl-hŏl'-stīn.
Fr. stä-ĕl'-ŏl-stăn'.

Stagira . . . . stā-jǐ'-rȧ.

Stagirite . . . . . . stăj'-ĭ-rīt.

Stagirus . . . . . . stā-jǐ'-rŭs.

Stamboul . . . . . . stäm-bōōl'.

Stambuloff . . . . . stäm-bōō'-lŏf.

Stanhope . . . . . . stăn'-ŏp.

Stanislas, see Stanislaus . stăn'-ĭs-lȧs.

Stanislas Lesczinski . . stăn'-ĭs-lȧs lĕsh-chĭn'-skē.

Stanislaus, see Stanislas . stăn-ĭs-lā'-ŭs.

Stanislaus (R.) . . . . stăn'-is-low.

Stanze . . . . ständ'-zĕ.

Starhemberg . . . . . stä'-rĕm-bĕrċh.

Statira . . . . stȧ-tī'-rȧ.

Staubbach . . . . . . stowb'-bäċh.

Stavanger . . . . . . stä-väng'-gĕr.

Stavropol . . . . . . stäv'-rō-pŏl.

Steen, Jan . . . . . yăn stān.

Steenkerke, or . . . . stān'-kĕrk-ĕ.

Steenkerken . . . . . stān'-kĕrk-ĕn.

Stefanie (L.) . . . . . stĕ-fä-nē'.

Stein, von . . . . . . fŏn stīn.

Steinau . . . . stī'-now.

Steinitz . . . . . . stīn'-ĭts.

Steinmetz . . . . . . stīn'-mĕts.

Steinwehr . . . . . . stīn'-vär.

Stelvio . . . . stĕl'-vǐ-ō.

Stendhal, De . . . . . dŭ stŏn-däl'.

Stéphanie . . . . . . stā-fä-nē'.

Stephano . . . . . . *Tempest,* stĕf'-ā-nō.
Merchant of Venice,
stĕf-ä'-nō.

Stephen Báthori . . . stē'-vĕn bä'-tō-rē.

Stepniak . . . . . . stĕp′-nē=äk.
Sterkstroom . . . . . stĕrk′-strōm.
Stettin . . . . stĕt-ēn′.
Steuben . . . . . . stū′-bĕn. *Ger.* stoi′-bĕn.
Steyn . . . . stīn.
Steyne . . . . stīn.
Stiberdigebit . . . . . stĭ′-bĕr-dĭ-jĕb″-ĭt.
Stigand . . . . stĭg′-ånd.
Stilicho . . . . stĭl′-ĭ-kō.
Stilliano . . . . . . stēl-ē-ä′-nō.
Stinnes, Hugo . . . . hoo′-gō stĭn′-ĕs.
Stockholm . . . . . . stŏk′-hōlm.
Stoke Poges . . . . . stōk pō′-jĕs.
Stolypin . . . . . . stŏ-lĭp′-ĭn.
Stolzenfels . . . . . stŏlt′-zĕn-fĕlz.
Stormberg . . . . . . stŏrm′-bĕrċh.
Stor-thing . . . . . . stōr′-tĭng.
Stötteritz . . . . . . stĕt′-tĕ-rĭts.
Stoughton . . . . . . stō-tŭn.
Stour . . . . stoor.
Strabo . . . . strā′-bō.
Strachey, Lytton . . . lĭt′-ŭn strā′-chĭ.
Stradivarius . . . . . străd-ĭ-vā′-rĭ-ŭs.
Strakosch . . . . . . strä′-kŏsh.
Stralsund . . . . . . sträl′-sŏond.
Strasbourg . . . . . *Fr.* sträs-boor′.
Strasburg, or . . . . străs′-bĕrg.
Strassburg . . . . . *Ger.* sträs′-boorċh.
Stratford-on-Avon . . străt-fōrd-ŏn-ā′-vōn.
Strauss . . . . strows.
Stravinsky . . . . . . strä-vĭn′-skĭ.
Strelitz . . . . *Ger.* shtrā′-lĭts.
Strelitzes . . . . . . strĕl′-its-ĕz.
Strephon . . . . . . strĕf′-ŏn.
Strindberg . . . . . strĭnt-bĕrċh.
Stromboli . . . . . . strŏm′-bō-lē.
Strophades . . . . . strŏf′-ă-dēz.

Strozzi . . . . strŏt'-zē.

Strumitza . . . . . . strōō'-mēts-à.

Struve . . . . strōō'-vŭ.

Stryj . . . . strē.

Strypa . . . . strē'-pä.

Stuhlweissenburg . . . shtōōl-vīs'-ĕn-bōōrċh.

Stürmer . . . . . . shtür'-mĕr.

Sturm und Drang . . . shtōōrm ŏŏnt dräng.

Stuttgart . . . . . . shtŏŏt'-gärt.

Stuyvesant . . . . . stī'-vĕ-sănt.

Stygian . . . . stĭj'-ĭ-àn.

Stylites . . . . stī-lī'-tēz.

Styr . . . . stēr.

Styx . . . . stĭks.

Suabia, see Swabia . . swā'-bĭ-à.

Suabian, see Swabian . . swā'-bĭ-àn.

Subiaco . . . . . . sōō-bē=ä'-kō.

Subig (Bay) . . . . . sōō-bēg'.

Sublime Porte . . . . sub-līm' pōrt.

Su-chau, or Suchow, see
 Soochow . . . . . sōō'-chow'.

Suchet . . . . sü-shä'.

Sucre, de . . . . . . dā sōō'-krā.

Sudan, see Soudan, Soodan sōō-dän'.

Sudanese, see Soudanese sōō-dăn-ēz', sōō-dăn-ēs'.

Sudermann . . . . . zōō'-dĕr-män.

Sudra, see Soodra . . sōō'-drä.

Sue, Eugène . . . . . yū'-jĕn sū. *Fr.* ē-zhān' sü.

Suetonius . . . . . . swē-tō'-nĭ-ŭs.

Suez . . . . sōō'-ĕz, sōō-ĕz'.

Suffeed Koh, see Safed Koh sŭf'-ēd-kō.

Suffren de Saint-Tropez . süf-frĕn' dŭ săṅ-trō-pĕss'.
  Fr. süf-frŏṅ' du săṅ trō-pā'.

Sufi, see Saffi, Sofii . . sōō'-fĭ.

Suhrab, see Sohrab . . *mod. Pers.* sōō-hrŏb'.
  Arab. sŏ-hrŏb'.

Suippe . . . . swēp.

Sukenobu . . . . . .   sōō'-kā'-nō'-bē'.
Sul, Rio Grande do . .   rē'-ō grän'-dā dōō sōōl.
Suleiman (Mosque of), see
  Solyman . . . . .   sōō-lā-män'.
Sulla . . . .   sŭl'-à.
Sully . . . .   sŭl'-ĭ.   Fr. sü-lē'.
Sully-Prudhomme . . .   sü-lē'-prü-dŏm'.
Sultanpur . . . . . .   sŭl-tăn-pōōr'.
Sulu, see Sooloo, Joló . .   sōō-lōō'.
Suluk . . . .   sōō-lōōk'.
Sumag . . . .   sōō-mäg'.
Sumatra . . . . . .   sōō-mä'-trä.
Sumbulpur, see Sambalpur   sŭm-bŭl-pōōr'.
Sundi . . . .   sōōn'-dē.
Sunna . . . .   sōŏn'-à.
Sunni . . . .   sōŏn'-ē.
Sun Yat Sen . . . . .   sōŏn yät sĕn.
Suppé, von . . . . .   fŏn zōŏp'-pä.
Surabaya, see Soerabaya   sōō-rä-bī'-ä.
Surajah Dowlah, see Siraj-
  ud-Daula . . . . .   sōō-rä'-jä dow'-lä.
Surat . . . .   sōō-rät'.
Surikoff . . . . . .   sōō'-rē-kŏf.
Surinam . . . . . .   sōō-rĭ-näm'.
Susa . . . .   sōō'-sà.   It. sōō'-zä.
Sutlej . . . .   sŭt'-lĕj.
Suvaroff, or . . . . .   sōō-vä'-rŏf.
Suvla . . . .   sōō'-vlà.
Suwalki . . . . . .   soo-väl'-kē.
Suwanee, or Suwannee .   sū-wô'-nē.
Suwaroff, or . . . . .   sōō-vä'-rŏf.
Suwarrow, see Suvaroff .   sōō-vä'-rŏv.
Suzuki Harunobu . . .   sōō'-zōō'-kē
                  hä'-rōō'-nō'-bē'.
Sverdrup . . . . . .   svĕr'-drōŏp
Swabia, see Suabia . .   swā'-bĭ-à.
Swabian, see Suabian . .   swā'-bĭ-àn.

Swansea . . . . swŏn'-sē.

Swartow, or . . . . . swär-tow'.

Swatow, see Shantow . . swä-tow'.

Swaziland . . . . . . swä'-zē-lănd.

Swedenborg . . . . . swē'-děn-bôrg.

        Sw. svĭd'-ĕn-bōrg.

Swedenborgian . . . . swē-děn-bôr'-jĭ-àn.

Swegen, or . . . . . svā'-gěn.

Swein, or . . . . . . swān.

Sweyn . . . . swān.

Sybaris . . . . sĭb'-à-rĭs, sĭb'-ā-rĭs.

Sybarite . . . . . . sĭb'-à-rīt.

Sybel, von . . . . . fŏn zē'-běl.

Sychar . . . . sī'-kär.

Sychem, see Sichem, She-
chem . . . . . . sī'-kĕm.

Sycorax . . . . . . sĭk'-ō-răks.

Sydenham . . . . . . sĭd'-ĕn-àm.

Sylhet, see Silhet . . . sīl-hĕt'.

Sylva, Carmen . . . . kär'-měn sĭl'-vä.

Sylvester . . . . . . sĭl-věs'-tĕr.

Sylvestre Bonnard . . . sĭl-věs'-tr bŏn-âr'.

Symonds . . . . . . sĭm'-ŭndz, sī'-mŭndz.

Symons . . . . sĭm'-ŭnz, sī'-mŭnz.

Symplegades . . . . . sĭm-plĕg'-à-dēz.

Synge . . . . sĭng.

Synod . . . . sĭn'-ŏd.

Synope . . . . sī-nō'-pē.

Syracuse . . . . . . sĭr'-à-kūs, sĭr'-à-kūz.

Syrinx . . . . sī'-rĭngks.

Szechenyi . . . . . . sā'-chĕn-yē.

Szechuen, see Sechuen,
Se Tchuen . . . . . sā-chōō-ĕn'.

Szegedin . . . . . . sĕg'-ĕd-ēn.

Sziget . . . . sĭg'-ĕt.

T

Taafe, von	fŏn tä′-fŭ.
Taal	täl.
Tabago, see Tobago . .	tä-bä′-gō.
Tabard	tăb′-ård.
Tabasco	tȧ-băs′-kō. Sp. tä-bäs′-kō.
Tablas	tä′-bläs.
Tabor	Mt. tā′-bŏr. Boh. tä′-bŏr.
Tacna	pop. tăk′-nȧ, täk′-nä.
Taddeo	täd-dā′-ō.
Tadema, Alma-	äl′-mä-tä′-dĕ-mä.
Tadmir	täd-mēr′.
Tadmor	tăd′-môr.
Taeping, see Tai-ping . .	tī-pĭng′.
Tafna	täf′-nä.
Tagal, see Tegal . . .	tä-gäl′. D. tä-ċhäl′.
Tagala	tä-gä′-lä.
Taganrog	pop. tăg-ȧn-rŏg′, tä-gän-rŏg′.
Tagle, Sanchez de . . .	sän′-chĕs dä tä′-glä.
Tagliacozzo	täl-yä-kŏt′-zō
Tagliamento	täl-yä-män′-tō.
Taglioni (Filippo) . . .	täl-yō′-nē.
Tagore, Rabindranath . .	rä′-bĭn′-drä′-näth′ tä′-gōr′.
Tagus, see Sp. Tajo, Port.	
Tejo	tä′-gŭs.
Tahamis	tä-ä′-mēs.
Tahiti	tä-hē′-lē.
Tahitian	tä-hē′-tĭ-ȧn.
Tahlequah	tä-lĕ-kwä′.
Tahoe	tä′-hō.
Tai, see Thai, or T'hai .	tī.
Tai-chau	tī′-chow′.
Taillebourg	tä=yŭ-bōōr′.
Taillefer	tä=yŭ-fâr′.
Taine	tän.

Tai-ping, see Taeping . . tī'-pǐng'.

Taiwan . . . . tī-wän'.

Tai-yuan . . . . . . tī-wän'.

Taj-e-mah (The) . . . täzh'-ĕ-mä'.

Taj Mahal, or Mehal . . täzh mä-häl', or mĕ-häl'.

Tajo, Sp. for Tagus . . tä'-ċhō.

Tajurrah . . . . . . '. tä-jōō'-rä.

Takahira . . . . . . tä'-kä'-hē'-rä'.

Takala, see Tekele . . . tä-kä'-lä.

Takao, or Takow . . . tä-kä'=ō, tä-kow'.

Taku . . . . tä'-kōō.

Talaut (Is.) . . . . . tä-lowt'.

Talavera de la Reina . . tä-lä-vä'-rä dä lä rä-ē'-nä.

Talbot . . . . tôl'-bŭt.

Talca . . . . täl'-kä.

Talfourd . . . . . . tôl'-fŭrd.

Taliaferro . . . . . . tŏl'-ĭ-vēr.

Ta Lien Wan, or Talien-
wan . . . . tä'-lēn'-wän'.

Taliesin . . . . . . tăl'-ĭ-sĭn.

Tallard . . . . tä-lär'.

Talleyrand-Périgord . . tăl'-ĭ-rănd. Fr.
täl-ā-räṅ'-pä-rē-gōr'.

Tallien . . . . tä-lē=ĕṅ'.

Talma . . . . tăl'-mȧ, täl-mä'.

Talmud . . . . . . tăl'-mŭd.

Talmudic . . . . . . tăl-mŭd'-ĭk.

Talmudist . . . . . . tăl'-mŭd-ĭst.

Tamalpais . . . . . . tăm-ȧl-pä'-ēs.

Tamanieb . . . . . . tä-mä-nē-ĕb'.

Tamar . . . . tä'-mär.

Tamaulipas . . . . . tä-mow-lē'-päs.

Tamboff . . . . . . täm-bŏf'.

Tamburlaine, or Tamber-
lane . . . . tăm-bēr-lān'.

Tamerlane, see Timur-
Leng . . . . tăm-ēr-lān'.

Tamils . . . . tăm′-ĭlz, tä-mēlz′.
Tammuz . . . . tăm′-ŭz.
Tamora . . . . . . tăm′-ō-rȧ.
Tampico . . . . . . tăm-pē′-kō. *Sp.* täm-pē′-kō.
Tamsui. . . . . . . täm-sōō′-ē.
Tanagra . . . . . . tăn′-ȧ-grä.
Tanais . . . . tăn′-ā-ĭs, tā′-nā-ĭs.
Tananerivo . . . . . tä-nä″-nä-rē′-vō.
Tancred . . . . . . tăng′-krĕd, tăn′-krĕd.
Tancrède . . . . . . täṅ-krĕd′.
Tancredi . . . . . . tän-krā′-dē.
Taneieff . . . . . . täṅ-yä′-ĕf.
Taney (Robert) . . . . tô′-nĭ.
Tanganyika (L.) . . . . tän-gän-yē′-kä.
Tanger, *Fr.,* or . . . . täṅ-zhä′.
Tanger, *Ger.,* see Tangier täng′-ĕr.
Tangerine . . . . . . tăn-jĕ-rēn′.
Tangier, or . . . . . tăn-jēr′, tän-jēr′.
Tangiers, or . . . . . tăn-jērz′, tän-jērz′.
Tanja, Native . . . . tän′-jä.
Tanjore . . . . . . tăn-jōr′.
Tan Kweilin . . . . . tän′-kwā′-lēn′.
Tannenberg . . . . . tän′-ĕn-bĕrċh.
Tannhäuser . . . . . tän′-hoi-zĕr.
Tännyu. . . . . . . tän′-n-yū′.
Tantalus . . . . . . tăn′-tȧ-lŭs.
Tao . . . . tä′-ō.
Taoism . . . . tä′-ō-ĭzm, tä′-ō-ĭzm,
                    tow′-ĭzm.
Taparelli, Massimo . . mäs′-sē-mō tä-pä-rĕl′-lē.
Tapia . . . . tä′-pē-ä.
Tappan Zee . . . . . tăp′-ȧn-zā.
Tapti (R.) . . . . . . tăp′-tē.
Tara . . . . tä′-rȧ.
Taranto . . . . . . tä-rän′-tō.
Tarapacá . . . . . . *pop.* tă-rȧ-păk′-ȧ.
                    Sp. tä″-rä-pä-kä′.

Tarascon . . . . . . tä-räs-kôṅ'.
Tarbes . . . . tärb.
Tardieu . . . . . . tär-dē̅=yē'.
Tarifa . . . . tä-rē'-fä.
Tárlac, or Tarlac . . . tär'-läk.
Tarn . . . . tärn.
Tarn-et-Garonne . . . tärn'-ä-gä-rŏn'.
Tarnopol . . . . . . tär-nō'-pŏl.
Tarnovo, see Tirnova . . tär'-nō-vō.
Tarpeia . . . . tär-pē'-yä.
Tarpeian . . . . . . tär-pē'-yȧn.
Tarquin . . . . . . tär'-kwĭn.
Tarquinio . . . . . . tär-kwē'-nē-ō.
Tarragona . . . . . tär-rä-gō'-nä.
Tarshish . . . . . . tär'-shĭsh.
Tartar, see Tatar . . . tär'-tär.
Tartarean . . . . . . tär-tā'-rē-ȧn.
Tartarin . . . . . . tär-tä-räṅ'.
Tartarus . . . . . . tär'-tȧ-rŭs.
Tartufe, or Tartuffe . . tär'-tŭf. *Fr.* tär-tüf'.
Tashkend, or Taschkend täsh-kend'.
Tasmania . . . . . . tăz-mā'-nĭ-ȧ.
Tasso, Torquato . . . . tōr-kwä'-tō tăs'-ō.
                       It. täs'-sō.
Tatar, see Tartar . . . tä'-tär.
Tatiana . . . . tät-yä'-nä.
Taubert . . . . . . tow'-bĕrt.
Tauchnitz . . . . . . towk'-nĭts.
                       Ger. towċh'-nĭts.
Taughannock . . . . tô-găn'-ŏk.
Tauler . . . . tow'-lĕr.
Taunton . . . . . . tänt'-ŏn.
Taunus . . . . tow'-nōōs.
Tauric . . . . tô'-rĭk.
Taurida . . . . . . tow'-rē-dä.
Taurus (Mt.) . . . . tô'-rŭs.
Tavannes . . . . . . tä-vän'.

Tavoy . . . . tä-voi'.
Tayabas . . . . . . tī-ä'-bäs.
Taygetus . . . . . . tā-ĭj'-ĕ-tŭs.
Taytay . . . . tä'=ē-tä'=ē.
Tchad (L.), see Chad,
  Tsad . . . . chäd.
Tchaikowsky . . . . . chī-kŏv'-skĭ.
Tcherepnin . . . . . chĕr-ĕp'-nĭn.
Tchernaya . . . . . . châr'-nī-ä.
Tchernigoff . . . . . chĕr-nē-gŏf'.
Tchernyshevsky . . . . chĕr-nē-shĕf'-skē.
Tchitcherin . . . . . chĭch'-ēr-ĭn.
Tchu . . . . chōō.
Tchukchis . . . . . chōōk'-chēz.
Tean, see Teian . . . tē'-ȧn.
Tebeth . . . . tĕ-bĕt'.
Teck . . . . tĕk.
Tecumseh . . . . . . tē-kŭm'-sĕ.
Te Deum . . . . . . tē dē'-ŭm.
Tegal, see Tagal . . . tĕ-gäl'.
Tegea . . . . tē'-jē-ä.
Tegetthoff . . . . . . tā'-gĕt-hŏf.
Tegnér . . . . tĕng-nâr'.
Teheran, or . . . . . tŏh č-rän'.
Tehran . . . . tčh-rän'.
Tehri . . . . tĕh-rē'.
Tehuantepec . . . . . tā-wän''-tā-pĕk'.
Teian, see Tean . . . . tē'-ȧn.
Te Igitur . . . . . . tē-ĭj'-ĭ-tēr.
Teignmouth . . . . . tān'-mŭth.
Tejo, Port. for Tagus . . tā'-zhōō.
Tekele, see Takala . . . tā-kā'-lĕ.
Telamon . . . . . . tĕl'-ā-mŏn.
Tel or Tell El Kebir . . tĕl ĕl kĕb-ēr'.
Telemachus . . . . . tĕ-lĕm'-à-kŭs.
Télémaque . . . . . tā-lā-măk'.
Tellez . . . . tĕl'-yĕth.

Teman . . . . tē'-măn.
Tembuland . . . . . těm'-bōō-lănd.
Téméraire . . . . . . tā-mā-râr'.
Temesvár . . . . . . těm'-ěsh-vär.
Temora . . . . . . tē-mō'-rȧ.
Tempe . . . . těm'-pā, těm'-pē.
Tenasserim . . . . . těn-ăs'-ēr-ĭm.
Tencin . . . . tŏṅ-săṅ'.
Tenebræ . . . . . . těn'-ē-brē.
Tenedos . . . . . . těn'-ē-dŏs.
Tenerife, or . . . . . tā-nā-rē'-fā.
Teneriffa, or . . . . . tā-nā-rēf'-fä.
Teneriffe . . . . . . těn-ēr-ĭf'.
Teniers (David) . . . . těn'-yěrz. *Fr.* tě-nē=âr'.
Tenniel . . . . těn'-yěl.
Teocalli . . . . . . tē-ō-kăl'-ē.
Tepic . . . . tā-pēk'.
Teplitz, see Töplitz . . těp'-lĭts.
Terauchi . . . . . . tā'-rä'=ōō-chē'.
Terburg . . . . . . těr'-bŭċh.
Terceira . . . . . . těr-sā'-rä.
Terek . . . . těr-ěk'.
Tergnier . . . . . . těrn-yā'.
Termonde . . . . . . tär-mōṅd'.
Ternina, Fräulein Milka . froĭ'-līn mēl'-kä těr-nē'-nä.
Terpsichore . . . . . těrp-sĭk'-ō-rē.
Terpsichorean . . . . těrp"-sĭ-kō-rē'-ȧn.
Terracina . . . . . . těr-rä-chē'-nä.
Terra del Fuego, see Tier-
  ra del Fuego . . . . těr'-rä děl fū-ē'-gō.
Terrazas . . . . . . těr-ä'-säs.
Terre, La . . . . . . lä târ.
Terre Haute . . . . . těr'-ě-hōt. *Fr.* târ-ōt'.
Tertullian . . . . . . těr-tŭl'-ē=ȧn.
Teruel . . . . tā-rōō-ěl'.
Teschen . . . . . . těsh'-ěn.
Tesla . . . . těz'-lä.

Tête-Noire . . . . . tāt-nwär'.
Tethys . . . . tē'-thĭs.
Tetrazzini . . . . . tā-träts-sē'-nē.
Tetuan . . . . tĕt-ōō-än'.
Teucer . . . . tū'-sĕr.
Teufelsdröckh, Herr . . hĕr toi'-fĕlz-drĕk.
Teuton . . . . tū'-tŏn.
Teutonic . . . . . . tū-tŏn'-ĭk.
Teviot . . . . tĭv'-ĭ-ŏt, tē'-vĭ-ŏt.
Tewfik Pasha . . . . tū'-fĭk păsh-ô', pà-shä'.
                      päsh'-à.
Texcoco, or . . . . . tās-kō'-kō.
Texel . . . . tĕks'-ĕl.
Tezcuco . . . . . . tās-kōō'-kō.
Thaba N'Chu, or Thaba
  Ntschu, or Thabanchu . tä'-bänts-chōō.
Thaddeus . . . . . . thăd'-ē-ŭs, thăd-ē'-ŭs.
Thai, see T'hi, Tai . . . tī.
Thais . . . . thā'-ĭs. *Fr.* tä-ēs'.
Thaisa . . . . thā'-ĭs-ä.
Thalaba . . . . . . thăl'-à-bà.
Thalberg . . . . . . täl'-bĕrċh.
Thales . . . . thā'-lēz.
Thalia . . . . thā-lī'-à.
Thamos, *Am.* . . . . thamz.
Thames, *Eng.* . . . . tĕmz.
Thanatopsis . . . . . thăn-à-tŏp'-sĭs.
Tharaud . . . . . . tă-rō'.
Theætetus . . . . . . thē-ē-tē'-tŭs.
Théâtre Antoine . . . tā-ătr' äṅ-twăn'.
Théâtre Chauve Souris . tā-ătr' shōv sōō-rē'.
Théâtre Comique . . . tā-ătr' kō-mēk'.
Théâtre Français, Le . . lē tā-ătr' frän-sā'.
Théâtre Italien . . . . tā-ătr' ē-tä-lē=ĕṅ'.
Thebaid (The) . . . . thē'-bā-ĭd, thē-bā'-ĭd.
Thébaide, La . . . . lä tā-bä-ēd'.
Thebais . . . . thē-bā'-ĭs, thĕb'-ā-ĭs.

The Hague, see Den Haag,
   La   Haye,   S'Graven
   Haage . . . . . . thē hāg.
Theiss, see Tisza, *Hung.*. . tīs.
Thekla . . . . těk'-lä.
Themis . . . . thē'-mǐs.
Themistocles . . . . . thē-mǐs'-tō-klēz.
Theobald (Lewis) . . . thē'-ō-bôld, tǐb'-ăld.
Theocritean . . . . . thē-ŏk″-rǐ-tē'-ȧn.
Theocritus . . . . . thē-ŏk'-rǐ-tŭs.
Theodoric . . . . . . thē-ŏd'-ō-rǐk.
Theodorus . . . . . thē-ō-dō'-rŭs.
Theodosia . . . . . . thē-ō-dō'-sǐ-ȧ, -shǐ-ȧ.
Theodosius . . . . . thē-ō-dō'-sǐ-ŭs,
                  thē-ō-dō'-shǐ-ŭs.
Theodota . . . . . . thē-ŏd'-ō-tȧ.
Theodotus . . . . . . thē-ŏd'-ō-tŭs.
Theophilus . . . . . thē-ŏf'-ǐl-ŭs.
Theophrastus . . . . thē-ō-frăs'-tŭs.
Theotocupuli . . . . . tä-ō″-tō-kōō-pōō'-lē.
Theresa . . . . . . tě-rē'-sä. *Ger.* tä-rā'-sä.
Thérèse . . . . . . tä-rěz'.
Thermidor . . . . . thĕr-mǐ-dôr'. *Fr.*
                  tĕr-mē-dōr'.
Thermopylæ . . . . thĕr-mŏp'-ǐ-lē.
Thersites . . . . . . thĕr-sī'-tēz.
Theseion . . . . . . thē-sē'-ŏn.
Theseum . . . . . . thē-sē'-ŭm.
Theseus . . . . . . thē'-sūs, thē'-sē-ŭs.
Thessalonica . . . . . thĕs″-sȧ-lō-nī'-kȧ.
Thetis . . . . thē'-tǐs.
Theuriet . . . . . . tĕr-ē-ā'.
T'hi, see Tai, Thai . . . tī.
Thiaucourt . . . . . tē-ō-kōōr'.
Thiaumont . . . . . tē-ō-mŏṅ'.
Thibaut . . . . . . tē-bō'.
Thibet, see Tibet . . . tǐb'-ět, tǐ-bět'.

Thibetan, see Tibetan . .	tĭ-bĕt'-àn, tĭb'-ĕt-àn.
Thielt	tēlt.
Thiepval	t-yĕp-väl'.
Thiergarten, see Tier-garten	tēr'-gär-tĕn.
Thierri, (or-ry) Amédée .	ăm-ā-dā'-tē-ĕr-ē'.
Thierry, Château . . .	shă-tō' tē-ĕr-ē'.
Thiers	tē-âr'.
Thing	*Dan.* tĭng.
Thionville	tē-ôn-vēl'.
Thisbe	thĭz'-bē.
Thogji Chumo (L.) . .	thŏg'-jē chōō'-mō.
Tholuck	tō'-lŭk. *Ger.* tō'-lŏŏk.
Thomas, Ambroise . .	än-brwäz' tō-mä'.
Thopas (Sir)	thō'-pàs.
Thor	thôr, tôr.
Thoreau	thō'-rō, thō-rō'.
Thorvaldsen, or often Thor-waldsen	tŏr'-väld-zĕn, tôr'-wôld-sĕn.
Thoth	tōt, thŏth.
Thothmes	thŏth'-mēz, tŏt'-mēz.
Thou	*Fr.* tōō.
Thouars	tōō-är'.
Thourout . .	tōō roo'.
Thrace	thrās. *Class.* thrā'-sē.
Thracian	thrā'-shĭ=àn.
Thrasybulus	thrăs-ĭ-bū'-lŭs.
Thrasymcnes	thrā-sĭm'-ē-nēz.
Thrasymenus	thrā-sĭ-mē'-nŭs.
Throndhjem, see Trondh-jem	trŏnd'-yĕm.
Thucydides	thū-sĭd'-ĭ-dēz.
Thugut	tōō'-gōōt.
Thule	thū'-lē.
Thun (L.)	tōōn.
Thurgau, or	tōōr'-gow.

Thurgovie, *Fr.* . . . . tür-gō-vĕ'.
Thüringen . . . . . . *Ger.* tü'-rĭng-ĕn.
Thuringia . . . . . . thū-rĭn'-jĭ-à.
Thuringian . . . . . thū-rĭn'-jĭ-àn.
Thurn . . . . tōōrn.
Thursby . . . . . . thĕrz'-bĭ.
Thyrsis . . . . thĕr'-sĭs.
Tibet, see Thibet . . . tĭb'-ĕt, tĭ-bĕt'.
Tibetan, see Thibetan . . tĭ-bĕt'-àn, tĭb'-ĕt'-àn.
Tibullus . . . . . . tĭ-bŭl'-ŭs.
Tiburzio . . . . . . tē-bōōrt'-zē-ō.
Ticao . . . . tē-kä'-ō.
Tichborne . . . . . . tĭch'-bŭrn, tĭch'-bŭn.
Ticino . . . . tē-chē'-nō.
Ticinus (R.) . . . . . tĭ-sī'-nŭs.
Ticinus . . . . tĭs'-ĭn-ŭs, tĭ-sī'-nŭs.
Tieck . . . . tēk.
Tien-Tsin, or Tientsin . tē-ĕn'-tsēn.
Tiepolo . . . . tē-ā'-pō-lō.
Tiergarten, see Thier-
garten . . . . . . tēr'-gär-tĕn.
Tierra del Fuego, see
Terra del Fuego . . tē=ĕr'-rä dĕl fwä'-gō.
Tiers État . . . . . tērz ā-tä', tē=âr'-zā-tä'.
Tietjens, see Titiens . . tēt'-yĕns.
Tiflis . . . . tĭf-lēs'.
Tighe (Mary) . . . . tī.
Tiglath-Pileser . . . tĭg'-lăth-pĭl-ē'-zēr.
Tigris . . . . tī'-grĭs.
Tilghman . . . . . . tĭl'-màn.
Tillemont . . . . . . tē=yŭ-môṅ'.
Tilly . . . . tĭl'-ĭ.
Tilsit . . . . tĭl'-sĭt.
Timæus . . . . . . tī-mē'-ŭs.
Timbuctoo, or Timbuktu . tĭm-bŭk'-tōō.
Timoleon . . . . . . tĭ-mō'-lē-ŏn.
Timon . . . . tī'-mŏn.

Timor	tē-mōr'.
Timotheus	tĭ-mō'-thē-ŭs.
Timour, or Timur, or. .	tē-mōōr'.
Timur Bey, or	tē-mōōr' bā.
Timur-Leng, see Tamer-	
lane	tē-mōōr'-lĕng.
Tinavelly, see Tinnevelli .	tĭn-à-vĕl'-ĭ.
Tinayre, Marcelle . . .	mär-sĕl tē-när'.
Tindale, see Tyndale . .	tĭn'-dàl.
Ting-hae, or Ting-hai . .	tĭng-hī'.
Tinnevelli, see Tinavelly .	tĭn-ĕ-vĕl'-ĭ.
Tino (Gen.)	tē'-nō.
Tintagel	tĭn-tăj'-ĕl.
Tintern	tĭn'-tĕrn.
Tintoret, or	tĭn'-tō-rĕt.
Tintoretto, Il	ēl tĭn-tō-rĕt'-ō,
	tēn-tō-rĕt'-ō.
Tioomen, or Tioumen, see	
Tiumen, Tyumen . .	tē-ōō-mĕn'.
Tipitapa (R.)	tē-pē-tä'-pä.
Tippecanoe	tĭp'-ē-kà-nōō'.
Tipperah	tĭp'-ĕ-rä.
Tipperary	tĭp-ĕ-rä'-rĭ.
Tippoo Sahib, see Tipu	
Saib	tĭp-ōō' sä'-hĭh
Tippoo Tib, or	tĭp-ōō' tĭb.
Tippoo Tip	tĭp-ōō' tĭp.
Tipu Saib, see Tippoo	
Sahib	tĭp-ōō' sä'-ĭb.
Tiresias	tĭ-rē'-sĭ-às.
Tirhakah	tĕr'-hà-kä.
Tirhoot	tĭr-hōōt'.
Tirlemont	tērl-mŏn'.
Tirnova, see Tarnovo . .	tēr'-nō-vä.
Tirpitz, von	fŏn tēr'-pĭts.
Tischendorf, von . . .	fŏn tĭsh'-ĕn-dôrf.
Tishri	tĭsh'-rĭ.

Tisiphone . . . . . . tī-sĭf'-ō-nē.
Tissot . . . . tē-sō'.
Tisza, see Theiss . . . tĭs'-ä. *Hung.* tĭsh'-à.
Titan . . . . tī'-tán.
Titania . . . . tī-tā'-nĭ-à.
Titanic . . . . tī-tăn'-ĭk.
Tithonus . . . . . . tĭ-thō'-nŭs.
Titian, see Tiziano . . tĭsh'-àn, tĭsh'-ē=àn.
Titicaca (L.) . . . . . tĭt-ē-kä'-kä.
Titiens, see Tietjens . . tēt'-yĕns. *pop.* tĭsh'-yĕnz.
Tito Melema . . . . . tē'-tō mä-lā'-mä.
Tittoni . . . . tēt-tō'-nē.
Titurel . . . . tĭt'-ū-rĕl.
Tityrus . . . . tĭt'-ĭ-rŭs.
Tiumen, see Tioomen,
    Tyumen . . . . . . tē-ōō-mĕn'.
Tivoli (Italy) . . . . . tē'-vō-lē.
Tivoli (New York) . . . tĭv'-ō-lĭ, tĭv-ō'-lē.
Tiziano Vecelli, It. . . . tēt-sē=ä'-nō vä-chĕl'-lē.
Tobago, see Tabago . . tō-bā'-gō, tō-bä'-gō.
Tobias . . . . tō-bī'-às.
Tobit . . . . tō'-bĭt.
Tobolsk . . . . . . tō-bŏlsk'.
Tocqueville, de . . . . dŭ tŏk'-vĭl. *Fr.* dŭ
    tŏk-vēl'.
Togoland . . . . . . tō'-gō-lănd.
Toison d'Or, La . . . . lä twä-zôǹ' dōr.
Tokaj, or Tokay . . . . tō-kā'. *Hung.* tō'-koi.
Tokio, Tokyo . . . . . tō'-kē=ō.
Tokugawa Shogunate . . tō-kōō'-gä'-wä'
    shō'-gŭn-āt.
Tolbooth . . . . . . tōl'-bōōth.
Toledo . . . . tō-lē'-dō. *Sp.* tō-lä'-dō.
Tolentino . . . . . . tō-län-tē'-nō.
Tolstoy . . . . tŏl'-stoi.
Tomaszov . . . . . . tō'-mä-shŏf.
Tommaseo . . . . . tŏm-mä-sā'-ō.

Tomsk	tŏmsk.
Tonga (Is.)	tŏng'-gä.
Tongaland, see Tongoland	tŏng'-gä-lănd.
Tong Chow, see Tung-	
chau	tŏng-chow'.
Tongking, see Tungking,	
Tonquin	tŏng-kĭng'.
Tongoland, see Tongaland	tŏng'-gō-lănd.
Tonkin, see Tonquin . .	tŏn-kēn'.
Tonnay-Charente . . .	tŏn-nā'-shä-rôṅt'ₒ
Tonquin, see Tonkin . .	tŏn-kēn'.
Tonquin, *Fr.*, see Tong-	
king	tôṅ-kăṅ'.
Tonstall, see Tunstall .	tŭn'-stál.
Toorkistan, see Turkestan	tōōr-kĭs-tän'.
Topeka	tō-pē'-kȧ.
Topete (Admiral) . . .	tō-pā'-tā.
Töplitz, see Teplitz . .	tēp'-lĭts.
Toral	tō-räl'.
Torcello	tŏr-chĕl'-lō.
Tordesilhas, *Port.*, or . .	tŏr-dä-sēl'-yäs.
Tordesillas, *Sp.*	tŏr-dä-sēl'-yäs.
Torgau	tŏr'-gow.
Torii	tō'-rē'-ē'.
Torino, see Turin . . .	*Il.* tō-rē'-nō.
Torquato Tasso	tŏr-kwä' tō täs'-sō.
Torquay	tôr-kē'.
Torquemada	tŏr-kä-mä'-dä.
Torregiano, see Torrigiano	tŏr-rä-jä'-nō.
Torres Vedras	tŏr'-rĕs vä'-dräsh.
Torricelli	tŏr-rĭ-sēl'-lĭ.
	It. tŏr-rē-chĕl'-lē.
Torricellian	tŏr-ĭ-sĕl'-ĭ-ȧn,
	tŏr-rĭ-chĕl'-ĭ-ȧn.
Torrigiano, see Torregiano	tŏr-rē-jä'-nō.
Torso Belvedere . . .	tôr'-sō bĕl-vĕ-dēr'.
Tortola	tôr-tō'-lä.

Tortuga . . . . . . tŏr-tōō'-gä.
Tortugas . . . . . . tôr-tōō'-gäz.
Tosca, La . . . . . . lä tŏs'-kä.
Toscanelli . . . . . . tŏs-kä-nĕl'-lē.
Tosti . . . . tōs'-tē.
Tostig . . . . tŏs'-tĭg.
Totila, or . . . . . . tŏt'-ĭ-lä.
Totilas . . . . tŏt'-ĭ-làs.
Toul . . . . tōōl.
Toulmin . . . . . . tōl'-mĭn.
Toulmouche . . . . . tōōl-mōōsh'.
Toulon . . . . tōō'-lŏn.   *Fr.* tōō-lôṅ'.
Toulouse . . . . . . tōō-lōōz'.
Touraine . . . . . . tōō-rĕn'.
Tourcoing . . . . . . tōōr-kwăṅ'.
Tour d'Auvergne . . . tōōr dō-vârn'=yŭ.
Tour de Nesle . . . tōōr dŭ nāl.
Tourgee . . . . . . tōōr-zhā'.
Tourgueneff, or Tourgué-
  nief, see Turgenieff . . tōōr'-gĕn-yĕf.
Tournai, or Tournay . . tōōr-nā'.
Tourneur . . . . . . tĕr'-nĕr, tōōr-nĕr'.
Tours . . . . tōōr.
Tourville . . . . . . tōōr-vēl'.
Toussaint Louverture, or
  L'Ouverture . . . . tōō-săṅ' lōō-vĕr-tür'.
Toxophilus . . . . . tŏks-ŏf'-ĭ-lŭs.
Toyoharu . . . . . . tō'-yō'-hä'-rē'.
Trachonitis . . . . . trăk-ō-nī'-tĭs.
Trafalgar (Battle of) . . trăf-ăl-gär', tră-făl'-gär.
Trafalgar (Square) . . . trăfăl'-gär.
Trani . . . . trä'-nē.
Transbaikalia . . . . trăns-bī-kä'-lĭ-à.
Transkei . . . . . . trăns-kē'.
Transvaal . . . . . . trăns-väl'.
Trapani . . . . . . trä'-pä-nē.
Trapezunt, see Trebizond   trăp-ĕ-zōōnt'.

Trasimenus (L.) . . . . trăs-ĭ-mē'-nŭs.
Tras-os-Montes, see Traz-
os-Montes . . . . . träs'-ōs-mŏn'-tĕs.
Trastevere . . . . . träs-tā'-vā-rĕ.
Trauttmansdorff . . . trowt'-mäns-dŏrf.
Travailleurs de la Mer . trä-vī-yēr' dŭ lä mâr.
Travancore . . . . . trăv-án-kōr'.
Traviata, La . . . . . lä trä-vē-ä'-tä.
Traz-os-Montes, see Tras-
os-Montes . . . . . träz'-ōs-mŏn'-tĕs.
Trebbia . . . . . . trĕb'-ē-ä.
Trebizond, see Trapezunt trĕb-ĭ-zŏnd'.
Tregelles . . . . . . trĕ-gĕl'-ĭs.
Treitschke . . . . . trīch'-kā.
Trek . . . . trĕk.
Trelawney . . . . . trē-lô'-nĭ.
Tremont . . . . . . trĕ-mŏnt', trē-mŏnt',
trĕm'-ŏnt.
Trench . . . . trĕnsh.
Trenck, von . . . . . fŏn trĕngk.
Trentino . . . . . . trĕn-tē'-nō.
Trevannion . . . . . trē-văn'-yŭn.
Trevelyan . . . . . . trĕ-vĕl'-yán.
Trevena . . . . . . trĕ-vē'-nä.
Treves . . . . trēvz.
Trèves . . . . trĕv.
Trevi (Fountain of) . . trä'-vē.
Trèvisa . . . . trĕ-vē'-sä.
Treviso . . . . trä-vē'-zō.
Trianon, Grand . . . . grän trē-ä-nôṅ'.
Trianon, Petit . . . . pē=tē' trē-ä-nôṅ'.
Trichinopoli . . . . . trĭch"-ĭn-ŏp'-ō-lĭ.
Tricoteuses, Les . . . lä trē-kō-tēz'.
Tricoupis, see Trikoupis . trē-kōō'-pĭs.
Trier, *Ger.* . . . . . trēr.
Triest, or . . . . . . trē-ĕst'.
Trieste . . . . trē-ĕst'. *It.* trē-ĕs'-tä.

Trifanum . . . . . . trī-fā'-nŭm.
Trikala, or Trikkala . . trē'-kä-lä.
Trikoupis, see Tricoupis . trē-kōō'-pĭs.
Trimalchio . . . . . trĭ-măl'-kĭ-ō.
Trinidad . . . . . . trĭn-ĭ-dăd'.
            Sp. trē-nē-däd'.
Trinkitat . . . . . . trĭng-kĭ-tät'.
Tripoli . . . . trĭp'-ō-lĭ.
Tripolitan . . . . . trĭ-pŏl'-ĭ-tàn.
Triptolemus . . . . trĭp-tŏl'-ē-mŭs.
Trisagion . . . . . . trĭ-sā'-gĭ-ŏn.
Tristan und Isolde . . . trĭs-tän' ŏŏnt ē-zŏl'-dŭ.
Triton . . . . trī'-tŏn.
Triumvirate . . . . . trī-ŭm'-vĭ-rāt.
Trivulzio . . . . . . trē-vŏŏl'-dzē-ō.
Trocadero . . . . . . trō-kä-dä'-rō.
Trocadéro . . . . . . *Fr.* trō-kä-dä-rō'.
Trochu . . . . trō-shü'.
Troilus . . . . trō'-ĭl-ŭs.
Troilus and Cressida . . trō'-ĭl-ŭs and krĕs'-ĭ-dà.
Trois Échelles . . . . trwä zä-shĕl'.
Trois Mousquetaires . . trwä mōōs=kĕ-târ'.
Trollope . . . . . . trŏl'-ŭp.
Trondhjem, see Thrond-
  hjem . . . . trŏnd'-yĕm.
Trophimus . . . . . trŏf'-ĭ-mŭs.
Troppau . . . . . . trŏp'-ow.
Trosachs, or Trossachs . trŏs'-ăks.
Trotzky . . . . . . trŏts'-kē.
Troubadours . . . . . trōō-bä-dōōrz'.
Troubetzkoy . . . . . trōō-bĕts'-kō-ē.
Trouvères . . . . . . trōō-vârs'.
Trouville . . . . . . trōō-vēl'.
Trovatore, Il . . . . . ēl trō-vä-tō'-rĕ.
Troyes . . . . trwä.
Troyes, Chrestien de . . krä-tē=ĕń' dŭ trwä.
Troyon . . . . trwä-yôń'.

Trübner . . . . . . trüb'-nĕr.
Trueba, Antonio de . . än-tō'-nē-ō dä troo-ä'-bä.
Trujillo, or Truxillo . . troo-ċhēl'-yō.
Tsad (L.), see Chad,
   Tchad, Tschad . . . tsäd.
Tsarevna, see Czarevna . tsär-ĕv'-nä.
Tsarina, see Czarina . . tsär-ē'-nä.
Tsaritsin . . . . . . tsär-ēt'-sēn.
Tsaritza . . . . . . tsär-ĭt'-zä.
Tsarovitch, see Czarevitch tsär'-ō-vĭch.
Tsarowitz, see Czarowitz . tsär'-ō-vĭts.
Tsarskoi Selo . . . . tsär-skō'-ĭ sä'-lō.
Tschad, see Chad, Tchad,
   Tsad . . . . . . chäd.
Tschaikovsky . . . . tshī-kŏf'-skĭ.
Tsech, see Czech . . . chĕk.
Tseng . . . . . . tsĕng.
Tsigane . . . . . . tsē-gȧn'.
Tsimshian, or Tsimsian . tsĭm-shē-än'.
Tsi-nan . . . . . . tsē-nän'.
Tsing . . . . . . tsēng.
Tsingtau (or -tao) Tsinan-
   fu . . . . tsĭng'-tow' tsē'-näm'-foo'.
Tsugaru Strait . . . . tsoo-gä'-roo strāt.
Tsunenobu . . . . . tsoo'-nä'-nō'-bĕ'.
Tsushima (Is.) . . . . tsoo'-shē'-mä'.
Tübingen . . . . . . tü'-bĭng-ĕn.
Tucson . . . . . . too-sŏn'.
Tuesday . . . . . . tūz'-dā.
Tugela (R.) . . . . . too-gä'-lä.
Tugendbund . . . . . too'-gĕnt-boont.
Tuh Chau . . . . . . too' chow'.
Tuileries . . . . . . twē'-lĕ-rĭz. _Fr._ twēl-rē'.
Tula . . . . too'-lä.
Tulle . . . . tül.
Tullia . . . . tŭl'-ĭ-ȧ.
Tully-Veolan . . . . tŭl'-ĭ-vē-ō'-lăn.

Tuncha . . . . tŭn-chä'.
Tung-chau, see Tong Chow tōōng-chow'.
Tungking, see Tongking . tōōng-kĭng'.
Tunis . . . . tū'-nĭs.
Tunisie, *Fr.* . . . . . tü-nē-zē'.
Tunstall, see Tonstall . . tŭn'-stȧl.
Turcaret . . . . . . tŭr-kä-rā'.
Turcoman, see Turkoman tẽr'-kō-mȧn, tōōr-kō-män'.
Turenne, de . . . . . dŭ tū-rẽr'. *Fr.* dŭ tü-rĕn'.
Turgai, or . . . . . . tōōr-gī'.
Turgansk . . . . . . tōōr-gänsk'.
Turgenieff (or -iev), see
   Tourgueneff . . . . tōōr'-gĕn-yĕf.
Turgot . . . . tür-gō'.
Turiddu . . . . . . tōō'-rēd-dōō.
Turin, It. Torino . . . tū'-rĭn, tū-rĭn'.
Turkestan, or . . . . tōōr-kĕs-tän'.
Turkistan, see Toorkistan tōōr-kĭs-tän'.
Turkoman, see Turcoman tẽr'-kō-mȧn, tōōr-kō-män'.
Turquino . . . . . . tōōr-kē'-nō.
Tuskeegee . . . . . tŭs-kē'-gē.
Tussaud's . . . . . . tü-sōz'.
Tutuila . . . . tōō-tōō-e'-lä.
Tver . . . . tvâr.
Twickenham . . . . . twĭk'-ĕn-ȧm.
Tybalt . . . . tĭb'-ȧlt.
Tyburn . . . . tī'-bẽrn.
Tychicus . . . . . . tĭk'-ĭ-kŭs.
Tycoon . . . . tī-kōōn'.
Tydeus . . . . tī'-dūs.
Tyndale, see Tindale . . tĭn'-dȧl.
Tynemouth . . . . . tīn'-mŭth, tĭn'-mŭth.
Typhon . . . . tī'-fŏn, tī'-fŏn.
Tyrol . . . . tĭr'-ŏl, tĭ-rōl'. *Ger.* tē-rōl'.
Tyrolean . . . . . . tĭr-ō'-lē-ȧn.
Tyrolese . . . . . . tĭr-ō-lēz', tĭr-ō-lēs'.
Tyrone . . . . tĭ-rōn'.

Tyrrhene . . . . . . tĭr′-ēn.
Tyrrhenian . . . . . tĭ-rē′-nĭ-ȧn.
Tyrtaean . . . . . . tĭr-tē′-ȧn.
Tyrtaeus . . . . . . tĭr-tē′-ŭs.
Tyrwhitt . . . . . . tĕr′-ĭt.
Tyumen, see Tioomen,
   Tiumen . . . . . . tē=ōō-mĕn′.
Tzigane, La . . . . . lä tsē-gӑn′.
Tzigany . . . . . . tsĭg′-ȧ-nĭ.

U

Uarda . . . . ōo-är′-dä.
Ubangi . . . . ōō-bäng′-gē.
Ubiquitarian . . . . ū-bĭk″-wĭ-tā′-rĭ-ȧn.
Uccello . . . . ōō-chĕl′-lō.
Uchatius . . . . . . ōō-ċhä′-tĭ-ōŏs.
Uclés . . . . ōō-klās′.
Udaipur, see Oodeypoor . ōō-dī-pōor′.
Udail (Nicholas) . . . yōō′-dȧl.
Udine . . . . ōō′-dē-nĕ.
Ufa . . . . ōō′-fä.
Uffizzi . . . . ōō-fēt′-sē.
Uganda . . . . . . ōō-gän′-dä.
Uggione, see Oggione . . ōōj-jō′-nĕ. [gä-rär-dĕs′-kä.
Ugolino della Gherardesca ōō-gō-lē′-nō dĕl′-lä
Uhland . . . . ōō′-länt.
Uhlans, see Ulans . . . ōō′-länz.
Uhrich . . . . *Fr.* ü-rēk′. *Ger.* ōō′-rĭċh.
Uitenhage . . . . . . oi-tĕn-hä′-ċhĕ.
Uitlander . . . . . . oit′-lӑn-dĕr.
Ujiji . . . . ōō-jē′-jē.
Ukerewe . . . . . . ōō-kĕ-rē′-wĕ.
Ukiyo-ye . . . . . . ōō′-kē′-yo-yä′.
Ukraine . . . . . . yū′-krān, ōō-krān′,
                ū′-krä-ĭn.
Ulalume . . . . . . ōō-lä-lōō′-mĭ.

Ulans, see Uhlans . . . ōō'-länz.
Ulfilas, see Ulphilas . . ŭl'-fĭ'-lås.
Ulleswater . . . . . ŭlz'-wô-tẽr.
Ulloa . . . . ŏŏl-yō'-ä.
Ulm . . . . ŏŏlm.
Ulphilas, see Ulfilas . . ŭl'-fĭ-lås.
Ulpian . . . . ŭl'-pĭ-ån.
Ulpianus . . . . . . ŭl-pĭ-ā'-nŭs.
Ulrica . . . . ŭl'-rĭ-kå. *It.* ŏŏl-rē'-kä.
Ulrich . . . . ŏŏl'-rĭċh.
Ulrici . . . . ŏŏl-rēt'-sē.
Ulrike Eleonore . . . . ŏŏl-rē'-kŭ ĕl″-ĕ-ō-nō'-rŭ.
Ultima Thule . . . . ŭl'-tĭm-å thū'-lē.
Ulundi . . . . ōō-lōōn'-dē.
Ulungu, see Urungu . . ōō-lōōng'-gōō.
Ulwar, see Alwar . . . ūl'-wär.
Ulysses . . . . yū-lĕs'-ēz.
Umar Khaiyàm, see Omar
  Khayyam . . . . . ōō'-mär kī-yäm'.
Umberto, Principe . . . prēn'-chē-pä ōōm-bĕr'-tō.
Umkomanzi . . . . . ŭm-kō-män'-sē.
Umritsir, see Amritsar . ŭm-rĭt'-sẽr.
Unalaska, see Oonalaska ōō'-nå-lăs'-kå,
  yū-nå-lăs'-kå.
Unao . . . . ōō'-nå-ō.
Un Ballo in Maschera . . ōōn bäl'-lō ēn mäs'-kä-rä.
Uncas . . . . ŭng'-kås.
Undine . . . . ŭn-dēn'. *Ger.* ŏŏn-dē'-nŭ.
Unitarian . . . . . . yū-nĭ-tā'-rĭ-ån.
Unser Fritz . . . . . ŏŏn'-zẽr frĭts.
Unter den Linden . . . ŏŏn'-tẽr dän lĭn'-dĕn.
Unterwalden . . . . . ŏŏn'-tẽr-väl″-dĕn
Unyoro, see Nyoro . . . ōō-nyō'-rō.
Upanishads . . . . . ōō-på-nĭ-shădz'.
Upernavik, Upernivik . . ōō-pẽr'-nå-vĭk.
Upolu (I.) . . . . . . ōō-pō-lōō'.
Upsal . . . . ŭp'-sål.

Upsala	ŭp-sä'-lä.
Ur	ēr.
Ural	ōō'-rȧl, yū'-rȧl.
Urania	yū-rā'-nĭ-ȧ.
Uranus	yū'-rȧ-nŭs.
Urban	ŭr'-bȧn.
Urbano, Pietro	pē-ā'-trō ōōr-bä'-nō.
Urbanus	ŭr-bä'-nŭs.
Urbino	ōōr-bē'-nō.
Urfé, Honoré d'	ō-nō-rā' dür-fā'.
Uri	ōō'-rĭ.
Uriah	ū-rī'-ä'.
Uriel	yū'-rĭ-ĕl.
Urquhart	ēr'-kärt.
Urraca	ŏŏr-rä'-kä.
Ursa Minor	ēr'-sȧ mī'-nŭr.
Ursula	ŭr'-sū-lä.
Ursule Mirouët	ür-sül' mē-rōō-ā'.
Ursulines	ŭr'-sū-lĭnz, ŭr'-sū-lĭnz.
Uruguay	yū'-rōō-gwä.
	Sp. ōō-rōō-gwī'.
Urundi	ōō-rōōn'-dē.
Urungu, see Ulungu . .	ōō-rōōng'-gōō.
Ushant	ŭsh'-ȧnt.
Uskiub, see Uskub . .	ōōs'-kē-ŭb.
Uskub, see Uskiub . . .	ŏŏs'-kub.
Usuramo	ōō-sōō-rä'-mō.
Utah	yū'-tä, yū'-tô.
Utamaro	ōō'-tä'-mä'-rō'.
Ute	yūt.
Utopian	yū-tō'-pĭ-ȧn.
Utraquist	yŭ'-trȧ-kwist.
Utrecht	yū'-trĕkt. *D.* ü'-trĕcht.
Uvaroff	ōō-vä'-rŏf.
Uzés	ü-zäs'.
Uzziah	ŭz-zī'-ä.
Uzziel	ŭz-zī'-ĕl, ŭz'-zĭ-ĕl.

V

Vaal (R.)	väl.
Vaca, Cabeza, or Cabeça de	kä-bä'-thä dä vä'-kä.
Vaccai, or Vaccaj . . .	väk-kä'=ē.
Vacuna	vä-kū'-nä.
Vaga	vä'-gä.
Vailima	vī-lē'-må.
Vaillant	vä-yäṅ'.
Valais	vä-lä'.
Val d'Arno	väl där'-nō.
Valdenses, see Waldenses	väl-děn'-sēz.
Valdensian, see Walden-	
sian	väl-děn'-sĭ-àn.
Valdés	*Sp.* bäl-děs'.
Valdéz	*Mex.* väl-děs.
	Sp. bäl-děth'.
Valdivia	väl-dē'-vē-ä.
Valée	vä-lä'.
Valence	*Fr.* vă-lŏṅs'.
Valencia	vă-lěn'-shĭ=à.
	Sp. vä-lěn'-thē-ä.
Valenciennes	vă″-lŏn-sĭ-ěnz', *or*
	vä″-lěn-sĭ-ěnz'.
	Fr. vă-lŏṅ-sē=ěn'.
Valens	vä'-lěnz.
Valentine	văl'-ěn-tīn.
Valentinian	văl-ěn-tĭn'-ĭ-àn.
Valentinois	văl-ŏṅ-tē-nwä'.
Valera	*Sp.* bä-lä'-rä.
Valère	vă-lâr'.
Valeria	vă-lē'-rĭ-à.
Val-es-Dunes . . .	văl-ä-dün'.
Valhalla	văl-hăl'-à.
Valjean, Jean . . .	zhäṅ văl-zhäṅ'.
Valjevo	väl'-yä-vō.
Valkyrie	väl-kē'-rē.

Valladolid	văl-lä-dō-lĭd'.
	Sp. bäl-yä-dō-lēth'.
Vallandigham	văl-lăn'-dĭ-găm.
Vallière, La	lä văl-ē=âr'.
Vallombrosa	väl-lŏm-brō'-zä.
Valmy	văl-mē'.
Valois	văl-wä'.
Valona, see Avlona . .	vä-lō'-nä.
Valparaiso	văl-pä-rī'-zō, väl-pä-rī'-zō.
	Sp. bäl-pä-rä'=ē-sō.
Valtellina, or	väl-tĕl-lē'-nä.
Val Tellina, or . . .	väl tĕl-lē'-nä,
Valtelline	väl-tĕl-lēn'.
Vámbéry	väṅ'-bä-rē'.
Van	vän.
Van Artevelde	văn är'-tĕ-vĕl-dĕ.
Vanbrugh	văn-broo'.
Vandalic	văn-dăl'-ĭk.
Vandamme	väṅ-däm'.
Van der Meulen . . .	văn dĕr mē'-lĕn.
Vandyck, Vandyke . . .	văn-dīk'.
Van Eyck	văn īk'.
Van Gogh	fän gŏgh. *Fr.* văn gŏf.
Van Hoeck	văn hōōk'.
Vanhomerigh, or . . .	văn-ŭm'-ēr-ĭ.
Vanhomrigh	văn-ŭm'-rĭ.
Valjevo	väl'-yä-vō.
Vanloo	*Fr.* väṅ-lō'.
Vannucchi	vän-nōōk'-kō.
Vannucci (Pietro) . . .	vän-nōōch'-ē.
Van Ostade	văn ŏs'-tä-dĕ.
Vanozza	vä-nŏt'-sä.
Van Schaick	văn skoik'.
Varanger Fjord, see Wa-	
ranger Fjord	vä-räng'-gĕr fē=ôrd'.
Varangians	vä-răn'-jĭ-änz.
Vardar	vär-där'.

Varennes	vä-rĕn'.
Varicourt	vä-rē-kōōr'.
Vari, or Varj dei Porcari .	vä'-rē dä'-ē pōr-kä'-rē.
Varna	vär'-nä.
Varnhagen von Ense . .	värn'-hä-gĕn fŏn ĕn'-sŭ.
Varus	vā″-rŭs.
Varzin	vär'-tsĭn.
Vasa	vä'-sä.
Vasari	vä-sä'-rē.
Vasco da Gama	väs'-kō dä gä'-mä.
Vashti	văsh'-tī.
Vasili	vä-sē'-lē.
Vasnietsof (-ov) . . .	väs-n-yĕts'-ŏf.
Vasquez de Coronado, see	
Vazquez	*Sp.* bäs-kĕth' dä
	kō-rō-nä'-dō.
Vassilenko	väs-ĭ-lĕn'-kō.
Vassy	vä-sē'.
Vathek	văth'-ĕk.
Vatican	văt'-ĭ-kăn.
Vauban, de	dŭ vō-bän'.
Vaucelles	vō-sĕl.
Vaucluse	vō-klüz'.
Vaucouleurs	vō-kōō-lĕr'.
Vaud, Pays de	pä=ē' dŭ vō'.
Vaudois	vō-dwä'.
Vaudreuil	vō-drē'-yŭ.
Vaughan	vôn, vô'-àn.
Vauvenargues	vōv-närg'.
Vaux	vôks. *Fr.* vō.
Vazquez de Coronado, see	
Vasquez de Coronado .	*Sp.* bäth-kĕth' dä
	kō-rō-nä'-dō.
Ve-Adar	vē'-ä-där.
Vecchio	vĕk'-ē-ō.
Vecellio	vä-chĕl'-ē-ō.
Veda	vä'-dȧ, vē'-dȧ.

Vedic	vā'-dĭk, vē'-dĭk.
Vega	vē'-gȧ. *Sp.* vā'-gä.
Vega Real	vā'-gä rā-äl'.
Vehmgerichte	fām'-gä-rĭċh"-tŭ.
Veile	vī'-lĕ.
Veit	fīt.
Veitch (John)	vēch.
Velalcazar, see Benalcazar	bā-läl-kä'-thär.
Velasco	*Sp.* bā-läs'-kō.
Velasquez, or	*Sp.* bā-läs'-kĕth.
Velazquez	*Sp.* bā-läth'-kĕth.
Velletri	vĕl-lä'-trē
Vendeans	vĕn-dē'-ȧnz.
Vendée, La	lä vŏṅ-dā'.
Vendémiaire	vŏṅ-dā-mē=âr'.
Vendidad	bĕn-dē-däd', vĕn-dē-däd'.
Vendôme, de	dŭ vôṅ-dōm'.
Venern (L.), see Wenern	vā'-nĕrn.
Venetia	vĕ-nē'-shĭ=ȧ.
Venezia	vā-nād'-zē-ä.
Veneziano	vā-nād"-zē-ä'-nō.
Venezuela	vĕn-ĕz-wē'-lä.
	Sp. vĕn-ċth-wā'-lä.
Venice	vĕn'-ĭs.
Venlo, or Venloo . . .	vĕn-lō'.
Ventersburg	fĕn-tĕrs-bŭrċh.
Venters' Spruit	fĕn'-tĕrs sproit.
Ventose	vôṅ-tŏz'.
Venus Anadyomene . .	vē'-nŭs ăn"-ȧ-dĭ-ŏm'-ĕ-nē.
Venus Callipyge	vē'-nŭs kă-lĭp'-ĭ-jē.
Vera Cruz	vā'-rä krōōz, *commonly*
	vĕr'-ȧ-krōōz.
	Sp. vā'-rä krōōth'.
Veragua, or	vā-rä'-gwä.
Veraguas	vā-rä'-gwäs.
Verazzano, see Verrazano	vā-rät-sä'-nō.
Verboeckhoven	fĕr-bōōk'-hō-fĕn.

Vercelli . . . . . . věr-chěl'-lē.
Vercingetorix . . . . věr-sǐn-jět'-ō-rǐks.
Verd (Cape), or Verde . vērd.
Verdi . . . . vâr'-dē.
Verdun . . . . věr-dǔn'.
Vereshagin, or . . . . vě-rē-shä'-gěn.
Verestchagin, Vassili . . *Russ.* vä-sē'-lē
                          vä"-rä-shä-gēn'.
Vergennes . . . . . věr-jěnz'. *Fr.* věr-zhěn'.
Vergil, see Virgil . . . věr'-jǐl.
Vergniaud . . . . . . věrn-yē=ō'.
Verhaeren, Émile . . . ä-mēl' věr-hä'-rěn.
Verlaine . . . . . . věr-lěn'.
Vermandois . . . . . věr-mǒn-dwä'.
Vermelles . . . . . . věr-měl'.
Verne, Jules . . . . . zhül věrn.
Vernet . . . . věr-nā'.
Verneuil . . . . . . věr-nē'-yǔ.
Vernéville . . . . . . věr-nā-vēl'.
Verocchio, see Verrocchio vä-rǒk'-kē=ō.
Verona . . . . vä-rō'-nä.
Veronese (Paul) . . . vä-rō-nä'-zě.
Veronese (adj.) . . . . věr-ō-nēz', věr-ō-nēs'.
Veronica . . . . . . věr-ō-nǐ'-kà, vě-rǒn'-ǐ-kà.
Verrazani, see Verazzano věr-räd-zä'-nē.
Verrazano, or . . . . věr-räd-zä'-nō.
Verrazzano . . . . . věr-rät-sä'-nō.
Verrocchio, see Verocchio vä-rǒk'-kē=ō.
Versailles . . . . . . věr-sālz'. *Fr.* věr-sä'=yǔ.
Vertumnus . . . . . věr-tǔm'-nǔs.
Verulam (Lord) . . . . věr'-ōō-lǎm.
Verus . . . . vē'-rǔs.
Verviers . . . . . . věr-vē=ā'.
Vervins . . . . věr-vǎn'.
Vesalius . . . . . . vě-sā'-lǐ-ǔs.
Vesle . . . . vāl.
Vespasian . . . . . . věs-pā'-zhǐ=àn.

Vespucci, Amerigo . . .   ä-mä-rē'-gō vĕs-pŏŏt'-chē.
Vespucius, Americus, Lat.   à-mĕ'-rĭ-kŭs
                 vĕs-pū'-shĭ=ŭs.
Veszprém, or . . . . .   vĕs'-prām.
Veszprim . . . . . .   vĕs'-prĭm.
Vet (R.) . . . . . .   fĕt.
Vevay, or Vevey   . . .   vĕv-ā'.
Via Æmilia . . . . .   vī'-ä ē-mĭl'-ĭ-ä.
Via Appia . . . . . .   vī'-ä ap'-pĭ-ä.
                 It. vē'-ä äp'-pē-ä.
Via Aurelia . . . . .   vī'-ä ô-rē'-lĭ-ä.
Via Dolorosa . . . . .   vī'-ä dŏl-ō-rō'-sä.
Via Mala . . . . . .   vē'-ä-mä'-lä.
Viardot-Garcia . . . .   vē=är-dō'-gär-thē'-ä.
Viareggio . . . . . .   vē-ä-rĕd'-jō.
Via Salaria . . . . .   vī'-ä sä-lä'-rĭ-ä.
Viatka, see Vyatka   . .   vē-ät'-kä.
Viaud . . . .   vē=ō'.
Via Valeria . . . . .   vī'-ä vä-lē'-rĭ-ä.
Vibert . . . .   vē-bâr'.
Viborg, see Wiborg   . .   vē'-bŏrg.
Vicenza . . . . . .   vĕ-sĕn'-zä. It. vē-chĕn'-zä.
Vichy . . . .   commonly, vĭsh'-ĭ.
                 Fr. vē-shē'.
Victor Amadeus . . . .   vĭk'-tôr äm-à-dē'-ŭs.
Victor-Perrin . . . . .   vēk-tōr'-pĕ-răṅ'.
Vidal (Pierre) . . . .   vē-däl'.
Vidocq . . . .   vē-dŏk'.
Vielé-Griffin . . . . .   vē-lä'-grē-făṅ'.
Vienna . . . .   vĭ-ĕn'-à.
Vieques . . . . . .   vē-ā'-kās.
Viersen . . . . . .   fēr'-sĕn.
Vierzehnheiligen . . .   fēr"-tsän-hī'-lĭg-ĕn.
Vieux Colombier, Le   . .   lē vē-ē' kŏl-ŏm-bē=ā'.
Vieuxtemps . . . . .   vē=ē-tŏṅ'.
Vigan . . . .   vē-gän'.
Vigée-Lebrun . . . .   vē-zhä'-lē-brŭṅ'.

Vigero (Marquis), di . . . dē vē-jā'-rō.
Vigneuilles . . . . . vē-nē'=yŭ.
Vignola . . . . vēn-yō'-lä.
Vignon, Claude . . . . klōd vēn-yôǹ'.
Vigny, de . . . . . . dŭ vēn-yē'.
Vigo . . . . vē'-gō.
Viljoen . . . . fĭl-yōōn'.
Villa Albani . . . . . vēl'-lä äl-bä'-nē.
Villa Aldobrandini . . . vēl'-lä äl"-dō-brän-dē'-nē.
Villa Borghese . . . . vēl'-lä bōr-gä'-zĕ
Villafranca, It., see Ville-
franche . . . . . . vēl-lä-fräng'-kä.
Villa Ludovisi . . . . vēl'-lä lōō-dō-vē'-zē.
Villa Medici . . . . . vēl'-lä mä'-dē-chē.
Villamil (Admiral) . . . vēl-yä-mēl'.
Villa Nazionale . . . . vēl'-lä nät"-zē-ō-nä'-lĕ.
Villani . . . . vēl-lä'-nē.
Villard . . . . vē-yär'.
Villa Real . . . . . . vēl'-lä rä-äl'.
Villari . . . . vēl'-lä-rē.
Villars . . . . vē-lär'.
Villebois- Mareuil . . . vēl-bwä'-mä-rē'=yŭ.
Villefranche, see Villa-
franca, It. . . . . . vēl-fräǹsh'.
Villehardouin . . . . vēl-är-dōō-ăǹ'.
Villemain . . . . . . vēl-măǹ'.
Villeroi . . . . vēl-rwä'.
Villers-Bretonneaux . . vē-yä' brä-tŏn-ō'.
Villers-Cotterets . . . vē-yä'-kŏt-rä'.
Villiers . . . . vĭl'-yērz.
Villiers de l'Isle Adam . vē-yä' dŭ lēl ä-däǹ'.
Villon . . . . vēl-yôǹ'.
Vilna, see Wilna . . . vĭl'-nä.
Vimeure . . . . . . vē-mēr'.
Viminal . . . . . . vīm'-ĭn-ȧl.
Vimy . . . . vē-mē'.
Vincennes . . . . . . vĭn-sĕnz'. Fr.văǹ-sĕn'.

Vincent de Paul . . . . vĭn'-sĕnt dŭ pôl'.
         Fr. văṅ-sŏṅ' dŭ pōl'.
Vincentio . . . . . . vĭn-sĕn'-shĭ=ō.
Vinci, da . . . . . . dä vĭn'-chē, dä vĭn'-chĭ,
         It. vēn'-chē
Vingt Ans Après . . . . văṅ täṅ zä-prä'.
Viola . . . . vī'-ō-lä. *It.* vē-ō'-lä.
Viollet-le-Duc . . . . vē-ō-lä' lē dük'.
Vionville . . . . . . vē=ôṅ-vēl'.
Viotti . . . . vē-ŏt'-tē.
Vira . . . . vē'-rä.
Virchow . . . . . . vĕr'-chow. *Ger.* fēr'-ċhō.
Virgil, see Vergil . . . vcr'-jĭl.
Virginia . . . . . . vēr-jĭn'-ĭ=à.
Virginian . . . . . . vēr-jĭn'-ĭ=àn.
Virginie . . . . . . vēr-zhē-nē'.
Virgo . . . . vẽr'-go.
Visayan . . . . . . vē-sä'-yän.
Viscaya, see Vizcaya . . *Sp.* bēs-kä'-yä.
Vischer, Peter . . . . pä'-tĕr fĭsh'-ĕr.
Visconti . . . . . . vĭs-kŏn'-tē.
Visigoths . . . . . . vĭz' ĭ-gŏthꜱ.
Vistula . . . . vĭs'-tū-lä, vĭst'-yū-lä.
Vita Nuova . . . . . vē'-tä nōō-ŏ'-vä.
Vitebsk . . . . . . vē-tĕbsk'.
Vitellius . . . . . . vĭ-tĕl'-ĭ-ŭs.
Viterbo . . . . vē-tĕr'-bō.
Viti Levu . . . . . . vē'-tē lĕv'-ōō.
Vitoria, or Vittoria . . vē-tō'-rē-à.
Vitry . . . . vē-trē'.
Vittoria Colonna . . . vē-tō'-rē-ä kō-lŏn'-nä.
Vittorio Emanuele . . . vēt-tō'-rē-ō
         ä-män"-ōō-ā'-lä.
Viviani . . . . vē-vē-ä-nē'.
Vizagapatam . . . . . vē-zä"gà-pà-täm'.
Vizcaya, see Viscaya . . *Sp.* bīth-kä'-yä.
Vizier . . . . vĭz'-yĕr, vĭz-ēr', vĭz'-yēr.

Vladikavkaz . . . . . vlä"-dē-käv-käz'.
Vladimir, see Wladimir . vlăd'-ē-mēr. *Russ. and Polish,* vlä-dē'-mĭr.
Vladislav, see Wladislaw . vlä'-dĭs-läv.
Vladivostok . . . . . vlä"-dē-vŏs-tŏk'.
Vogelweide . . . . . fō'-gĕl-vī"-dŭ.
Vogesen, see Vosges . . vō-gä'-zĕn.
Vogler, Abbé, or Abt . . ăb-ā' (äpt) fō'-glĕr.
Vogt . . . . fŏċht.
Vogüé . . . . vō-gü-ā'.
Voiture . . . . vwä-tür'.
Volapük . . . . . . vō-lä-pük'.
Volga . . . . vŏl'-gä.
Volhynia . . . . . . vō-lēn'-yȧ.
Volsci . . . . vŏl'-sī.
Volksraad . . . . . . fŏlks'-rät.
Vologda . . . . . . vō-lŏg-dä'.
Von Essen . . . . . fŏn ĕs'-ĕn.
Volscian . . . . . . vŏl'-shĭ=ȧn.
Volsung . . . . . . vŏl'-sŭng.
Volta . . . . vŏl'-tä.
Voltaire . . . . . . vŏl-târ'.
Voltas (Cape) . . . . vŏl'-täs.
Volterra, da . . . . . dä vŏl-tĕr'-rä.
Voltigeurs . . . . . . vŏl-tē-zhēr'.
Vondel . . . . vŏn'-dĕl.
Von Kluck . . . . . fŏn klŏŏk.
Von Spee . . . . . . fŏn spā.
Voortrekkers . . . . . fōr'-trĕk-ĕrs.
Vorarlberg . . . . . fōr'-ärl-bĕrċh.
Voronetz, or . . . . . vō-rō'-nĕts.
Voronezh . . . . . . vō-rō'-nĕzh.
Vosges, see Vogesen . . vōzh.
Voynich . . . . . . voi'-nĭch.
Vrede . . . . frä'-dĕ.
Vryburg . . . . . . vrī'-būrg. *D.* frī'-bŭrċh.
Vrigny . . . . vrēn'-yē'.

Vroubel . . . . . . vroō-bĕl.
Vryheid . . . . . . *D*. frī'-hīt.
Vuelta Abajo . . . . . *Sp.* boō=ĕl'-tä ä-bä'-ċhō.
Vuelta Arriva . . . . *Sp.* boō=ĕl'-tä är-rē'-bä.
Vuillard . . . . . . vwē-yär'.
Vulgate . . . . vŭl'-gāt.
Vyatka, see Viatka . . . vē-ät'-kä.

W

Wacace . . . . . . wä-shä'-shā.
Wace . . . . wäs.
Wacht am Rhein, Die . . dē väċht äm rīn.
Wadai . . . . wä-dī'.
Waddington . . . . . wŏd'-ĭng-tŭn.
                      Fr. vä-dăṅ-tôṅ'.
Wadelai . . . . . . wä-dĕ-lī'.
Wady-Halfa . . . . . wä'-dē-häl'-fä.
Wagner . . . . . . wăg'-nĕr. *Ger.* väg'-nĕr
Wagnerian . . . . . wăg-nē'-rĭ-àn.
Wagram . . . . . . vä'-gräm.
Wahabee . . . . . . wä-hä'-bē.
Wahabis, see Wahhabees wä-hä'-bēz.
Wahaby . . . . . . wä-hä'-bē.
Wahhabees, see Wahabis wä-hä'-bēz.
Wahlstatt (Battle of) . . väl'-stät.
Wahnfried . . . . . vän'-frēt.
Wahrheit, Dichtung und . dĭċh'-tōŏng ŏŏnt vär'-hīt.
Wahsatch . . . . . . wô-săch'.
Wailuku . . . . . . wī-loō'-koō.
Wakkerstroom . . . . văk'-ĕrs-strōm.
Walachia, see Wallachia . wŏ-lä'-kĭ-à.
Walcheren . . . . . väl'-ċhĕr-ĕn.
Waldeck . . . . . . wŏl'-dĕk. *Ger.* väl'-dĕk.
Waldemar . . . . . . wŏl'-dĕ-mär.
                      Ger. väl'-dĕ-mär.
Walden . . . . . . wôl'-dĕn.

Waldenses, see Valdenses   wäl-děn'-sēz.
Waldensian, see Valdensian   wäl-děn'-sĭ=an.
Waldersee . . . . . väl'-děr-zā.
Waldshut . . . . . . välts'-hōot.
Waldstätter, Die Vier . . dē fēr vält'-stět-ěr.
Waldstein . . . . . . vält'-stīn.
Waldteufel . . . . . vält'-toi-fěl.
Walewski . . . . . . vä-lěv'-skē.
Walhalla . . . . . . väl-häl'-lä.
Walküre, Die . . . . dē väl'-kü-rŭ.
Walkyrie . . . . . . wäl-kĭr'-ĭ.
Wallachia, see Walachia . wŏl-lä'-kĭ-á.
Wallenstein . . . . . wŏl'-ĕn-stīn.
              Ger. väl'-lĕn-stīn.
Waller . . . . wŏl'-ĕr.
Wallis, *Ger.* for Valais . väl'-lĭs.
Walloon . . . . . . wäl-ōōn'.
Walpole . . . . . . wŏl'-pōl.
Walpurgis . . . . . . väl-pōōr'-gēs.
Walsingham . . . . . wŏl'-sĭng-ám.
Waltham (U. S.) . . . wäl'-thám.
Waltham (Eng.) . . . . wôlt'-hám, wŏlt'-hám.
Walther von der Vogel-
   weide . . . . . . väl'-tĕr fŏn dĕr
              fō'-gĕl-vī"-dŭ.
Wamba . . . . . . wäm'-bä.
Wan-chow-fu . . . . wän'-chow'-fōō'.
Waranger Fjord, see Var-
   anger Fjord . . . . vä-räng'-gĕr fē=ôrd'.
Warbeck . . . . . . wôr'-běk.
Wartburg . . . . . . värt'-bōōrċh.
Warwick . . . . . . wŏr'-ĭk.
Warwickshire . . . . wŏr'-ĭk-shĭr.
Wasulu . . . . . . wä-sōō'-lōō.
Waterloo . . . . . . wô-tĕr-lōō'.   *D.* vä-tĕr-lō'.
Watervliet . . . . . . wô-tĕr-vlēt'.   [vä-tō'.
Watteau . . . . . . *commonly,* wŏt'-tō.   *Fr.*

Wauchope (Gen.) . . .	wô'-chōp.
Waugh (Edwin)	wô.
Waukegan	wô-kē'-gàn.
Waukesha	wô'-kĕ-shô.
Wavre	vävr'.
Wawre	vä'-vrĕ.
Weald (The)	wēld.
Wealden	wēld'-n.
Weber, von	fŏn vä'-bĕr.
Weeninx	wä'-nĭnks.
Wei-hai-wei	wä'-hī-wä.
Wei-ho	wä'-ē-hō.
Weimar	vī'-mär.
Weissenburg	vīs'-sĕn-bōōrćh.
Weissnicht-wo	vīs'-nĭćht-vō.
Welsbach	wĕlz'-băk. *Ger.* vĕlz'-bäćh.
Wellesley	wĕlz'-lĭ.
Wemyss (Castle) . . .	wēms, wē'-mĭs.
Wenceslaus	wĕn'-sĕs-lôs, wĕn'-sĕs-làs.
Wen-chau	wĕn-chow'.
Wenern, see Venern . .	vä'-nĕrn.
Wenzel	vĕnt'-zĕl.
Wepener	vä'-pā-nĕr.
Werder, von	fŏn vĕr'-dĕr.
Werdt, see Werth . . .	vĕrt.
Werra	vĕr'-rä.
Werrenrath	vĕr'-ĕn-rät.
Werth, see Werdt . . .	vĕrt.
Werther	wĕr'-tĕr. *Ger.* vĕr'-tĕr.
Wesel	vä'-zĕl.
Weser	wē'-zĕr. *Ger.* vä'-zĕr.
Wesleyan	wĕs'-lĭ-àn.
Westmoreland	wĕst'-mŏr-lănd.
Westphalia	wĕst-fä'-lĭ-à.
Weyden, van der . . .	văn dĕr vī'-dĕn.
Weyler	wä'-lĕr.
Weyman	wī'-màn.

Weymouth	wā'-mŭth.
Whewell	hū'-ĕl.
Whitefield, or Whitfield .	hwĭt'-fēld.
Whydah, see Widah . .	hwĭd'-ä.
Wiborg, see Viborg . . .	vē'-bôrg.
Wickliffe, see Wyclif . .	wĭk'-lĭf.
Widah, see Whydah . .	wĭd'-ä.
Widdin, or Widin . . .	vĭd'-ĭn.
Widor	vē'-dōr.
Widukind, see Wittekind	wĭd'-oo-kĭnd.
Wied	vēt.
Wieland	wē'-lănd. *Ger.* vē'-länt.
Wien	vēn.
Wieniawski	vē-nē-ŏf'-skē,
	vē=yä-nē-äv'-skĭ.
Wiertz	vērts.
Wiesbaden	vēs'-bä-dĕn.
Wigan	wĭg'-ȧn.
Wildenbruch	vĭl'-dĕn-brooċh.
Wilhelm	vĭl'-hĕlm.
Wilhelmine	*Ger.* vĭl-hĕl-mē'-nŭ.
Wilhelmj	vĭl-hĕl'-mĭ.
Wilhelm Meister's Lehr-	
jahre	vĭl'-hĕlm mīs'-tĕrz'
	lâr'-yär"-ŭ.
Wilhelmshöhe	vĭl'-hĕlmz-hē-yŭ.
Wilhelmsthal	vĭl'-hĕlmz-täl.
Wilkesbarre, or Wilkes-	
Barre	wilks'-băr-ĭ.
Willamette	wel-ä'-mĕt.
Wilna, see Vilna . . .	vĭl'-nä.
Wiltshire	wĭlt'-shĭr.
Wimpffen (de)	*Fr.* văṅ-fŏṅ'. *Ger.*
	vĭmp'-fĕn.
Winburg	vĭn'-bŭrċh.
Winckelmann	wĭngk'-ĕl-măn. *Ger.*
	vĭngk'-ĕl-män.

Windischgrätz . . . . vĭn'-dĭsh-grâts.
Windsor . . . . . . wĭnd'-zôr.
Winkelried, von . . . . fŏn wĭng'-kĕl-rēd.   *Ger.*
                        vĭng'-kĕl-rēt.
Winnepesaukee, or Winni-
  piseogee . . . . . wĭn"-ē-pē-sô'-kē.
Wirth . . . . vērt.
Witenagemot . . . . . wĭt'-ĕ-nä-gĕ-mōt".
Witte . . . . vĭt'-ŭ.
Wittekind, see Wittikind . wĭt'-ĕ-kĭnd.
Wittelsbach . . . . . vĭt'-tĕls-bäċh.
Wittenberg . . . . . wit'-ĕn-bērg.   *Ger.*
                        vĭt'-tĕn-bĕrċh.
Wittgenstein . . . . . vĭt'-gĕn-stīn.
Wittikind, see Wittekind . wĭt'-ĭ-kĭnd.
Wittstock . . . . . . vĭt'-stŏck.
Wituland . . . . . . vē'-tōō-lănd.
Witwaterstrand . . . . vĭt-vä'-tĕr-stränd.
Wladimir, see Vladimir . vlăd'-ē-mēr.
                        Russ. vlä-dē'-mĭr.
Wladislaw, see Vladislav . vlä'-dĭs-läv.
Woden . . . . wō'-dĕn.
Wodenowski . . . . . vŏ-dĕn-ŏf'-skĭ.
Woerth, see Wörth . . . vērt.
Woevre . . . . . . vĕvr.
Wöhler . . . . vē'-lĕr.
Wohlgemuth . . . . . vōl'-gä-mōōt.
Wolcott . . . . . . woŏl-kŭt.
Wolf, von, see Wolff . . *Ger.* vŏlf.
Wolfenbüttel . . . . . vŏlf'-ĕn-büt"-ĕl.
Wolff, see Wolf . . . . *Ger.* vŏlf.
Wolfgang . . . . . . vŏlf'-gäng.
Wolfram von Eschenbach vŏlf'-räm fŏn ĕsh'-ĕn-bäċh.
Wolgast . . . . . . vŏl'-gäst.
Wolkonsky . . . . . vŏl-kŏn'-skē.
Wollaston . . . . . . woŏl'-äs-tŭn.
Wollstonecraft . . . . woŏl'-stŭn-krăft.

Wolowski . . . . . . vō-lŏv'-skē.

Wolseley . . . . . . wŏŏlz'-lĭ.

Wolsey . . . . wŏŏl'-zĭ.

Wolzogen . . . . . . vōl-tsō'-gĕn.

Woochang, see Wuchan . wōō-chăng'.

Woolwich . . . . . . wŏŏl'-ĭch, wŏŏl'-ĭj.

Worcester (Eng.) . . . wŏŏs'-tĕr, wōōs'-tĕr.

Worcester (U. S.) . . . wōōs'-tĕr, wŏŏs'-tĕr.

Worcestershire . . . . wŏŏs' or wōōs'-tĕr-shĭr.

Worms . . . . vŏrms.

Wörth, see Woerth . . . vĕrt.

Wouverman, or Wouwer-

   man . . . . wow'-vĕr-măn.

Wouvermans . . . . . wow'-vĕr-mănz.

Wrangel . . . . . . räng'-gĕl. *Ger.* vräng'-ĕl.

Wrede . . . . vrä'-dĕ.

Wren . . . . rĕn.

Wriothesley . . . . . rŏts'-lĭ, rŏt'-ĕs-lĭ.

Wuchan, see Woochang . wōō-chăn'.

Wun . . . . wŏŏn.

Wundt . . . . vŏŏnt.

Wurmser . . . . . . vōōrm'-zĕr.

Wurtemberg . . . . . vür'-tĕm-bĕrċh.

Würzburg . . . . . . vürts'-bōōrċh.

Wyandot, or Wyandotte . wī-ăn-dŏt'.

Wyborg, see Viborg . . vē'-bôrg.

Wycherley . . . . . wĭch'-ĕr-lĭ.

Wyclif, or Wycliffe, see

   Wickliffe . . . . . wĭk'-lĭf.

Wykeham . . . . . . wĭk'-ăm.

Wyndham . . . . . . wĭnd'-ăm.

Wyoming . . . . . . wī-ō'-mĭng.

Wyss . . . . vĭs.

Wythe . . . . wĭth.

Wytschaete . . . . . wīts-ċhā'-tŭ.

X

Xalapa, see Jalapa . . . ċhä-lä'-pä.
Xalisco, see Jalisco . . ċhä-lēs'-kō.
Xanadu . . . . zăn-á-dōō'.
Xanthippe, see Xantippe . zăn-thĭp'-ē.
Xanthippus . . . . . zăn-thĭp'-ŭs.
Xanthus . . . . . . zăn'-thŭs.
Xantippe, see Xanthippe . zăn-tĭp'-ē.
Xauxa, see Jauja . . . 'how'-ċhä.
Xaver . . . . ksä'-věr.
Xavier . . . . zăv'-ĭ-ēr. *Fr.* zăv-ē-ā'.
           Sp. ċhä-vē-âr'.
Xenia . . . . zē'-nĭ-á.
Xenocrates . . . . . zĕn-ŏk'-rá-tēz.
Xenophon . . . . . . zĕn'-ō-fŏn.
Xeres, see Jeres, or . . 'hā'-rĕs.
Xerez, see Jerez . . . 'hā-rĕth'.
Xerez de la Frontera, see
  Jerez de la Frontera . 'hā-rĕth' dā lä frŏn-tā'-rä.
Xerona, see Gerona, Jerona 'hā-rō'-nä.
Xerxes . . . . zĕrk'-sēz.
Ximena, see Jimena . . ċhē-měn'-ä.
Ximenez, see Jimenez . zĭm-ē'-nēz.
           Sp. ċhē-měn'-āth.
Ximenez de Quesada . . ċhē-měn'-āth dā kā-sä'-dü.
Xingú . . . . shēn-gōō'.
Xorullo, see Jorullo . . ċhō-rōōl'-yō.
Xucar, see Jucar . . . 'hōō'-cär.
Xury . . . . zū'-rĭ.

Y

Yafa, see Jaffa, Japho . . yä'-fä.
Yahoo . . . . yä-hōō'.
Yahveh . . . . yä-vä'.
Yaka . . . . yä'-kä.

Yakama, or	yăk′-ā-må.
Yakima	yăk′-ĭ-må.
Yakonan	yă′-kō-năn.
Yakootsk, see Yakutsk, Jakutsk	yä-koŏtsk′.
Yakub Khan	yä-koŏb′ khän.
Yakutsk, see Yakootsk, Jakootsk	yä-koŏtsk′.
Yalu	yä-loŏ′.
Yana	yä′-nā.
Yang-chau	yäng′-chow.
Yang-tse-Kiang, or	yäng″-tsē-kĭ-äng′.
Yang-tze	yäng′-tsĕ.
Yanina, see Janina	yä′-nē-nä.
Yankton	yăngk′-tŭn.
Yap, see Guap	yäp.
Yaqui	yä′-kē.
Yare	yâr.
Yarkand, or	yär-känd′.
Yarkend	yär-kĕnd′.
Yarmouth	yär′-mŭth.
Yaroslaff, or	yä-rō-släv′.
Yaroslavl, see Jaroslaff	yä-rō-slä′-vl.
Yarra-Yarra	yä′-rä-yä′-rä.
Yarriba, see Yoruba	yä′-rē-bä.
Yasunobu	yä′-soŏ′-nō′-bĕ′.
Yauco	yä′–oŏ-kō.
Yazoo	yăz′-oŏ.
Youghiogheny	yŏ-hŏ-gä′-nĭ.
Youmans	yoŏ′-månz.
Ypres	ēpr.
Ypsilanti	ĭp-sĭl-ăn′-tĭ.
Yradier	ē-răd-ē=ā′.
Yriarte, see Iriarte	ē-rē-är′-tä.
Ysaye	ē-zī′-yŭ.
Yser	ē-zĕr′.
Yseult, see Isolde, Iseult	ē-sēlt′, ē-soŏlt′.

Ysoude, see Isoude . . ē-sōōd'.
Yssel . . . . ī'-sĕl.
Yuan Shi Kai . . . . yōō-än'-shē-kī.
Yucatan . . . . . . yōō-kä-tän'.
Yuen . . . . yōō-ĕn'.
Yugoslavia, see Jugoslavia yū'-gō slăv'-ĭ-à.
Yukon . . . . yōō'-kŏn.
Yungchau . . . . . yōōng-chow'.
Yunnan-fu . . . . . yŭn-nän'-fōō'.
Yuste . . . . yōōs'-tä.
Yvetot, Le Roi d' . . . lĕ rwä dĕv-tŏ'.
Yeats . . . . yāts.
Yeddo, see Jeddo, or . . yĕd'-dō.
Yedo . . . . yĕd'-ō.
Yegoroff . . . . . . yā'-gôr-ŏf.
Yaisen . . . . yā'-ĭ'-sĕn.
Yeishí . . . . yā'-ē'-shē'.
Yeisk, see Jeisk . . . . yā'-ĭsk.
Yeizan . . . . yā'-ĭ'-zăn'.
Yekaterinburg, see Eka-
  terinburg . . . . yĕ-kä''-tĕ-rēn-bōōrg'.
Yekaterinodar . . . . yĕ-kä''-tĕ-rē-nō-där'.
Yekaterinoslaff . . . . yĕ-kä''-tĕ-rē-nō-släv'.
Yelisavetpol, or Yelizavetpol yĕ-lē''-zä-vĕt-pŏl'=yĕ.
Yellala . . . . yĕl-lä'-lä.
Yemen . . . . yĕm'-ĕn.
Yenesei . . . . . . yĕn-ē-sā'-ē.
Yenikale (Strait) . . . yĕn-ē-kä'-lä.
Yeniseisk . . . . . . yĕn-ē-sä'-ĭsk.
Yesso, see Jesso, or . . yĕs'-sō.
Yezo . . . . yĕz'-ō, yā'-zō.
Yggdrasil, see Igdrasil . ĭg'-drà-sĭl.
Yguerne, see Igerna,
  Igerne . . . . . . ĭ-gĕrn'.
Y-lin . . . . ē-lēn'.
Yoga . . . . yō'-gà.
Yohchau . . . . . . yō-chow'.

Yokohama . . . . . yō-kō-hä'-mä.
Yonge . . . . yŭng.
Yonkers . . . . . . yŏngk'-ērz.
Yonne . . . . yŏn.
Yorick . . . . yŏr'-ĭk.
York von Wartenburg . . yōrk fŏn vär'-tĕn-bōōrċh.
Yoruba, see Yarriba . . yō'-rōō-bä.
Yosemite . . . . . . yō-sĕm'-ĭt-ē.
Youghal . . . . . . yôl, yô'-hȧl.

Z

Zaandam, see Saandam . zän-dăm'.
Zaardam, see Saardam . zär-dăm'.
Zab . . . . zäb.
Zabulon . . . . . . zăb'-yū-lŏn.
Zacatecas . . . . . . dzä-kä-tä'-käs,
                       sä-kä-tä'-käs.
Zacchaeus, or Zaccheus . zăk-ē'-ŭs.
Zacconi, Ermete . . . ĕr-mā'-tä dzäk-kō'-nĕ.
Zachariah . . . . . . zăk-ȧ-rī'-ȧ.
Zadkiel . . . . zăd'-kĭ-ĕl.
Zadok . . . . zā'-dŏk.
Zahara, see Sahara, Sahhra zä-hä'-rä, zä'-hȧ-rä.
Zahn . . . . tsän.
Zama . . . . zā'-mȧ.
Zamacoïs . . . . . . thä-mä-kō'-ĭs.
Zambales . . . . . . zäm-bä'-lĕs. Sp.
                      thăm-bä'-lĕs.
Zambesi . . . . . . zäm-bä'-zē, pop.
                      zăm-bē'-zĭ.
Zambezia . . . . . . zăm-bē'-zhĭ=ȧ.
Zamboanga . . . . . zäm-bō-äng'-gȧ.
Zamora . . . . thä-mō'-rä.
Zampieri . . . . . . dzäm-pē-ä'-rē.
Zand (R.) . . . . . . zănt.
Zanguebar . . . . . zäng-gä-bär'.

Zangwill . . . . . . săng'-wĭl.
Zankoff . . . . zän'-kŏf.
Zanoni . . . . ză-nō'-nĭ.
Zante . . . . zän'-tĕ, zän'-tā.
Zanzibar . . . . . . zän-zĭ-bär'.
Zaragoza, see Saragossa . thä-rä-gō'-thä.
Zarathushtra . . . . . ză-rà-thōōsh'-trà.
Zauberflöte, Die . . . dē tsow'-bĕr-flē''-tŭ.
Zaylah, see Zeila . . . zā'-lä.
Zealand, see Zeeland . . zē'-lănd.
Zebedee . . . . . . zĕb'-ĕ-dē.
Zebú, see Cebú . . . . zē-bōō'. *Sp.* thä-bōō'.
Zebulon, or . . . . . zĕb'-ū-lŏn.
Zebulun . . . . . . zĕb'-ū-lŭn.
Zechariah . . . . . . zĕk-à-rī'-à.
Zedekiah . . . . . . zĕd-ĕ-kī'-ä.
Zeebrugge . . . . . . zā'-brŏŏg-ŭ.
Zeeland, see Zealand . . zā'-länt.
Zeila, see Zaylah . . . zā'-lä.
Zela . . . . zē'-lä.
Zelaya . . . . sä-lä'-yä.
Zenaida . . . . . . zē-nā'-ĭ-dä.
Zeno . . . . zē'-nō.
Zenobia . . . . . . zĕ-nō'-bĭ-à.
Zenta . . . . zĕn'-tä.
Zephaniah . . . . . . zĕf-à-nī'-à.
Zephon . . . . zē'-fŏn.
Zeppelin . . . . . . zĕp'-ĕ-lĭn. *Ger.* tsĕp'-ā-ɪen
Zephyrus . . . . . . zĕf'-ĭ-rŭs.
Zerafshan . . . . . . zĕr-äf-shän'.
Zerin . . . . zĕ-rēn'.
Zerlina . . . . dzĕr-lē'-nà.
Zermatt . . . . . . zĕr-mät', tsĕr-mät'.
Zerubbabel, see Zorobabel zĕ-rŭb'-à-bĕl.
Zeus . . . . zūs.
Zeuxis . . . . zūk'-sĭs.
Zhitomir, see Jitomir . . zhĭt-ōm'-ēr.

Zidon, see Sidon . . . . zī'-dŏn.
Ziethen, or Zieten . . . . tsē'-tĕn.
Zimri . . . . zĭm'-rī.
Zincali . . . . zĭng'-kä-lē.
Zingara . . . . dzēn-gä'-rä.
Zingarelli . . . . . . dzēn-gä-rĕl'-lē.
Zion, see Sion . . . . zī'-ŏn.
Zipporah . . . . . . zĭp'-ō-rä.
Ziska, or . . . . . . zĭs'-kä.
Zižka . . . . zhĭzh'-kä.
Znaim . . . . tsnīm.
Zobeidah, or Zobeide . . zō-bā'-dä, zō-bī'-dä,
. . . . zō-bī-dā.
Zoë . . . . zō'-ē.
Zola . . . . zō'-lä. *Fr.* zō-lä'.
Zollverein . . . . . . tsŏl'-fä-rīn.
Zoloaga . . . . . . thō-lō-ä"-gȧ.
Zombor . . . . . . zŏm'-bŏr.
Zonurko . . . . . . zō-nōōr'-kō.
Zophiei . . . . . . zō'-fī-ĕl.
Zorilla, see Zorrilla . . thōr-rēl'-yä.
Zorn . . . . tsôrn.
Zorndorf . . . . . . tsôrn'-dôrf.
Zoroaster . . . . . . zō-rō-ăs'-tēr.
Zorobabel, see Zerubbabel zō-rŏb'-ā-bĕl.
Zorrilla, see Zorilla . . thōr-rēl'-yä.
Zorrilla y Moral . . . thōr-ēl'-yä ē mō-räl'.
Zouave . . . . zōō-äv'.
Zoutpansberg . . . . zowt'-păns-bĕrċh.
Zschokke . . . . . . tshŏk'-kŭ.
Zuccarelli . . . . . . dzōōk-kä-rĕl'-lē.
Zucchero . . . . . . tsōōk'-ā-rō.
Zuccoli . . . . tsōōk'-kō-lē.
Zug . . . . zōōg. *Ger.* tsōōċh.
Zuider Zee, see Zuyder
Zee . . . . zī'-dĕr zē. *D.* zoi'-dĕr zā.
Zuinglius . . . . . . zwĭng'-glĭ-ŭs.

Zukertort . . . . . . tsŏŏk′-ĕr-tōrt.
Zuleika . . . . zū-lē′-kȧ.
Zulu . . . . zōō′-lōō.
Zululand . . . . . . zōō′-lōō-lănd.
Zumpt . . . . tsŏŏmpt.
Zuñi . . . . zōōn′-yē.
Zunz . . . . tsŏŏnts.
Zurbaran . . . . . . thōōr-bä-rän′.
Zurich, or . . . . . . zōō′-rĭk.
Zürich, *Ger.* . . . . . tsü′-rĭċh.
Zurlinden (Gen.) . . . zür-lĭn-dĕn′.
Zütphen . . . . . . züt′-fĕn.
Zuyder Zee, see Zuider
    Zee . . . . zī′-dĕr zē.   *D.* zoi′-dĕr zā.
Zwartkopjesfontein . . zvärt′-kŏp-yĕs-fŏn′-tīn.
Zweibrücken . . . . . tsvī′-brük-ĕn.
Zwickau . . . . . . tsvĭk′-ow.
Zwingle . . . . . . zwĭng′-gl.
Zwingli . . . . zwĭng′-glē.   *Ger.*
                     tsvĭng′-lē.
Zwolle . . . . zwŏl′-lĕ.